GIVING BACK

GIVING BACK

A Tribute to Generations of African American Philanthropists

VALAIDA FULLWOOD

PHOTOGRAPHY BY CHARLES W. THOMAS JR.

Published by Foundation For The Carolinas
FFTC is the host community foundation for
New Generation of African American Philanthropists
CHARLOTTE, NORTH CAROLINA

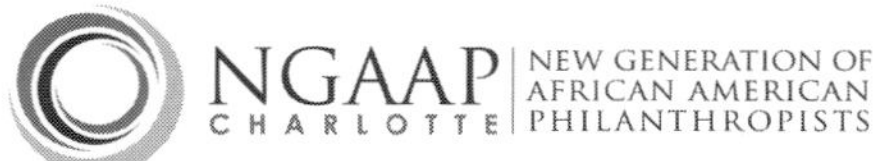

Published by Foundation For The Carolinas
220 North Tryon Street, Charlotte, North Carolina 28202

FFTC is the host community foundation for New Generation of African American Philanthropists
www.NewPhilanthropists.org

Manufactured in the United States of America

This book project was made possible, in part, through grants and contributions from:

Foundation For The Carolinas
John S. and James L. Knight Foundation
Harvey B. Gantt Center for African-American Arts + Culture
The Duke Endowment
NCGives
Charlotte Post Foundation
Community Investment Network
Piedmont Natural Gas
Blue Cross and Blue Shield of North Carolina Foundation

Library of Congress Cataloging-in-Publication Data

Fullwood, Valaida.
Giving back : a tribute to generations of African American philanthropists / Valaida Fullwood ; photography by Charles W. Thomas, Jr.
p. cm.
Includes bibliographical references and index.
ISBN 978-0-89587-564-8 (alk. paper)
1. African American philanthropists. 2. African Americans--Charities--History. 3. Endowments--United States--History. I. Title.
HV91.F85 2011
361.7092'396073--dc23
2011015919

Book design by Casajulie Visual Communications

for Love

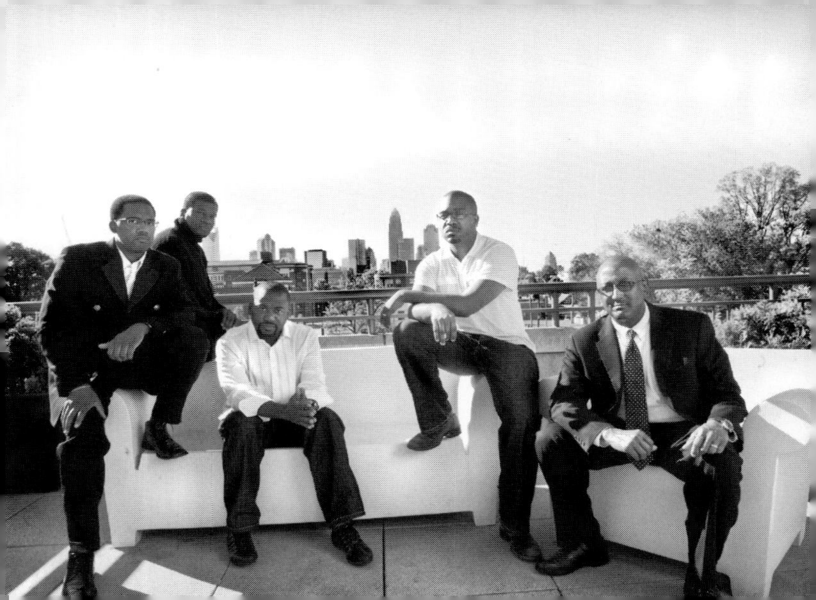

Reframing portraits of philanthropy,
because we have always been philanthropists

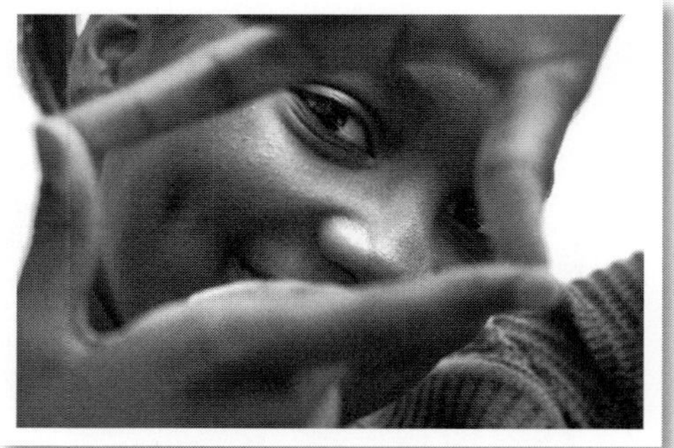

Contents

Truth Be Told

Let us be clear: Black philanthropy is no mere tinted twin.
It is of another Mother land, and in its entirety entirely apart, as revealed herein.

Africa taught its lessons about *we* ages ago with love and vigor.
America tested it though. Still does, with regularity and rigor.

No titan of wealth from this fine nation; instead, faith and unity laid its foundation.
Did somebody say, *Noblesse oblige*? Please. Nearer to négresse oblige in deed.

It is a proclivity for civility. A style of a generic generosity,
borne of a mentality of mutuality. A study in radical reciprocity.

Caring for folks in need. Sharing in a pinch. Giving gifts in any amount.
Even when some come deemed, by some counts, no account.

Mindless, yet heart-full kindness. Just being plain nice. Bread lent without a fuss.
Forever rooted in a most sacred sacrifice, it is of ties that bind the least of us.

To help a sister out. Be a brother's keeper. Next door, the widow might
need a hand to quit slipping deeper and have her back next time, but trust, she's got mine tonight.

It is a responsibility. A seldom-questioned duty.
A thing of supreme Black beauty.

Shut out of places that claimed to aid, the ancestry sure enough came around
with their own homegrown, gracious goodness profound.

Treasure scarce; time a measly ration, the kin back then gazed back on their teaching.
Measuring out lessons in Old World fashion, stirring in truths the faith-filled, still, believe in

Mixing in heaps of talent seasoned with courage of the valiant, they made a way.
As if of loaf and fish, *we* still feed on their soulful gifts today.

Once dark coast plunder, our people afore here ashore honed a niche and a knack.
And lo and behold a curious wonder: From scraps and lack

Least, need and hunger sprang forth feast, good deeds and compassion abundant.
Lavishly ladled love and humanity with rare fever poured out by a people who ironically got neither.

Despite centuries of bullies, blocks and blows
in a land designed to keep us down, *we* instead rose.

Overcoming wrongs, woulds, coulds and shoulds,
we didn't just make do, *we* attained greatness in our doing good.

A long, lasting legacy of benevolence, absent need for further evidence.
Forget the twisted myths. *We* have always given our gifts.

Since my aha on what it is and ain't, I can no longer justify undue restraint.
With newfound awe and ardor, I think, harder.

Choose, wiser. Weigh every factor.
Give and strategize, Blacker.

No more am I among the ranks of the fooled.
Knowing this now too, consider yourself schooled.

So recognize.

— *Ava Wood*

Foreword

Being a blessing to somebody *is* philanthropy.

Sometimes it takes a while to embrace that simple truth. Some folks never get it, but the lucky ones learn it early or soon enough and then choose giving and sharing as a way of life. As we have grown in how we give our gifts, immeasurable inspiration has come from our Black heritage and traditions. African American ancestors who have passed on and elders living today may seem unlikely philanthropists by conventional definitions, but their deeds amply prove otherwise. These way-makers exhibited an astonishing capacity for transcending circumstance to give thus earning their standing among other beacons of philanthropy. Calls for sacrifice, sometimes beyond reason, never diminished their bigheartedness or deep concern for generations to come.

Born enslaved, Harriet Tubman gave freedom. Robbed of education, Catherine Ferguson started a school. After shattering ceilings, Madam C.J. Walker opened doors. Forklift driver by trade, Matel Dawson lifted hopes. Retired from postal work, Thomas Cannon delivered assistance. Dealt hardships, Oseola McCarty granted scholarships. Grace and gratitude thread each of these stories, which are among the finest examples of philanthropy around.

Within these stories of note and in the lives of countless African American philanthropists lies a blueprint for philanthropy today. Instead of giving up or holding back, many ordinary people of past generations chose to give back in bold and unexpected ways. Despite rough times and raw deals, they clung to compassion and found ways to become a blessing to other people. They could have made excuses, but did not. Our predicaments rank petty in comparison and so do our excuses for not doing more. Look closely at their stories: *What they achieved. How they engaged. Why they decided to act. Who benefited from their actions. Where they made an impact.* The insights gained can guide our philanthropy and thereby strengthen our communities.

We have discovered the joy of creating a lasting legacy through philanthropy. With every blessing received, we pay it forward by investing in people and communities with our wealth, our work and our wisdom. You too can move past your struggles and build on your triumphs to find a path to give with purpose. Be a blessing.

— *Members of New Generation of African American Philanthropists*

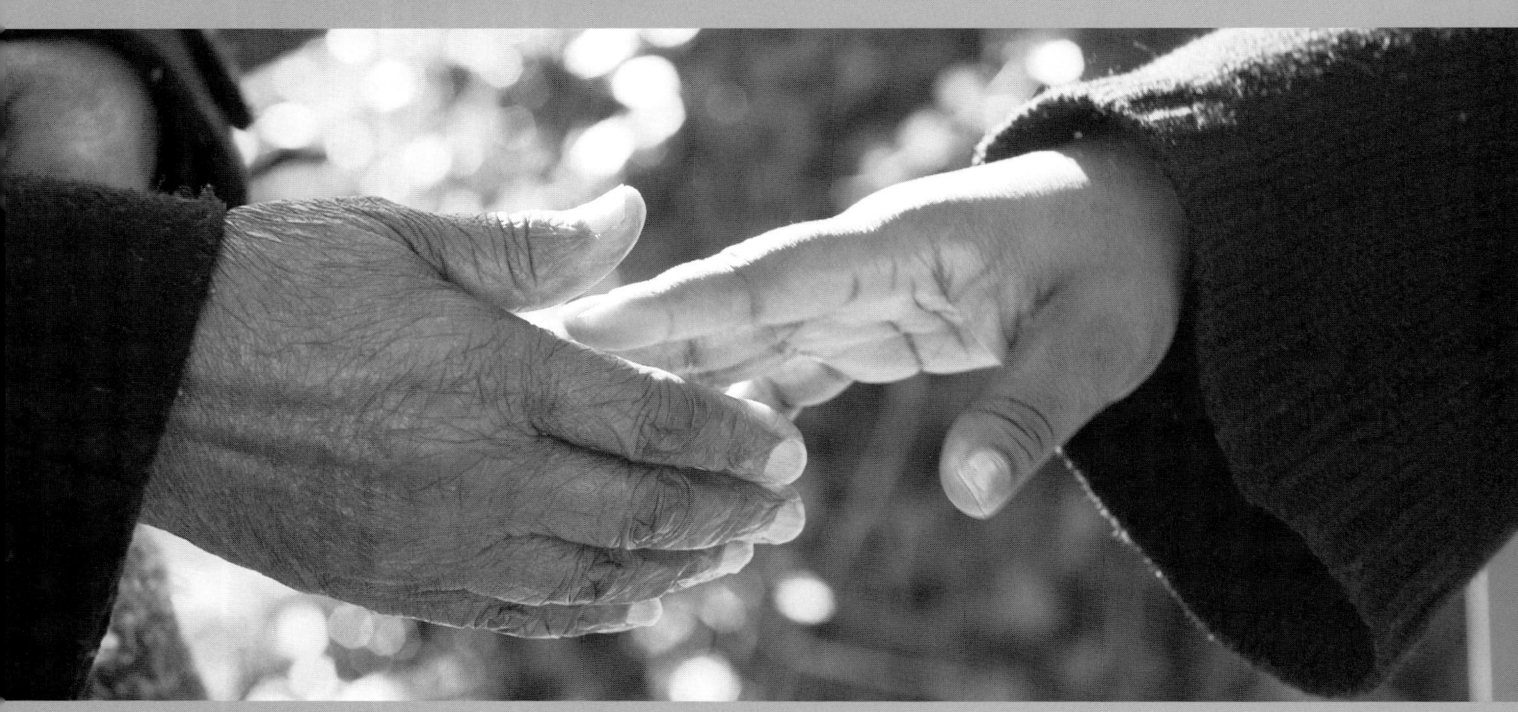

Give, and it shall be given to you. For whatever measure you deal out to others, it will be dealt to you in return.

LUKE 6:38

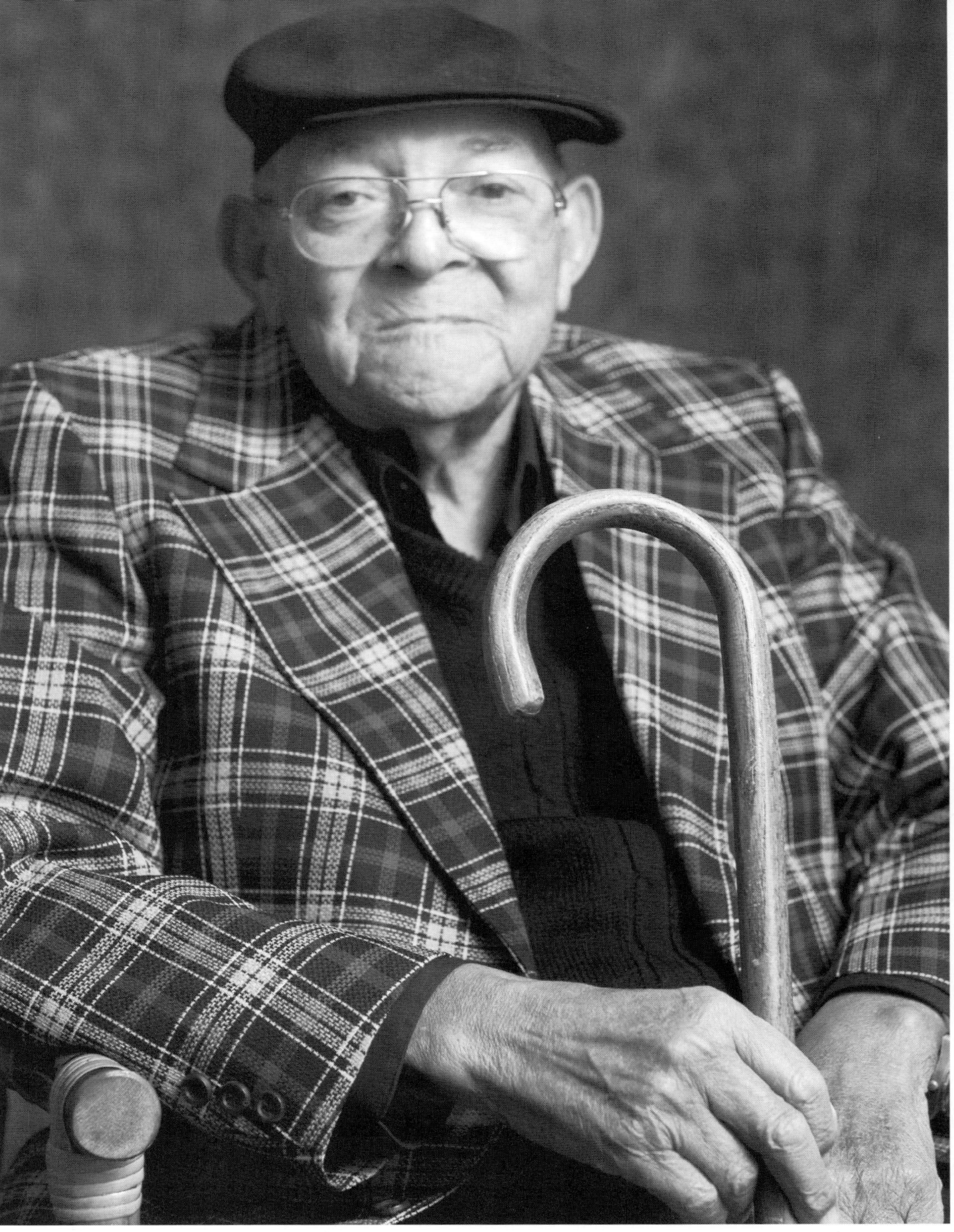

Giving Back

GIVING BACK

A Tribute to Generations of African American Philanthropists

VALAIDA FULLWOOD

PHOTOGRAPHY BY CHARLES W. THOMAS JR.

Published by Foundation For The Carolinas
FFTC is the host community foundation for
New Generation of African American Philanthropists
CHARLOTTE, NORTH CAROLINA

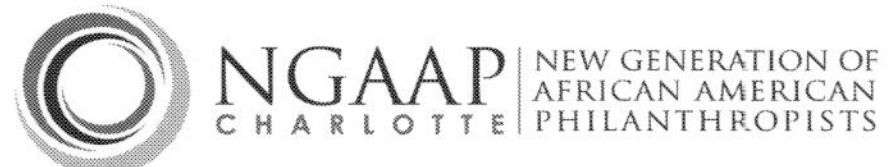

Published by Foundation For The Carolinas
220 North Tryon Street, Charlotte, North Carolina 28202

FFTC is the host community foundation for New Generation of African American Philanthropists
www.NewPhilanthropists.org

Manufactured in the United States of America

This book project was made possible, in part, through grants and contributions from:

Foundation For The Carolinas
John S. and James L. Knight Foundation
Harvey B. Gantt Center for African-American Arts + Culture
The Duke Endowment
NCGives
Charlotte Post Foundation
Community Investment Network
Piedmont Natural Gas
Blue Cross and Blue Shield of North Carolina Foundation

Library of Congress Cataloging-in-Publication Data

Fullwood, Valaida.
Giving back : a tribute to generations of African American
philanthropists / Valaida Fullwood ; photography by Charles W. Thomas, Jr.
p. cm.
Includes bibliographical references and index.
ISBN 978-0-89587-564-8 (alk. paper)
1. African American philanthropists. 2. African
Americans--Charities--History. 3. Endowments--United States--History.
I. Title.
HV91.F85 2011
361.7092'396073--dc23
2011015919

Book design by Casajulie Visual Communications

for Love

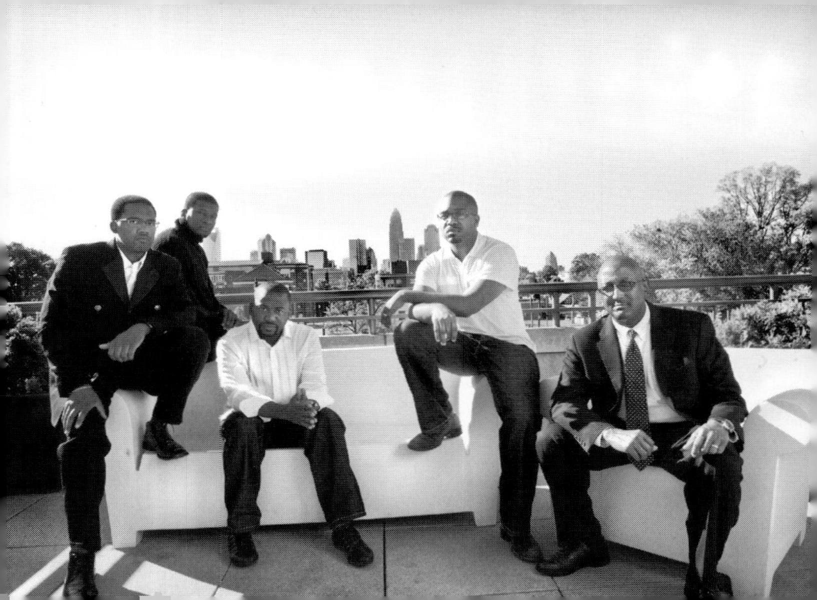

Reframing portraits of philanthropy,
because we have always been philanthropists

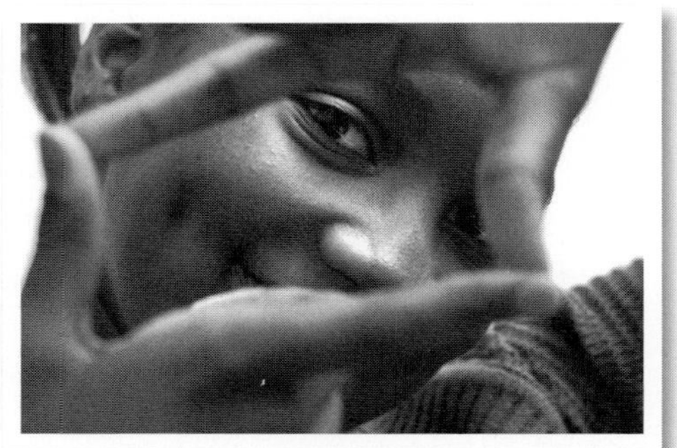

Contents

Truth Be Told

Let us be clear: Black philanthropy is no mere tinted twin.
It is of another Mother land, and in its entirety entirely apart, as revealed herein.

Africa taught its lessons about *we* ages ago with love and vigor.
America tested it though. Still does, with regularity and rigor.

No titan of wealth from this fine nation; instead, faith and unity laid its foundation.
Did somebody say, *Noblesse oblige*? Please. Nearer to négresse oblige in deed.

It is a proclivity for civility. A style of a generic generosity,
borne of a mentality of mutuality. A study in radical reciprocity.

Caring for folks in need. Sharing in a pinch. Giving gifts in any amount.
Even when some come deemed, by some counts, no account.

Mindless, yet heart-full kindness. Just being plain nice. Bread lent without a fuss.
Forever rooted in a most sacred sacrifice, it is of ties that bind the least of us.

To help a sister out. Be a brother's keeper. Next door, the widow might
need a hand to quit slipping deeper and have her back next time, but trust, she's got mine tonight.

It is a responsibility. A seldom-questioned duty.
A thing of supreme Black beauty.

Shut out of places that claimed to aid, the ancestry sure enough came around
with their own homegrown, gracious goodness profound.

Treasure scarce; time a measly ration, the kin back then gazed back on their teaching.
Measuring out lessons in Old World fashion, stirring in truths the faith-filled, still, believe in

Mixing in heaps of talent seasoned with courage of the valiant, they made a way.
As if of loaf and fish, *we* still feed on their soulful gifts today.

Once dark coast plunder, our people afore here ashore honed a niche and a knack.
And lo and behold a curious wonder: From scraps and lack

Least, need and hunger sprang forth feast, good deeds and compassion abundant.
Lavishly ladled love and humanity with rare fever poured out by a people who ironically got neither.

Despite centuries of bullies, blocks and blows
in a land designed to keep us down, *we* instead rose.

Overcoming wrongs, woulds, coulds and shoulds,
we didn't just make do, *we* attained greatness in our doing good.

A long, lasting legacy of benevolence, absent need for further evidence.
Forget the twisted myths. *We* have always given our gifts.

Since my aha on what it is and ain't, I can no longer justify undue restraint.
With newfound awe and ardor, I think, harder.

Choose, wiser. Weigh every factor.
Give and strategize, Blacker.

No more am I among the ranks of the fooled.
Knowing this now too, consider yourself schooled.

So recognize.

— *Ava Wood*

Foreword

Being a blessing to somebody *is* philanthropy.

Sometimes it takes a while to embrace that simple truth. Some folks never get it, but the lucky ones learn it early or soon enough and then choose giving and sharing as a way of life. As we have grown in how we give our gifts, immeasurable inspiration has come from our Black heritage and traditions. African American ancestors who have passed on and elders living today may seem unlikely philanthropists by conventional definitions, but their deeds amply prove otherwise. These way-makers exhibited an astonishing capacity for transcending circumstance to give thus earning their standing among other beacons of philanthropy. Calls for sacrifice, sometimes beyond reason, never diminished their bigheartedness or deep concern for generations to come.

Born enslaved, Harriet Tubman gave freedom. Robbed of education, Catherine Ferguson started a school. After shattering ceilings, Madam C.J. Walker opened doors. Forklift driver by trade, Matel Dawson lifted hopes. Retired from postal work, Thomas Cannon delivered assistance. Dealt hardships, Oseola McCarty granted scholarships. Grace and gratitude thread each of these stories, which are among the finest examples of philanthropy around.

Within these stories of note and in the lives of countless African American philanthropists lies a blueprint for philanthropy today. Instead of giving up or holding back, many ordinary people of past generations chose to give back in bold and unexpected ways. Despite rough times and raw deals, they clung to compassion and found ways to become a blessing to other people. They could have made excuses, but did not. Our predicaments rank petty in comparison and so do our excuses for not doing more. Look closely at their stories: *What they achieved. How they engaged. Why they decided to act. Who benefited from their actions. Where they made an impact.* The insights gained can guide our philanthropy and thereby strengthen our communities.

We have discovered the joy of creating a lasting legacy through philanthropy. With every blessing received, we pay it forward by investing in people and communities with our wealth, our work and our wisdom. You too can move past your struggles and build on your triumphs to find a path to give with purpose. Be a blessing.

— *Members of New Generation of African American Philanthropists*

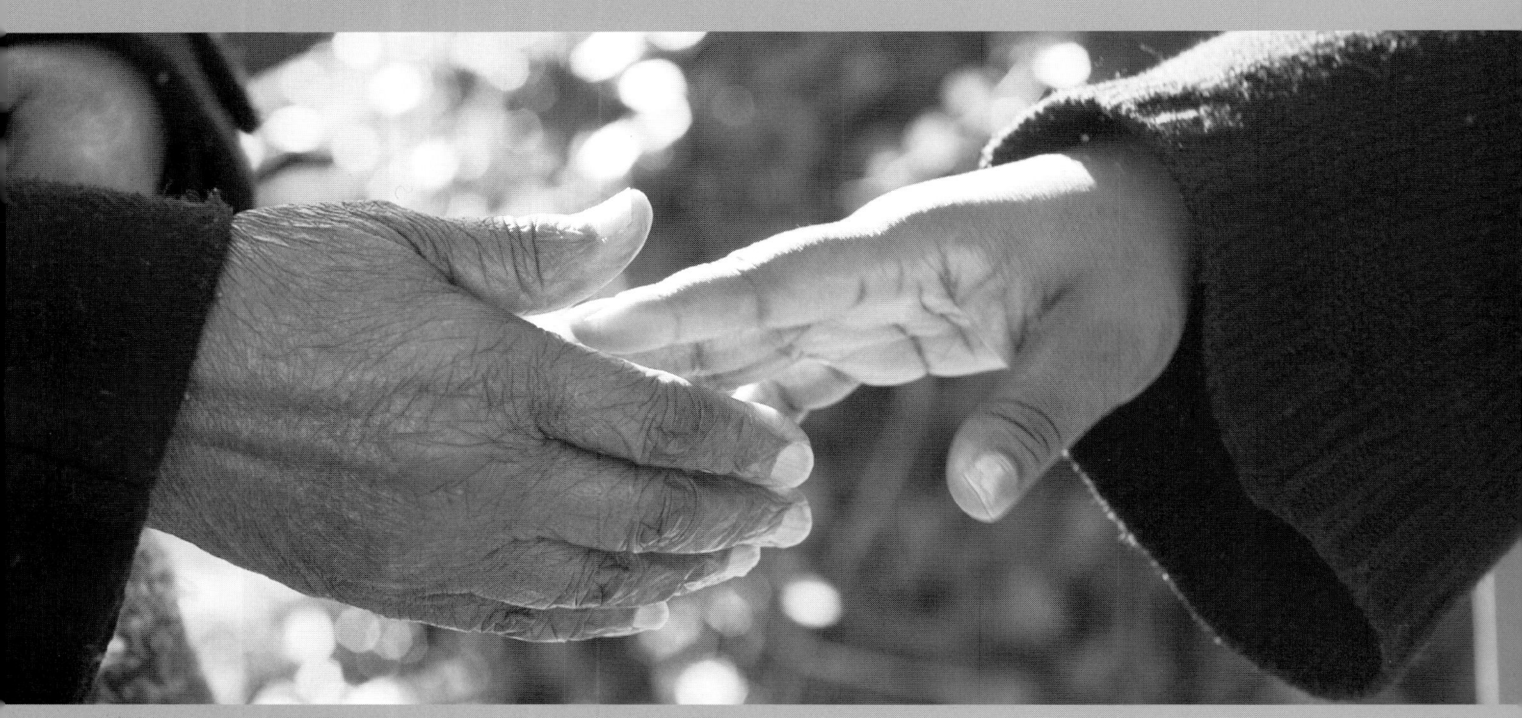

Give, and it shall be given to you. For whatever measure you deal out to others, it will be dealt to you in return.

LUKE 6:38

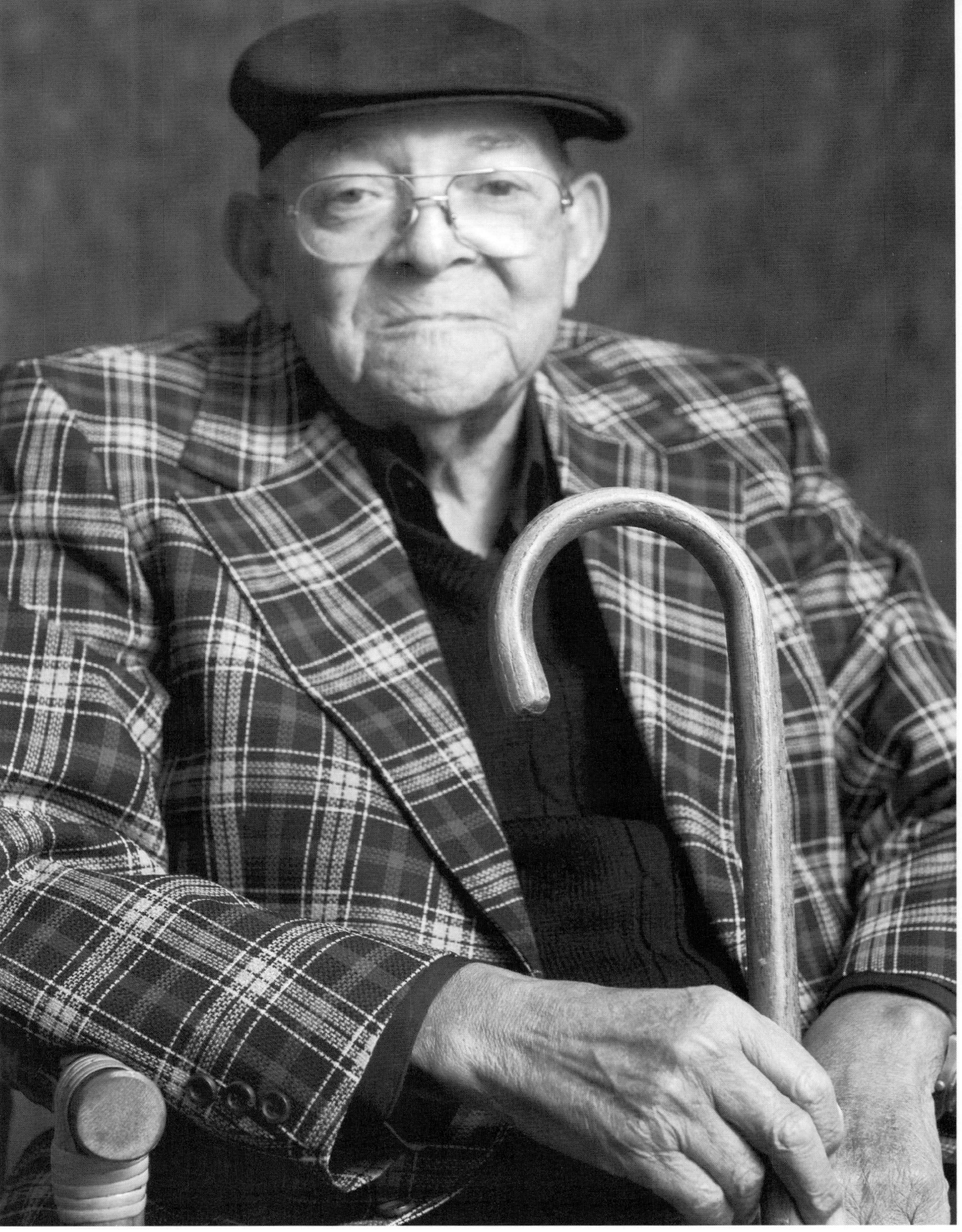

We Have Always Been Philanthropists

Reframing, Redefining, Re-imagining Philanthropy

No building bears their names. No boardroom displays their portraits. No foundation sustains their legacy. And yet, the philanthropists best known to me are the ones in my family, church and hometown. These are people who showed a profound love for humankind and taught me about giving. Freely sharing things of value to benefit others—the essence of philanthropy—these unassuming, everyday people had monumental influences on me and on the lives of many.

Though conventional places offer few traces of African American philanthropists, ample evidence of their generosity can be found all around. The photography and stories collected for this book are but a representative sample of the Black philanthropy that has shaped our communities and nation. In presenting illustrative stories about a select few, I venture to pay tribute to all African Americans whose sacrifices and gifts, whether modest or grand, honor past generations, inspire current generations and clear the way for posterity.

"To whom much is given much is expected."

This biblical passage from the Gospel of Luke conveys a belief that I and many of my African American family and friends hold dear. Many of us recall a defining moment or childhood lessons that influence our philanthropic giving.

A 2004 study of Black philanthropy by The Twenty-First Century Foundation found that for many African American donors a core value is "repaying family, community, and, perhaps, society at large." We are acutely aware of what others have given or given up to pave the way and contribute to our successes. As a result, we share a sense of responsibility about honoring and sustaining that legacy.

Historically, African Americans have created and supported their own systems for giving—often informally, yet always generously—to members of the community, neighbors and kinfolk needing assistance. Culturally significant vehicles of giving include the Underground Railroad, Black churches, Masonic societies, Greek sororities and fraternities, mutual aid societies, social clubs and civic, alumni and professional associations.

While this cultural legacy of "giving back" prevails today, it is often overlooked by mainstream society and rarely celebrated within the African American community. Indeed, in the community it is seldom even described as philanthropy.

Today, common public perceptions of charitable giving and philanthropy not only underestimate levels of giving within the African American community, they also undermine the veritable power of Black philanthropy. Too often, images, media coverage and reports of prominent philanthropic leaders and institutions advance a false view, which places African Americans only on the demand side, and not on the supply side of philanthropy. The consumers, not the donors. The source of problems, not a resource for solutions. In need, not influential. Beneficiaries, not benefactors. Not only are African Americans shortchanged by these erroneous propositions, a host of philanthropic causes and nonprofit institutions as well as the broader community lose out on an expansive pool of prospective contributors.

The truth of the matter:

- African Americans give 8.6 percent of their discretionary income to charity—more than any other racial group in America.

- Further, African Americans donate 25 percent more of their discretionary income than do Americans of European descent.

- Nearly two-thirds of African American households give to charity more formally, to the tune of $11 billion each year.

— *From 2003 study in* The Chronicle of Philanthropy

Vibrant traditions and beliefs about giving are indeed flourishing in the African American community. It is interesting to take a closer look at our generous giving and increased wealth, education and opportunities juxtaposed with seemingly unshakable disparities and inequities. It suggests African Americans, collectively, could gain from deeper knowledge about the breadth of options for giving and a sharper focus on investing strategically for social change.

Such shifts in awareness and intent require broader recognition of the power of Black philanthropy and greater understanding about philanthropic vehicles. Stronger and more strategic alliances also are needed among African American donors as well as between Black communities and a wide range of nonprofit organizations and charitable foundations.

I am a part of New Generation of African American Philanthropists, a giving circle based in Charlotte, North Carolina. Much like members of a book club or investment club, our giving circle members share an interest. Our group's shared interest is philanthropy. Members of the giving circle pool their money to fund community projects and to support the work of nonprofit organizations.

Our giving circle also engages in community service and learns together by studying and discussing innovations and trends in the field of philanthropy. One of our aims is to reclaim the root meaning of philanthropy—the love of humankind—by celebrating our African American roots and traditions, promoting new as well as time-honored ways of giving and expanding the term's definition to encompass gifts of not only money, but also time and talent.

Exploring our own philanthropy and cultural connections as a giving circle made clear the strength of images, stories and tradition to create breakthroughs in thinking and inspire giving. *Giving Back* is a product of that insight. Members of New Generation of African American Philanthropists are vested in educating ourselves and others about community issues, in building bridges and in expanding philanthropy with inclusive giving and problem solving. Our journey and mission as a giving circle led me to conceive this book in April 2007.

Seeking creative expression through arts and culture, I set out to shed light on my American heritage, reveal the layers of philanthropy within Black communities and engender greater giving. All along, my aspiration has been to bring new content to the discourse on philanthropy and on African American giving as a complement to explorations by scholars and researchers. I also hold hopes of reaching new audiences, stirring discovery and knowledge and shifting how people view and do things.

Photography with its visceral potency, fortified by personal revelation and unfiltered truths, seemed apt ingredients for a book that could captivate, educate, honor and inspire. In mixing the oral history of community elders, candid commentary from my contemporaries, adages from ancestors and a myriad of memories about giving, I found the breadth of illuminating stories I hoped for.

Mindful that photographs on society pages and headlines in celebrity news feature philanthropists every day, I chose instead the unsung and the familiar but overlooked. *Giving Back* profiles everyday givers whose philanthropy seldom makes the news and rarely fits the standard frame for being heralded as philanthropists. Contained in the following pages are photographic images and narrative snapshots of ordinary people, from ages two to ninety-two, who inspire and motivate us to do our part to change the world. Their stories of generosity vary yet convey a common simplicity, authenticity and dignity that are sure to influence how you think about philanthropy.

— *Valaida Fullwood*

Reader's Guide to the Stories and Photography of *Giving Back*

Throughout this book, pages of photography alternate with pages of narrative that fall into four main categories. The collection of photographs is defined by two approaches. Descriptions of and background on the book's narrative and photographic content follow.

The stories and narrative content

- *Tribute vignette:* This is a story that honors a role model or community elder. A "tribute sponsor" tells the story. The book's writer interviewed the tribute sponsors and crafted their stories based on what they shared. In most cases, giving by the tribute sponsor was inspired by his or her honoree.

  Each tribute vignette is part of a two-page spread. The story falls on the left-hand page and a corresponding portrait featuring the honoree and/or tribute sponsor is on the right.

  A bold header identifies each honoree. The tribute sponsor's name is shown at the end of the vignette, along with a bit of background information: "connection" (the tribute sponsor's relationship to the honoree), "channel" (an organizational affiliation that illustrates the tribute sponsor's philanthropy) and "cause" (a philanthropic passion carried by the tribute sponsor).

- *Micro story:* This is a brief personal narrative about a tradition or aspect of Black philanthropy. A variety of givers contributed micro stories. The book's writer interviewed some people to capture and craft their story, and other people wrote their own. Each story contributor's name and philanthropic passion are noted in italics.

  Micro stories are paired with editorial photography, which feature people and objects that are generally unaffiliated with the story contributor but express some aspect of the story.

- *Quotes from everyday givers:* Most chapters open with a question followed by a series of quoted answers from everyday givers. Totaling ten, these questions shape the titles and content of the ten chapters.

- *Quotes from the ages:* Scattered throughout the book are motivational messages and wise words from distinguished people across cultures and centuries. The selected quotes give insight and commentary on the African American experience, community building, philanthropy and love. Names of the people quoted appear in capital letters and their distinguishing achievement or title is noted. These quotes are paired with a photographic interpretation of the passage.

The photographs

- *Tribute portraits:* Portraiture paired with tribute vignettes is generally found on the right page. In most cases, the photograph features honorees and sometimes it includes his or her tribute sponsor, too. In instances when honorees had passed on, their posthumous tribute includes a photograph of the tribute sponsor, a photo from the tribute sponsor's family album or a still-life composition.

- *Editorial photographs:* This type of photography introduces each chapter and is paired with micro stories, quotes and other photographs. These photographs fall mostly on the left page. The editorial photographs capture various everyday philanthropists—some of whom are also featured in tribute portraits—as well as children and evocative places and objects.

  These images were selected for artistic commentary and to provide a photographic interpretation of the corresponding or preceding pages. By design, the page does not include names of the people and locations.

At the back of the book, two appendices and an index provide useful information and insights. The list of photography (Appendix I) corresponds to each chapter and identifies people, places and objects that appear in each photograph. The list of organizations (Appendix II) catalogs the charitable organizations, educational institutions and community-based groups mentioned in stories. The scope and breadth of organizations, alone, should go far in dispelling the notion that we give only at church.

It is our hope that you savor the stories and imagery and that you digest everything *Giving Back* offers.

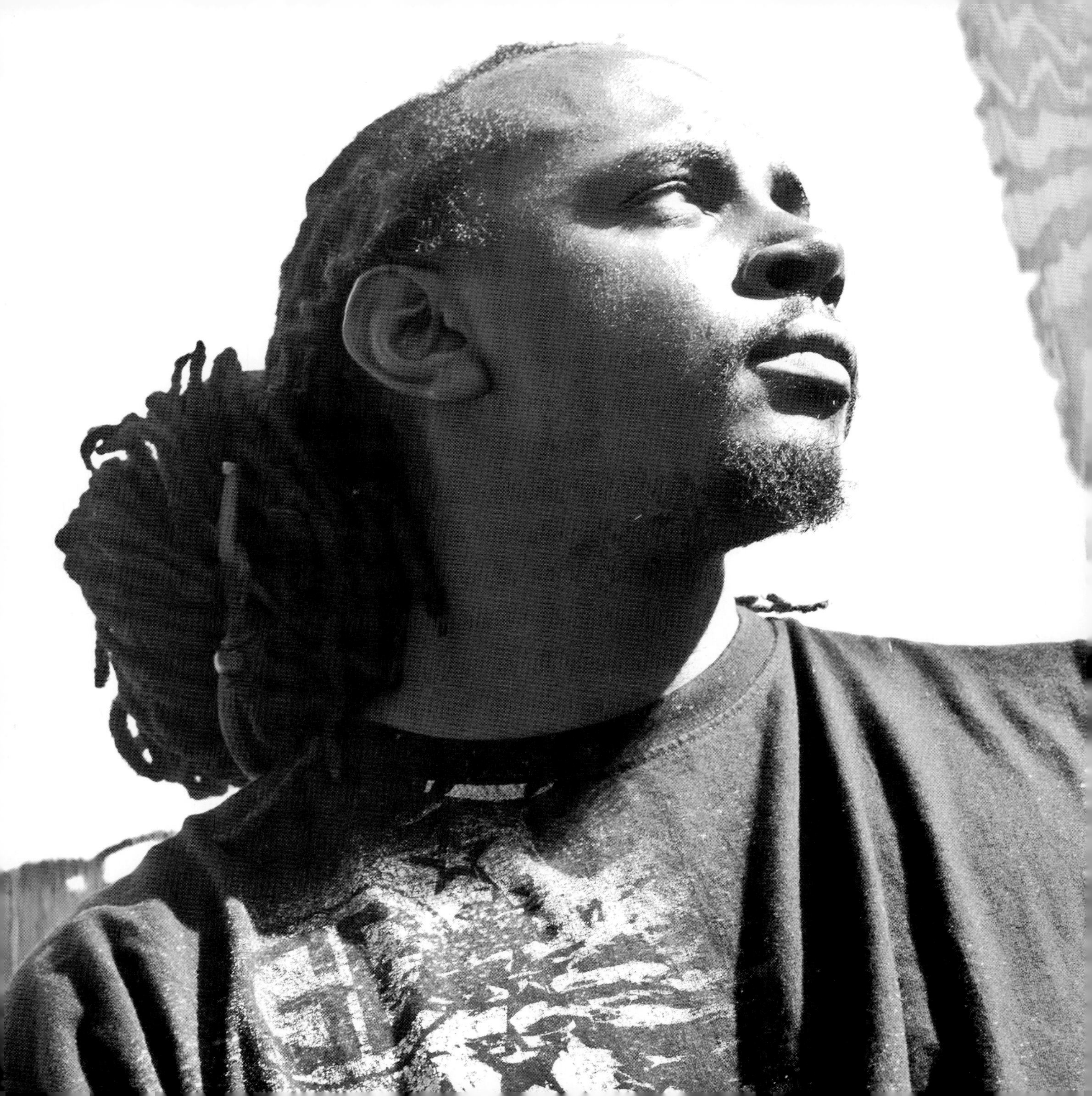

DEFINITIONS

How do you define philanthropy?

Philanthropy is sharing yourself by giving your time, talent or treasure for the benefit of a cause or person. — *Ohmar Land*

It is making an effort to give of your time, knowledge, experience, and finances to help make a positive difference in the lives of fellow citizens. — *Britt Brewer Loudd*

Philanthropy is the extension of one's self in the form of volunteering, know-how, and resources, including money and other things of value. — *Darryl K. Lester*

Philanthropy is the love of humankind. That basic definition really works for me. Philanthropy is expressed in multiple ways. The Christian challenge to give 'time, talent and treasure'—not valuing one gift over another—is the expression of true love of humankind. — *Jennifer Henderson*

The giving of time, talent and funding with a target and specific purpose — *Christian Friend*

I define philanthropy as using the abundance of any or all resources that one has to benefit an individual or group. — *Dan Nunn*

Philanthropy is giving from the heart and sharing one's special gifts and talents with humanity. — *Mattie Marshall*

Voluntary support for the betterment of peoplekind — *LaDawn Sullivan*

It's giving back to a cause you are passionate about. — *Joy Webb*

Realizing how blessed you are, believing that you are your brother's keeper and giving your time, talents and treasures to make a difference in the lives of others — *Cathy Peterson*

Philanthropy is about being inspired by your faith, then taking action and being a good steward of your gifts, time and resources. — *Sherry Waters*

Making a financial contribution to a worthy cause or a nonprofit organization — *Jeanene Thompson*

Sharing financial and developmental resources to aid in the development of a great vision that serves mankind — *Vikkii Beckwith Graham*

The giving of time, talent and treasure — *Edgar Villanueva*

Giving something of yourself to others in need — *Belinda E. Alston*

Giving back — *Robert Hill*

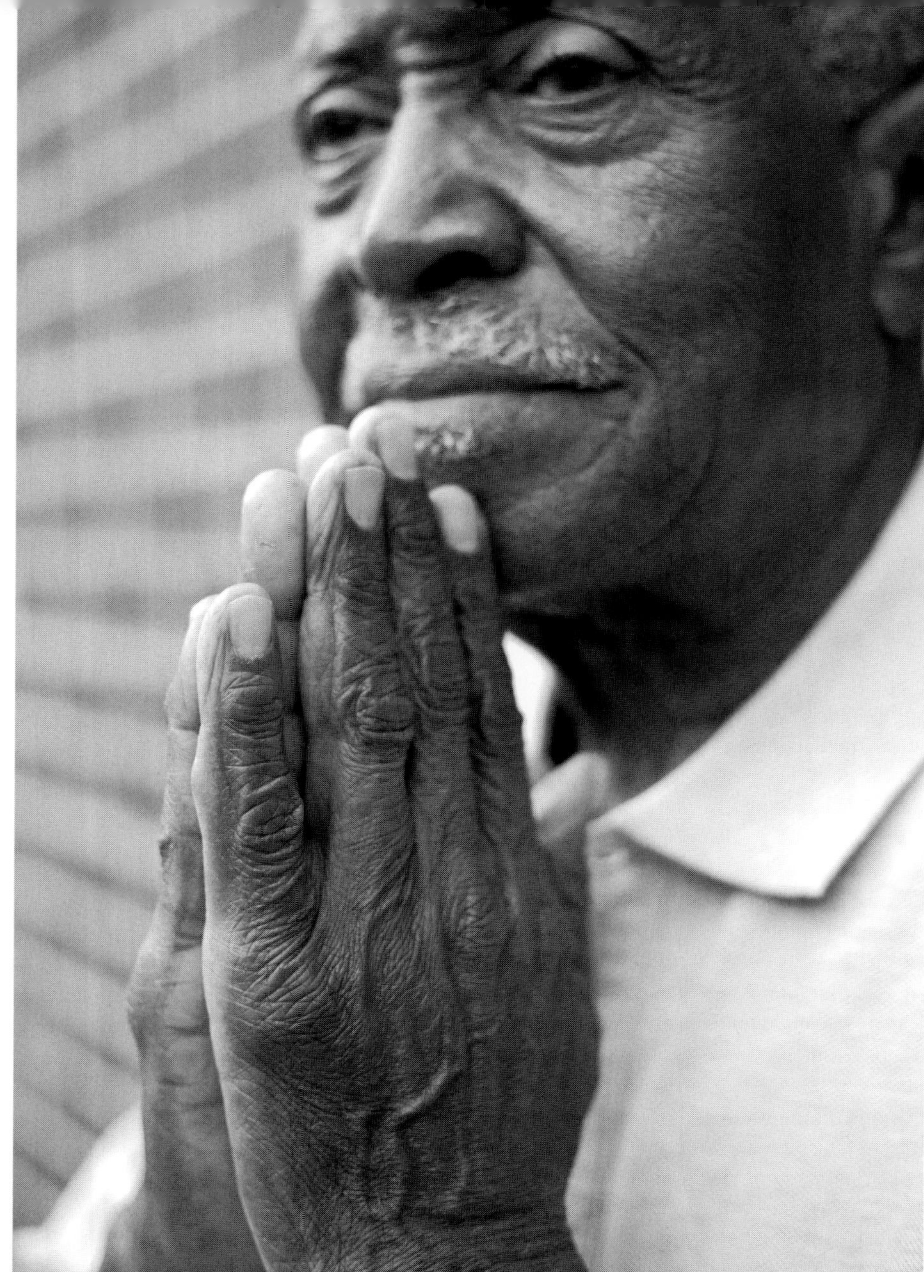

Philanthropy is commendable, but it must not cause the philanthropist to overlook the circumstances of economic injustice which make philanthropy necessary.

DR. MARTIN LUTHER KING JR.
American civil rights leader
(1929-68)

Dora Atlas | RICH AUNT

A soup kitchen? The morning my mother called with news that a great-aunt had begun organizing free daily meals in a fragile part of town is as vivid to me today as it was nearly twenty years ago.

Expectations of service are handed down like heirlooms in my family, and Aunt Dora figured prominently in a long line of givers. Even so, I had never imagined such a bold move or demanding commitment from my grandmother's reserved younger sister. Widowed and seventy-something at the time, Aunt Dora had selflessly looked after people her entire life as a mother, grandmother, foster mother, den mother and church pastor. I was at a loss as to why she was launching a community food program on the heels of her retirement from the church. *Hadn't she given enough? Wasn't it time to pull back?* To the contrary: It was precisely at this point she sought to commit herself anew.

I later learned it was in meditation during a silent spiritual retreat that Aunt Dora received the answer to her quest. "Feed the hungry" was her directive from God, and she founded Our Daily Bread Kitchen Inc. Since that day, the kitchen has flourished and now serves free meals to over ten thousand people a year. Aunt Dora's lifelong series of callings and her obedient responses—constructing a larger, new facility and preparing meals, still, as she nears ninety—have removed any of my questions about the ceaseless bounty of service for fortunate heirs.

VALAIDA FULLWOOD

Connection: *Grandniece* • Channel: *Founding member, New Generation of African American Philanthropists* • Cause: *Social justice and racial equity*

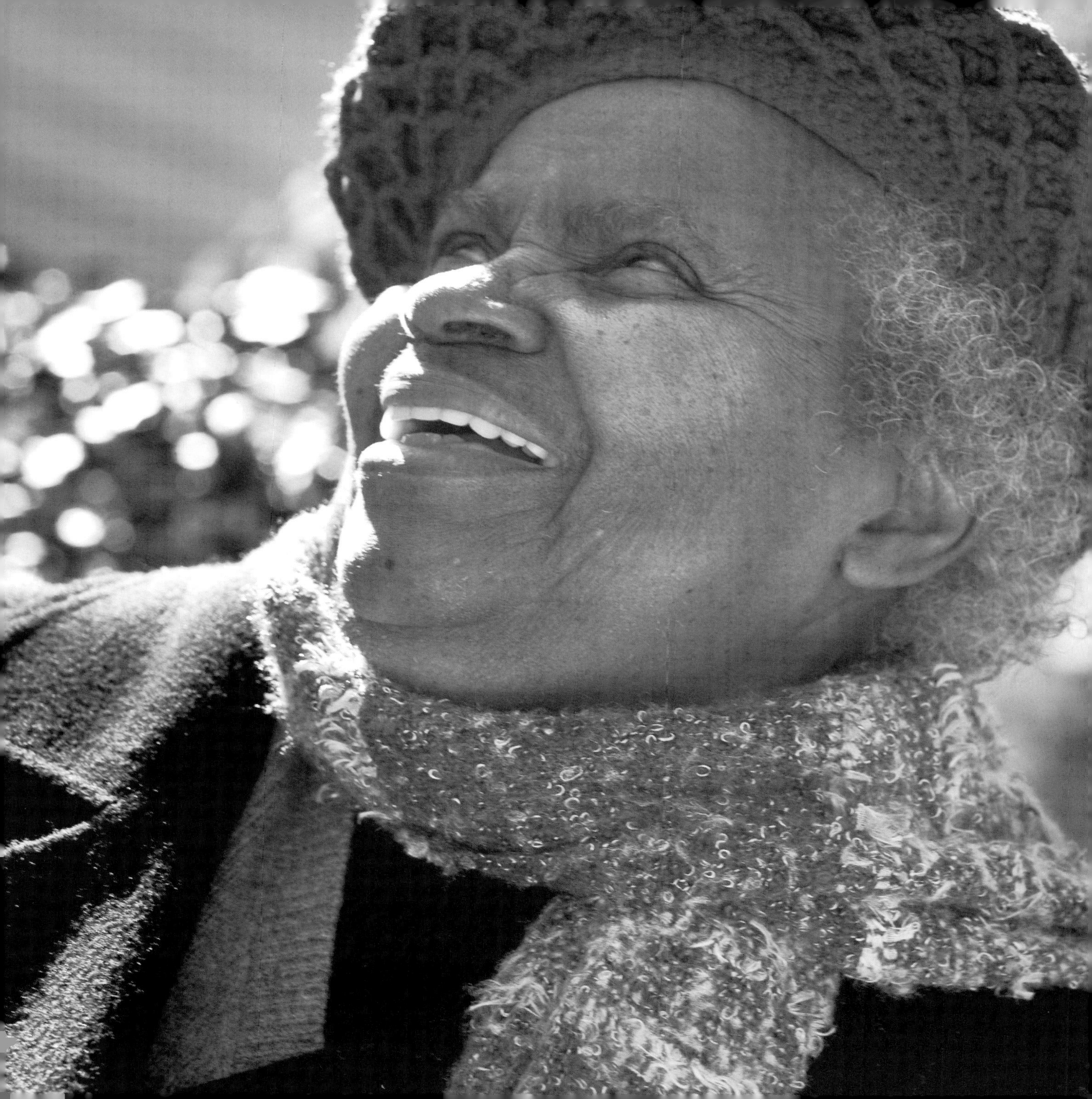

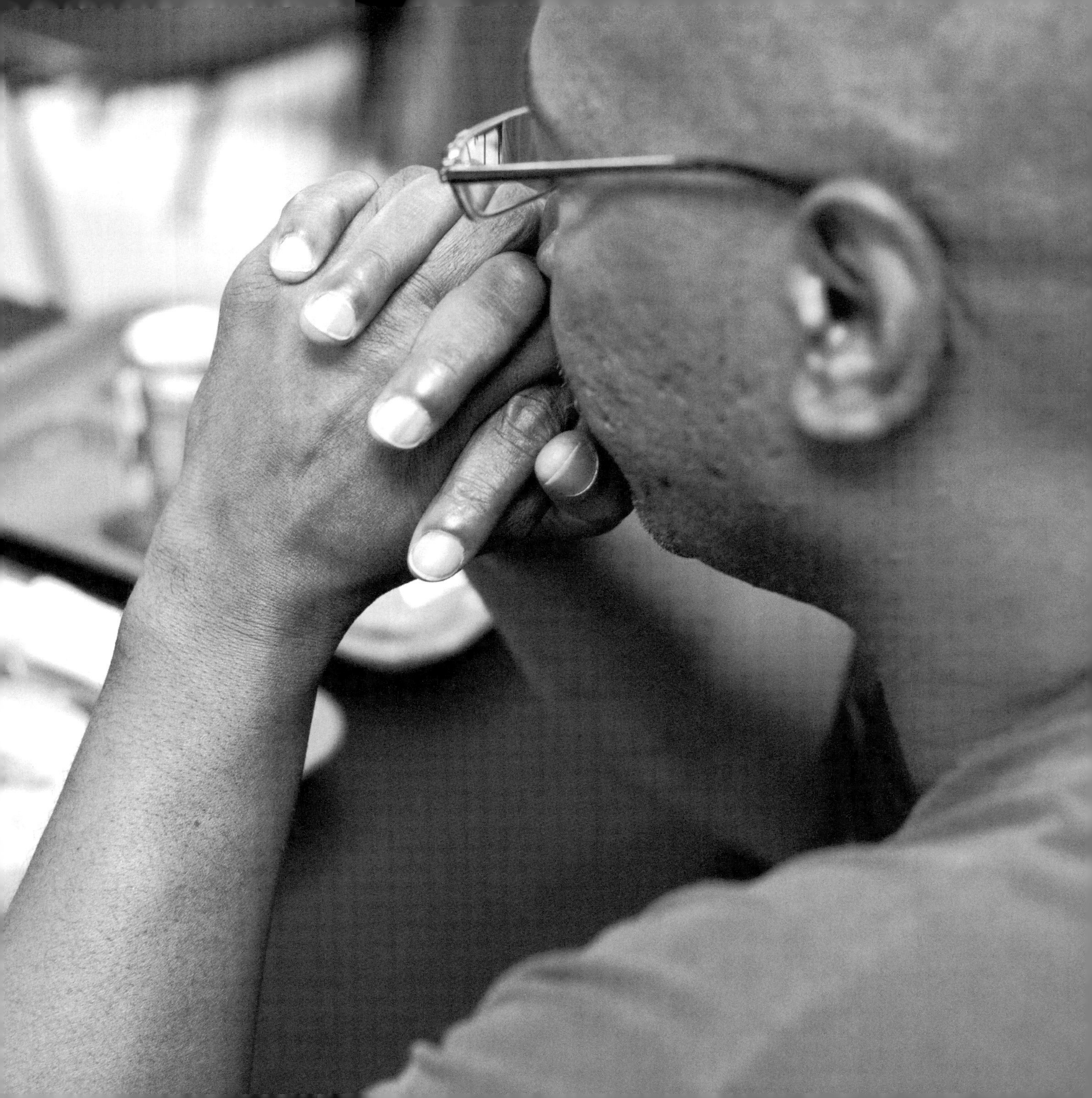

If you can't feed a hundred people, then feed just one.

MOTHER TERESA
Humanitarian
(1910-97)

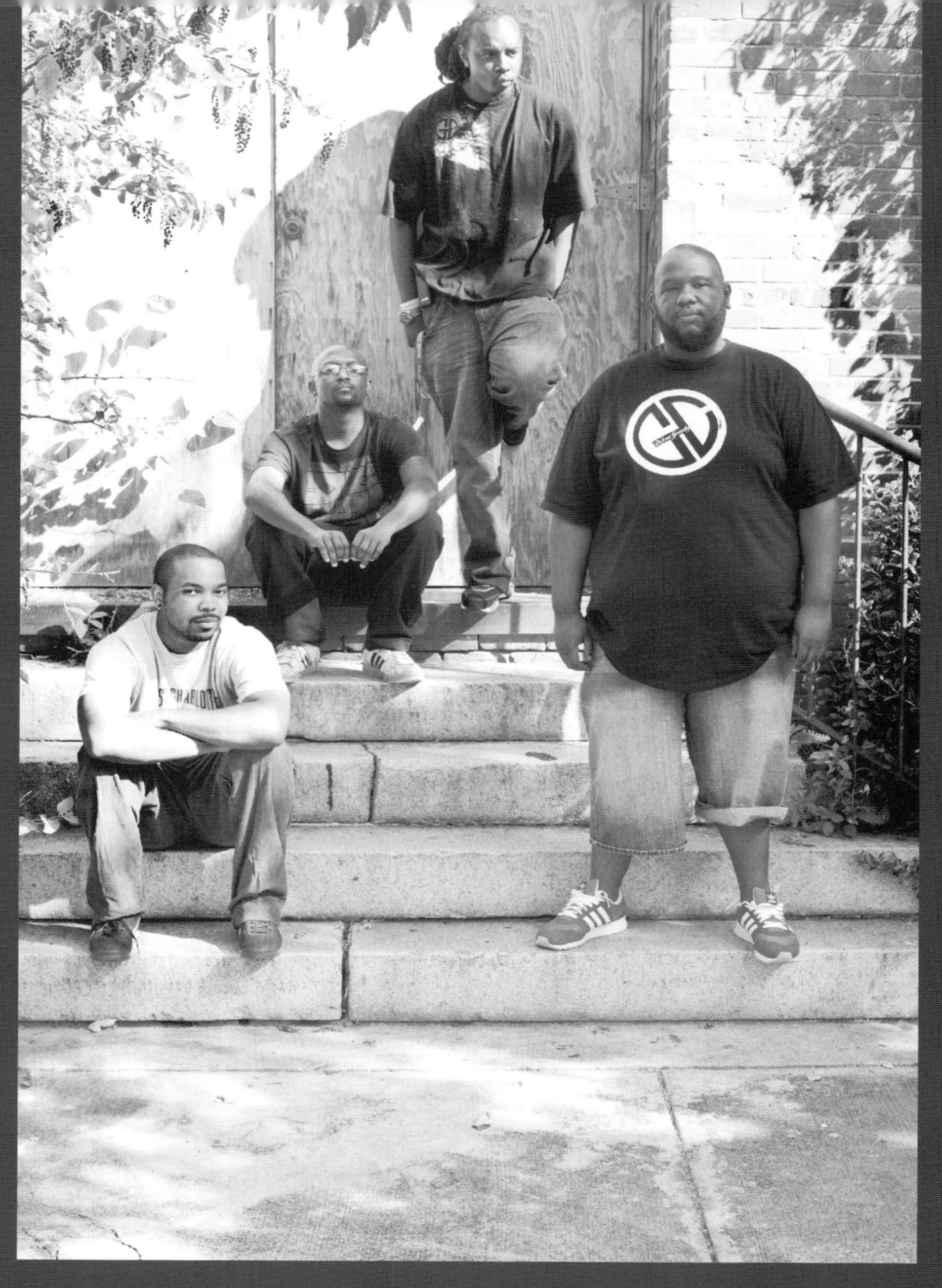

"FOR BLACK PEOPLE *philanthropy* is not a luxury, it's a survival technique. Our extended family culture requires us to look at the helpless and needy not as a 'wayward other,' but as a brother, sister, cousin or uncle. But what's most remarkable is that even as we help others who are 'at risk,' we ourselves are often at risk at the same time."

Michael Sales
artistic mentoring

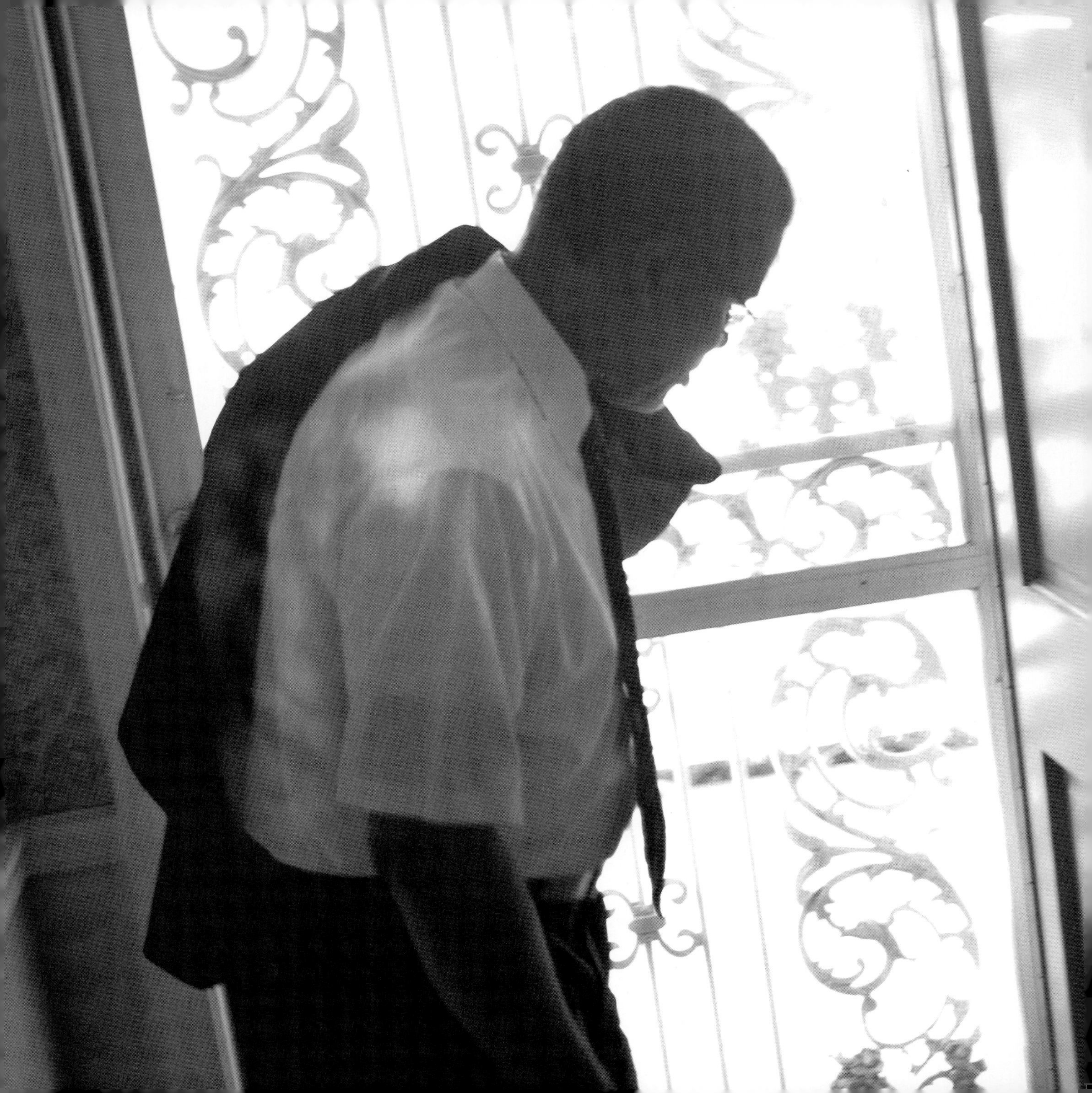

Never respect men merely for their riches, but rather for their philanthropy; we do not value the sun for its height, but for its use.

GAMALIEL BAILEY
American journalist and abolitionist
(1807-59)

Robert Harrington, J.D. | CIVIC SERVANT

I met my husband Rob while in law school at Duke University. He was two years ahead, but his reputation preceded our introduction. Rob had attended Duke as an undergrad and was active in student government and at the top of his class. He was one of those people everybody—students, faculty and staff—thought *everyone* should get to know. Once we met, I understood why.

Rob grew up in Florence, South Carolina, the youngest of five children. Like all of his siblings, he is brilliant, caring and wonderful. If you are around him for even a short time, you will come to know he is passionate about history, public policy and civic involvement. He has always been community-minded, a quality reinforced at Duke Law, which expects graduates to give back to the community.

After law school, Rob clerked for a federal judge in New Orleans. Given his passions, it is not surprising that he also began volunteering with the Lawyers' Committee for Civil Rights Under Law. In 1963, at the height of civil rights turmoil, the Lawyers' Committee formed at the behest of JFK, who wanted the country's best advocates working on issues. Rob began by providing pro bono services through this historic nonprofit organization. Soon he was invited to join the board and eventually co-chaired it. Now, almost two decades later, he serves on the executive board and still finds his involvement a meaningful convergence of his interests.

Today in Charlotte, Rob's community service ranges from grassroots advocacy to large-scale catalytic work. His passions continue to drive his involvement whether at the Mecklenburg Bar Association or at Levine Museum of the New South or while mentoring young attorneys. Rob exudes a quiet humility and serves admirably. Even so, I look for ways to acknowledge his dedication and renew his spirit. Community work is not easy. Servant leaders deserve a nod or collective pat on the back. Every now and then we would be wise to slow down, take stock and acknowledge the good people doing good work around us.

SHARON HARRINGTON, J.D.
Connection: *Wife* • Channel: *Founding board member, Women's Impact Fund*
Cause: *Issues of equity, social justice and the ending of disparities in public education*

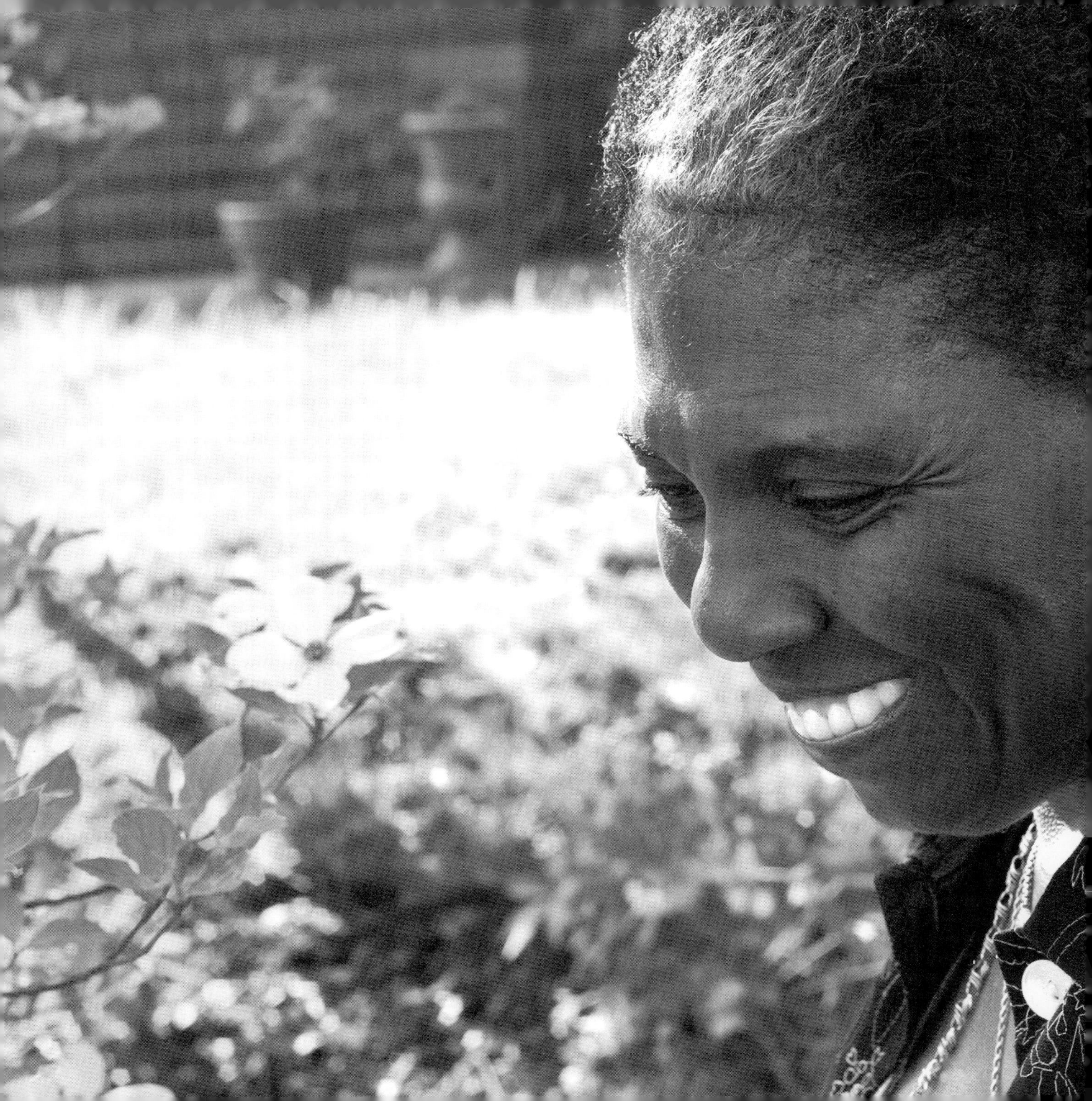

Generosity is the flower of justice.

NATHANIEL HAWTHORNE
American novelist
(1804-64)

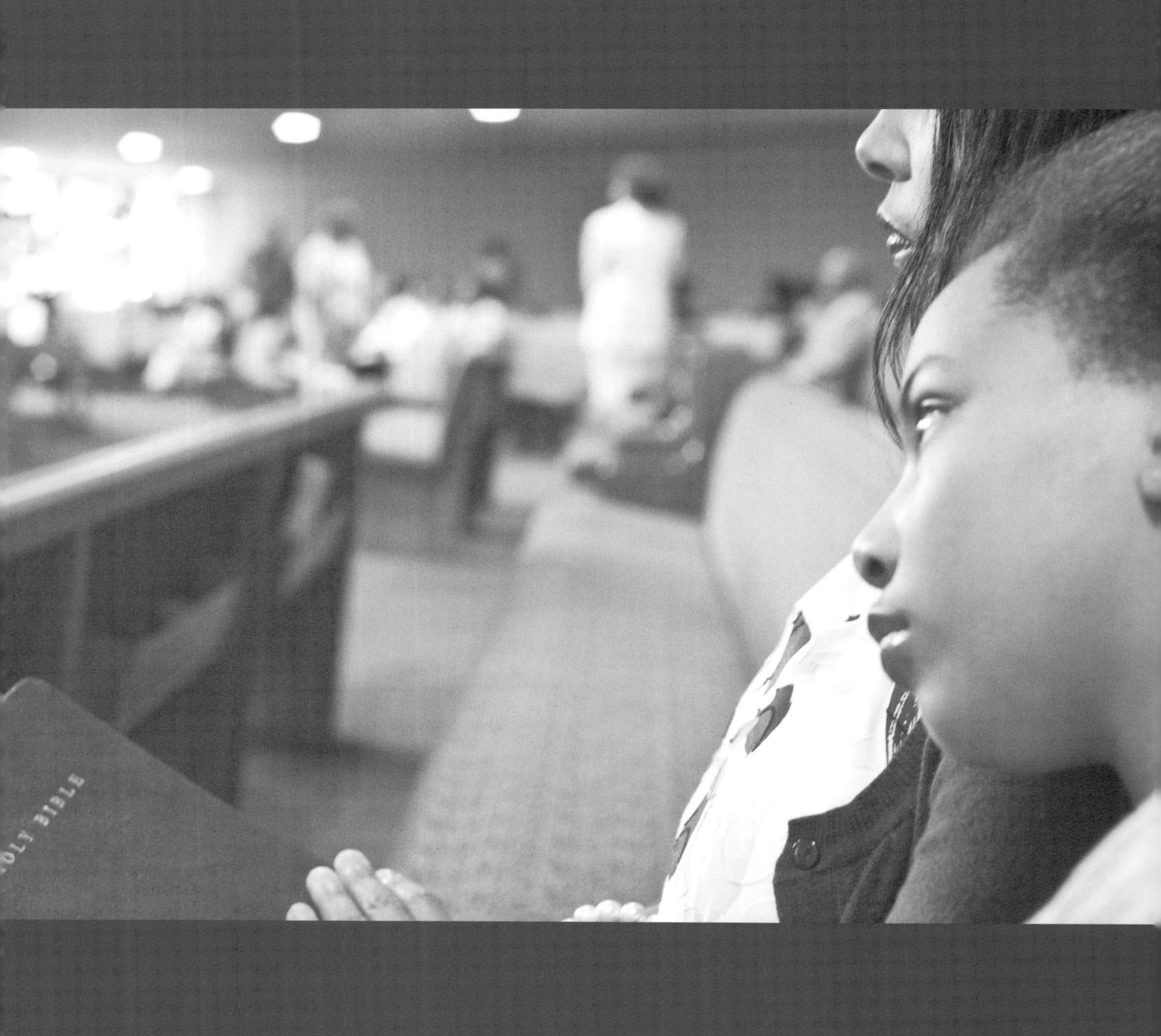
OLY BIBLE

"WHEN I WAS FIVE years old sitting in church and clutching my two-dollar offering, I asked my mother why God—who has control over everything—needed *my* money. She told me an answer that shapes my giving to this day: 'God needs your money for his *Earth operations.* He looks to us to be his team here on Earth. He's counting on us.' I have never forgotten that brief, yet pivotal conversation."

Jennifer Henderson
board chair of Sweet Beginnings, a social enterprise that provides transitional jobs and support to formerly incarcerated men and women

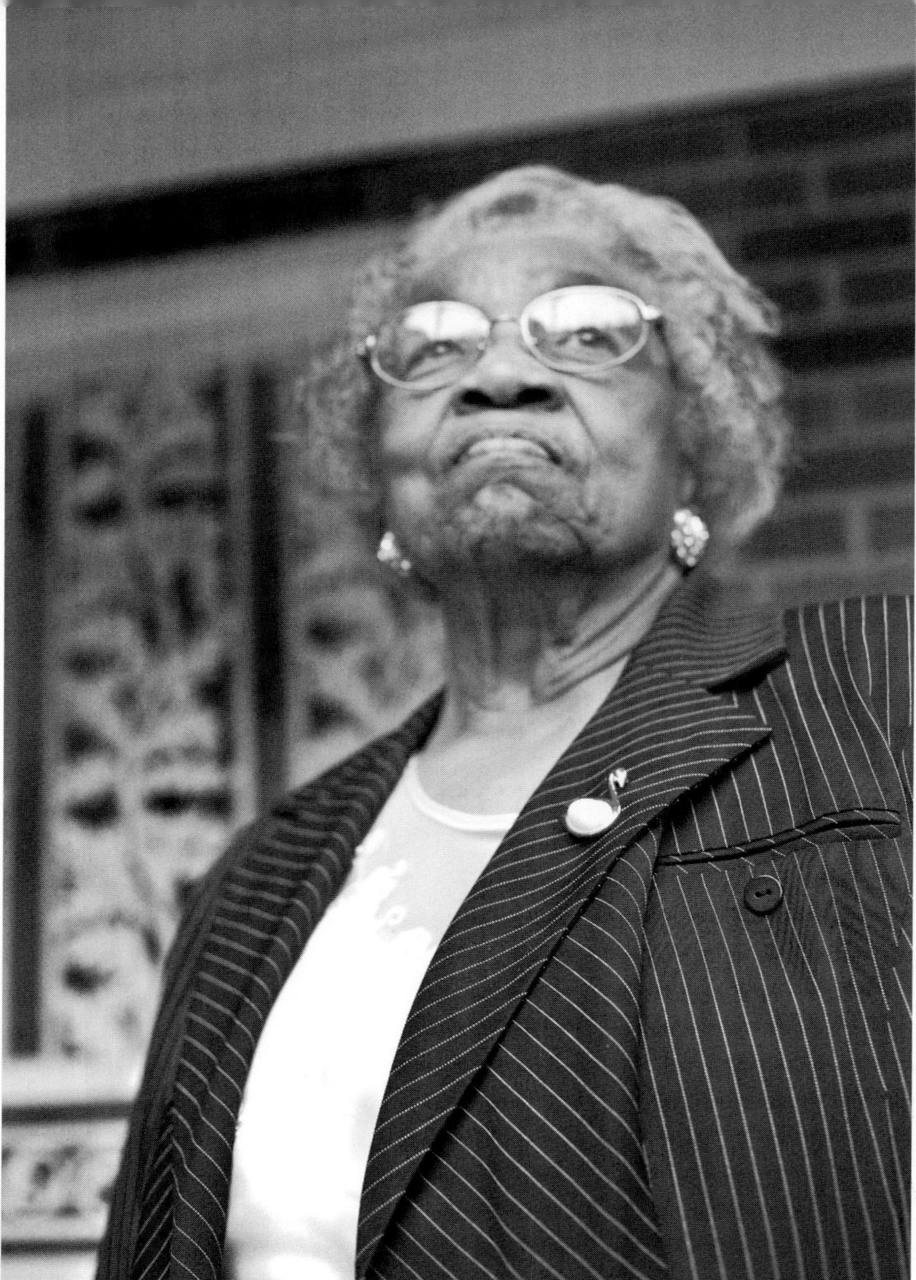

Those who have no record of what their forebears have accomplished lose the inspiration which comes from the teaching of biography and history.

CARTER G. WOODSON, PH.D.
American historian and writer
(1875-1950)

Doris Ann Fullwood | MOTHERING TEACHER & TEACHING MOTHER

Long before Hillary Clinton wrote a book, Doris Fullwood knew it takes a village to raise children. Her daughter and I became best friends in kindergarten, so Mrs. Fullwood has been part of my life for ages. Along with my parents, she schooled me on many lifelong lessons.

While I was growing up, my friend's mother was fun-loving, but I also knew she didn't play. I attribute her mix of gentleness and sternness to being a classroom teacher for so many years. She understood children at a level few adults do. Frequently, she would start conversations and pose questions in a way that made us feel safe enough to answer honestly. And whenever we expressed views that were naïve or misguided, she cared enough to set us straight.

One funny, teachable moment that I'll never forget happened when I was in fifth grade. As was often the case, Mrs. Fullwood was chauffeuring her girls and me around town after school. A few blocks from my family's house, I carelessly tossed out a candy-bar wrapper from an open window of the car. Mrs. Fullwood immediately stopped the station wagon, voiced her dismay and instructed me to retrieve the littered scrap of paper. Though shocked, I didn't dare hesitate but swiftly hopped out to find the wrapper. I arrived home embarrassed but wiser.

That day she raised my consciousness about protecting Mother Earth, and she also showed me how influential other mothers can be in a child's life. Just as she had an impact on me, my mother was a positive influence on her daughter, too. Now, as an adult and a parent, I exercise every opportunity to be a role model for youth and to give back in ways that tend the "village." I tie it back to the enduring lessons Mrs. Fullwood taught. And to this day, litterbugs exasperate me.

LISA NANNETTE MOORE
Connection: *Family friend* • Channel: *Mentor, YMCA Black Achievers, founded in 1971*
Cause: *Influencing the lives of children*

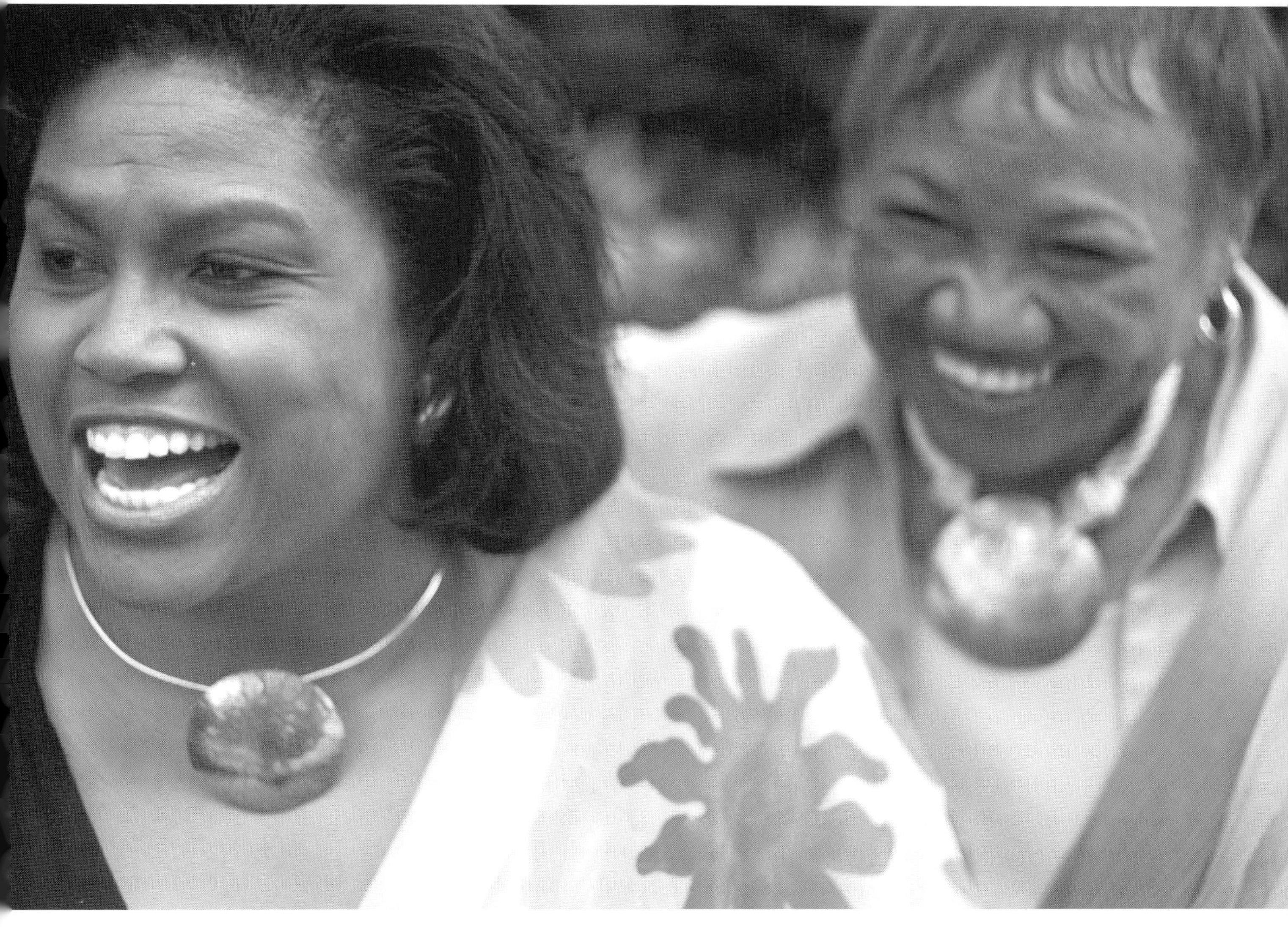

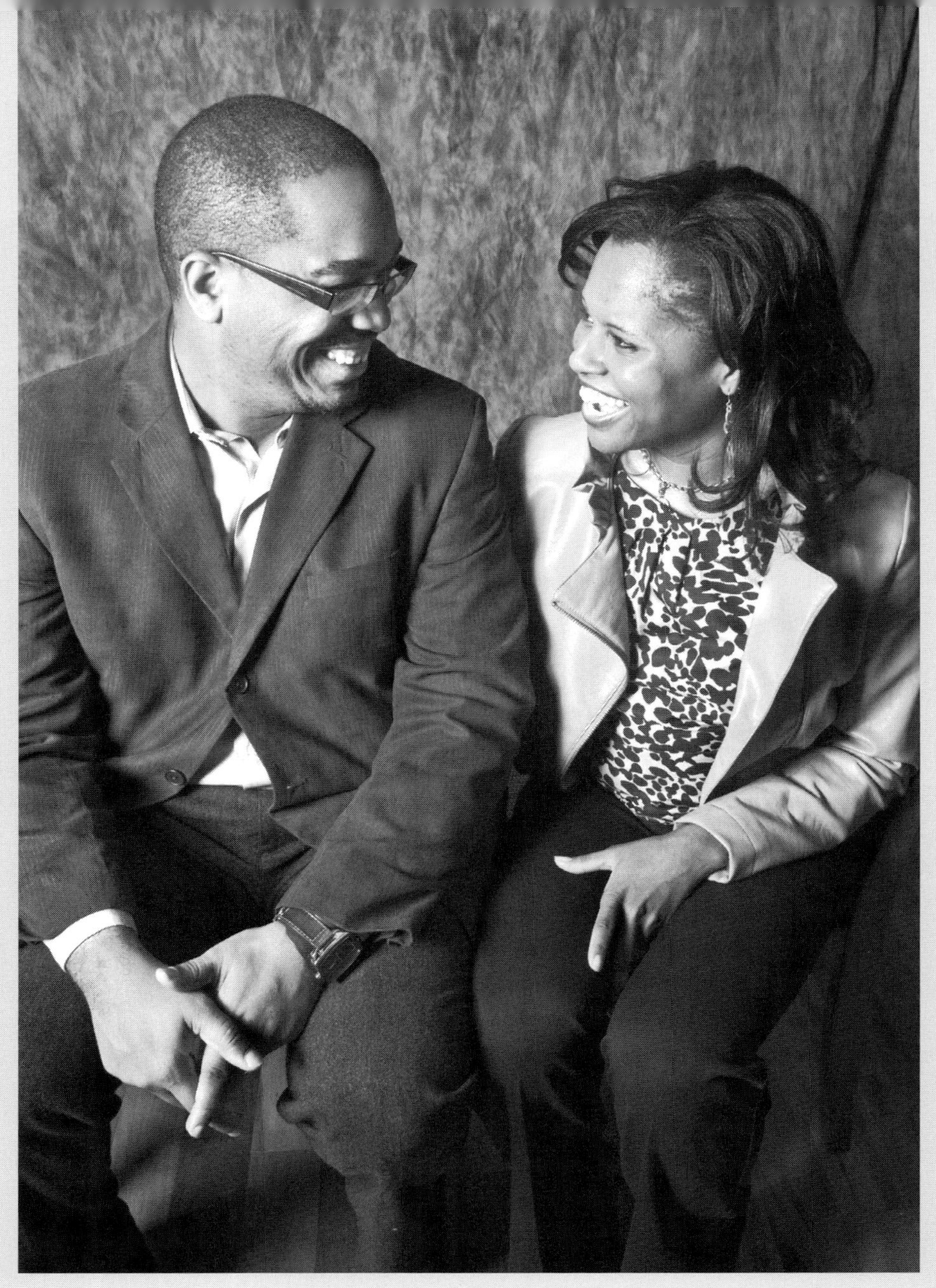

To laugh often and much. To win the respect of intelligent people and the affection of children; to earn the appreciation of one's critics and endure the betrayal of false friends. To appreciate beauty, to find the best in others, to leave the world a bit better, whether a healthy child, a redeemed social condition, or a job well done. To know even one other life has breathed easier because you live. This is to have succeeded.

RALPH WALDO EMERSON
American philosopher and poet
(1803-82)

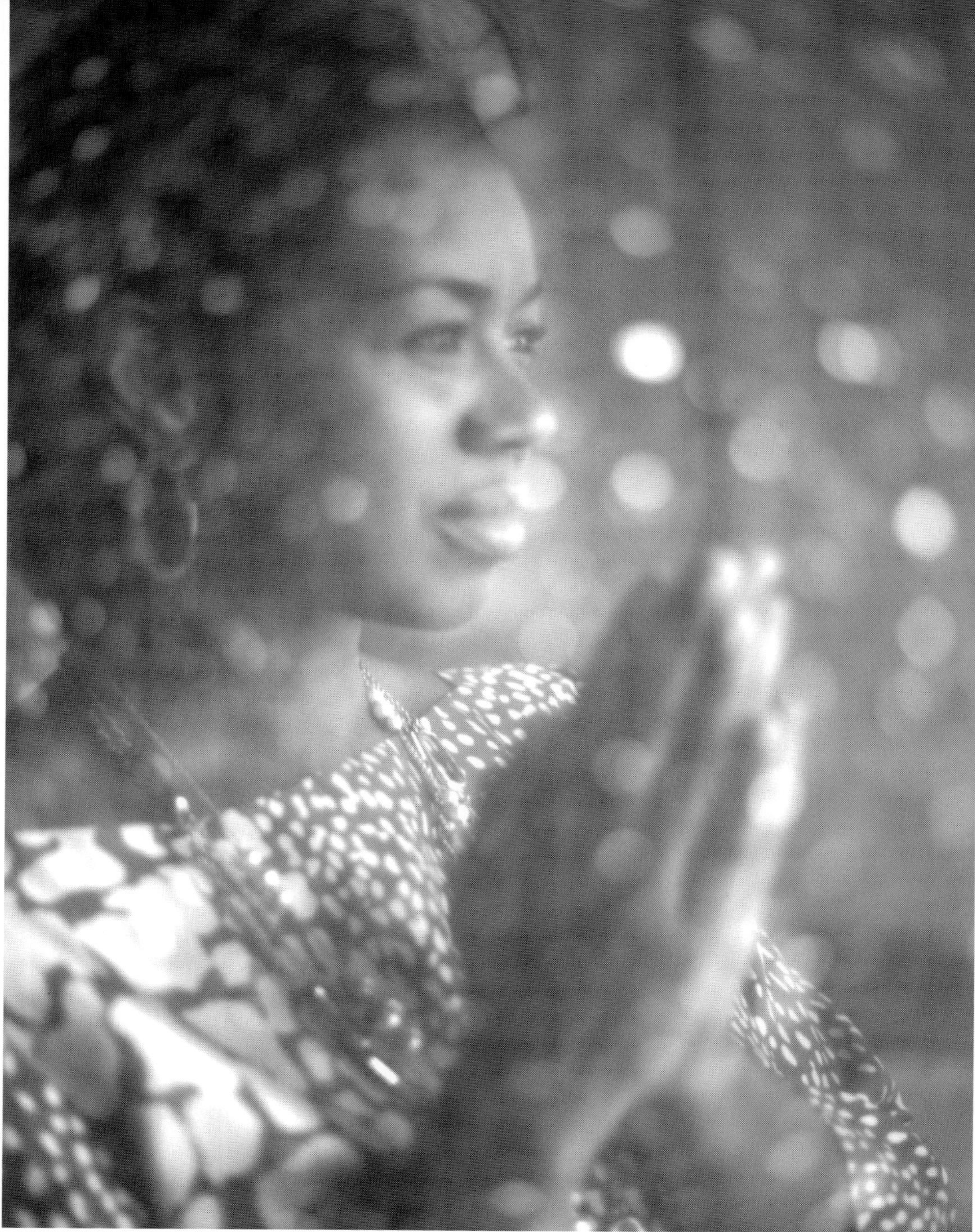

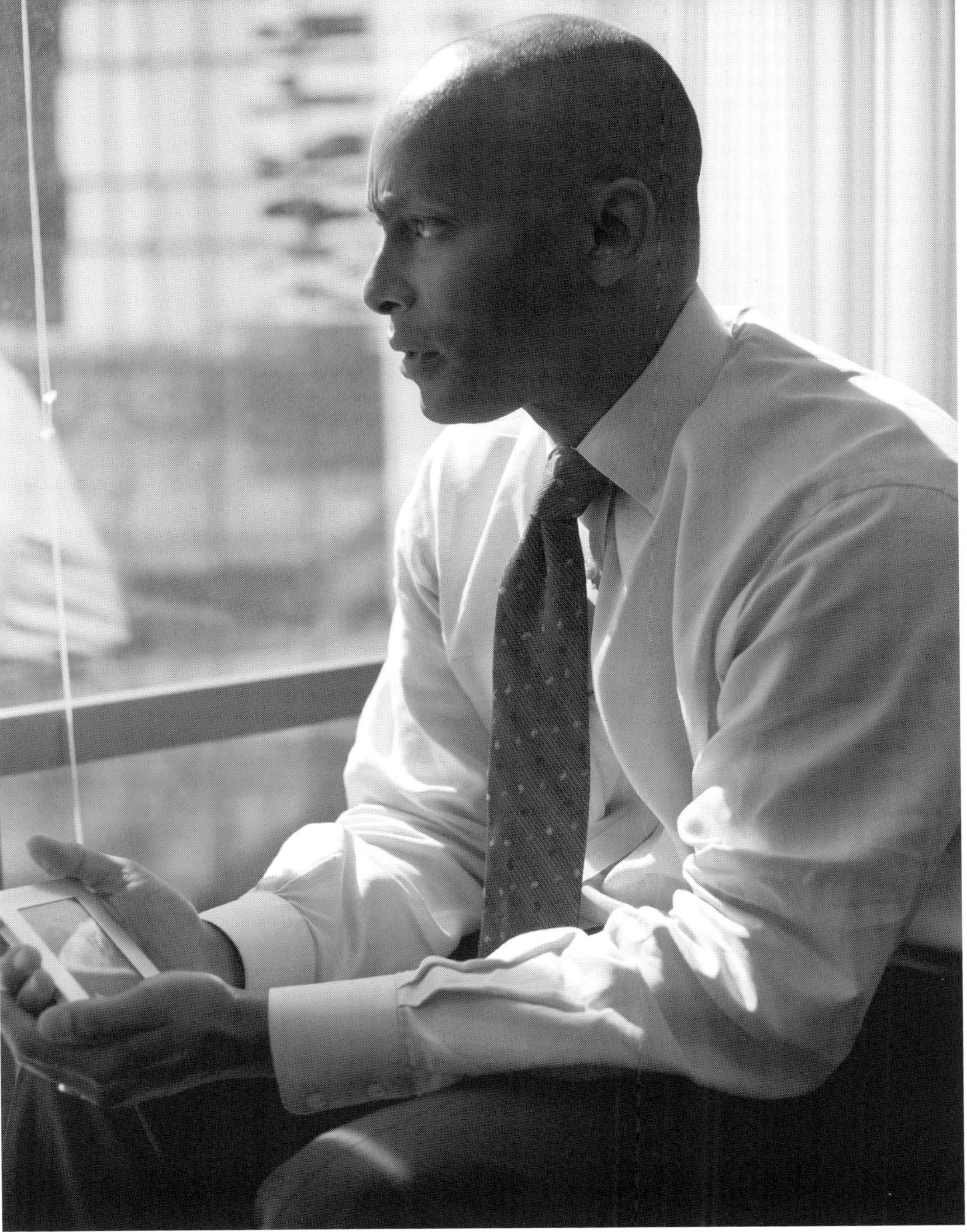

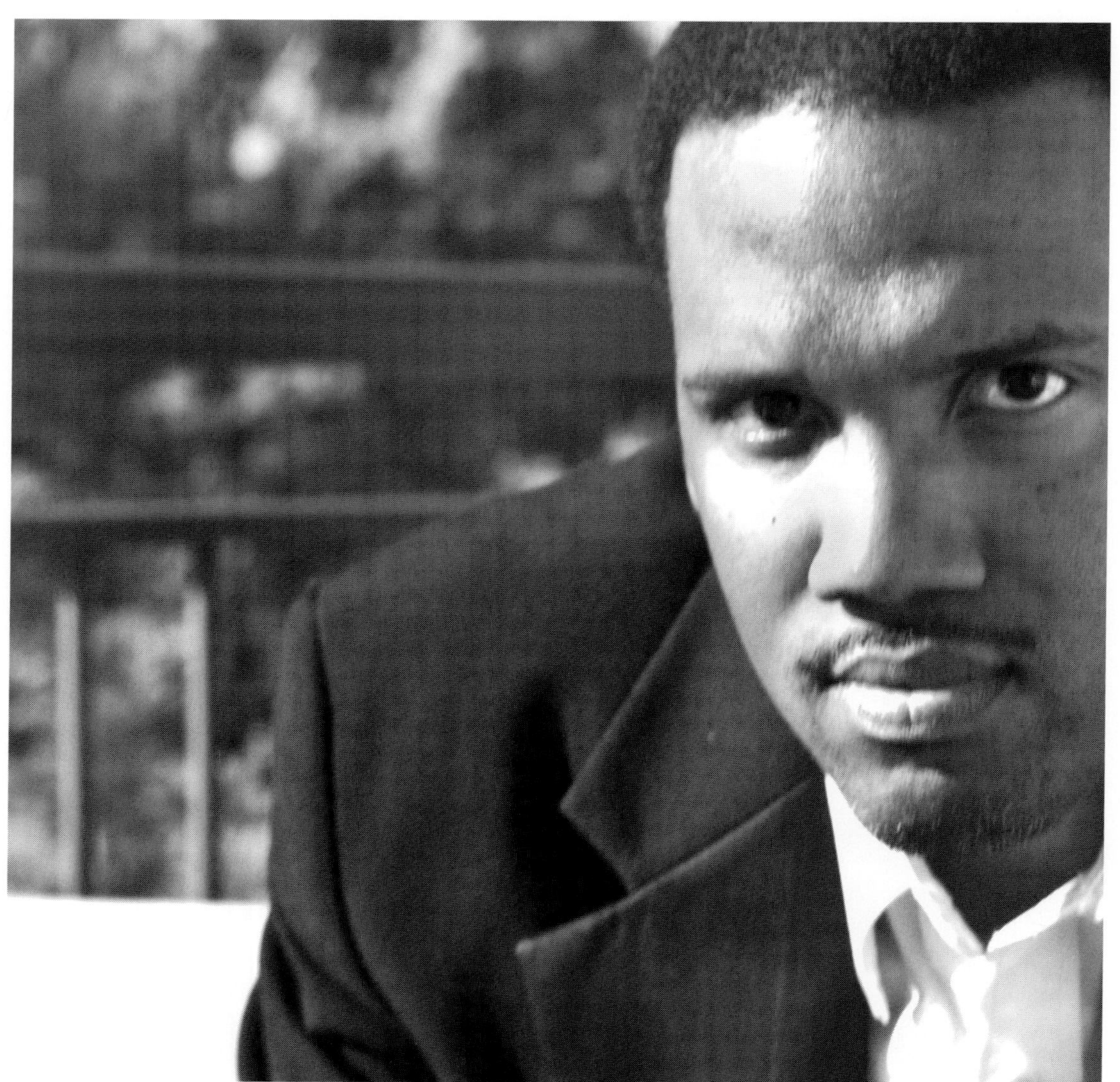

The wise man does not lay up his own treasures.
The more he gives to others, the more he has for his own.

LAO TZU
Chinese philosopher and founder of Taoism
(circa sixth century BC)

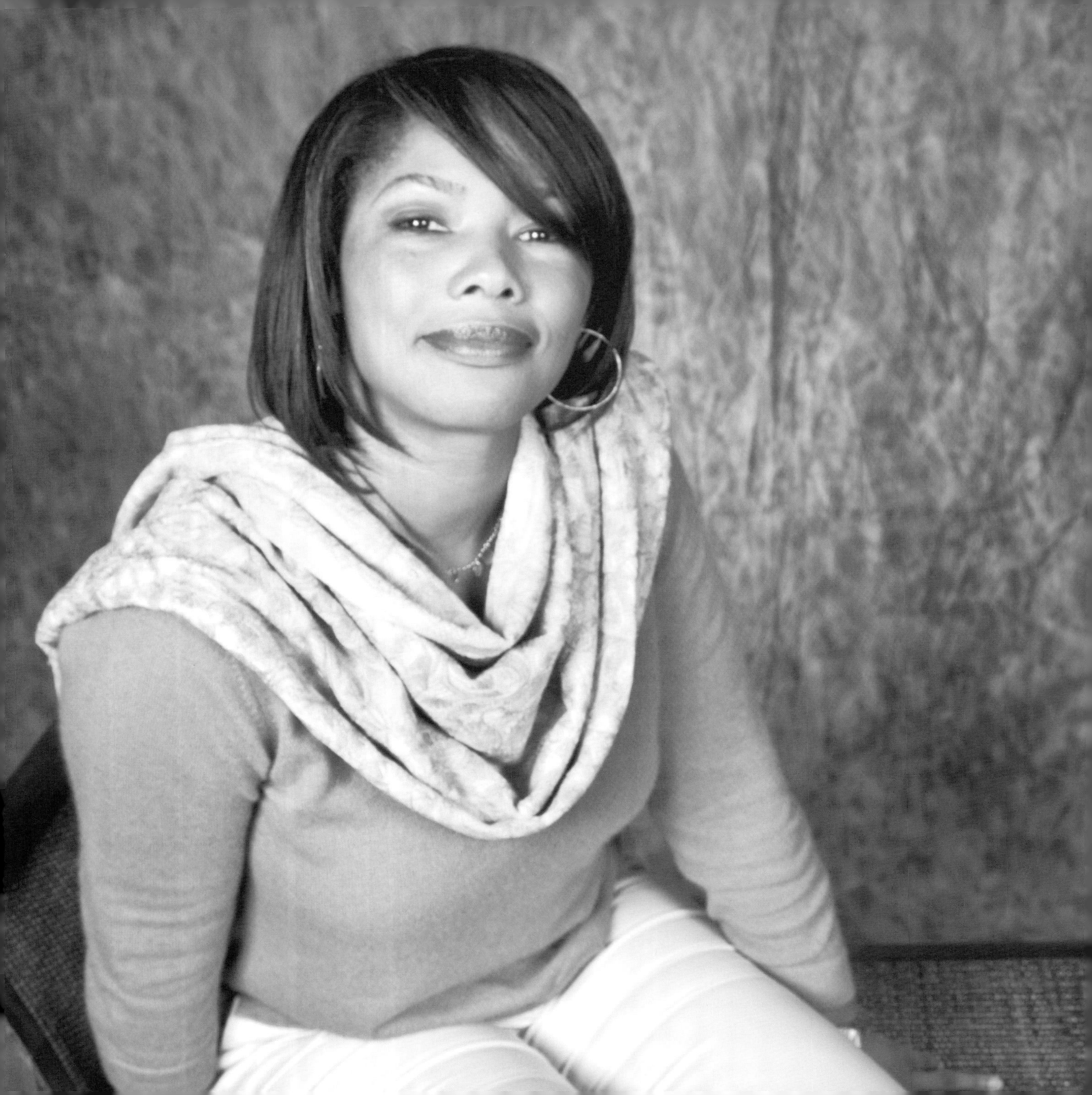

FRAMEWORK

A philanthropist is . . .

A philanthropist is one who seeks to understand the human condition and responds to needs with financial and human resources. — *Jereann King Johnson*

Someone who recognizes the 'linked destiny' of all people of the Earth and works beyond her or his self-interest to improve the quality of life for others. Everyone has the opportunity to be a philanthropist by deciding to live their life in a way that reflects empathy for others. — *Jennifer Henderson*

One who gives financial resources and/or talents and skills in the support of causes that serve to enrich and or enhance others that are in need — *Daryl Parham*

An individual who gives their time, talent and skills and/or financial support to positive community-changing efforts — *LaDawn Sullivan*

Anyone who translates his or her love of humanity into action with a gift of time, talent or treasure — *Eric Law*

Someone who is intentional about giving of time, talent and funding for a specific purpose — *Christian Friend*

An individual or group of individuals who share their wealth to support identified causes — *Ihsan Abdin*

Someone who cares and shows it — *Joy Webb*

A faithful steward — *Sherry Waters*

It's a person who is constantly assessing how he or she can be of service to others through the giving of one's know-how and money. — *Darryl K. Lester*

A person who gives out of the goodness of the hearts without any expectations or strings attached — *Jeanene Thompson*

Someone who is willing to share his or her abundance with others to make a positive difference in others' lives — *Dan Nunn*

Any individual or organization that works to uplift humanity with dignity and respect — *Mattie Marshall*

Someone who gives selflessly so others can have more — *Ohmar Land*

Anyone that gives — *Edgar Villanueva*

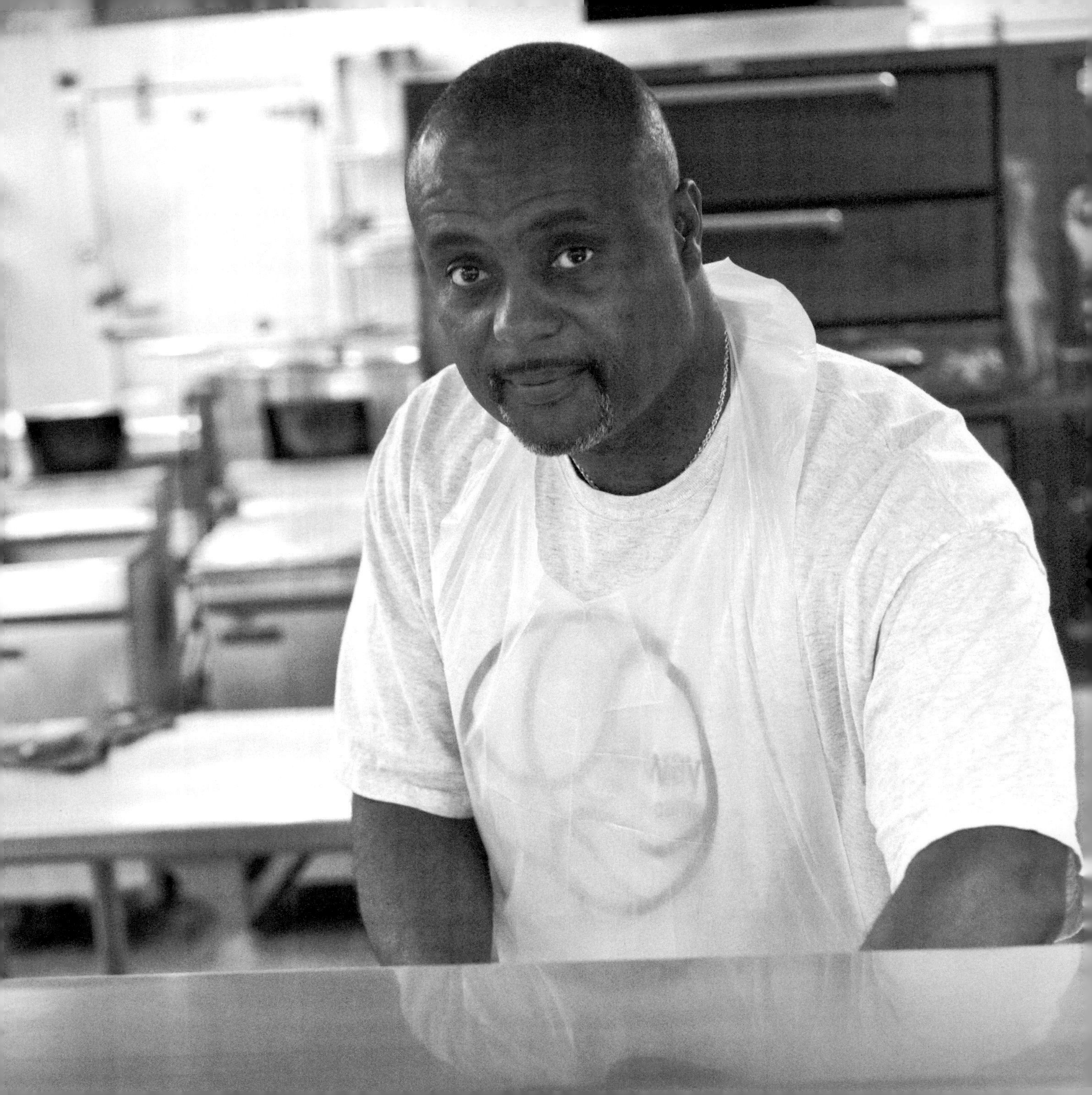

I can't do everything, but I can do something to help somebody. And what I can do, I will do. I wish I could do more.

OSEOLA MCCARTY
American washerwoman and major donor to the University of Southern Mississippi
(1908-99)

Lois Jamison | LOVER OF HUMANKIND

Funny, I was going through one of the drawers in the den brimming with cards and thank-you notes organizing my mother's things, when I decided to start a list of charities represented in that cramped little archive. According to Daddy, Mommy and he would select two or three charities each month to donate a few dollars toward. I don't think it was ever more than ten, maybe forty dollars.

When there was a child from the family or the church who was graduating, money would more often go to one of them than a charitable organization. Mind you, my parents, on a fixed income, were simultaneously tithing to their church. When Mommy started getting ill, I considered putting a stop to what seemed like her helter-skelter "gifting." I chalked it up to boredom and her increasing dementia. Then I thought about how blessed and peaceful the lives of my parents had been. They didn't lack or want for anything and reveled in the love of each other. Who was I to upset the graceful balance of their blessing others and being blessed in return?

So, now I just lay aside the Native American blankets, St. Jude commemorations, Veterans of Foreign Wars tributes, rosaries and so forth. It hadn't struck me until the preacher used the word *philanthropist* in my mother's eulogy that that was in essence who she was. Over the years, she had been spreading a little love and blessings . . . with a few checks a month.

SANDRA JAMISON
Connection: *Daughter* • Channel: *Soror, Alpha Kappa Alpha Sorority, founded in 1908*
Cause: *Arts*

Thank You

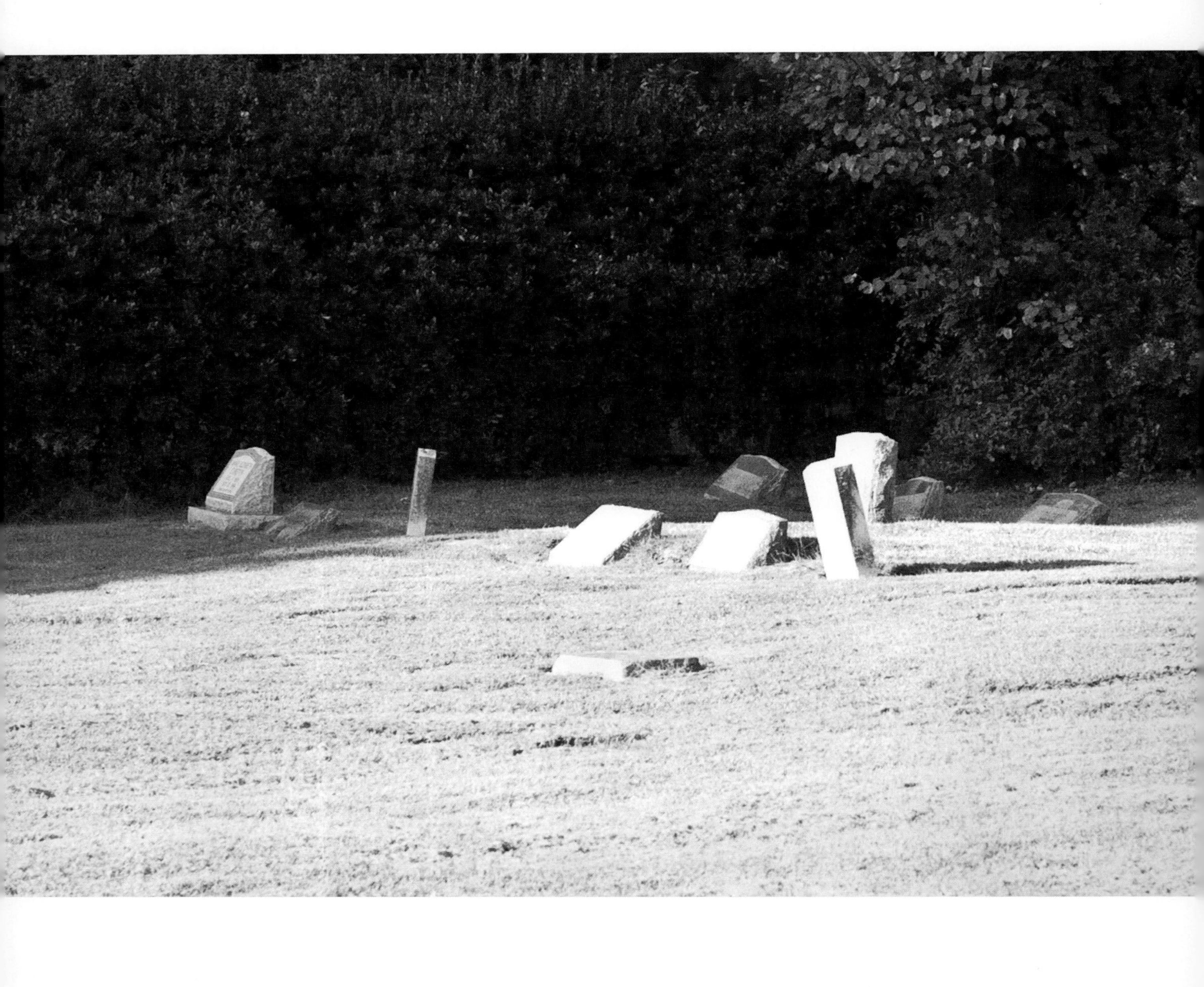

All you have shall some day be given; Therefore give now, that the season of giving may be yours and not your inheritors.

KAHLIL GIBRAN
Lebanese-born artist and poet
(1883-1931)

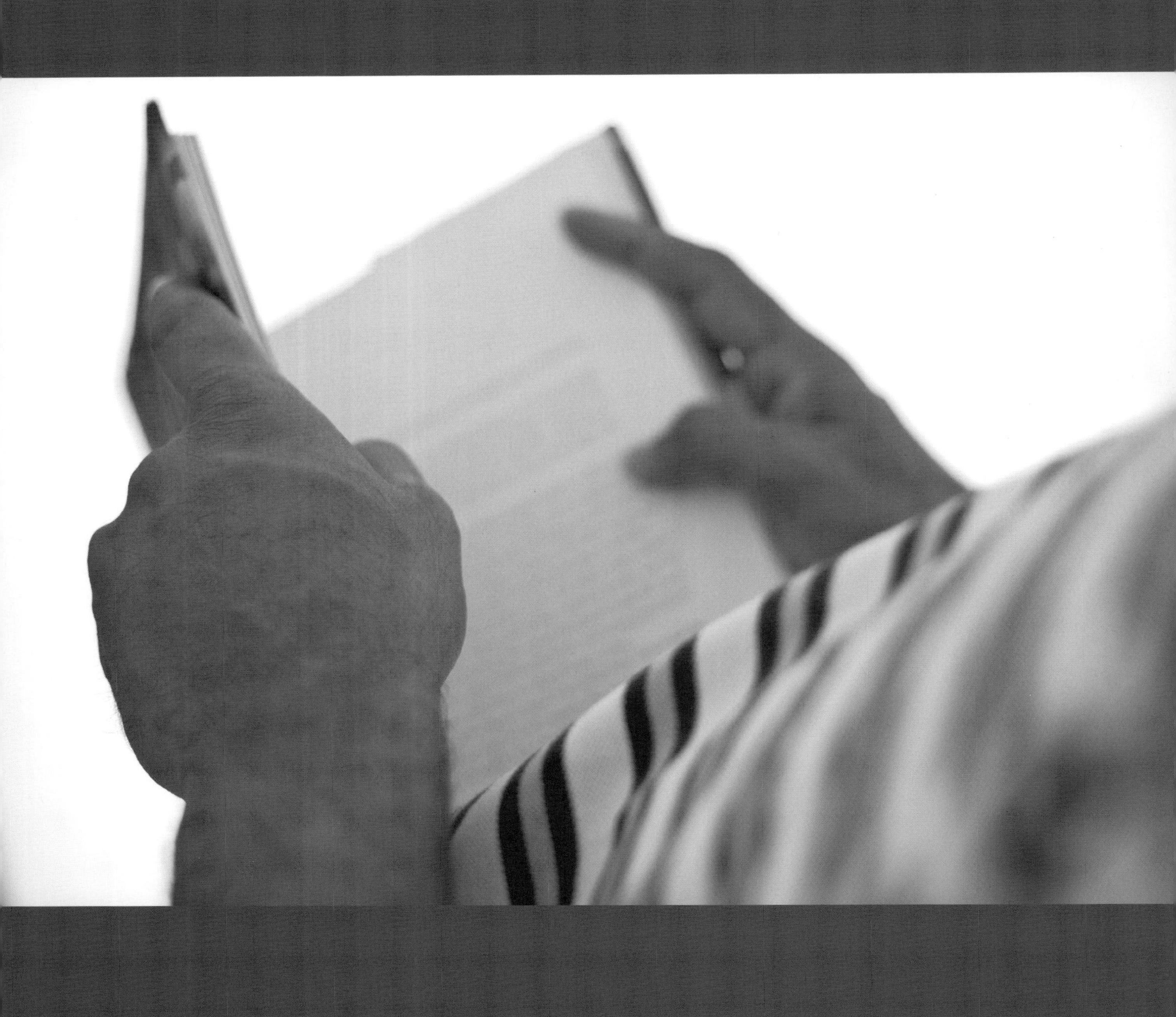

"I USED TO READ about the wealthy giving thousands of dollars to this charity and that institution and thought I would never be in a position to give. Later, when I began earning more than what housework had paid, I still thought I didn't make enough to donate a substantial amount. A church tithe, a few dollars to United Way or dropping two or three dollars in a cheer bucket was all I thought my budget could handle, after all I was married with two children. Eventually, I learned it didn't have to be about giving only money but about time and talent, too. Not that I had an abundance of that either. Looking back, I now realize that I did give, in a variety of ways, but at the time I thought it was insignificant. . . . You don't have to be wealthy to be a philanthropist."

Mary Peterson
president of Morganton chapter of Bethune Women's Club

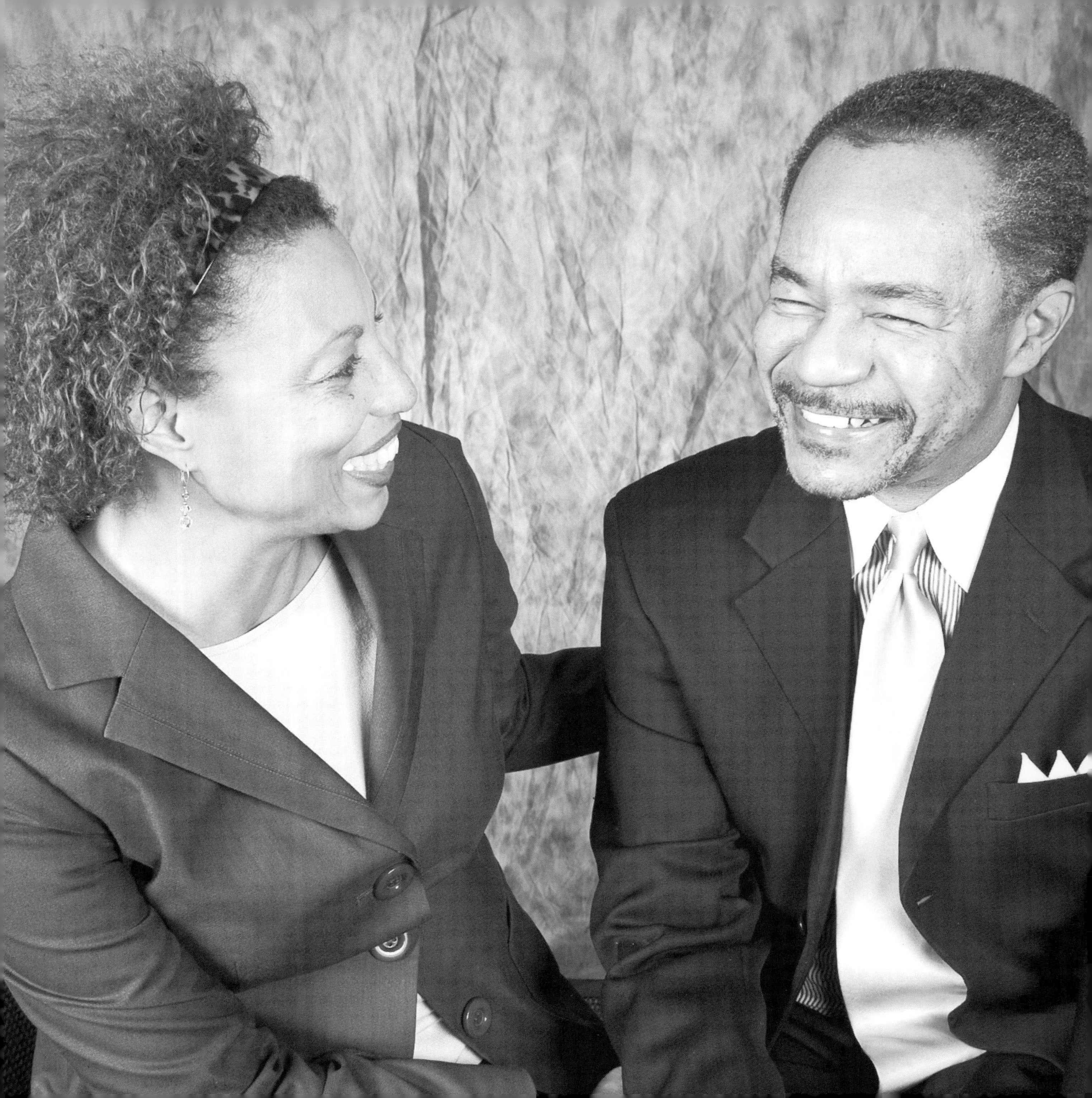

The place to improve the world is first in one's own heart and head and hands.

ROBERT M. PIRSIG
American writer and philosopher
(b. 1928)

Endia Brabham | VOICE COACH

Wow. That's what entered my mind after first encountering Endia during a site visit to Jacob's Ladder Job Center. Jacob's Ladder helps unemployed and underemployed people find and keep living-wage jobs. Two years ago, I visited the center, which was a finalist in my giving circle's grant process. As is customary of grantmakers, a small group of us made a round of site visits to nonprofits under consideration for a grant.

Much to our surprise and delight, the center's staff had assembled an impressive mix of a dozen or so stakeholders—board members, staff, volunteers and clients. We listened as the various stakeholders took turns giving testimony to how Jacob's Ladder was changing lives. Then Endia Brabham arrived. She settled quietly into an open seat. When it was Endia's turn, she apologized for being late and explained that she had just come from a college class but felt compelled to participate in the site visit.

Endia began sharing her story, and I was struck by how generous she was with what she revealed. She told us about her experiences with joblessness and homelessness and gave a vivid account of hardships she had faced. She credited Jacob's Ladder for how her life had turned around. Endia also made it clear that since regaining her footing she had become an advocate and mentor for others and transitioned from client to volunteer at the center. When she finished, I was wowed by the program's impact on her life. I was equally awed by her command of the room and eloquence in conveying the challenges and barriers when chronically unemployed.

Impressions from that site visit are still with me. Endia demonstrated how people in crisis can come to harness their power when caring people are willing to open doors and dedicate time to bolster their skills and confidence. I remember Endia saying she used to aspire to become a voice for others but learned everyone has his own voice and that she can only help people find it. Memory of her voice—authentic, strong and passionate—continues to be a force in my philanthropy and advocacy.

DAWN FISHER

Connection: *Admirer* • Channel: *Donor, WFAE 90.7 FM Public Radio* • Cause: *Arts & culture*

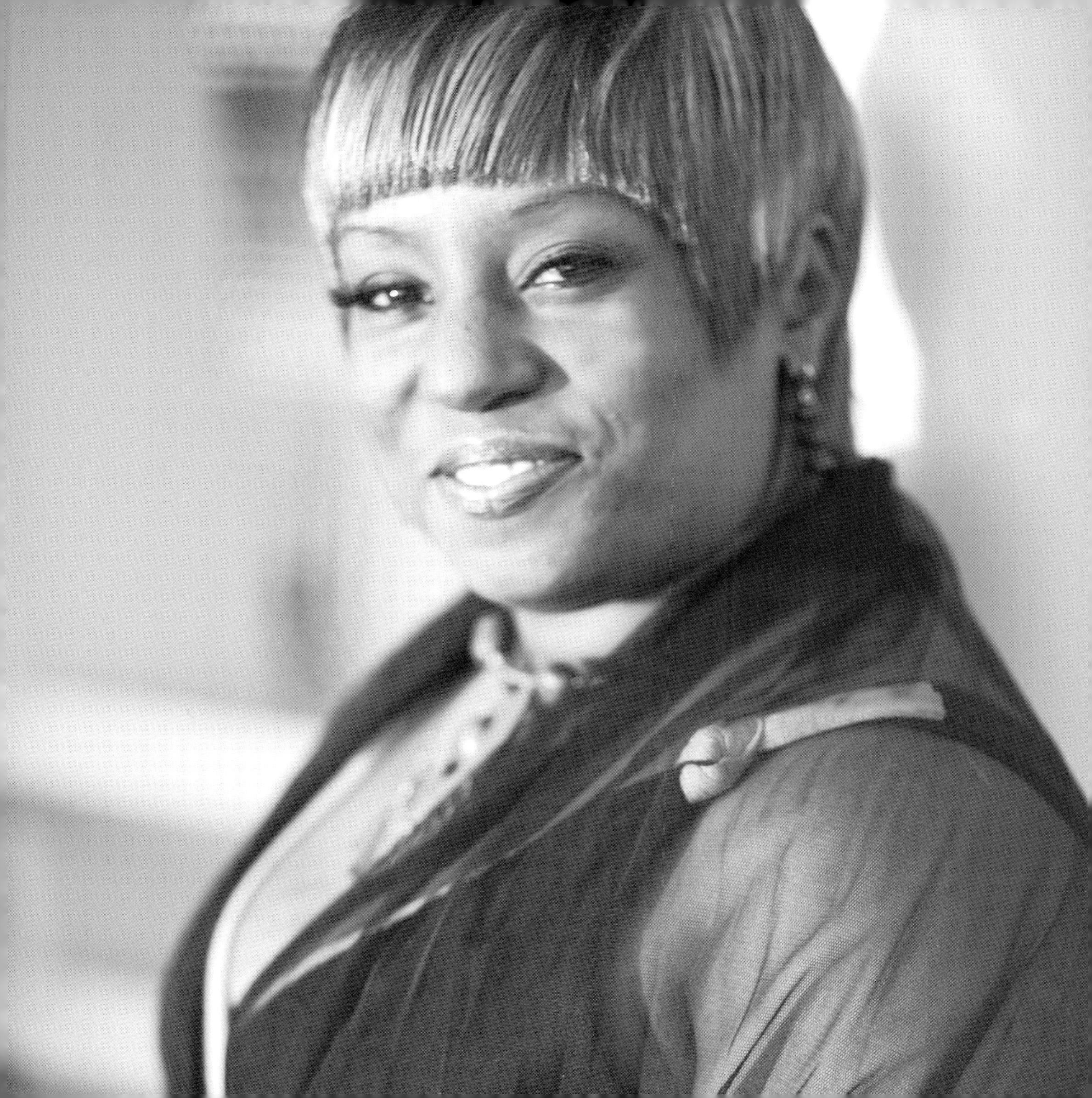

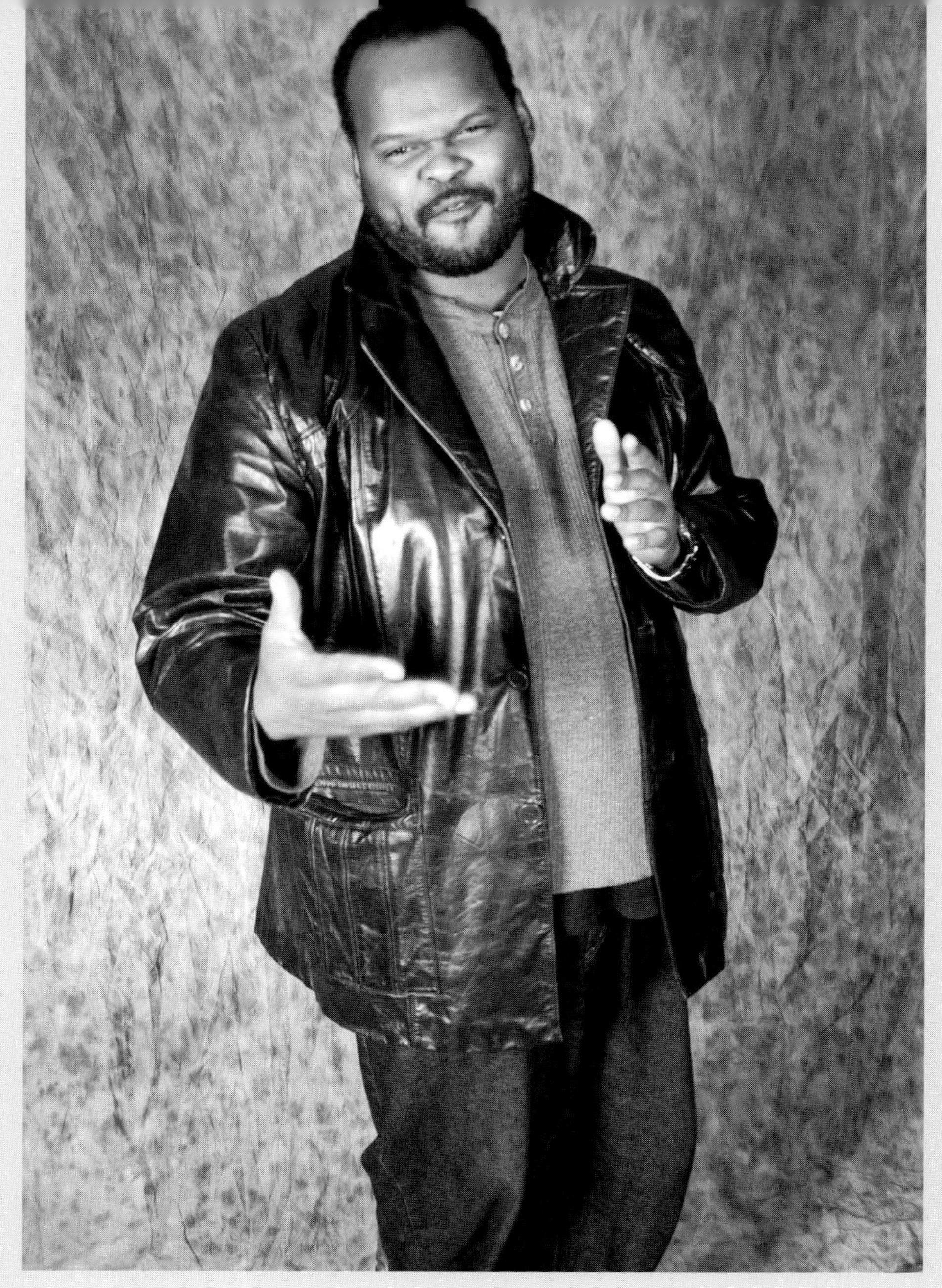

The mind has exactly the same powers as the hands;
not merely to grasp the world, but to change it.

COLIN WILSON
British writer and philosopher
(b. 1931)

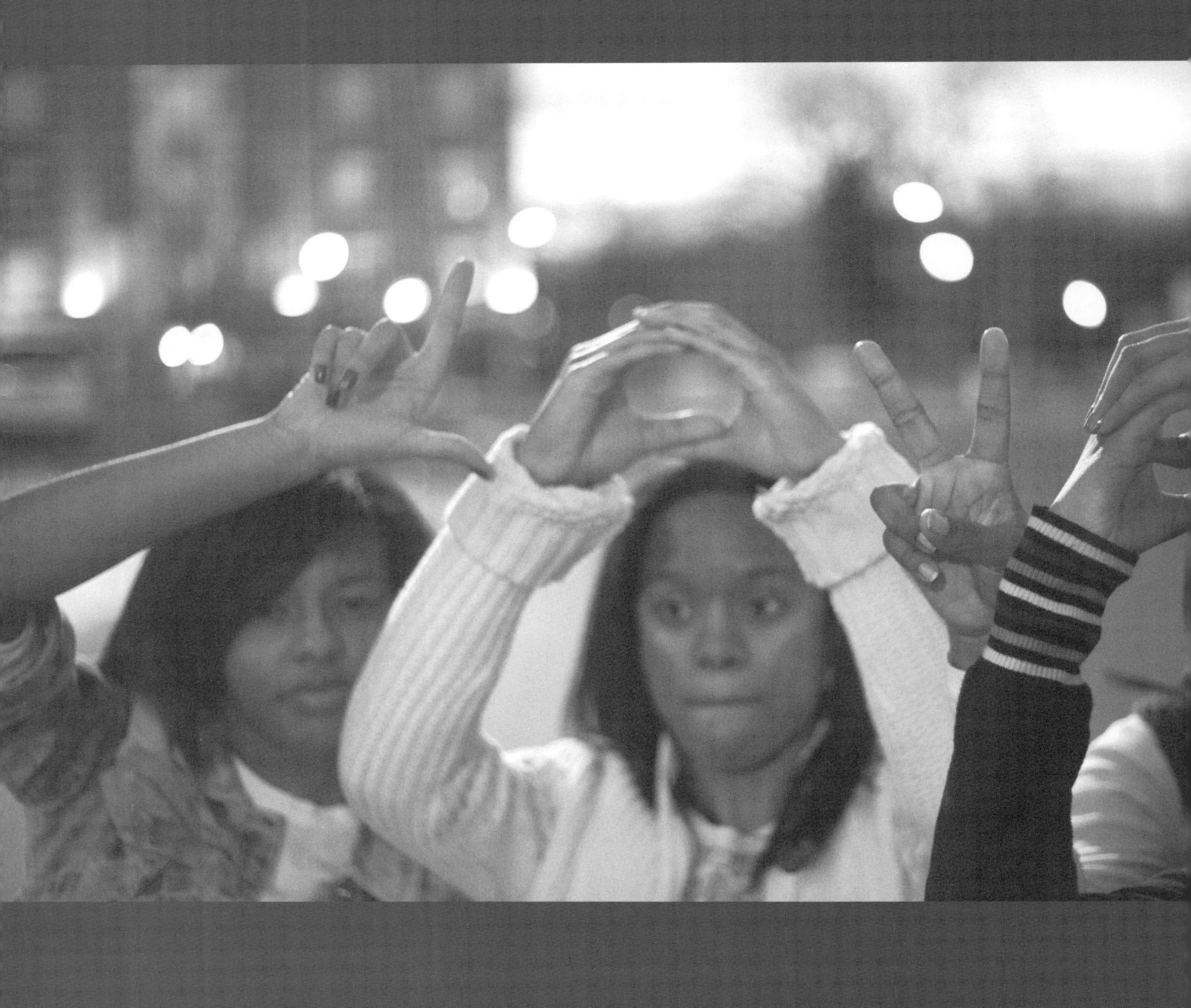

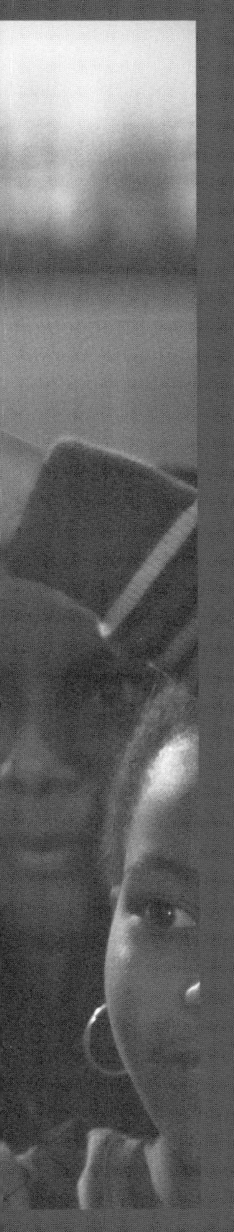

"A COUPLE OF TIMES a year my parents used to let me skip school to spend the day with my Granddaddy. I would ride with Granddaddy in his beat up yet sturdy Ford truck and shuttle people around the small Alabama town of Loxley all day long. But, Granddaddy wasn't a taxi driver; he was a farmer. Every election day he would volunteer to shuttle people to and from the polls. It wasn't until I was an adult that I realized the significance of those truck rides.

"Granddaddy was always hiring young men and giving them odd jobs to help out at the farm. He would stay late after church on Sunday to count the day's offerings. I never consciously associated Granddaddy's life with one of a philanthropist . . . I just thought that was who Granddaddy was. But, now I get it. It is indeed who he was. Thanks, Mom and Dad, for letting me skip school on those days to see my Granddaddy model philanthropy for me. My story, my motivation for giving is my pursuit of purpose and character, and the love for mankind that my Granddaddy showed me."

Marcus Littles
member, Emmanuel Baptist Church , Brooklyn

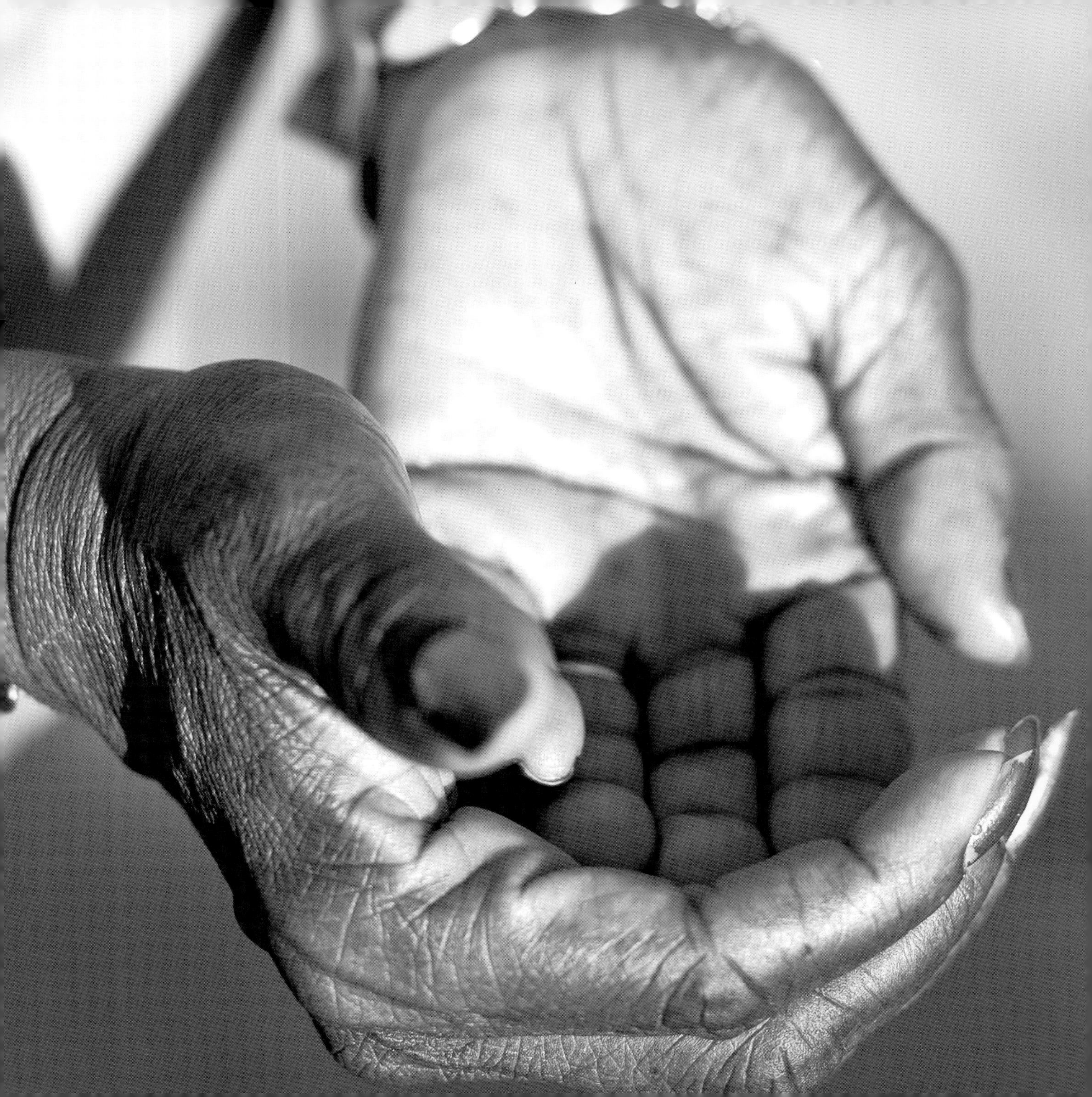

Charity is no substitute for justice withheld.

ST. AUGUSTINE
Theologian and philosopher of the ancient world
(354-430)

Robert J. Brown | PASSIONATE COMMUNITARIAN

I have known Bob Brown pretty much all my life. We both grew up in High Point. When I was about nine years old, he was working as a parks and recreation counselor. I came to know him well through the student activities he organized. Over the years, we shared turning-point experiences, and he eventually became my mentor. His generous spirit reveals an abiding concern for the quality of life of all people, especially young people who are striving for better lives.

Bob Brown introduced me to South Africa. It started when he invited me to make some arrangements for one of Nelson and Winnie Mandela's daughters, which led to my traveling to the family's homeland. Eventually, I began working with Bob on an initiative to provide books to young children in South African townships lacking adequate educational facilities. Together, we brought a lot of creativity to the project, and it grew by leaps and bounds.

Without a doubt, our relationship helped mold me into the *passionate communitarian* that I am today. He is one of many people who made a way when I could not see a way and helped me financially when my parents did not have the resources. I cannot act as if I have made it by pulling up my own bootstraps. That is not my life story. I am here because there have been a lot of people coaching and mentoring me. So, it is my responsibility to do likewise when a young person wants to realize a passionate dream, but obstacles block the way. If I have the strength and resources to remove those obstacles then I am obligated to do it.

RONALD CARTER, PH.D.
Connection: *Protégé* • Channel: *President, Johnson C. Smith University, an HBCU founded in 1867* • Cause: *Foster children*

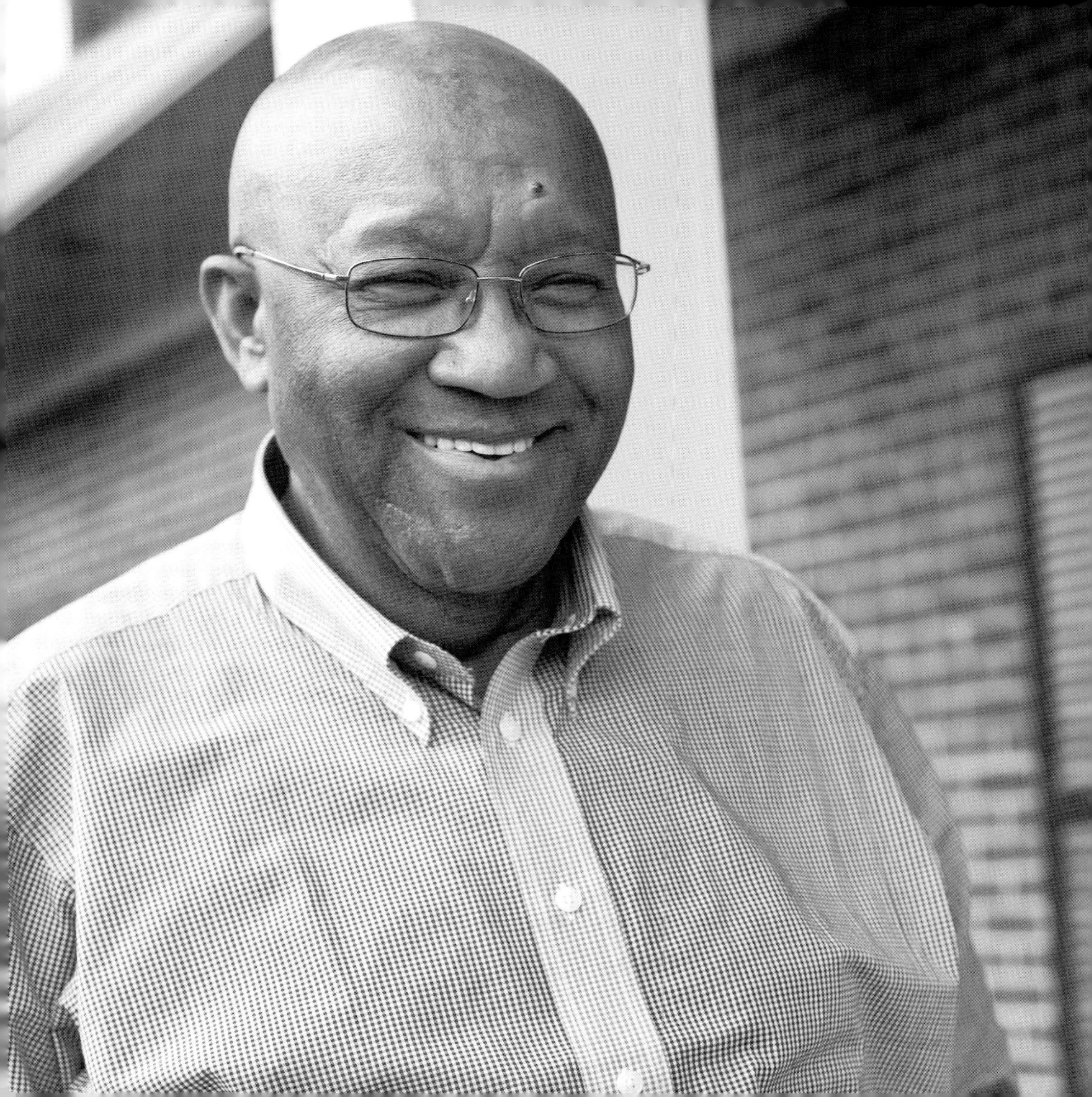

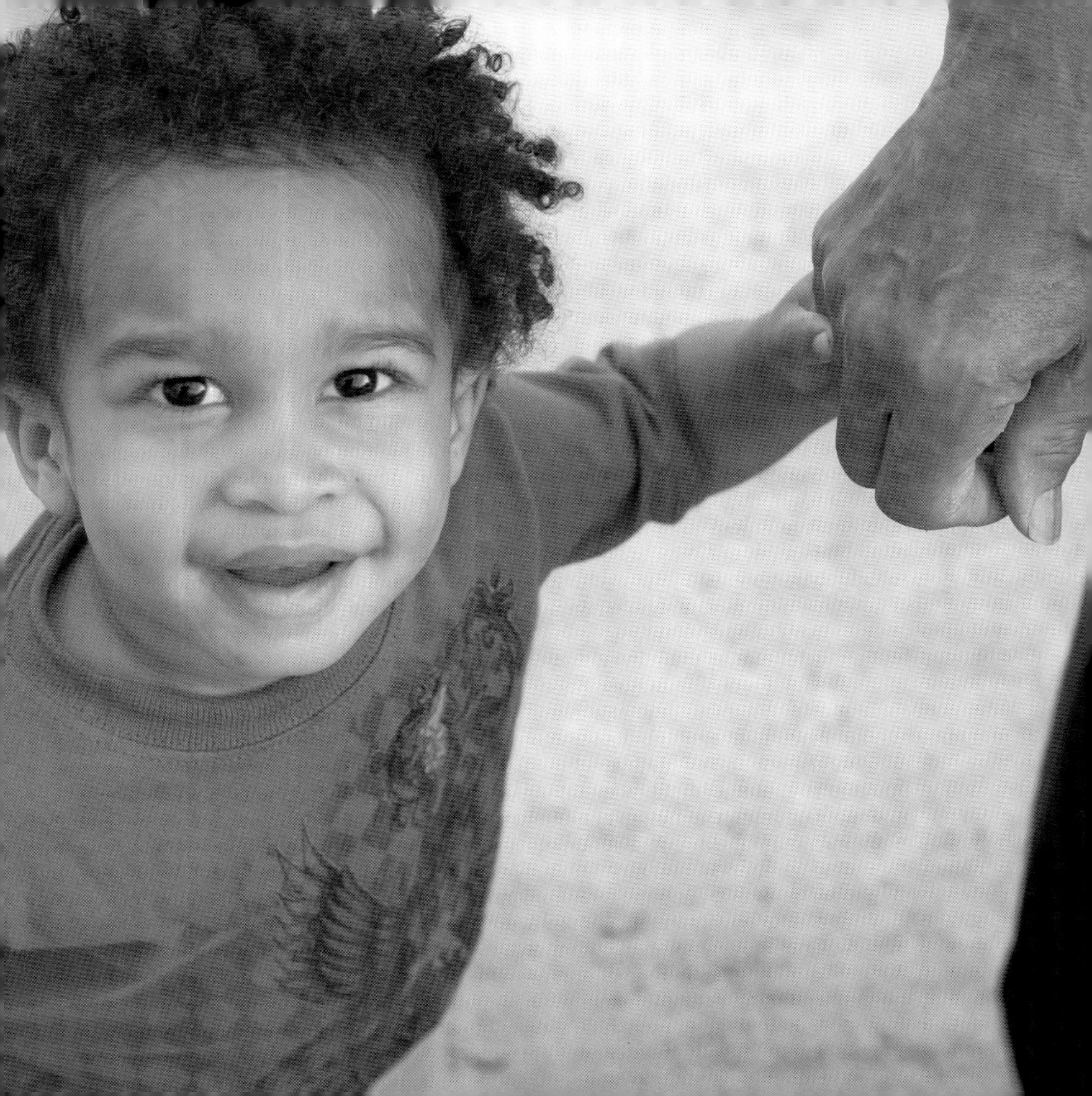

Our children's lives are in our hands, but our future is theirs.

AFRICAN PROVERB

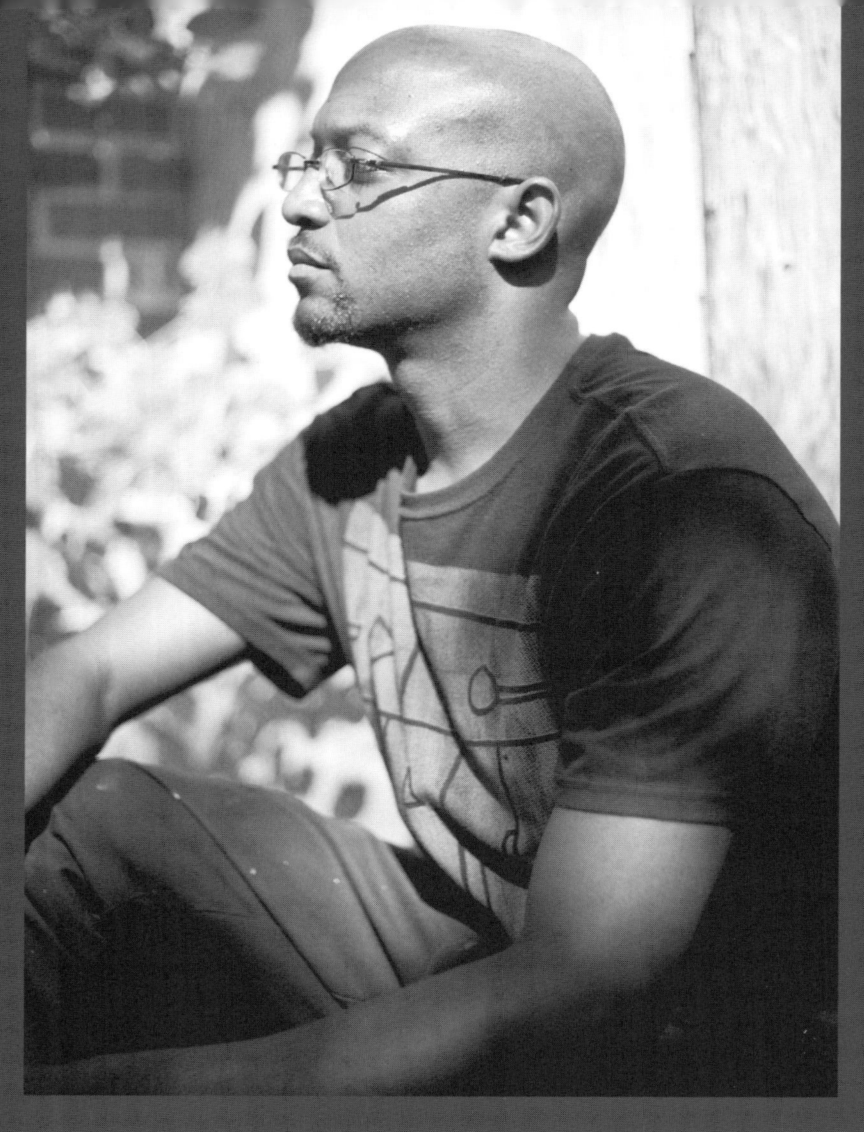

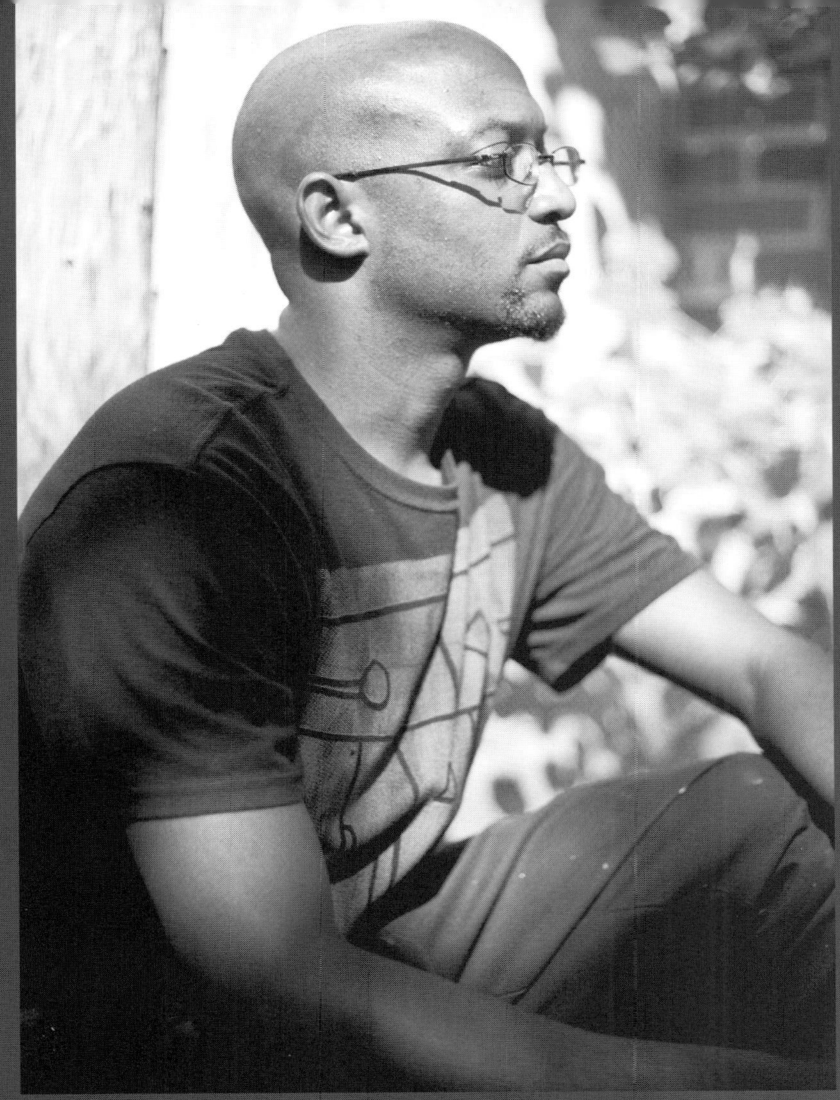

IT IS A PECULIAR SENSATION, this double-consciousness, this sense of always looking at one's self through the eyes of others, of measuring one's soul by the tape of a world that looks on in amused contempt and pity. One ever feels his twoness, an American, a Negro; two warring souls, two thoughts, two unreconciled strivings; two warring ideals in one dark body, whose dogged strength alone keeps it from being torn asunder.

— *W.E.B. Du Bois,* American intellectual leader, author and civil rights activist

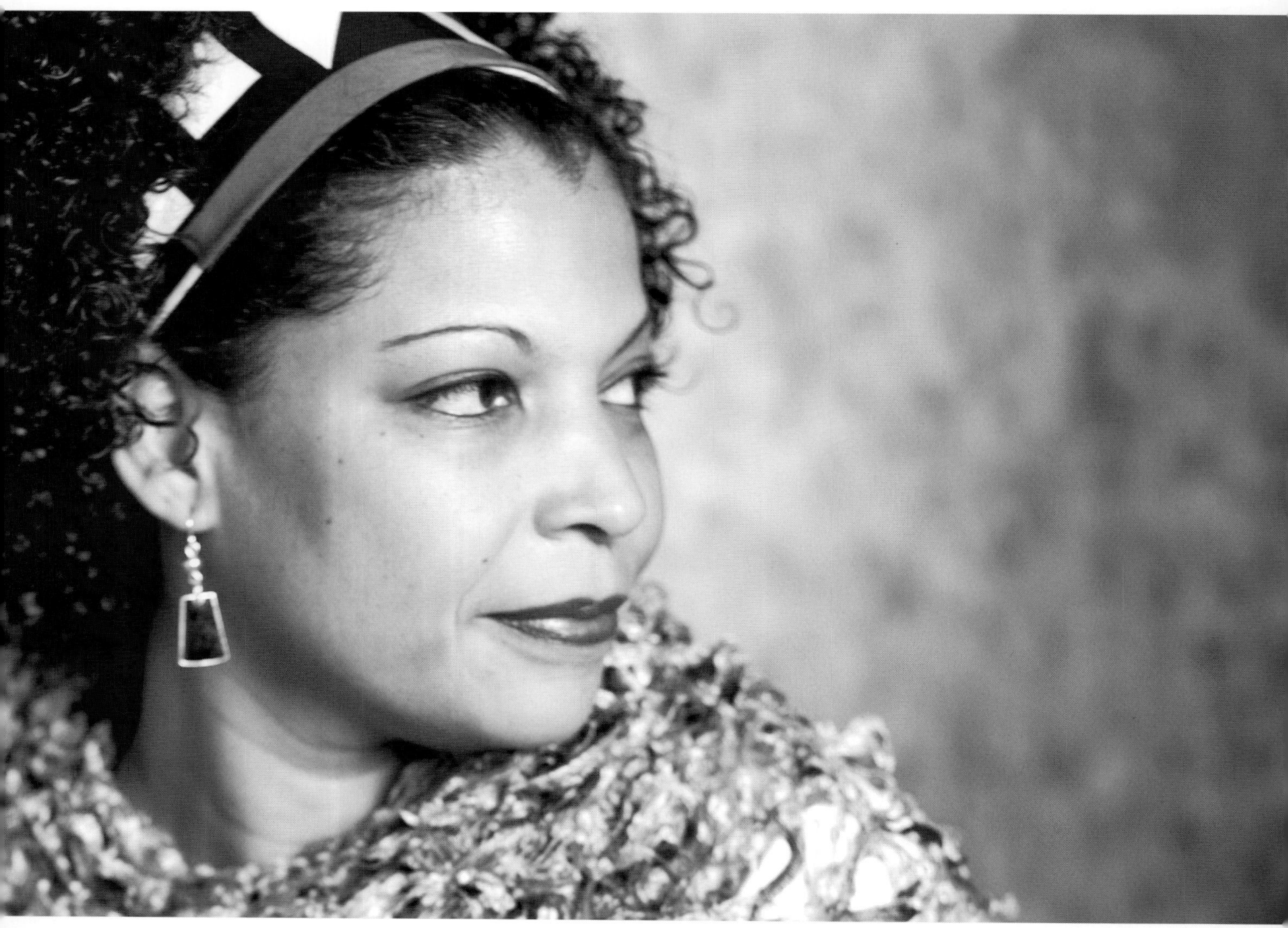

What you leave behind is not what is engraved in stone monuments, but what is woven into the lives of others.

PERICLES
Greek statesman, orator and military general
(circa 495-429 BC)

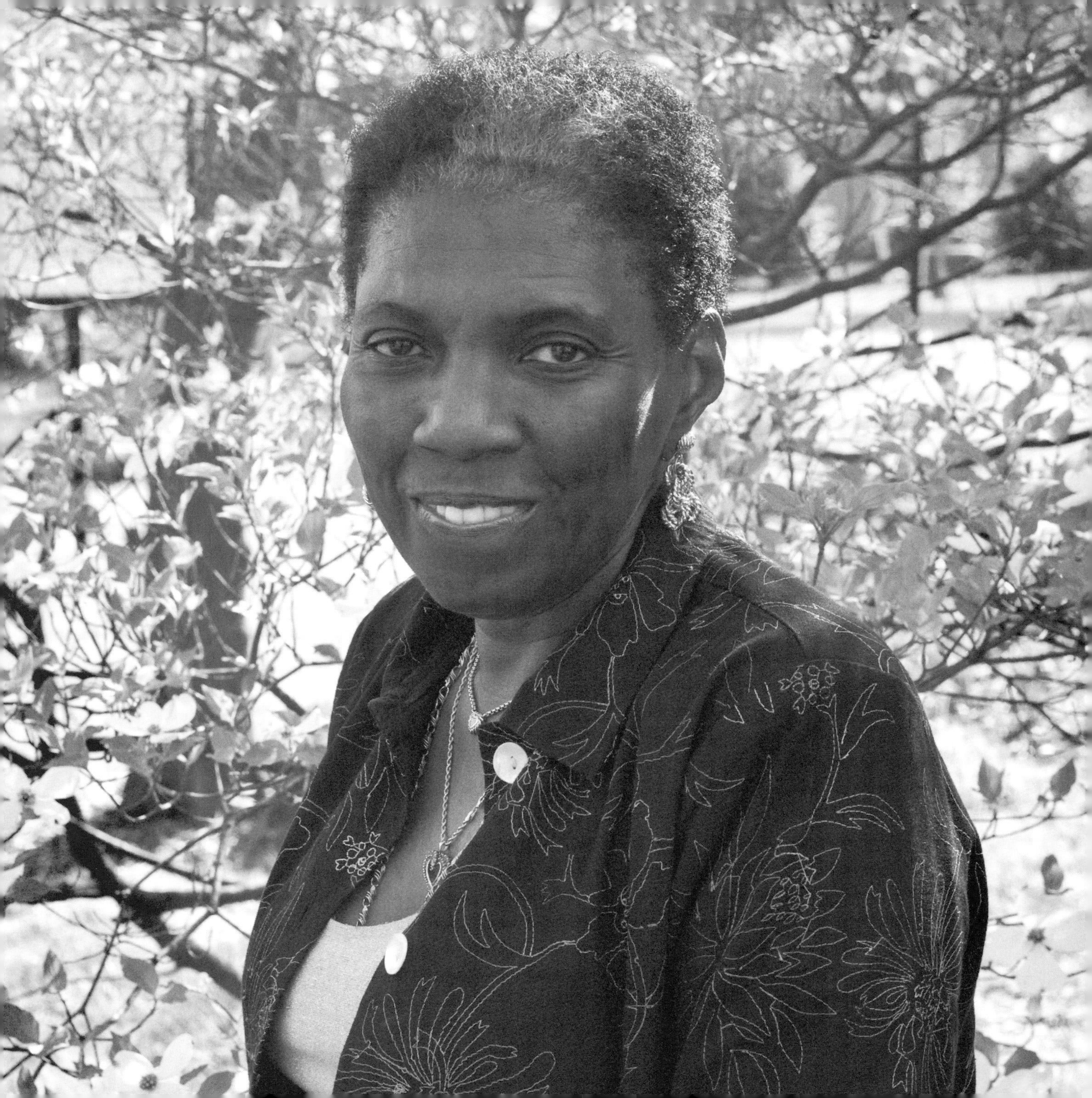

Distinctions

What's distinctive about Black philanthropy?

African Americans tend to give much more of their time, love, food and clothing as opposed to large monetary spending. Attention is paid to real needs for everyday people. — *Britt Brewer Loudd*

Philanthropy is part of the culture, and many philanthropists don't know that they are philanthropists. — *Edgar Villanueva*

That we've been actively involved and engaged in philanthropy, even before it was 'cool.' Our elders did it mostly through their service in church or other grassroots vehicles in our communities. — *Sherry Waters*

African American philanthropy is a stunning example of 'populist philanthropy.' We as a people have been able to demonstrate how philanthropy is a form of relationship with others that everyone can practice. Children to seniors in our community have a long history of giving selflessly to those we know intimately as well as to total strangers. I am very proud of our cultural history as philanthropists! — *Jennifer Henderson*

I find it remarkable that the early Black philanthropists, who had access to less financial capital, were able to leave a huge legacy for us today. — *Darryl K. Lester*

We have given throughout our history and have used philanthropy to overcome what may be thought to be insurmountable challenges. When we are in need, we will give to those who need more. — *LaDawn Sullivan*

How dynamic it is—just like African Americans. Our philanthropy can take on many shapes and forms, from taking care of neighborhood children to preparing meals, from sharing our artistic talents to braiding hair or donating dollars. — *Meka S. Sales*

The humility, sincerity and genuine spirit of African American philanthropy are what move me the most. There is not a sense of needing to advertise or make political plays—it's a sincere desire to help another human being, and that is the true meaning of philanthropy. Our community is great at this and has a great tradition of giving, sharing and caring. — *Melandee Jones*

That we have been philanthropists for years but were not given recognition in the community or in the public eye — *Belinda E. Alston*

It is engrained in who we are and deeply rooted in the tradition of our people and culture. — *Ohmar Land*

[African Americans have] An opportunity to address the specific needs of our community in a way that others might overlook. — *Christian Friend*

It is part of our culture. It is part of who we are. — *Denise Rowson*

It can be a new form of ownership for Black folks who have had a 'consent mentality.' — *Ed Fields*

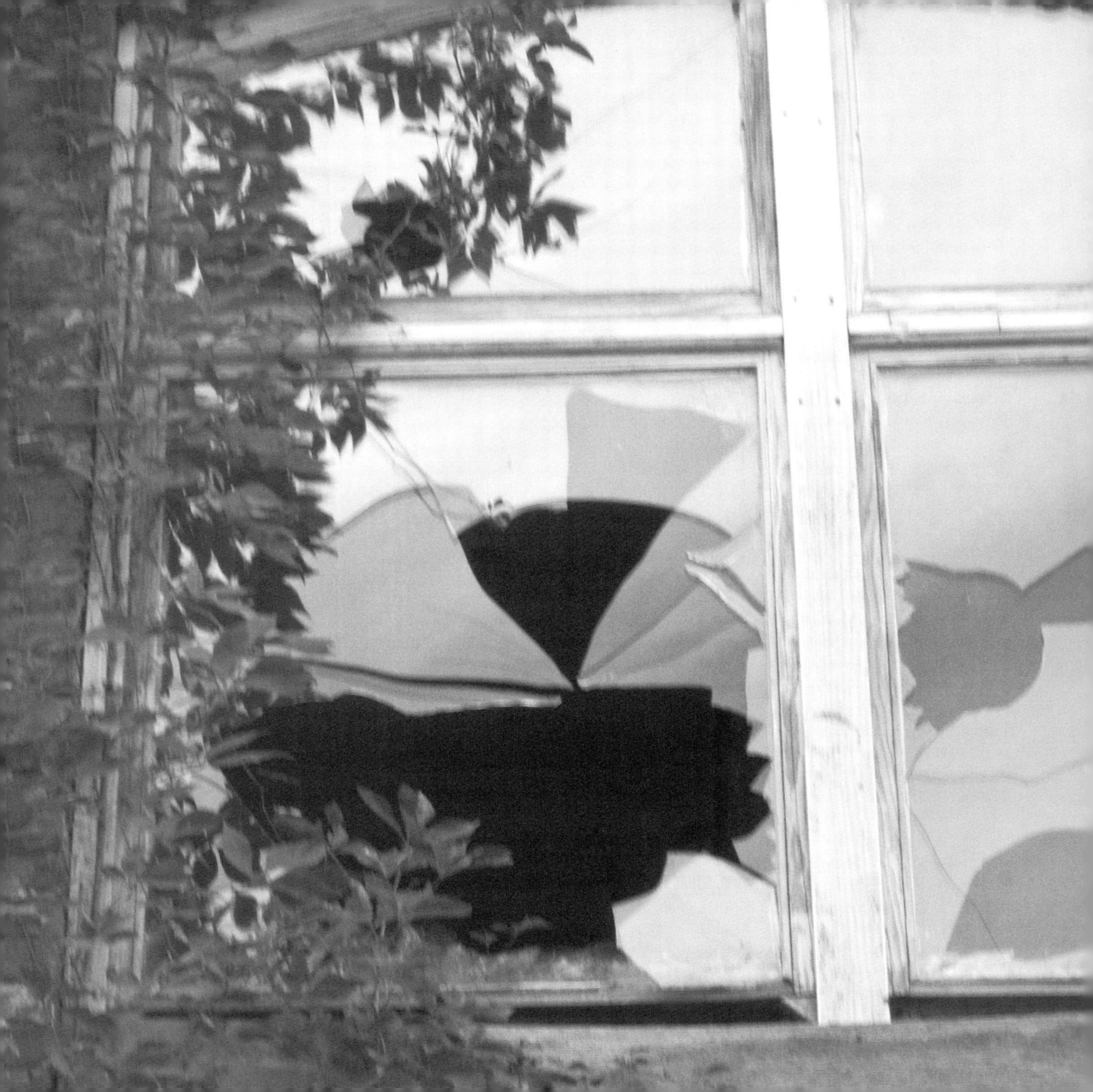

We are responsible for the world in which we find ourselves, if only because we are the only sentient force which can change it.

JAMES A. BALDWIN
American writer and civil rights activist
(1924-87)

Darryl K. Lester | NETWORK ANCHOR

Passion fuels Darryl's consulting practice in the field of philanthropy. Though he is passionate about giving in general, his deep love for Black people is most striking. He clearly would pursue his life's work without pay or recognition.

I remember at first people seriously questioned Darryl's interest in organizing African Americans around philanthropy. For years, he had observed how our community was disregarded and, in effect, invisible in the philanthropic mainstream. This persisted, even though African American history overflows with examples of generous giving. Darryl believed more inclusive dynamics could exist. He set out to make strategic inroads—in both philanthropy and Black communities—by making the right tools and information accessible to African American donors and by leveraging their expressed willingness to invest time, talent and treasure in response to community issues.

Still, some people Darryl encountered seemed to believe that mainstream philanthropy would require most African Americans to operate outside their "comfort zone." It was as if they thought that, culturally, we were limited to only fish-fry fundraising and bake sales and lacked motivation to do anything greater. Or, for our people, tithing in church was the most anyone could expect.

Darryl sees things differently. Rather than philanthropy being alien to our culture, to the contrary, he considers it central to who we are as a people. He shares this belief at every turn. His message resonates and has given rise to numerous giving circles and donors participating in strategic, community-based philanthropy all across the country. One of Darryl's best gifts is how he connects with people, which is why he has found success in organizing giving circles and creating the Community Investment Network.

When detractors tell you "no" and you move forward anyway that shows passion. In fact, doubts and cynicism drive Darryl all the more. His perseverance is unsurprising to me. That was apparent sixteen years ago when he showed up in my aerobics class and persisted at asking me out. Little did I know that the cute guy from the health club would not only become my husband but also seed innovative ideas about philanthropy that would move so many people.

DIONNE LESTER

Connection: *Wife* ◆ Channel: *Parent volunteer, Sassafras All Children's Playground*
Cause: *Unconventional projects for children with special needs*

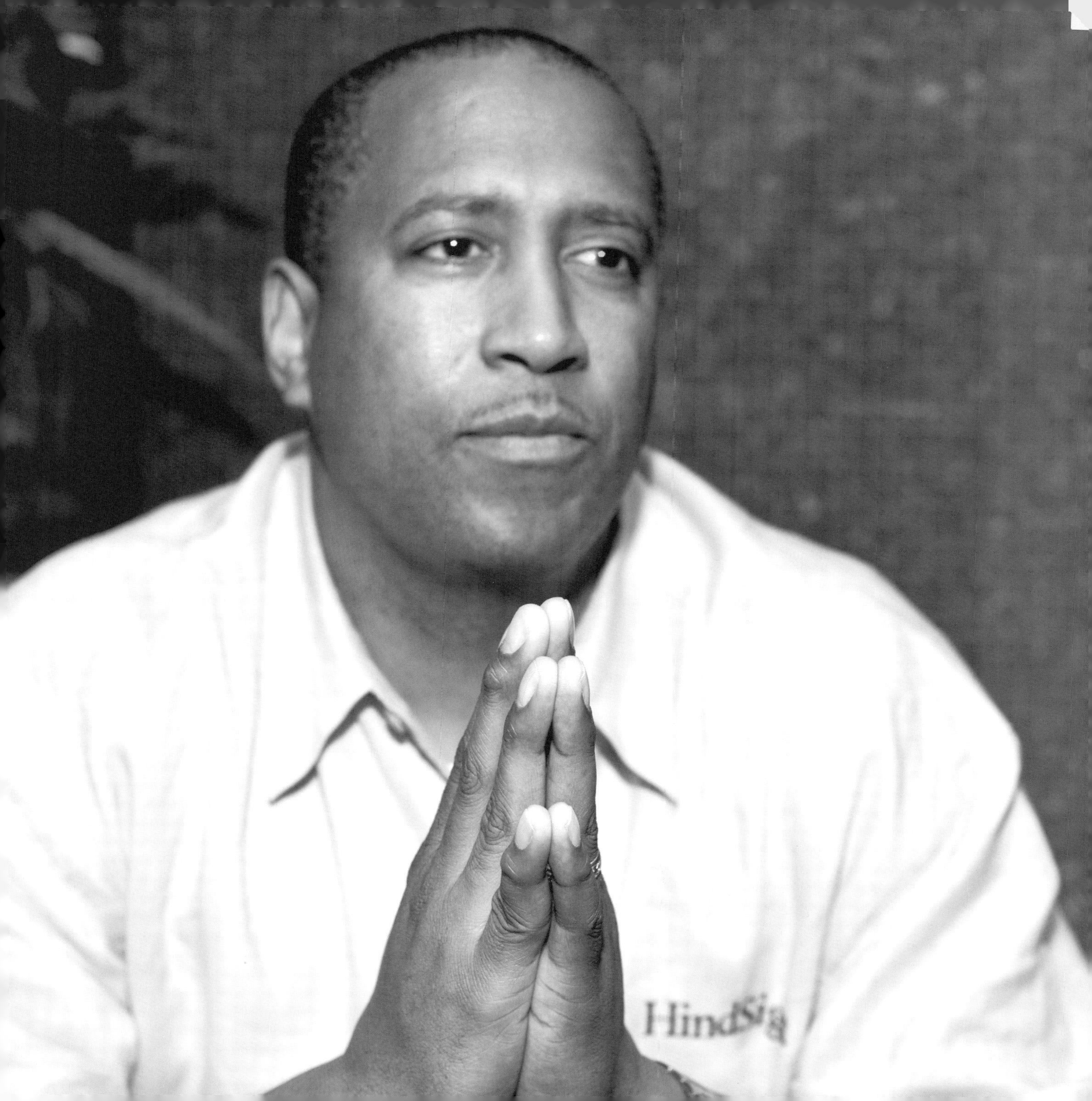

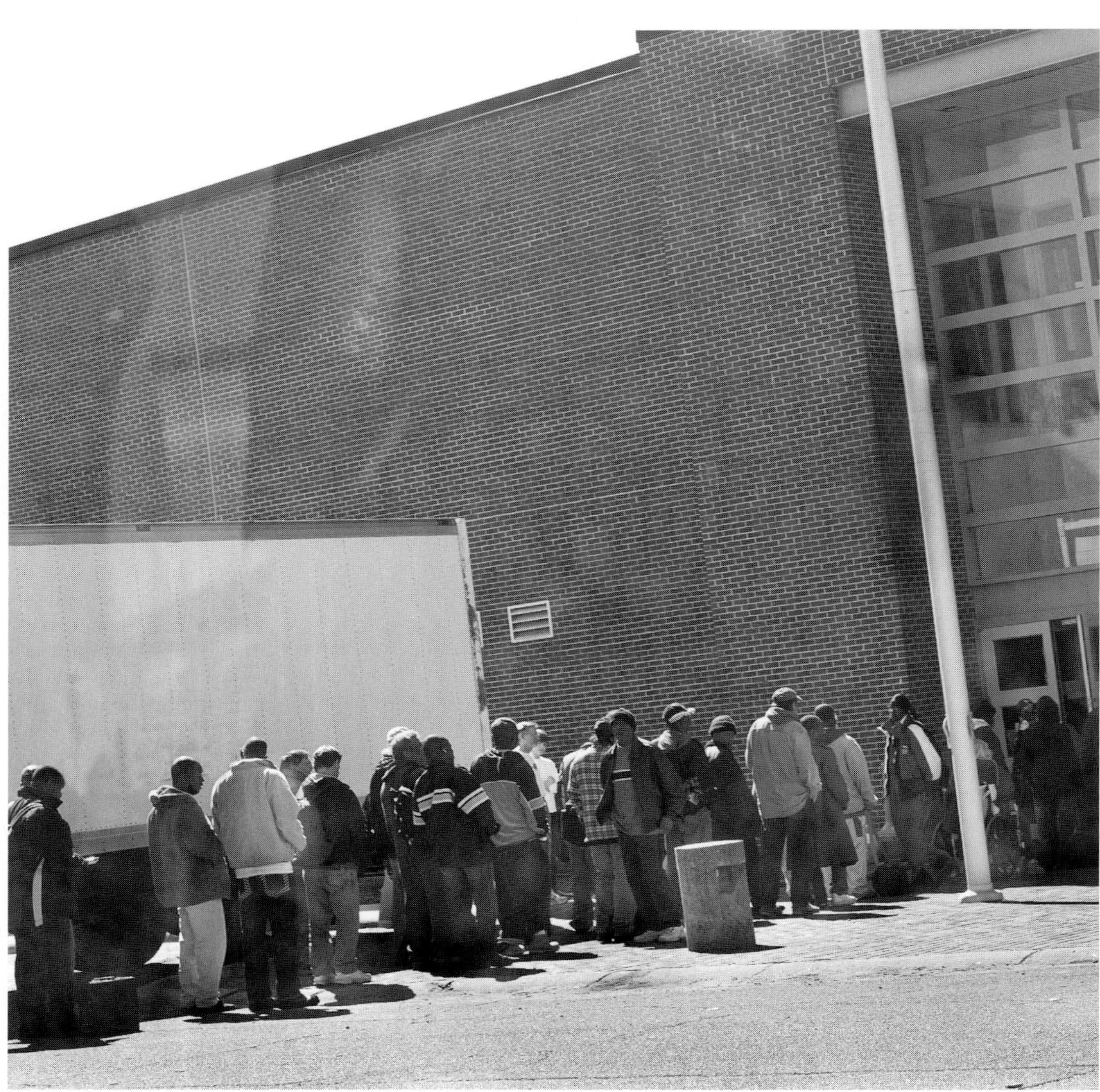

To be a poor man is hard, but to be a poor race in a land of dollars is the very bottom of hardships.

W.E.B. DU BOIS
American intellectual leader, author and civil rights activist
(1868-1963)

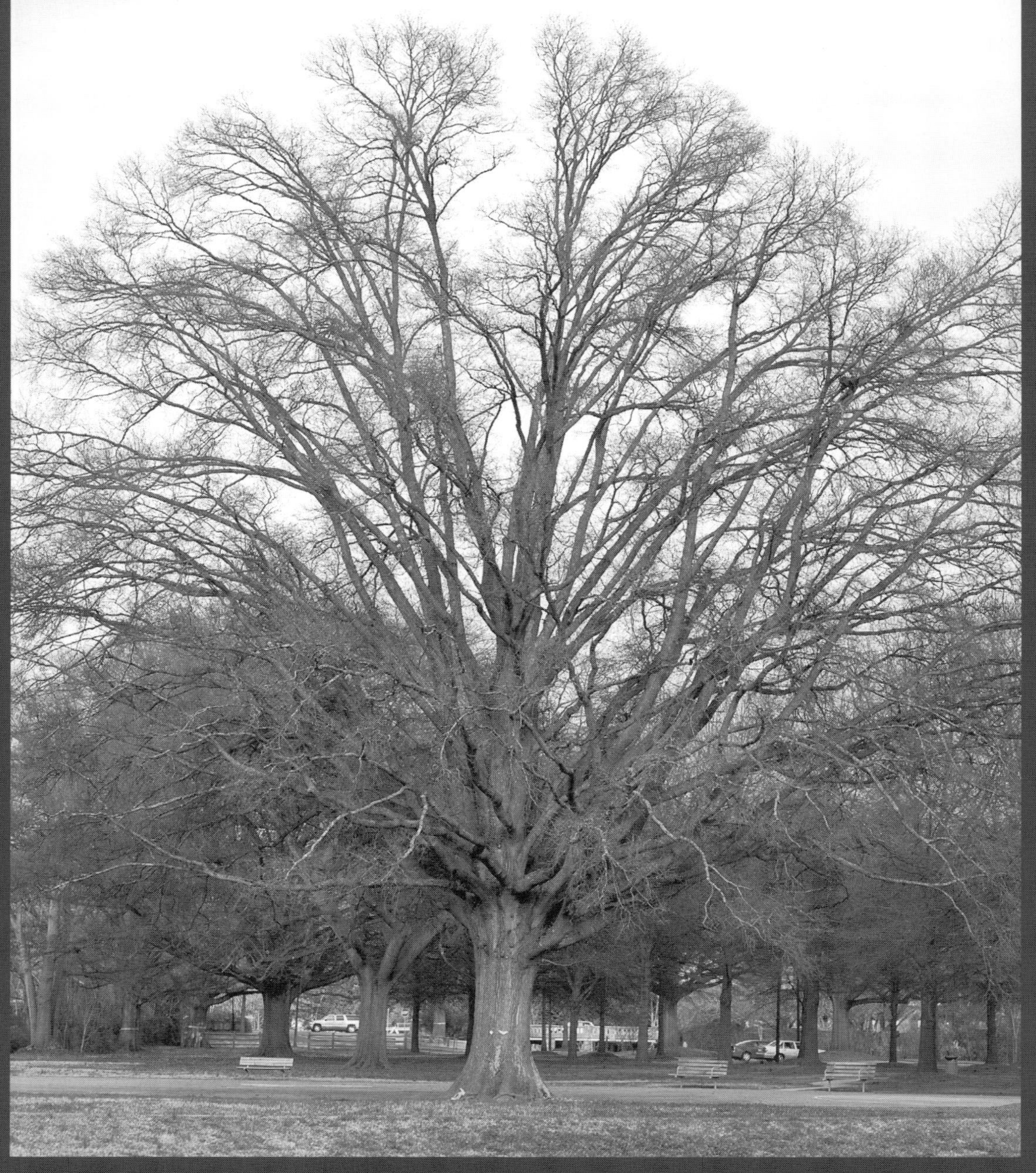

"PHILANTHROPY IS AN INDEPENDENT RESOURCE, with an option to focus on re-generating energy, fervor, knowledge, inventiveness and loyalty to community—either a community of interest or place. I believe that investing in thoughtful inclusive leadership strengthens present possibilities as well as insures future opportunities of many generations.

"What strikes me most about Black philanthropy is that Black donors seem to have recognized early the importance of giving for the present as well as for the future. Historically, Blacks gave time, talent and money recognizing the need to establish immediate capacity *and* institutions for to sustain capacity for the long-term development of Black people. Our DNA for giving is to identify issues today demanding a response from a Black perspective. The wisdom of our giving expects that the results of our philanthropy will also benefit many beyond our communities."

Linetta J. Gilbert
senior program officer at the Ford Foundation and
founder and board member of the Louisiana Disaster Recovery Foundation

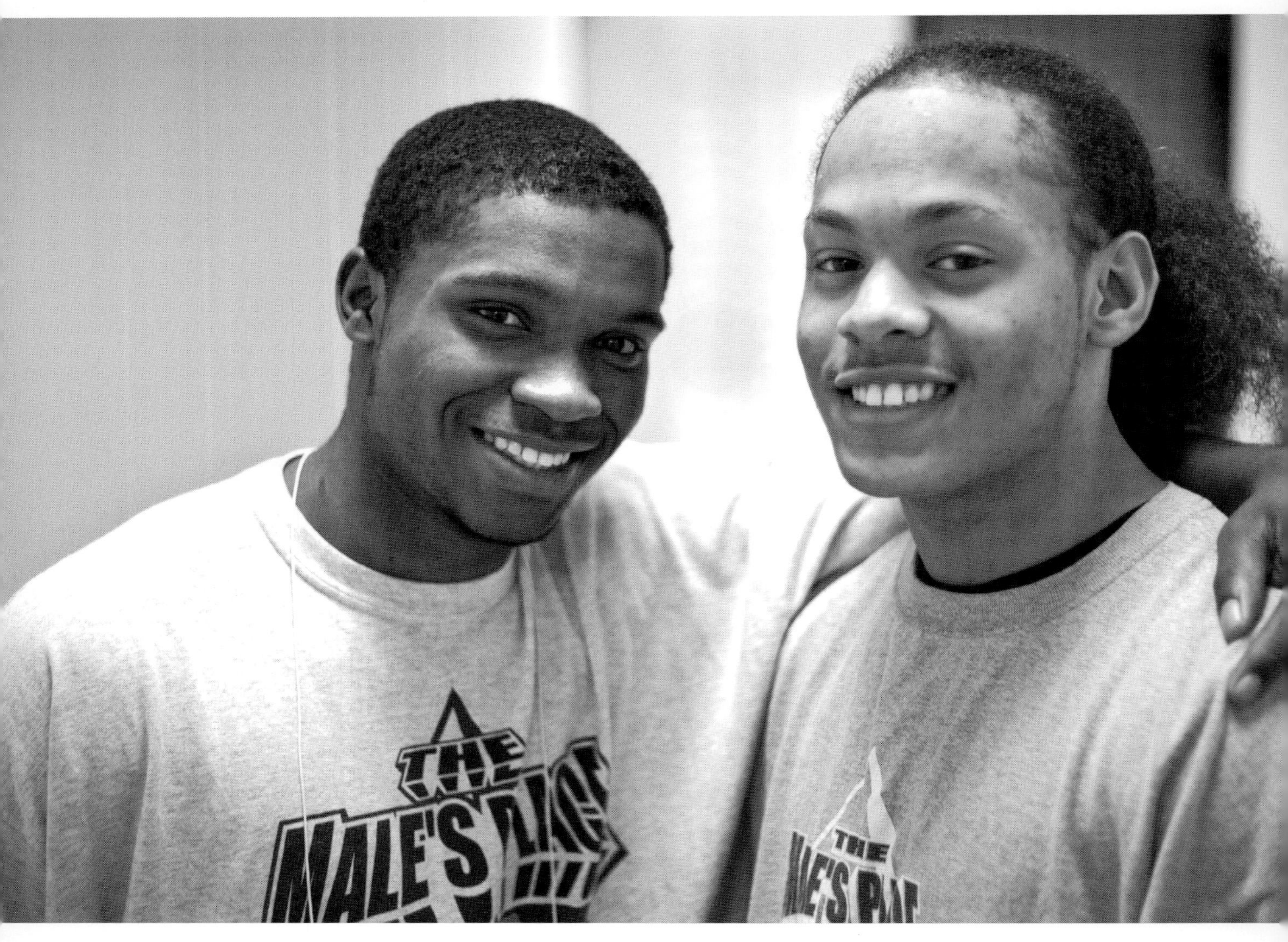
THE
MALE'S

Bringing the gifts that my ancestors gave,
I am the dream and the hope of the slave.

MAYA ANGELOU
American writer and poet
(b. 1928)

Annie Brewer | WONDER WOMAN

Growing up I honestly believed my grandmother was a superhero. She has long been known both for model good looks and model goodness and she is more wondrous than ever well into her eighties.

Granny's house was just doors from ours during my childhood, so I saw her every day. Awestruck by her ability to handle just about everything, I was her shadow and saw up close how she was always going and doing for others. The little things she did are what I remember most. So many times, I watched curiously as she reached into her bottomless basket of greeting cards when somebody needed lifting up and for folks to know they were not forgotten.

My fondest memories are of how she would cook and bake for everyone. Since Granny didn't drive, Papa would load up the car with pots and dishes and then my grandparents, with me in tow, would deliver food to people who were sick or going through something. Even through a child's eyes, I could see the impact of her generosity in each person's face. Though she was not a wealthy woman in terms of finances, Granny was doing what she knew to do best. Fixing a home-cooked meal or whipping up a cake was my grandmother's way of sharing her riches.

I still walk in her shadow today. Sometimes between picking up kids at school, assembling prizes for the youth choir raffle, hauling Girl Scout cookies across town and organizing my precinct meeting, I pause and think, *just like Annie Brewer*, and a little smile comes over my face.

BRITT BREWER LOUDD
Connection: *Granddaughter* ◆ Channel: *Member, Greenville Memorial AME Zion Church*
Cause: *Social justice*

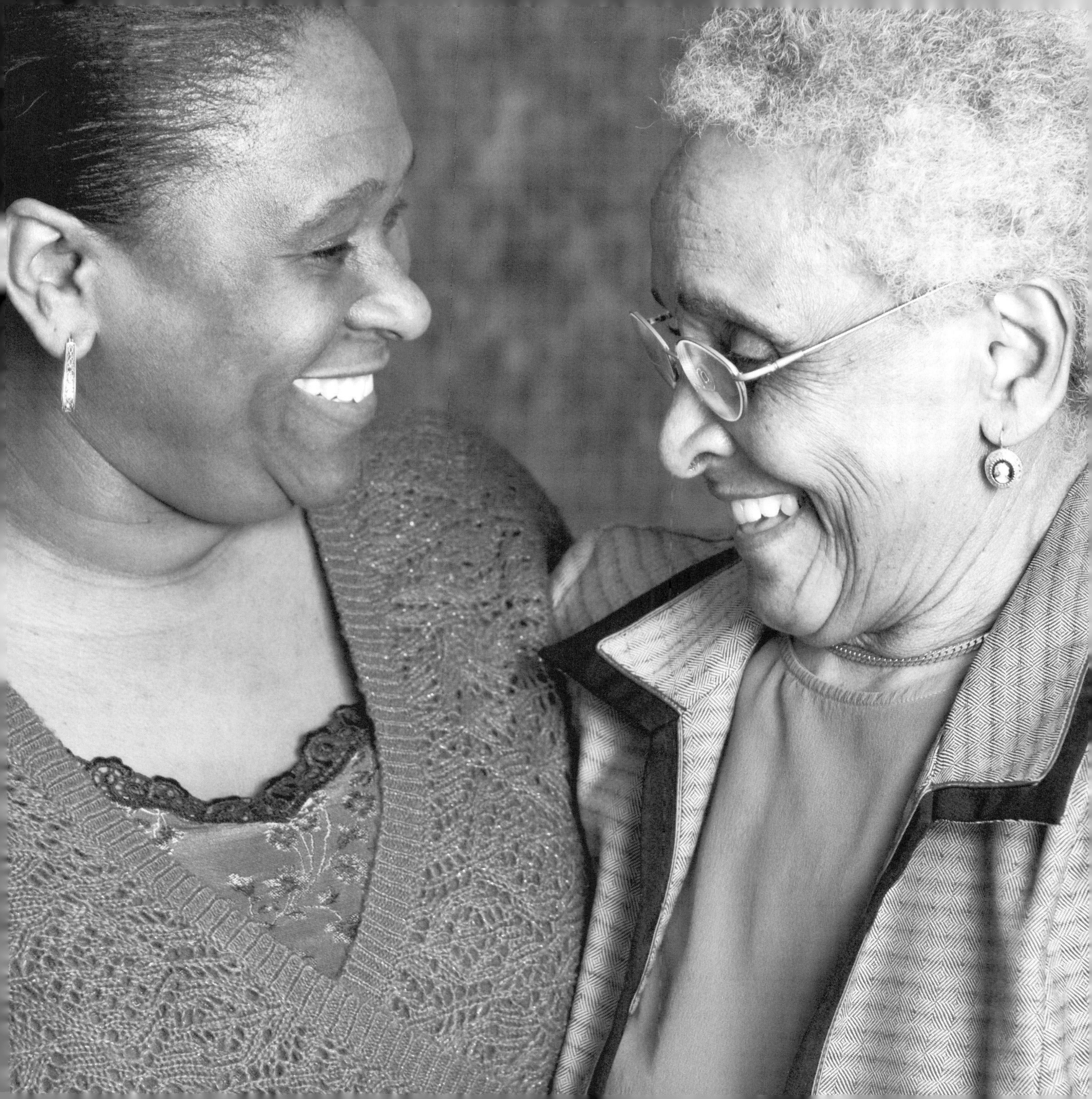

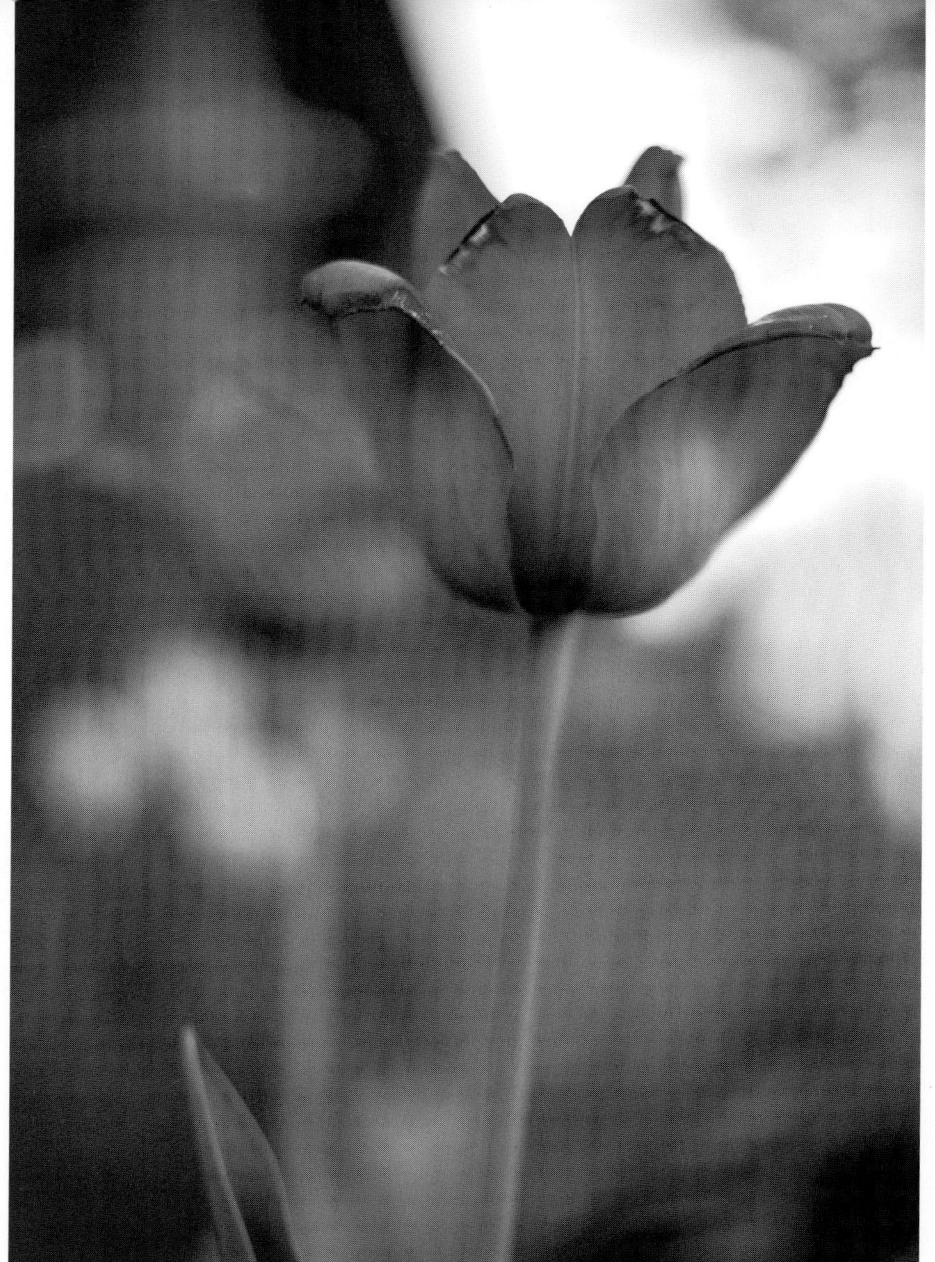

Love's in need of love today.

STEVIE WONDER
American songwriter and singer
(b. 1950)

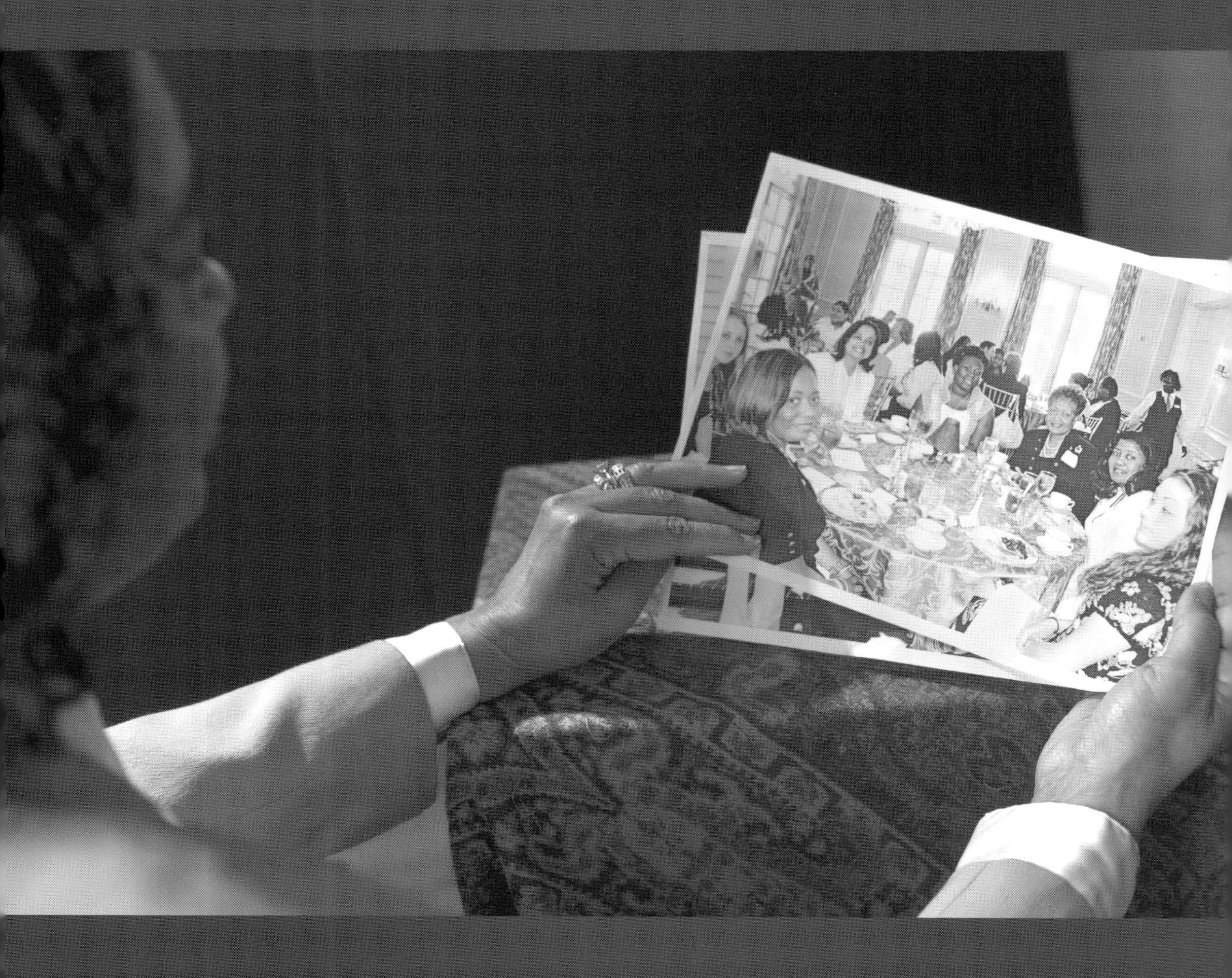

"WHEN I THINK OF effective collective giving groups that promote philanthropy for social justice, The Links, Incorporated stands foremost in my mind.

"The Links is a nonprofit organization founded in 1946 to enhance friendship and community service within small groups of African American women. Today, the organization flourishes with a membership of more than 12,000 women of color in 270 chapters across the United States and abroad. An early goal was to give financial contributions to promote civil and human rights, economic development and educational equality. The NAACP Legal Defense and Educational Fund, the Urban League and UNCF have all benefited from The Links' support.

"As a Charter member of Charlotte's Crown Jewels Chapter, I am proud to continue a tradition that was begun more than sixty years ago. With my Link sisters, we carry the ideals of dedicated concern for the welfare of others and the promotion of social action programming and philanthropic support for major African American civil rights, educational and arts organizations."

Ruth L. Greene, Ed.D.
charter member of the Crown Jewels Chapter, established in 1993 and part of the national network of The Links, Incorporated, a philanthropic staple in the African American community since 1946

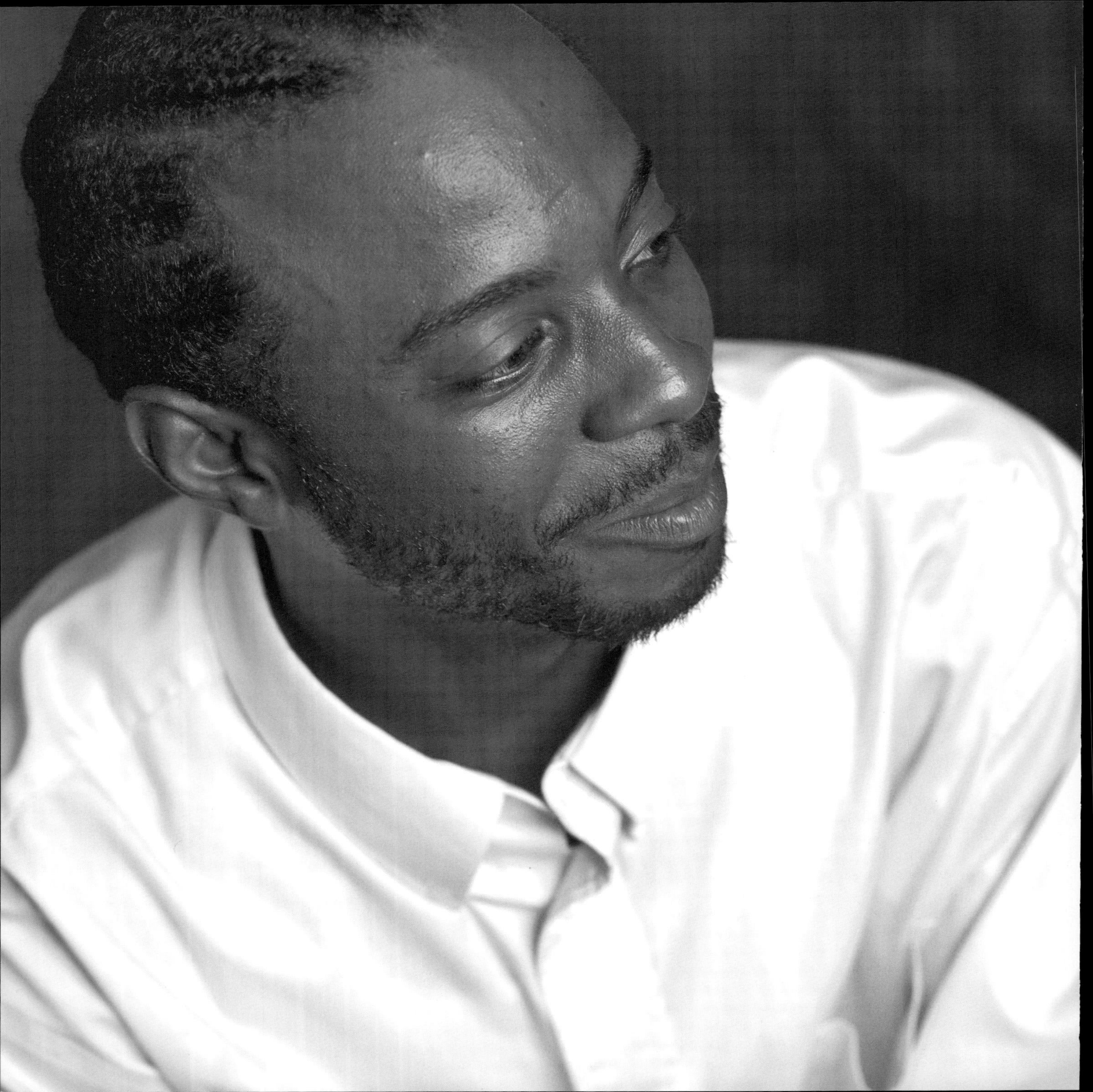

If you're not part of the solution, you're part of the problem.

ELDRIDGE CLEAVER
American writer and Black Panther leader
(1935-98)

Carlenia Ivory | CHAMPION FOR CHILDREN

When Carlenia Ivory enters a room, you take notice. Her tall stature and strong presence command attention. Most striking, however, is that she is of a rare breed that may not give millions to a program but makes magic every day by working on the frontline with children.

Long before I was ever mayor, I came to know Carlenia, largely through her husband. I played tennis with Titus Ivory, and he always talked about her. While the Ivorys were best described as acquaintances rather than close friends, my wife and I heard about their generosity through mutual friends and admired them from afar.

The Ivorys were an unusual family. Unusual in how they earned affection from kids and adults alike. Carlenia and Titus were devoted to not only their boys but also young people across the city. Their home in Hyde Park was a frequent hangout and center of activity for teenagers. When Titus died suddenly and too soon, I listened to the testimonials at his funeral. They were clearly a selfless couple and a light in many lives. As a widow, Carlenia has kept the torch lit.

With Titus gone, Carlenia poured herself into her sons and the wellbeing of sons and daughters throughout the community. She honored his commitments and redoubled her own, carrying on an annual golf tournament to benefit the McCrorey YMCA and championing a teen center in Titus' memory. And she didn't stop there. Through the school system, Carlenia became a child and family advocate in Double Oaks, a challenged, low-income neighborhood. Resources have flowed into Double Oaks because Carlenia beats the drum and then pulls and pushes politicians to make things happen. I still marvel at how her efforts took the Anita Stroud Youth Development Center from a trailer to a modern-day learning facility. She has given far more than any salary she receives.

But that's the thing, Carlenia doesn't do it for a paycheck. It is part of her DNA—an imprint from perhaps a grandma or teacher long ago. Her kind is not in it for a sprint. Transforming lives is a long-term commitment requiring the same tenacity, zeal and energy evident on day one being maintained through the long haul of a lifetime. The life's work of real philanthropists is more like a marathon, and Carlenia possesses the heart and stamina of a long-distance runner for kids.

HARVEY B. GANTT

Connection: *Friend* • Channel: *Member, Friendship Missionary Baptist Church, founded in 1890*

Cause: *Education that supports youngsters facing challenges and inspires them to do better*

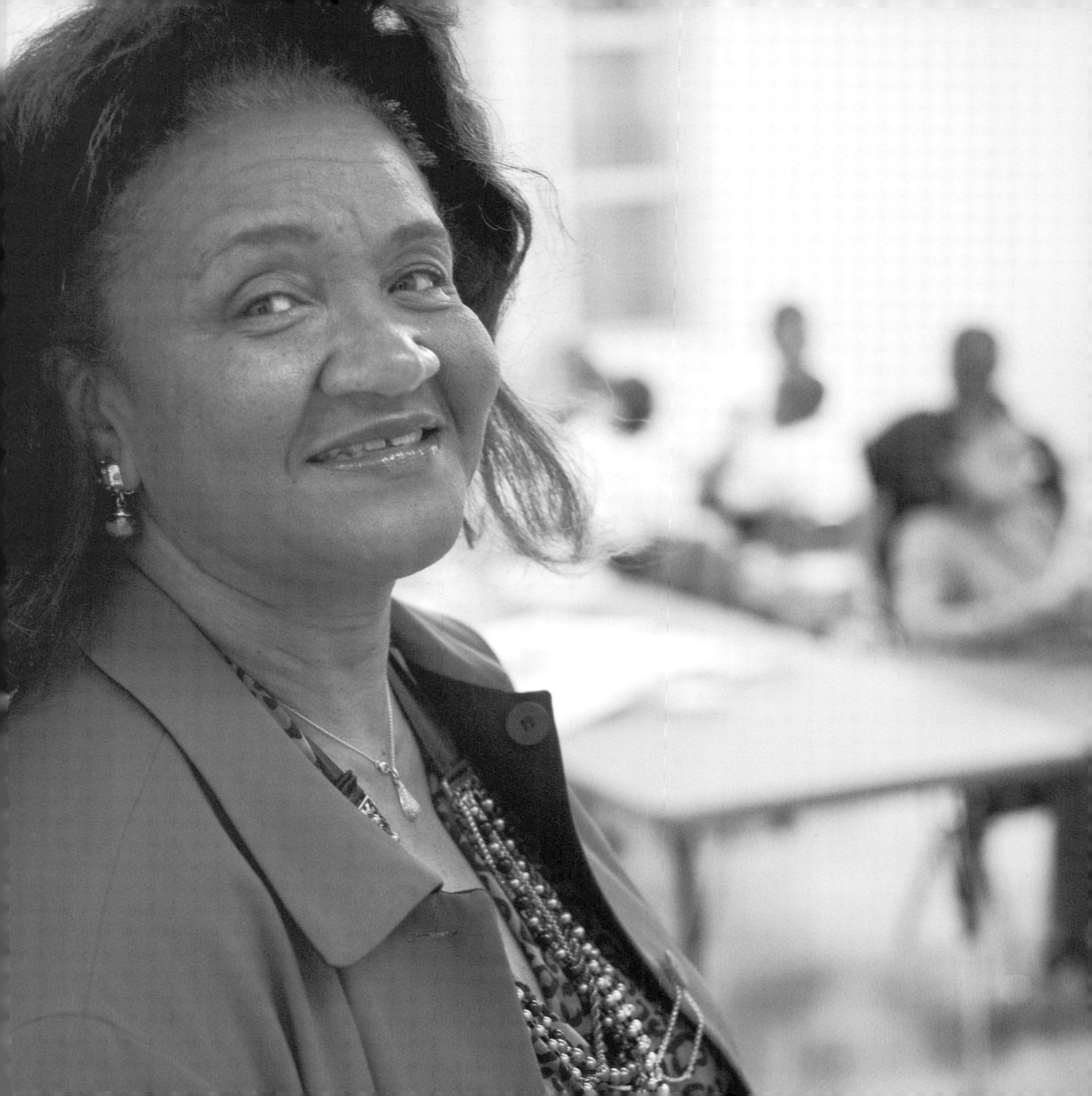

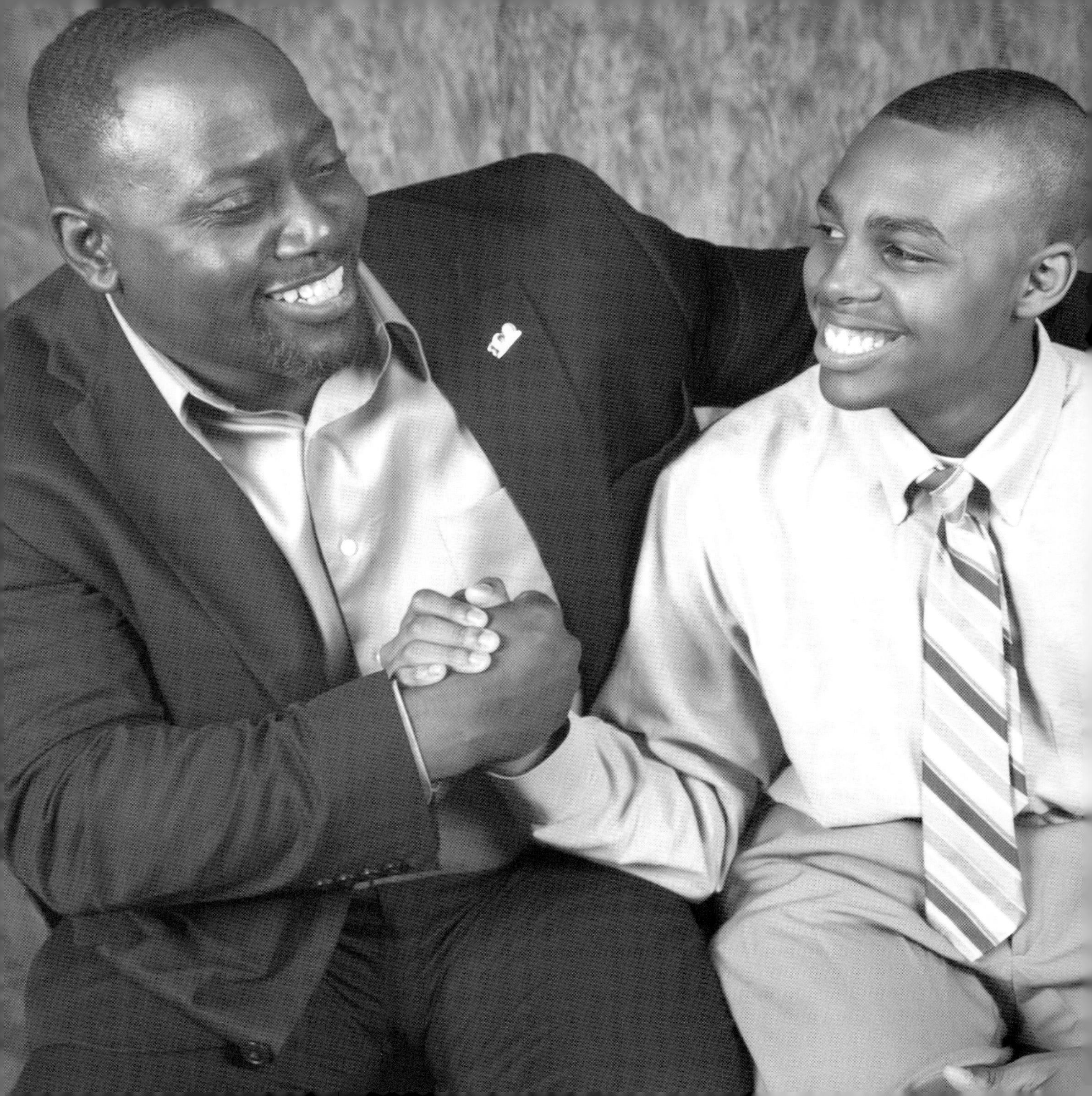

Everyone has been made for some particular work, and the desire for that work has been put in every heart.

RUMI
Persian philosopher, theologian and poet
(1207-73)

"I FIRST KNEW I'd be an educator when as a senior at Morehouse a guy from Teach For America spoke at a colloquium and declared: 'If you want to change the community, you have to change the kids.'

"Until that moment, I had been on a public-health track throughout undergrad. His words struck me so deeply that I wrote them down. Once my mind turned to education, I didn't look back. I wanted to do school leadership and to start a bunch of schools—before I even knew about KIPP, the Knowledge Is Power Program. Right after college, I became a Teach For America volunteer and was humbled by my first teaching assignment. I still kept my sights on eventually opening a school.

"Four years after graduation we got a greenlight and the next year we opened KIPP Charlotte. Integral to our school is *Ubuntu*, a Zulu concept about the power of the collective. We teach our students that their personal best makes the whole group better. An example we use is that the strength of the pride lies with the lions, and the strength of a lion is its pride. We are hoping our kids develop a sense of responsibility to their community, and we are modeling who and what they will be. We want them to see service as love, and then love being the choice to make."

Keith Burnam
co-founder and co-leader of KIPP Charlotte, a charter school founded in 2007
and graduate of Morehouse College, an HBCU founded in 1867

"'DON'T LET YOUR BACKGROUND DEFINE YOU.' That's the biggest piece of advice I always give children. 'You can't always change your circumstances. And while you may not be able to control your mom or your dad or your auntie, you can control how you perform in school, and your education shapes your future.'

"Our school is 97 percent African American and Spelman is a historically Black college. Spelman focused on empowering students and taught us that we were part of a group of people who had pride about their history and heritage. When I think about KIPP, we have an opportunity to help kids in the same way. Our students must understand where they come from, in the broadest sense, not their neighborhood or their street.

"I have always wanted to be an advocate for children and to help reunite the Black family. My role in giving back is to make sure that through my actions and words I'm sowing seeds so a future generation gets to live out its dreams and change the world."

Tiffany Flowers Washington
co-founder and co-leader of KIPP Academy of Charlotte, a charter school founded in 2007 and alumna of Spelman College, an HBCU founded in 1881

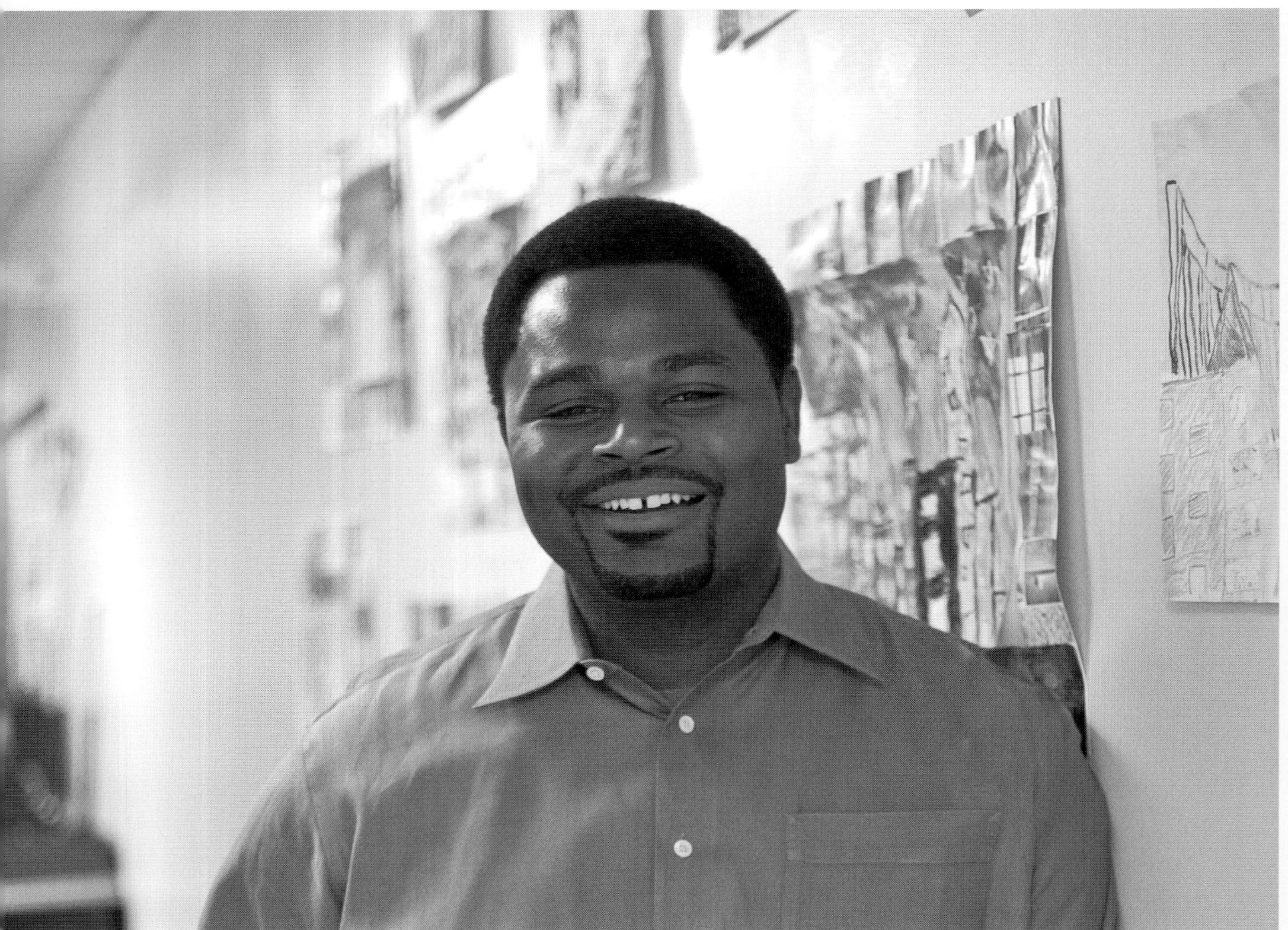

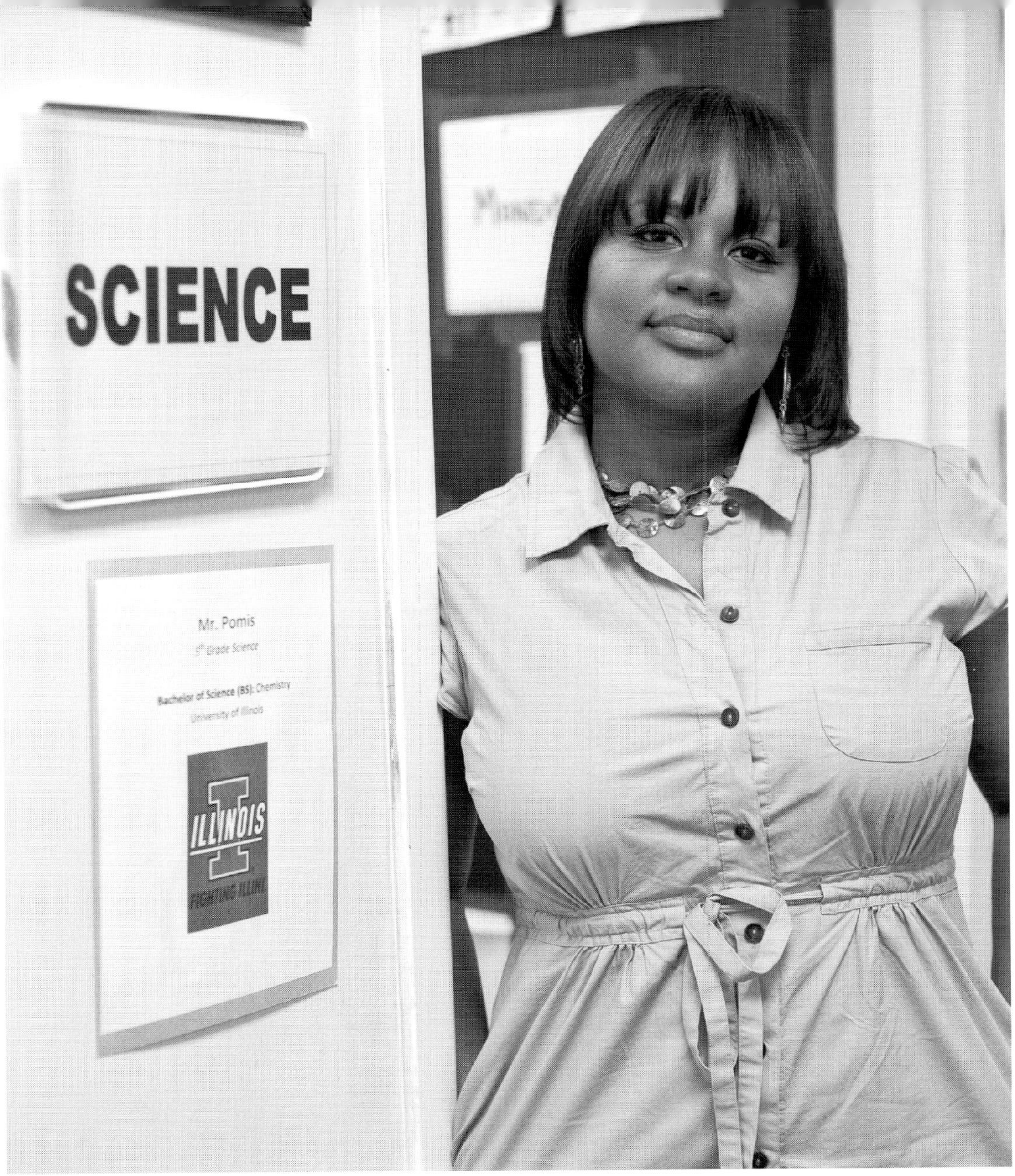

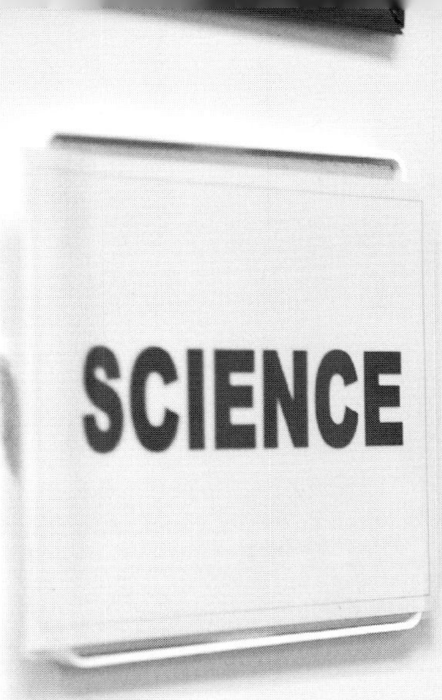
SCIENCE

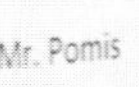
Mr. Pomis
5th Grade Science
Bachelor of Science (BS): Chemistry
University of Illinois

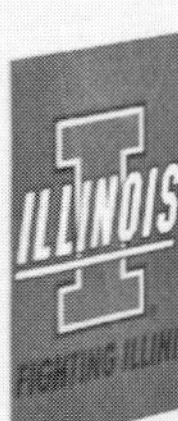
ILLINOIS
FIGHTING ILLINI

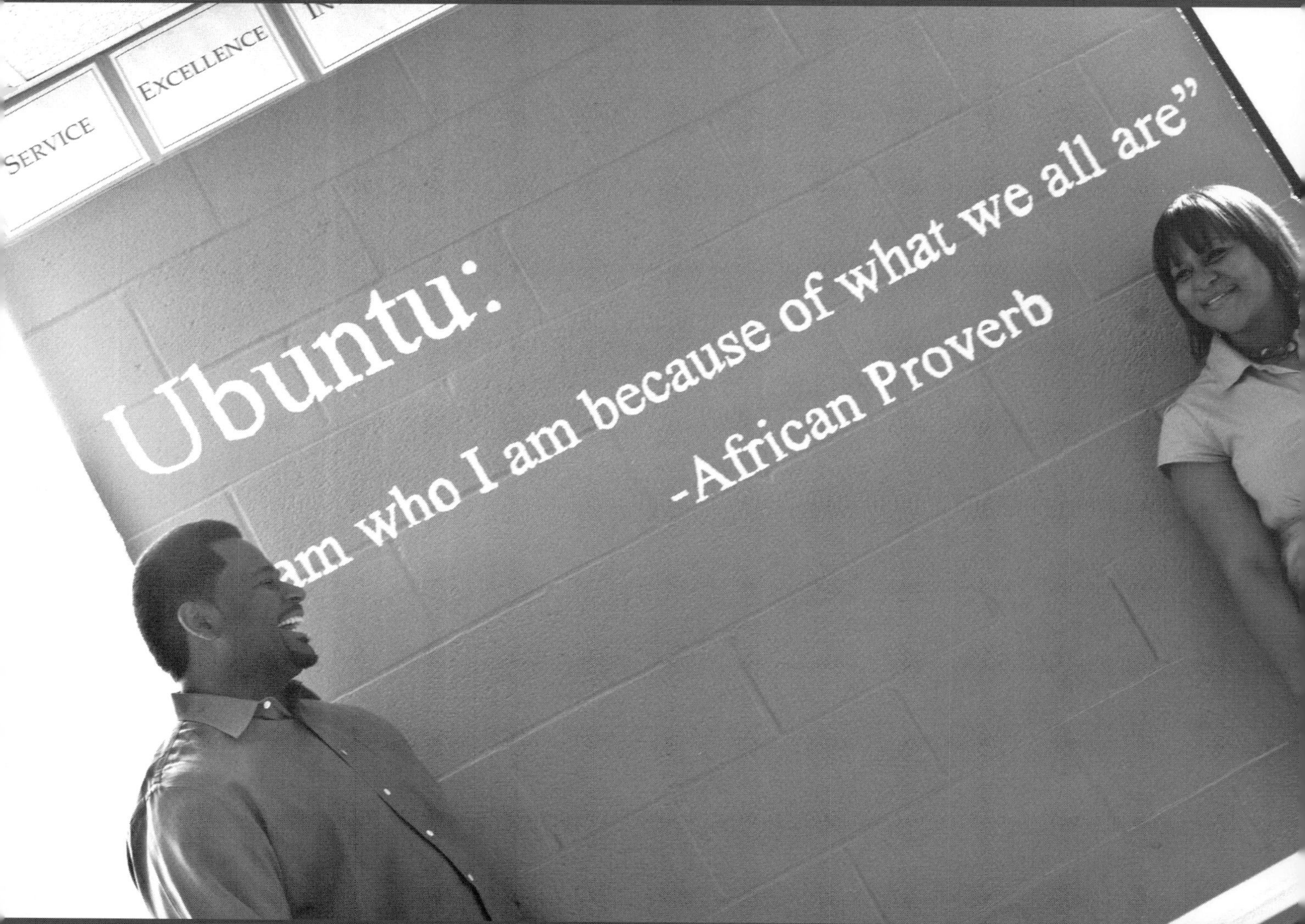

SERVICE

EXCELLENCE

Ubuntu:

am who I am because of what we all are"

-African Proverb

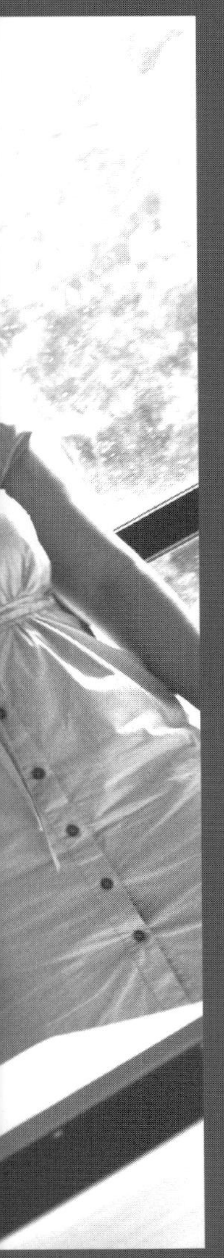

One of the sayings in our country is Ubuntu: the essence of being human. Ubuntu speaks particularly about the fact that you can't exist as a human being in isolation.

ARCHBISHOP EMERITUS DESMOND TUTU
South African cleric and activist
(b. 1931)

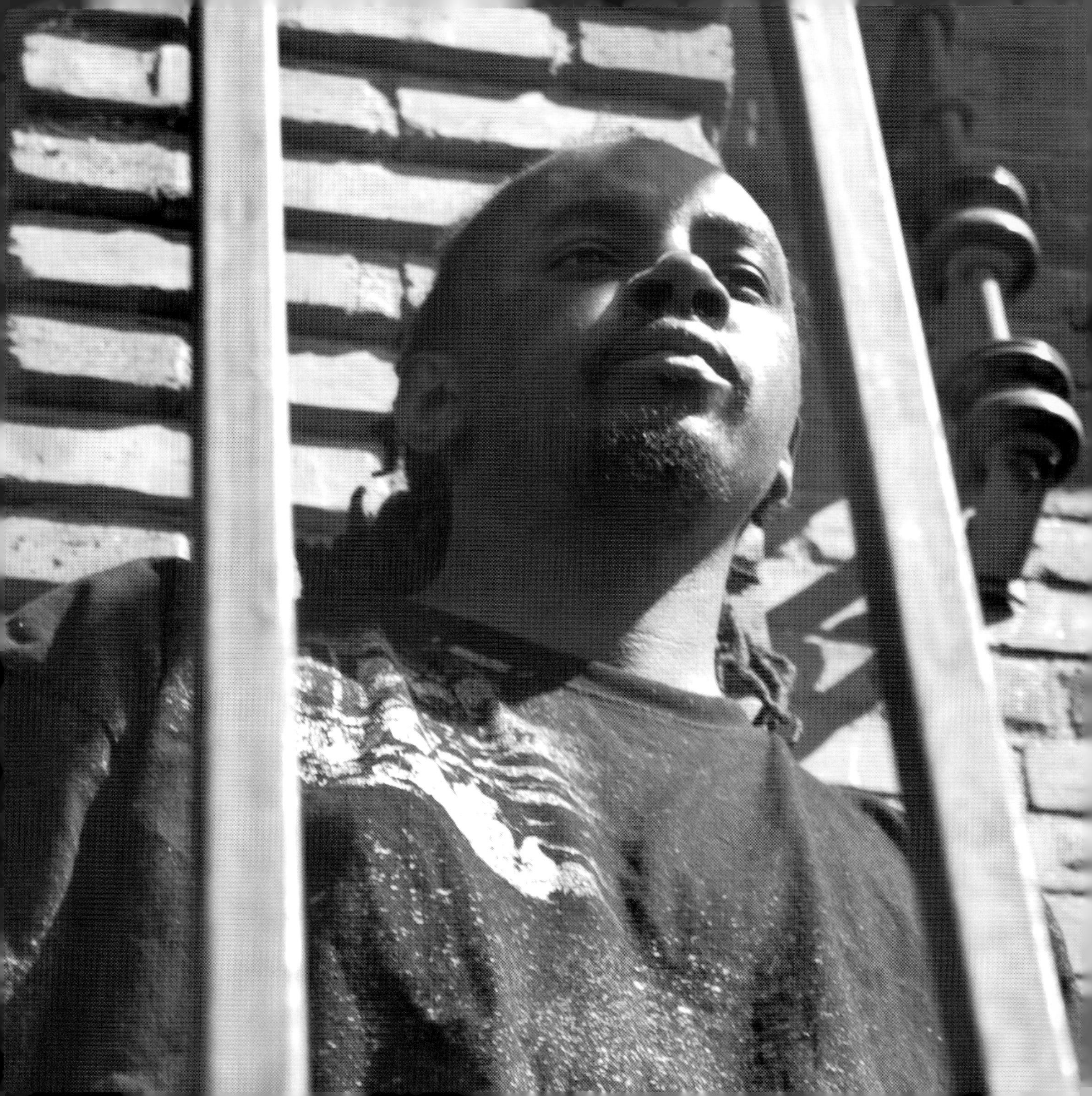

Gave away my soul.
Giving back to get it back.
Given what I know.

Ava Wood
poet

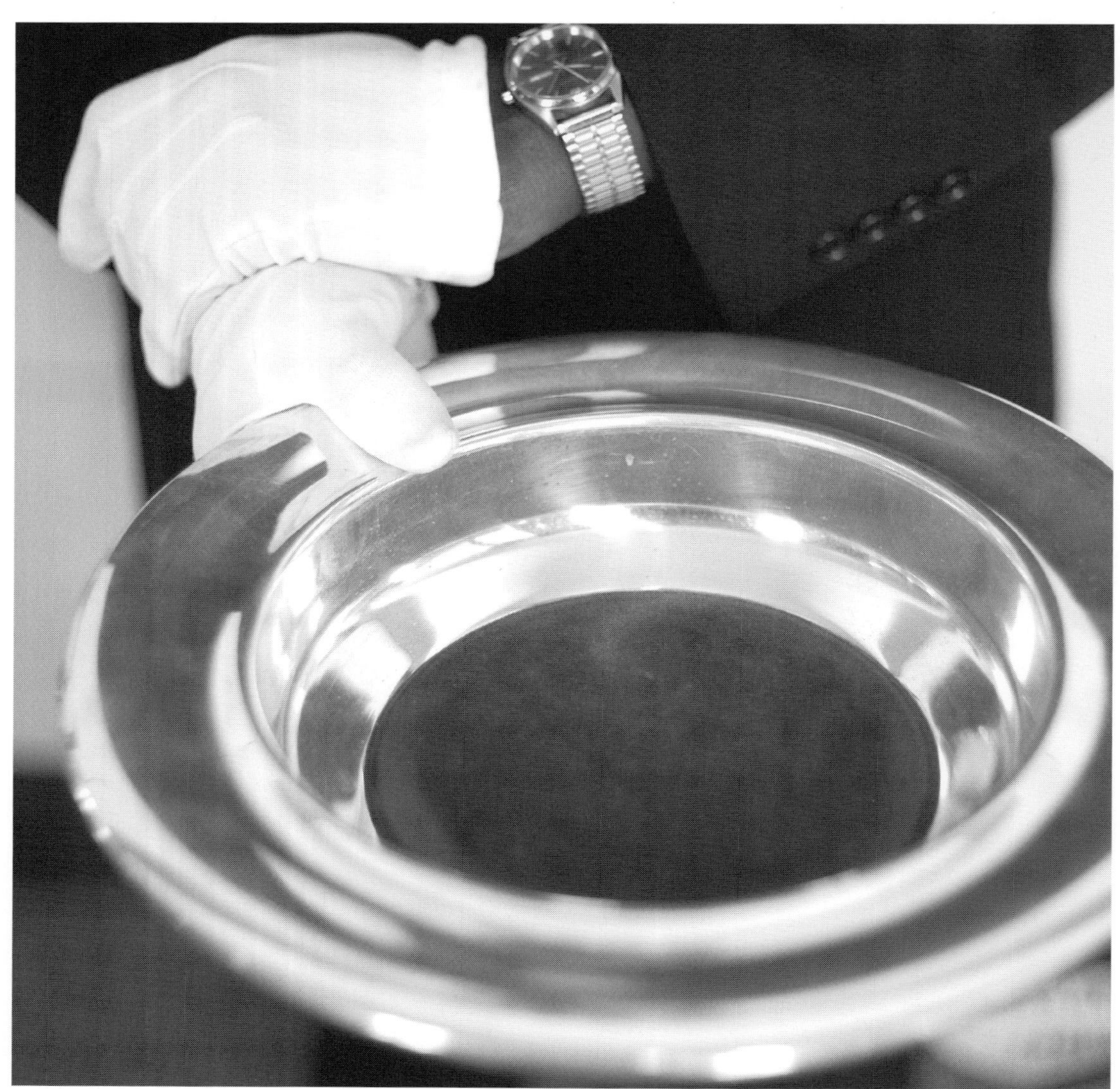

Shadowed beneath Thy hand, may we forever stand,
True to our God, true to our native land.

JAMES WELDON JOHNSON
American diplomat, educator, journalist and songwriter
(1871-1938)

From the lyrics of "Lift Every Voice And Sing,"
also known as the Black National Anthem, 1899

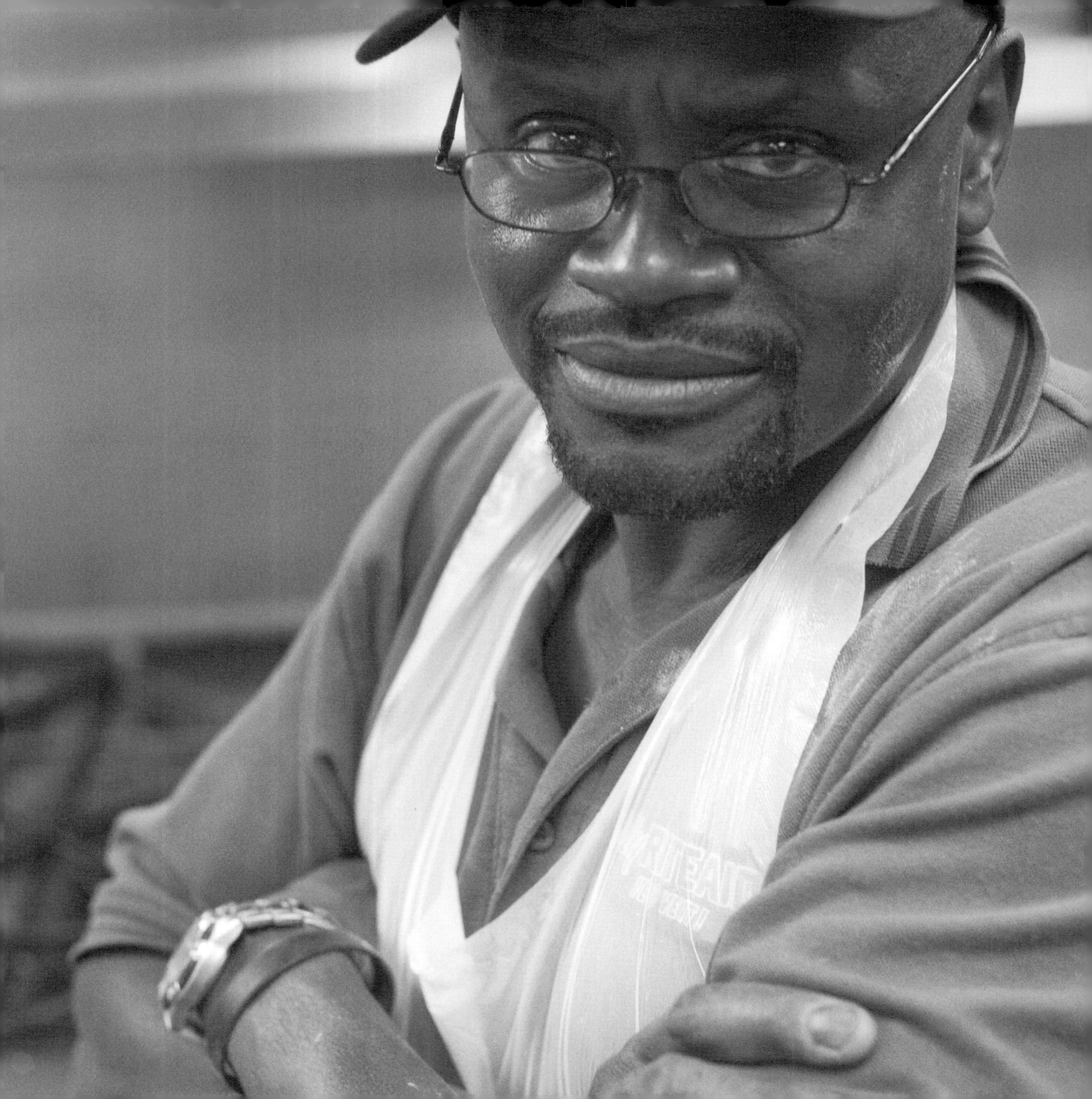

MOTIVATIONS

What motivates you to give?

Love — *Ed Fields*

Seeing organizations that improve and help the community — *Charles Smith*

My father modeled giving. His generous spirit touched everyone he met. And I came to realize that giving begins with belief—the belief that the smallest gift can make a difference, belief that everyone is worthy of a chance and belief that each of us can provide that opportunity. — *Ruthye Cureton-Cooley*

The desire to serve others. Showing others how to give freely. Freely I give, freely I receive. Being a steward of God's blessings — *Rashad Davis*

My faith motivates me most to give. — *Dan Nunn*

Passion and strong belief in the organization — *Jeanene Thompson*

When I can see the measurable impact of that giving — *Christian Friend*

I want to be a part of strong, healthy communities, and I want other people to be a part of strong healthy communities. The reason I give is because I want to make sure that there are other people who are able to contribute to making strong, healthy communities. — *Lyord Watson Jr.*

I am inspired to change the face of philanthropy by doing all I can to leave a legacy as a young, African American woman who gives out of her love for humanity. — *Renee L. Bradford*

Realizing that I have the ability to give something back to the community — *Ihsan Abdin*

I think that this is what God has called me to do: To show His goodness. — *Denise Rowson*

Knowing that someone is better off than they were and that I made a difference in someone's life. Also, being blessed that I have something to share with others — *Ohmar Land*

My family has a tradition of giving back and reaching back to carry our community with us as we advance in any area of our lives. — *LaDawn Sullivan*

Helping others live better lives — *Linsey Mills*

It is my duty as a Christian and a citizen. Giving gives me satisfaction knowing that as little as I have, I may have 'more' than my neighbor, and it is my obligation to share. — *Coron Jordan*

The need to help our community learn more and do better — *Britt Brewer Loudd*

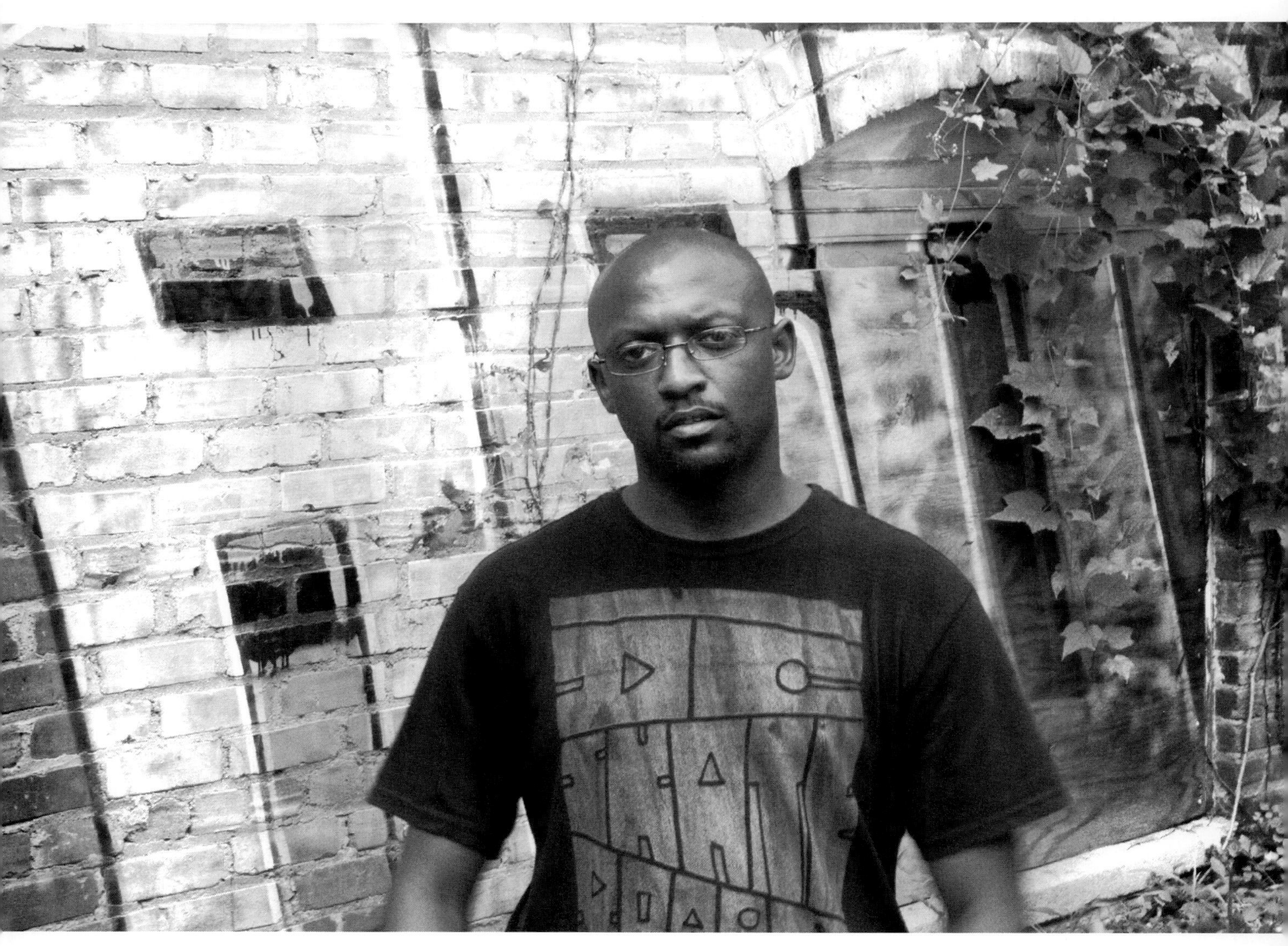

I'm for truth, no matter who tells it. I'm for justice, no matter who it is for or against. I'm a human being, first and foremost, and as such I'm for whoever and whatever benefits humanity as a whole.

MALCOLM X
American civil rights activist and Muslim minister
(1925-65)

Jeanne M. Brayboy | SERIOUS GIVER

Strong and authoritative describe how some people view my mother. I definitely held that perspective as a child. I was twelve and my brother Jack was seventeen when my father died, and my mother faced raising us as a single parent. She had a strong work ethic and was insistent about certain things. As children, we thought she was strict.

I see things differently now. My respect for her increased exponentially as our relationship evolved from mother and child to mother and adult daughter. Now my brother and I often tease her about that serious persona and those exacting ways. She laughs while denying it and insists we are exaggerating. She has a lighthearted and fun side that I rarely noticed as a child.

One thing I did notice growing up was how committed she was to the community. She is a retired music teacher and has long held a special interest in the arts. With growing children and teacher's pay, she did not have a lot of personal wealth to donate. Nevertheless, she believed it was important to give, even if the gift was small. Whether it was the church, the Afro-American Cultural Center, Johnson C. Smith University, Bennett College, Crisis Assistance Ministry or a political candidate, she made a contribution when the opportunity arose. She also contributed her time as a volunteer to too many organizations to name. Lessons unspoken about my responsibility to the community still speak volumes.

To this day, my mother continues setting examples about giving back. She has for years belonged to a "lunch bunch" made up of half a dozen women who celebrate each other's birthday over a meal. At a certain point, they ran out of gift ideas. I mean, *How many scarves can you have?* At Mom's suggestion, instead of exchanging gifts, the group now makes a donation to the birthday girl's charity of choice. For a woman who herself has celebrated eighty birthdays, she forever gives me more to aspire to be.

JOYCE MARTIN BRAYBOY

Connection: *Daughter* • Channel: *Founder, African American Women On The Hill Network*
Cause: *Political action and advocacy*

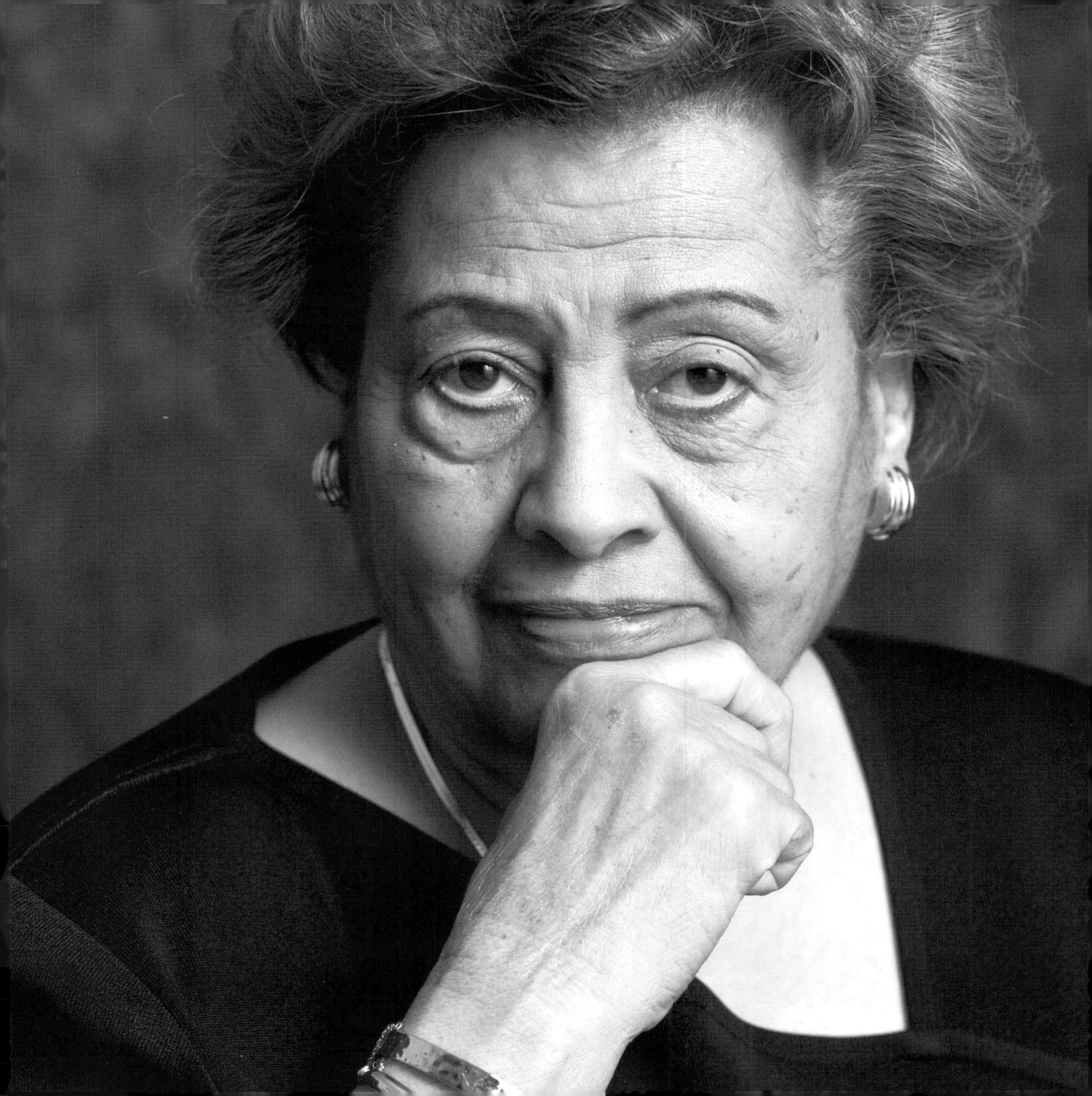

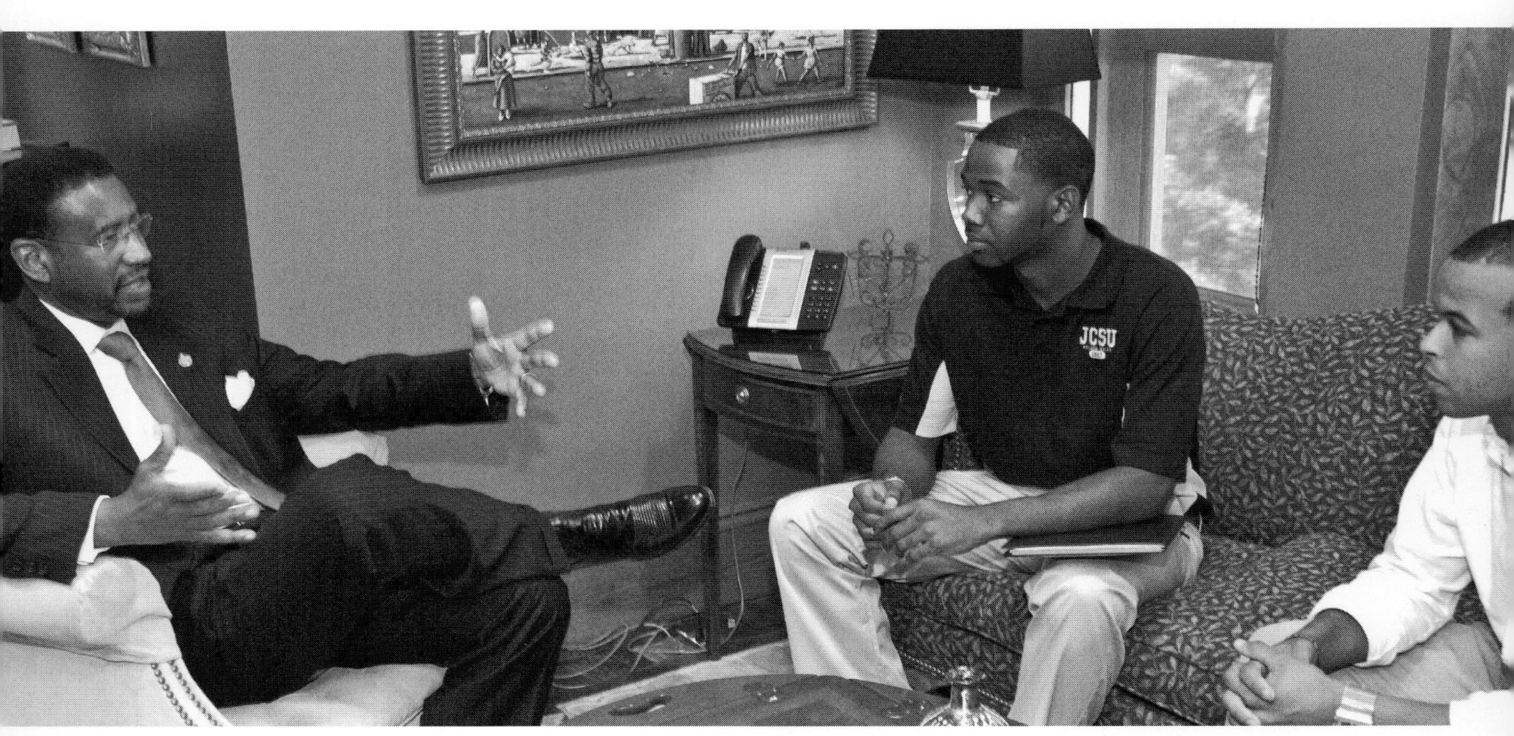
JCSU

We've got to work to save our children and do it with full respect for the fact that if we do not, no one else is going to do it.

DOROTHY I. HEIGHT
American educator and social activist
(1912-2010)

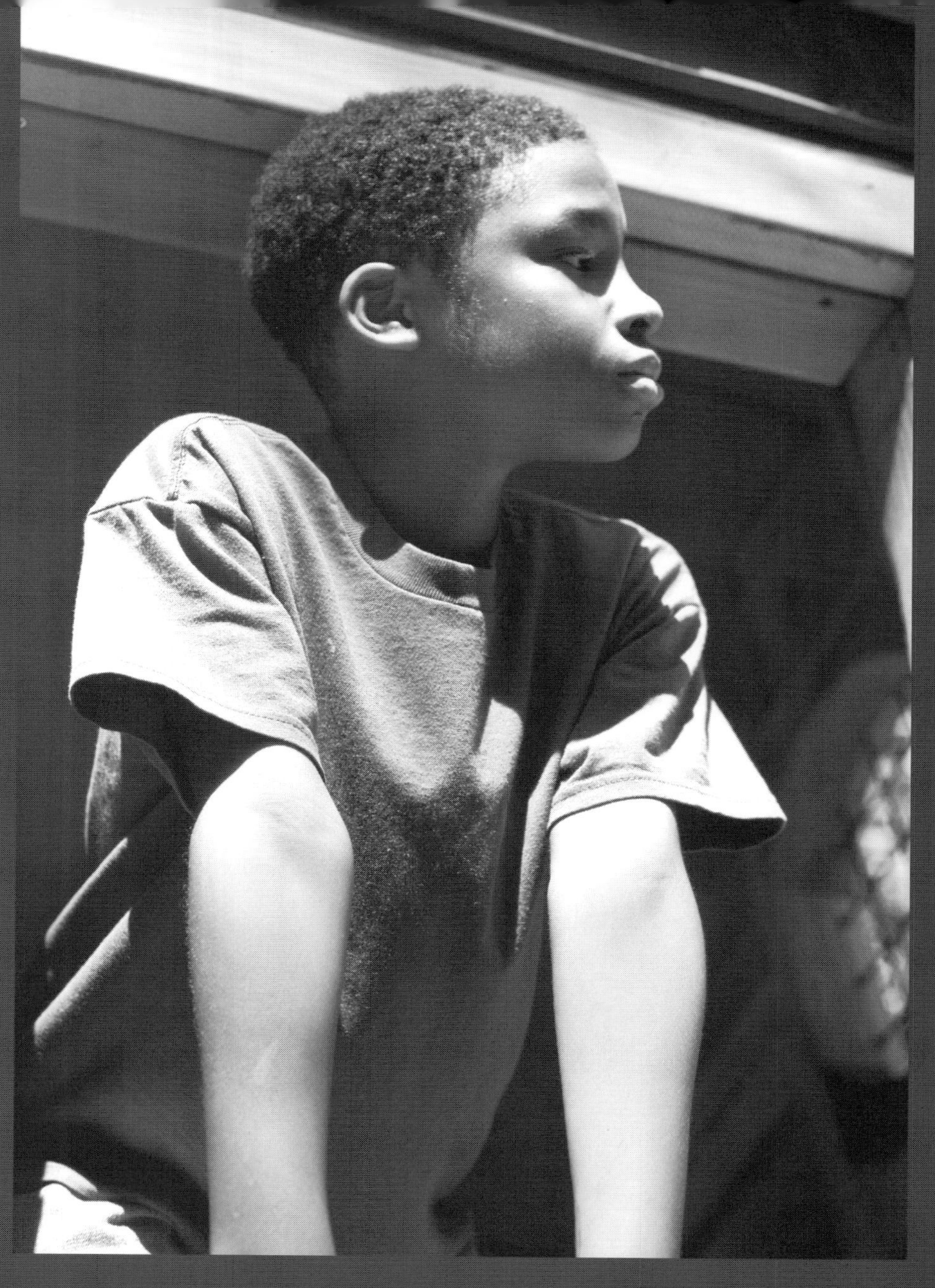

"IT WAS CHRISTMAS SEASON 1999. I didn't need anything, I didn't want anything and neither did my wife. We had a new house, no kids and our families lived in the Midwest. The idea of going to the mall held little allure. So, we decided to adopt a family in need for Christmas—a single father with three kids. This, we reminded ourselves, was what Christmas giving was really about.

"Our idea was to secretly meet the father outside his apartment to deliver the toys. Instead, the boys got wind of our plan and happily met us in the parking lot. We helped carry the presents inside and placed them under their tree. It was quite enjoyable. As we pulled out to head home, it hit me. No one said thank you—not the kids or the father. When I pointed that out to my wife, she reminded me that thank you was not the goal. And as wives often are, she was right.

"I also realized it was not the boys' fault. There are generations of families born into circumstances beyond their control. In this case, these boys were born into a life of public assistance. They were raised to expect someone or some group would always bring needed items. That was deeply troubling to me.

"Every child should have a chance. Every child should understand that there is a world of opportunities outside of their home, neighborhood and city. And for that reason, I launched the Bay Area Leadership Foundation. The program provides mentoring, coaching and scholarships for low-income kids from Northern California enabling them to successfully graduate high school and college. It is our goal that kids have hope and vision."

Vintage Foster
founder and chairman of the Bay Area Leadership Foundation, established in 2000
to provide support and resources for youth from economically disadvantaged communities

I am not tragically colored. There is no great sorrow dammed up in my soul, nor lurking behind my eyes. . . . Even in the helter-skelter skirmish that is my life, I have seen that the world is to the strong regardless of a little pigmentation more or less. No, I do not weep at the world—I am too busy sharpening my oyster knife.

ZORA NEALE HURSTON
American author and anthropologist
(1891-1960)

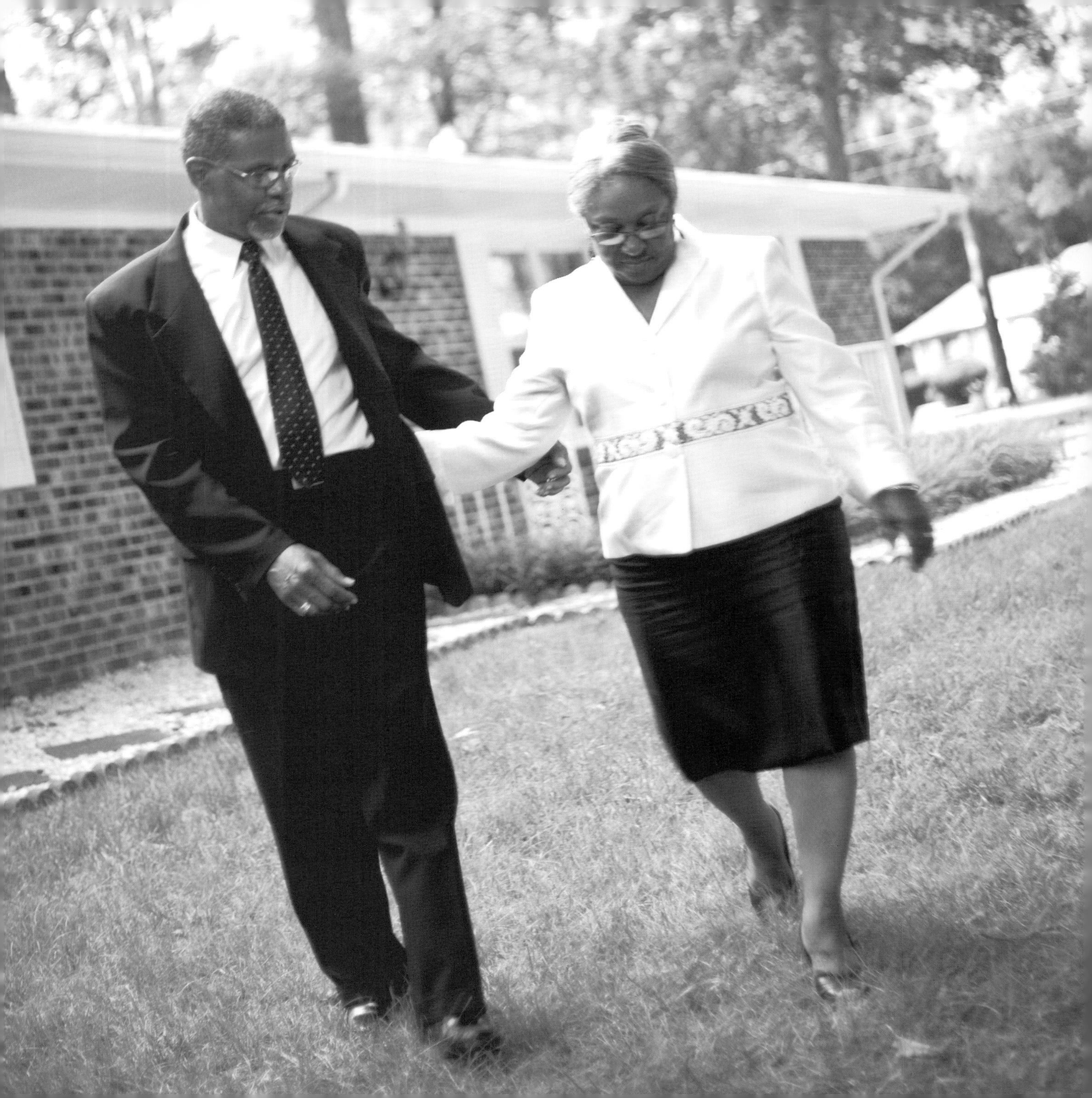

Those whose minds are shaped by selfless thoughts give joy when they speak or act. Joy follows them like a shadow that never leaves them.

BUDDHA
Eastern spiritual leader and founder of Buddhism
(circa 563 BC-483 BC)

John Crawford | OPPORTUNITY'S USHER

Giant. That's what I see when I think of my father. From childhood, I have cast my eyes up to a man of tall, powerful stature and a huge, radiant persona. As I have grown older, the hugeness of his heart has become more apparent. It is wonderful looking up to a person who wants to see you do well and the whole world, too.

When I was a kid and did not know any better, I was a little jealous of all of the giving Daddy did. During his career at the public housing authority, he treated the kids in the communities he served as if they were his own. I thought, "I'm your only child!" With maturity came understanding that there was enough of him to share. I lacked for nothing because of the concern he showed for other children; in fact, I gained.

Recently, while out at breakfast, a guy approached Daddy and me. He was a kid from dad's public housing days that he had not seen in years. The bond was still there and a glimmer of my father's big spirit was obvious in this guy's personality. In their brief reunion, I observed fruit of a seed planted long ago.

"Give a youth a chance" is almost a cliché, but as dad's mantra it is so much more than that. Giving kids a chance for a decent life led him to found the Charlotte Housing Authority Scholarship Fund. The college scholarships he helped make possible have had an impact on thousands of families. I cannot express how much pride I feel for what he has accomplished as a pillar in the community and as a father.

Daddy's example influenced my giving, even though our styles differ. He is soft and fuzzy. I am more matter of fact. Nonetheless my mother calls us both visionaries: We see things as they should be and then go about making it so. Like my dad did for those kids, I have dedicated myself to Mothers Of Murdered Offspring, a nonprofit support group for families of homicide victims. We both give because we have learned that it is what you do for others that matters most.

LISA CRAWFORD

Connection: *Daughter* • Channel: *Mothers of Murdered Offspring* • Cause: *Compassion for people facing grief and crisis*

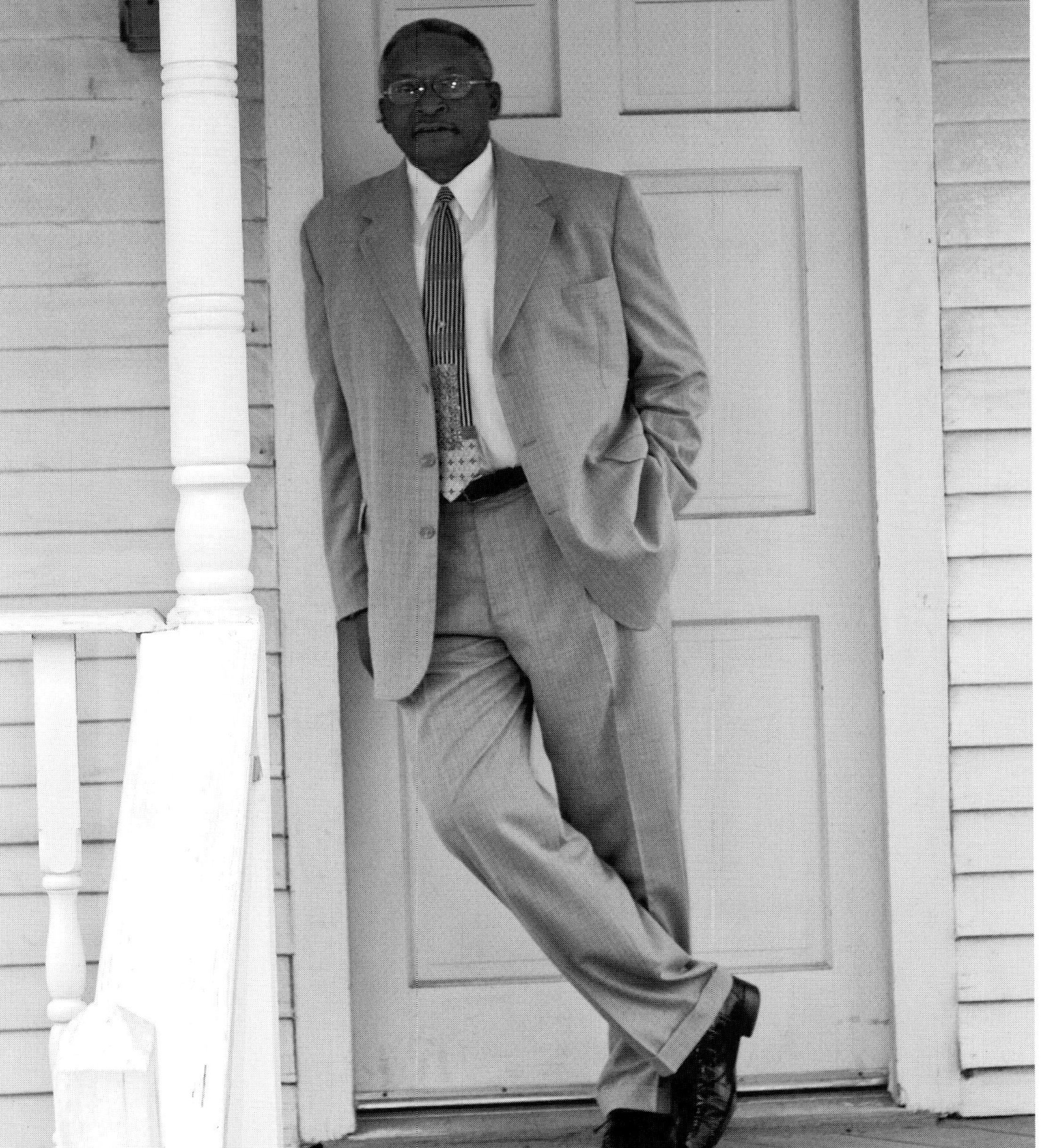

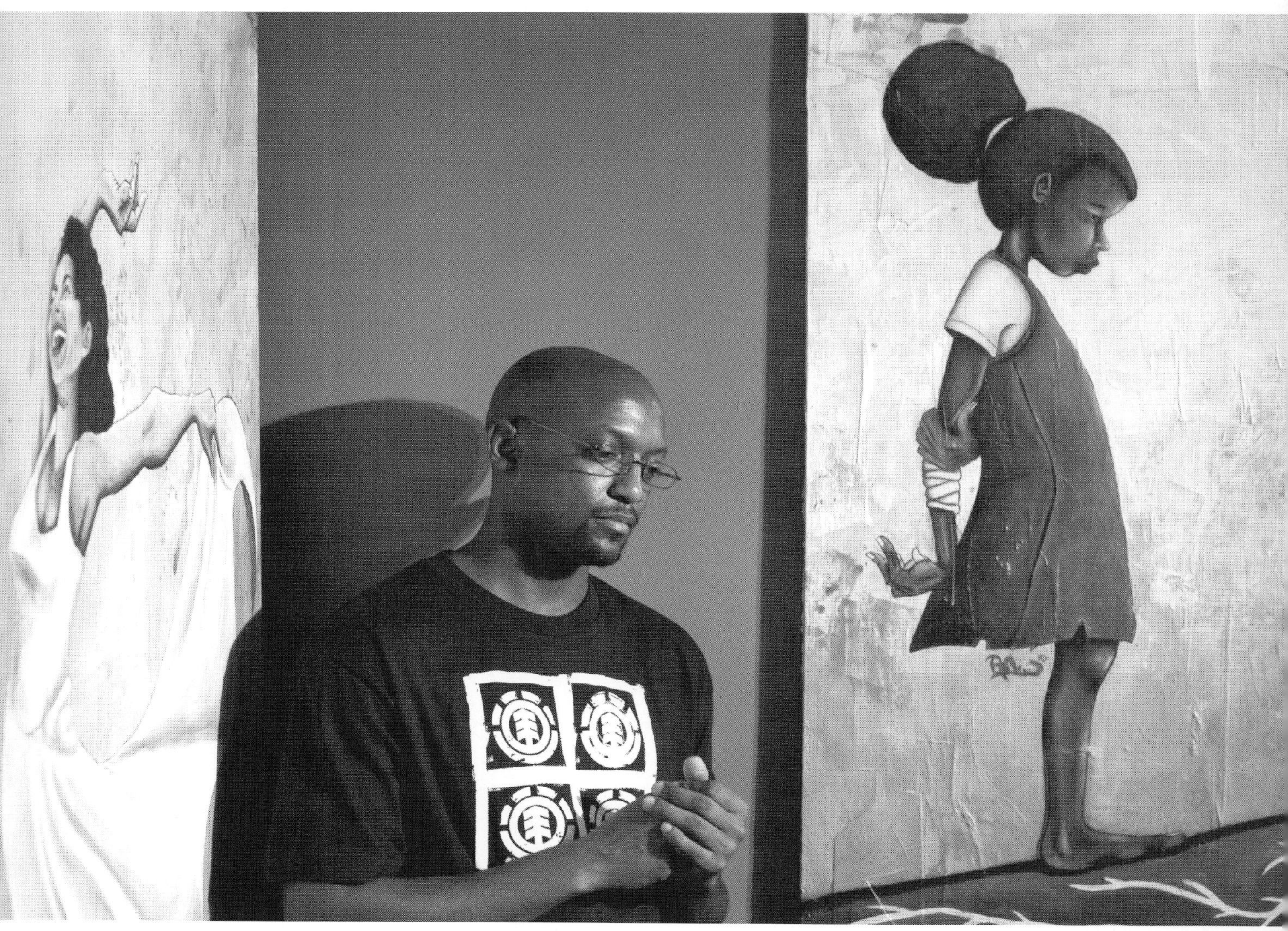

You give but little when you give of your possessions.
It is when you give of yourself that you truly give.

KAHLIL GIBRAN
Lebanese-born artist and poet
(1883-1931)

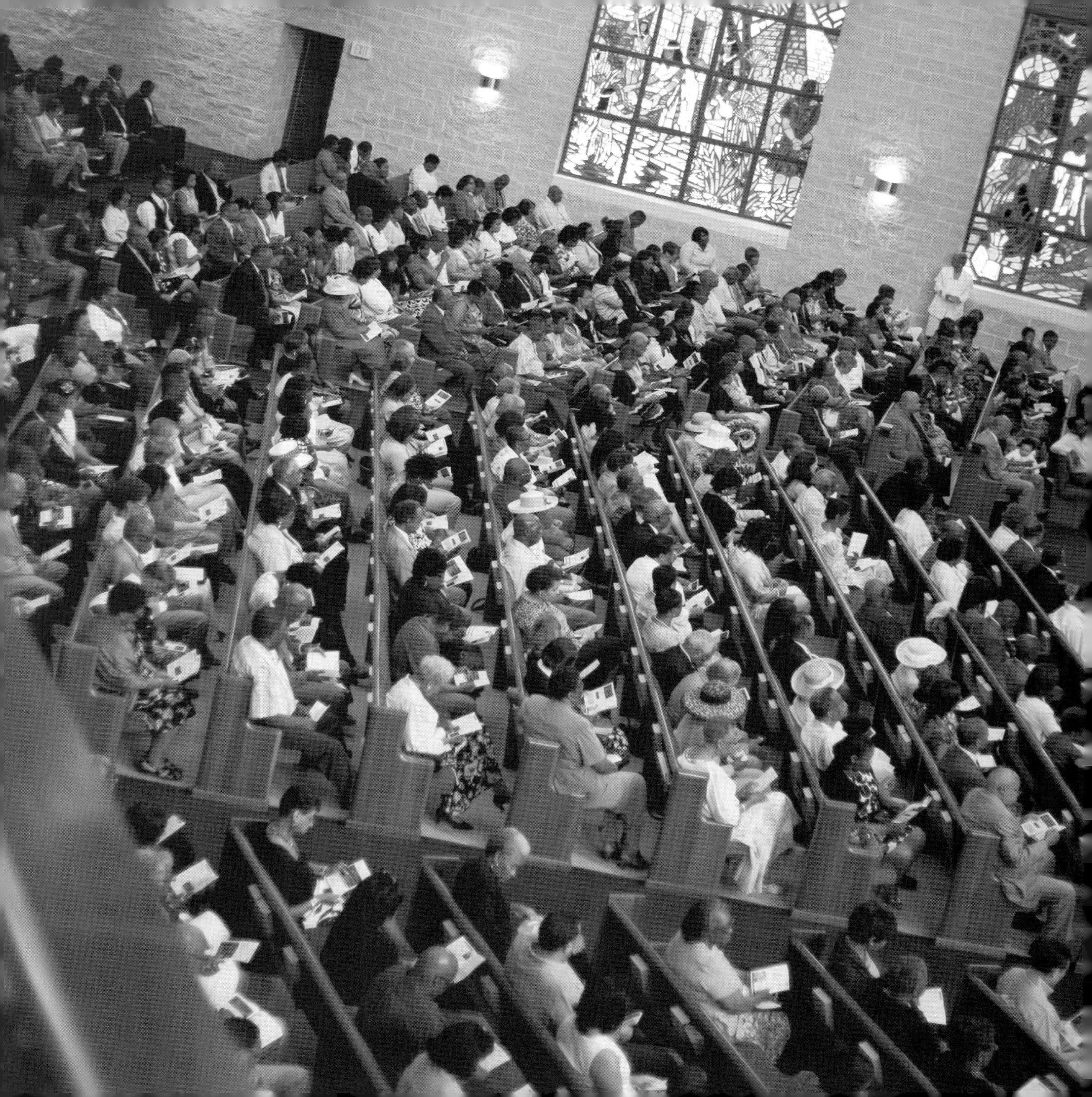
EXIT

Religion without humanity is poor human stuff.

SOJOURNER TRUTH
American abolitionist and women's rights activist
(1797-1883)

Maldonia McGimpsey Fullwood | THE ROSE GARDENER

Cherished times grew plentiful on the front porch of my grandmother's home. My sister, cousins and I spent a large share of our childhood playing up and down Bouchelle Street and around Mama's house. Mama Fullwood is what the other grandchildren called her, but to me she was always just *Mama*.

Mama's porch was a beloved gathering spot for extended family while I was coming up. During the long stretch of summer in the South, you could find Mama sitting in her favorite chair, uncles and aunts perched on the banister and visitors often overflowing to the lawn. One too many cousins and I usually pressed our luck to sit snugly together in the porch swing that hung by a slim chain. As passersby neared the house, Mama would invite them to come sit a spell. Unless something was pressing, refusals were few.

At the corner of the porch sprung a beautiful rosebush that bloomed bountifully around Mother's Day. It was sort of a tradition for neighbors along Bouchelle to stop by Mama's house Sunday morning or the day before for a red blossom clipped from her rosebush. This simple gift was emblematic of her generosity, and I can picture her smile as she graciously gave each rose.

Monetary wealth was not found in our family, yet Mama earned a reputation for being a generous woman who loved her family deeply, served her church devoutly and gave to all freely. Her manner of treating people provided lessons every day about giving of yourself, your time, your energy and a kind word. When called to give material objects including money, she taught us to give ungrudgingly.

Mama cared for her family like she tended her rosebush. She exposed each of us to the light of church and faith, rooted us in tradition, nurtured us with encouragement and was prompt to prune us when we grew unwieldy and wild. Her good deeds were a trellis during our upbringing. She likely smiles among the clouds as she watches the seeds of her generosity blossoming today.

ALLEN W. FULLWOOD
Connection: *Grandson* • Channel: *Board member, Flynn Christian Fellowship Home*
Cause: *Enriching the lives of people with special needs*

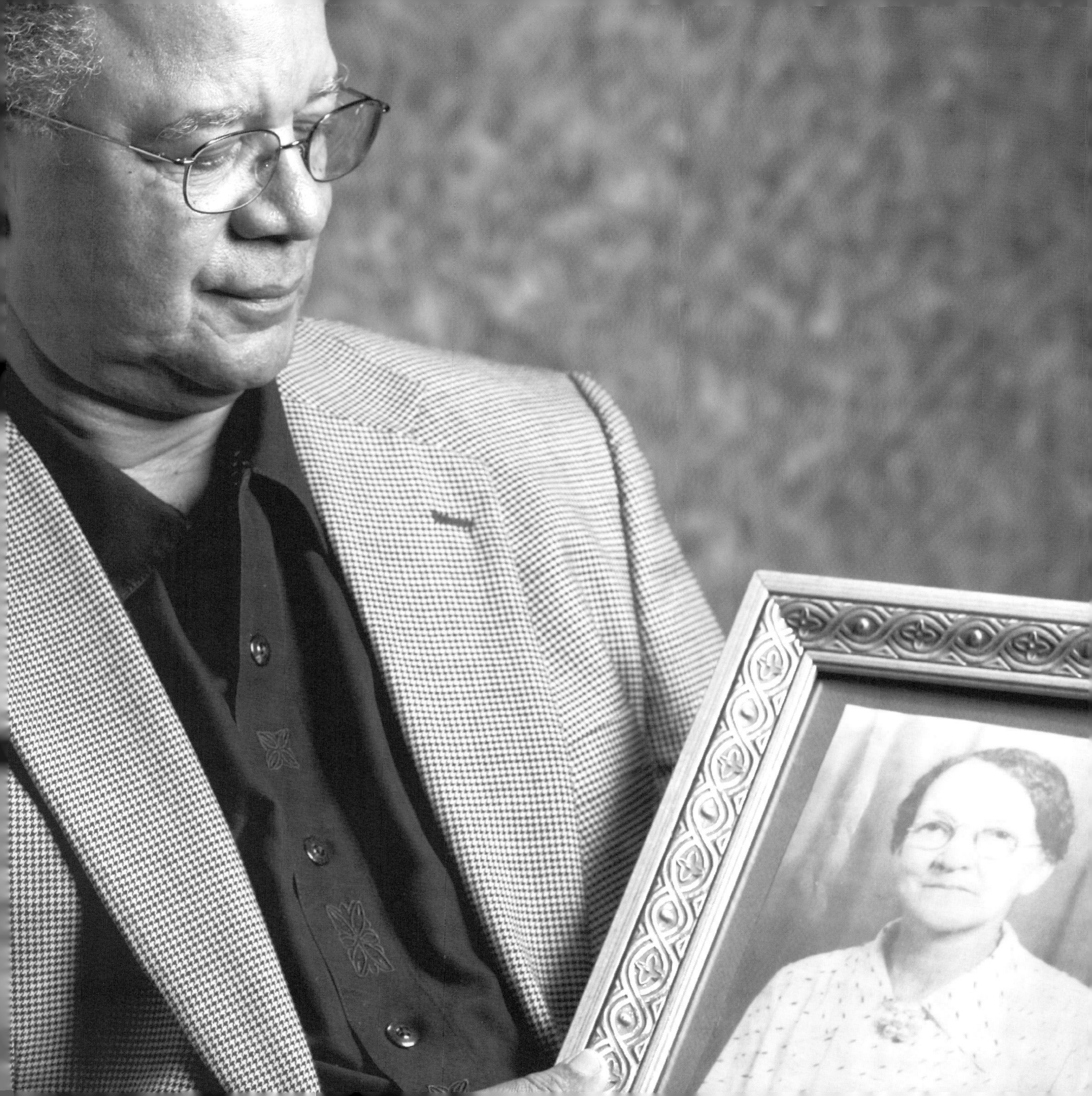

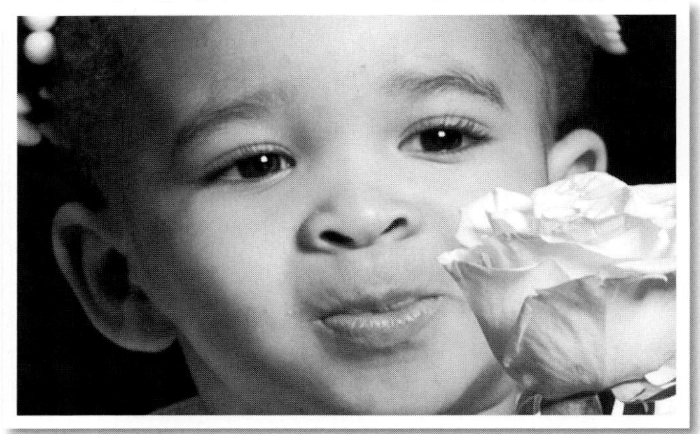

The fragrance always remains in the hand that gives the rose.

CHINESE PROVERB

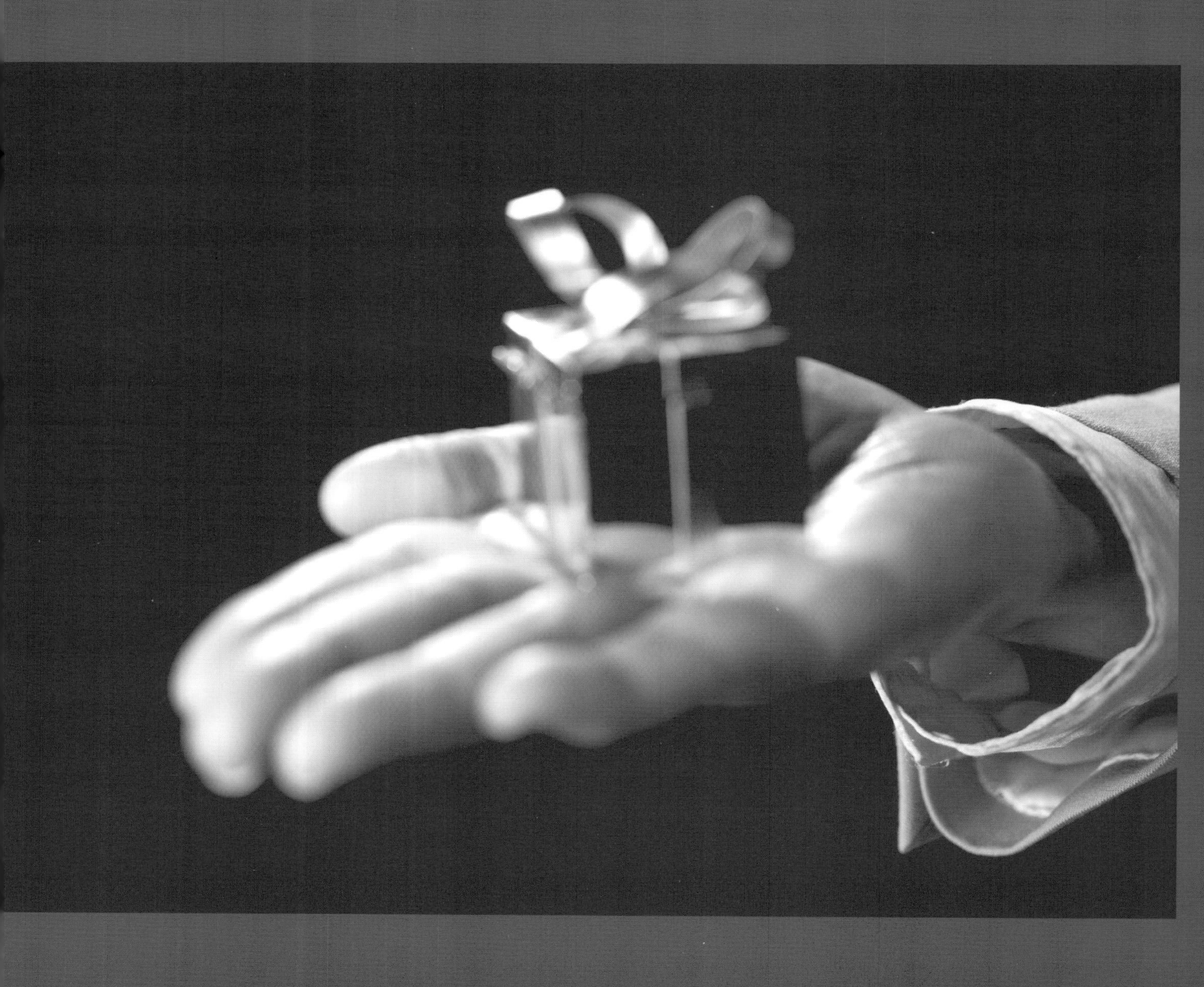

"ZAWADI is a Swahili word meaning 'gift.' The seed for our giving circle, Zawadi, was planted in 2004 at a conference on Black philanthropy in Baton Rouge. It was there that I, along with my friend and co-worker Ivette Smythe-Macaulay, heard the story of Oseola McCarty, an African American woman who saved enough of her modest earnings from washing and ironing clothes to donate $150,000 to the University of Southern Mississippi for scholarships for Black students.

"It was also at that conference that Ivette and I first heard about giving circles and met another colleague in philanthropy, Samantha Bickham. The three of us, all living in New Orleans at the time, began meeting and brainstorming how they could convince other people to join a giving circle. We'd had so many conversations with friends about all the things wrong with New Orleans that we wanted to take a more active role in becoming part of the solution. We thought we were going to face a lot of apathy and possibly even opposition to starting a circle.

"As it turned out, I was at a friend's home with about seven other women and mentioned, in the course of conversation, that Ivette, Samantha and I were trying to figure out how to start a circle. Incredulous, the rest of the group said, 'What are you waiting for? Let's do it!' The first meeting of our giving circle was held the very next week."

Christine Jordan
founding member of Zawadi, a CIN giving circle, and
grantmaker for corporate philanthropy and social responsibility at Entergy Corporation

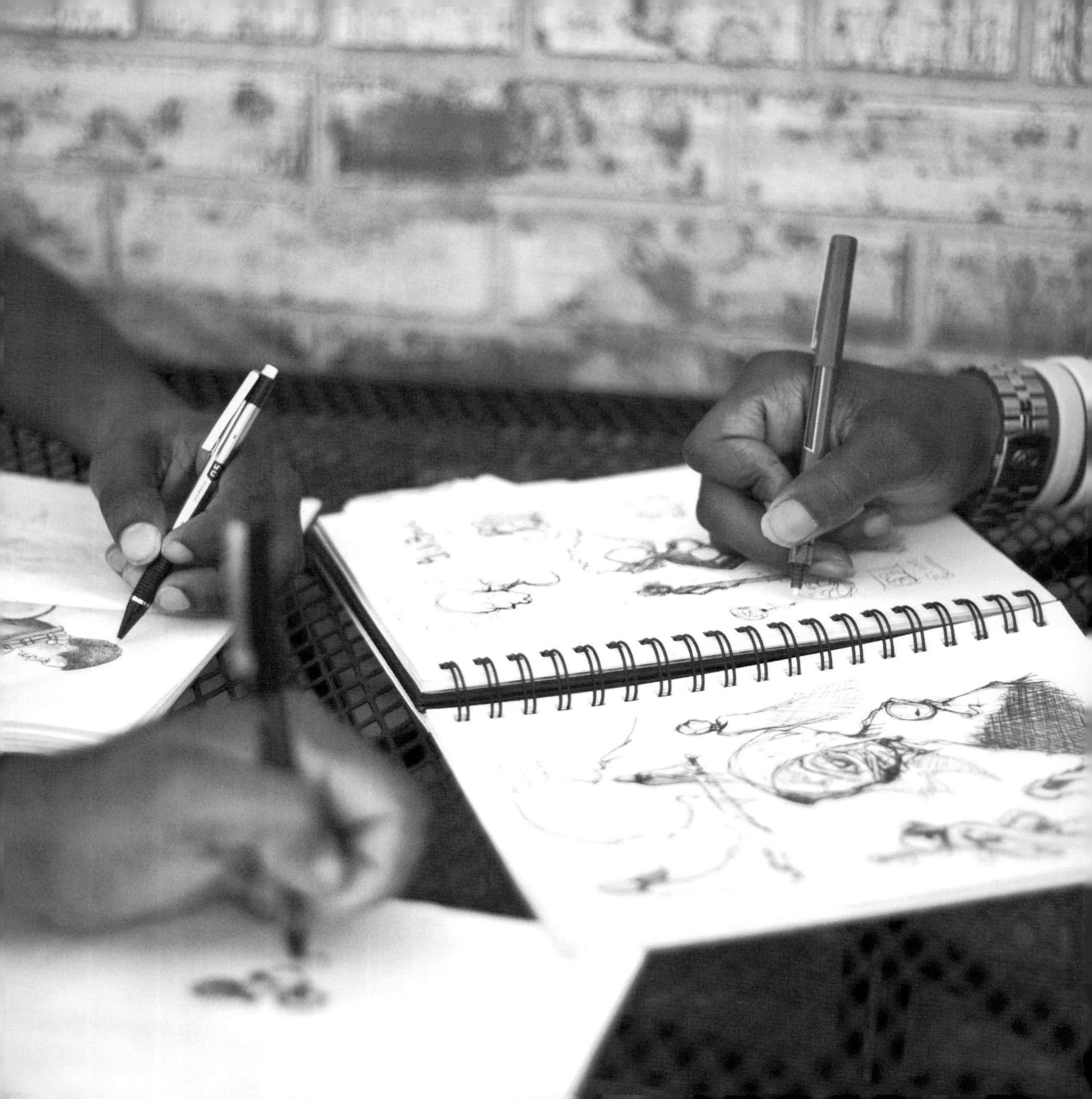

We are all gifted. That is our inheritance.

ETHEL WATERS
American jazz vocalist and actress
(1900-77)

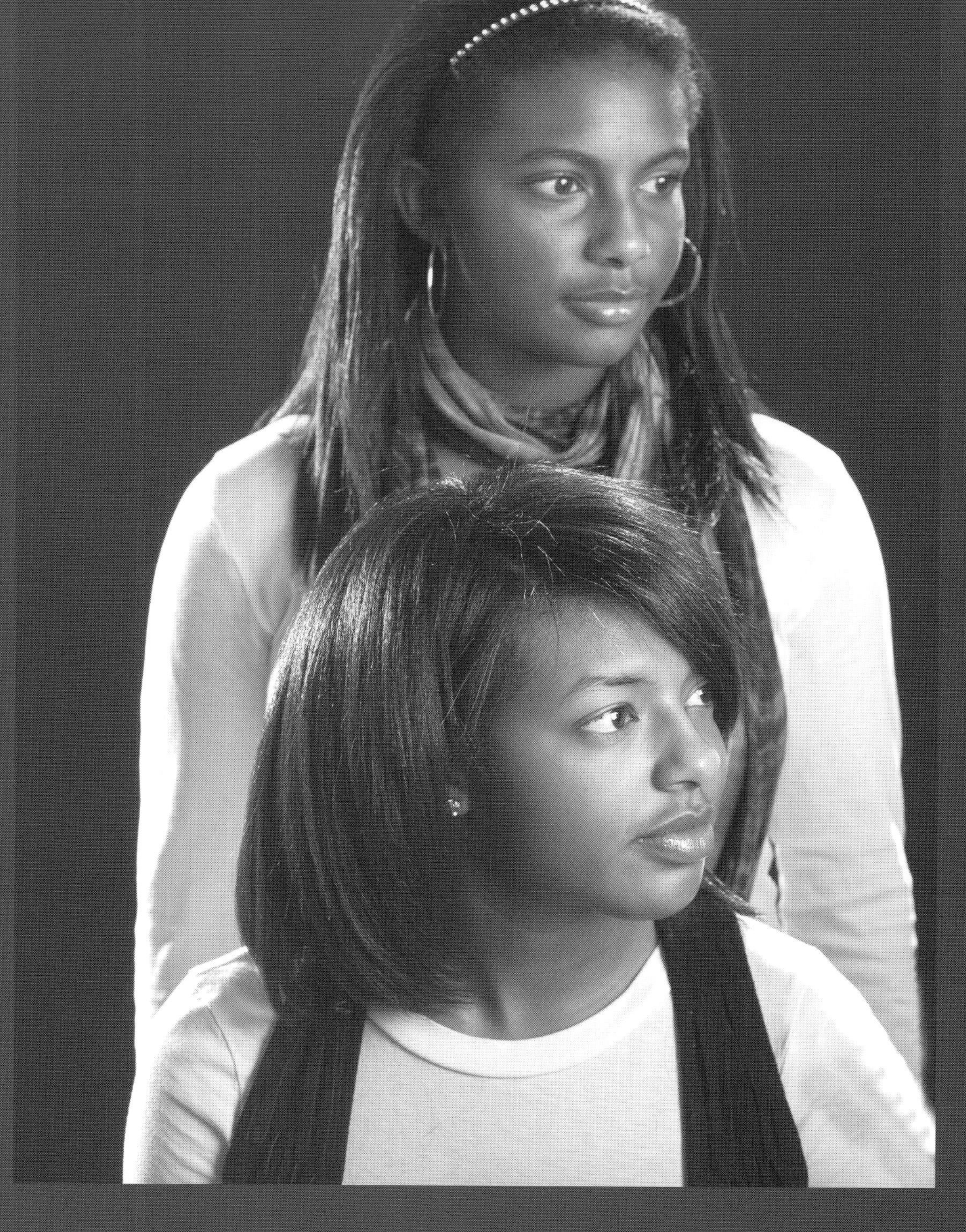

"A GREAT SENSE OF PRIDE and commitment filled me when I served as president of our alumnae chapter. I am a Bennett College Legacy, and the education I received there carries tremendous significance. My father graduated from Bennett prior to it becoming a women's college. An aunt and cousin were graduates, and my daughter attended, too.

"During my presidency, I focused on the *Little Miss Bennett Pageant,* which is one of the chapter's fundraisers. The annual pageant provided an opportunity to bring together talented and poised little girls from various towns in our area. The churches, schools and families of the girls were always excited about contributing to a good cause. Everyone helped their contestant compete for the winning crown and a chance to take home a trophy and savings bonds and to ride in North Carolina A&T University's homecoming parade.

"Our chapter was able to give scholarships to deserving students with the dollars the pageant generated. The pageant has a rich legacy in the community that is important to continue. I carry a hope that the little pageant participants will someday attend Bennett College and that the scholarship recipients will become as dedicated to Bennett as our chapter's alumnae."

Ernestine Paschall Shade
charter member of the Southern California Bennett College Alumnae Chapter and former president of the Western North Carolina Bennett College Alumnae Chapter, both of which support an HBCU founded in 1873

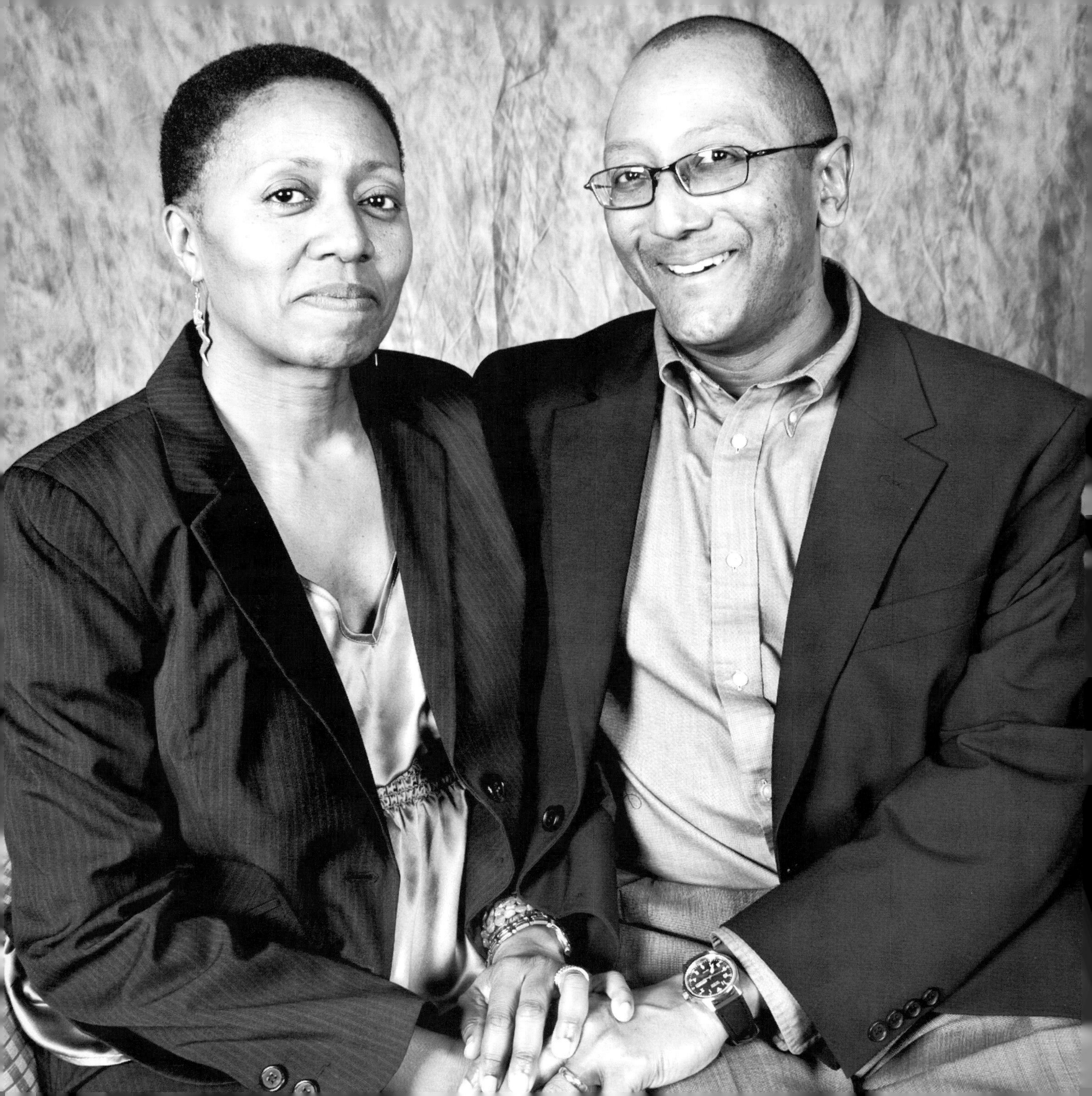

Thousands of candles can be lighted from a single candle,
and the life of the candle will not be shortened.
Happiness never decreases by being shared.

BUDDHA
Eastern spiritual leader and founder of Buddhism
(circa 563 BC-483 BC)

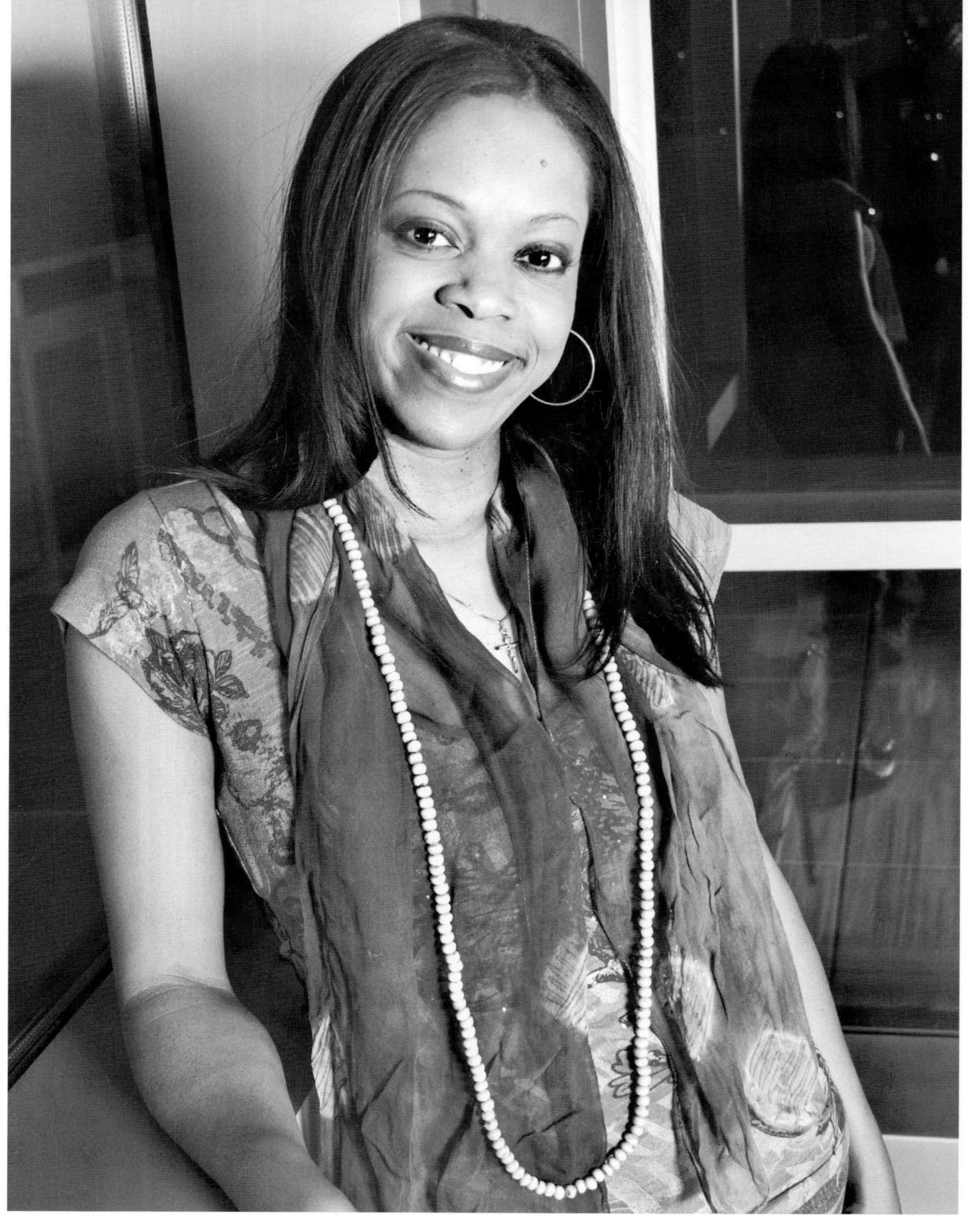

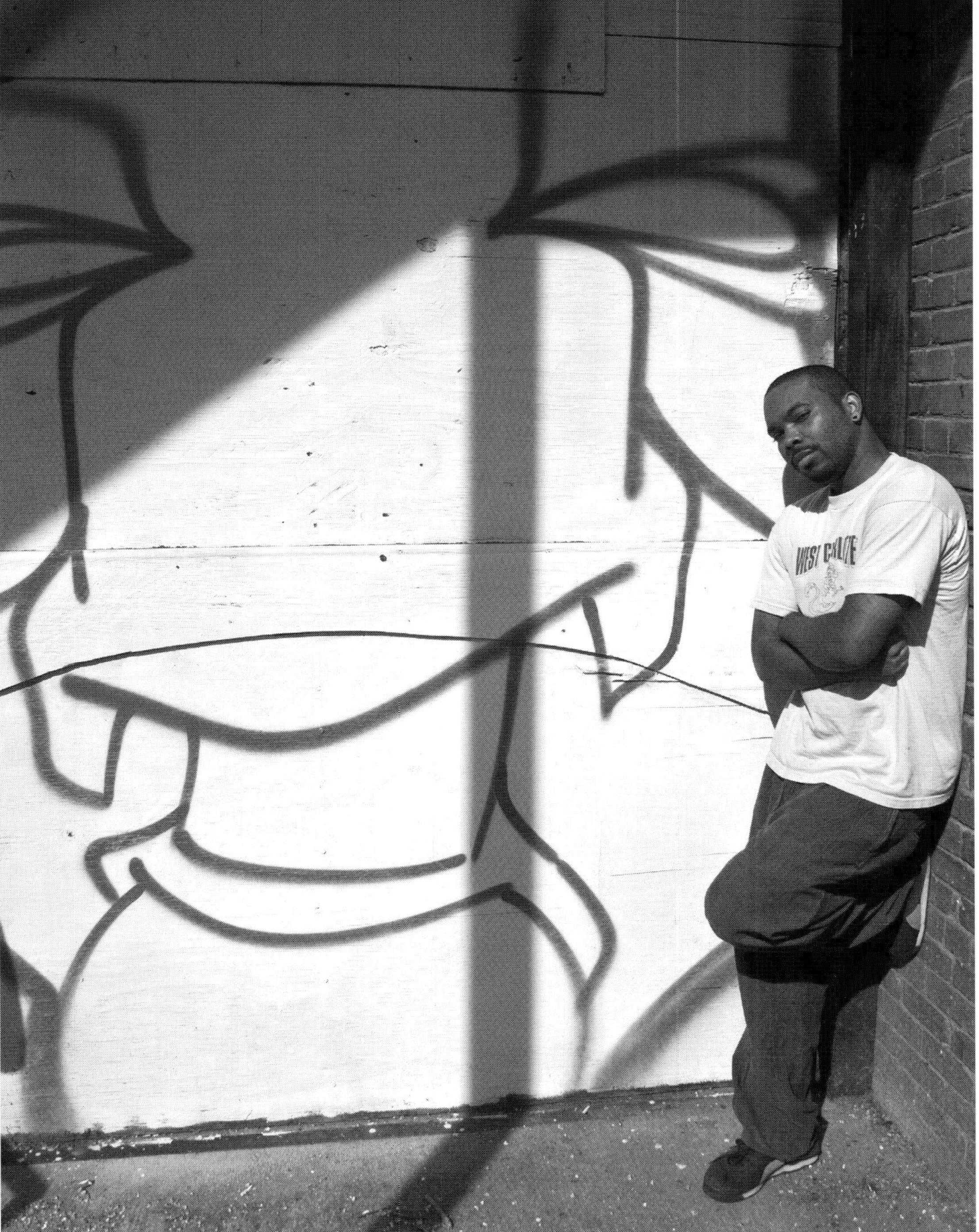

No individual has any right to come into the world and go out of it without leaving behind him distinct and legitimate reasons for having passed through it.

GEORGE WASHINGTON CARVER
American scientist, educator and inventor
(1864-1943)

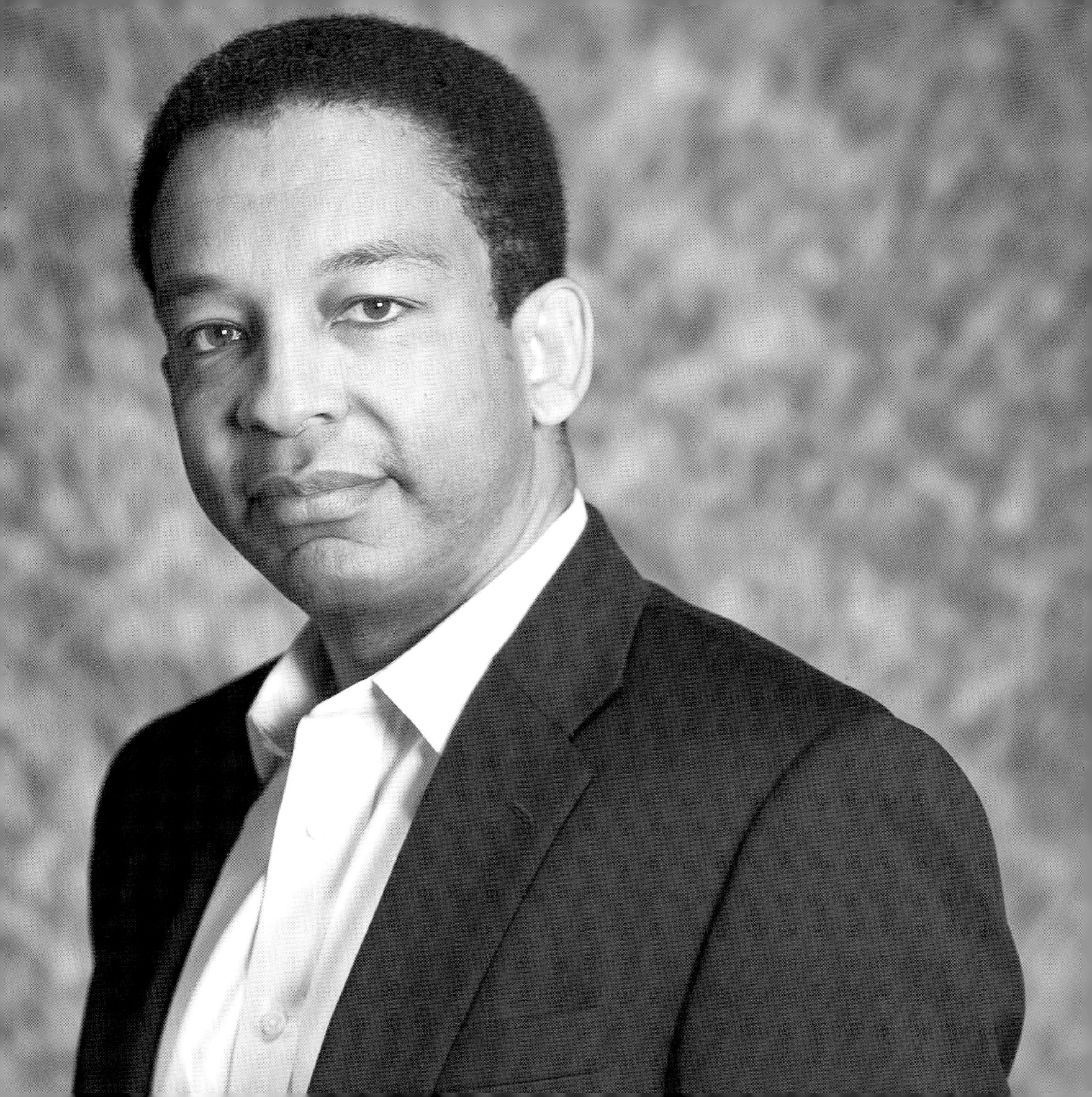

INFLUENCES

Who or what shaped why and how you give?

My parents shaped my approach to giving. — *Dan Nunn*

Being a part of a group of people who are focused on giving back to the community — *Ihsan Abdin*

Women in need would come to me asking for help, and I would do so. I learned that collective giving goes so much further. — *Denise Rowson*

Ms. Ella Talley. She always told me to help others through my time, talents or money. She was one to give back to her community, and I was always right by her side. — *Gelisa Stitt*

My mother, because in her own nontraditional way, she would give. There were many times that she would give to others when we really didn't have much to give. At the time, I was upset and couldn't really understand it, but now I appreciate her for it. — *Patricia Martelly*

Seeing others giving back as I was growing up. Relatives gave money to their church, and my Girl Scout leader gave so much time and attention to our troop over the years. — *Diatra Fullwood*

My giving was shaped by my family—a family of twelve brothers and sisters—where you learned the importance of sharing and giving. — *Mattie Marshall*

My family: parents, grandparents, extended family. It's in the blood! — *Britt Brewer Loudd*

Having an opportunity to go to school for free through a scholarship, because someone decided to give. Their gifts helped to position me to give and help groom others to give as well. — *Ohmar Land*

Mother and church — *Edgar Villanueva*

My parents, through their service and tireless dedication to church and family — *Sherry Waters*

My grandmother was a civil rights activist and stressed to us that it is up to us to make change in our community—be it through education, success or our financial investment in our community. — *LaDawn Sullivan*

My spiritual beliefs and social consciousness shape my giving. — *Christian Friend*

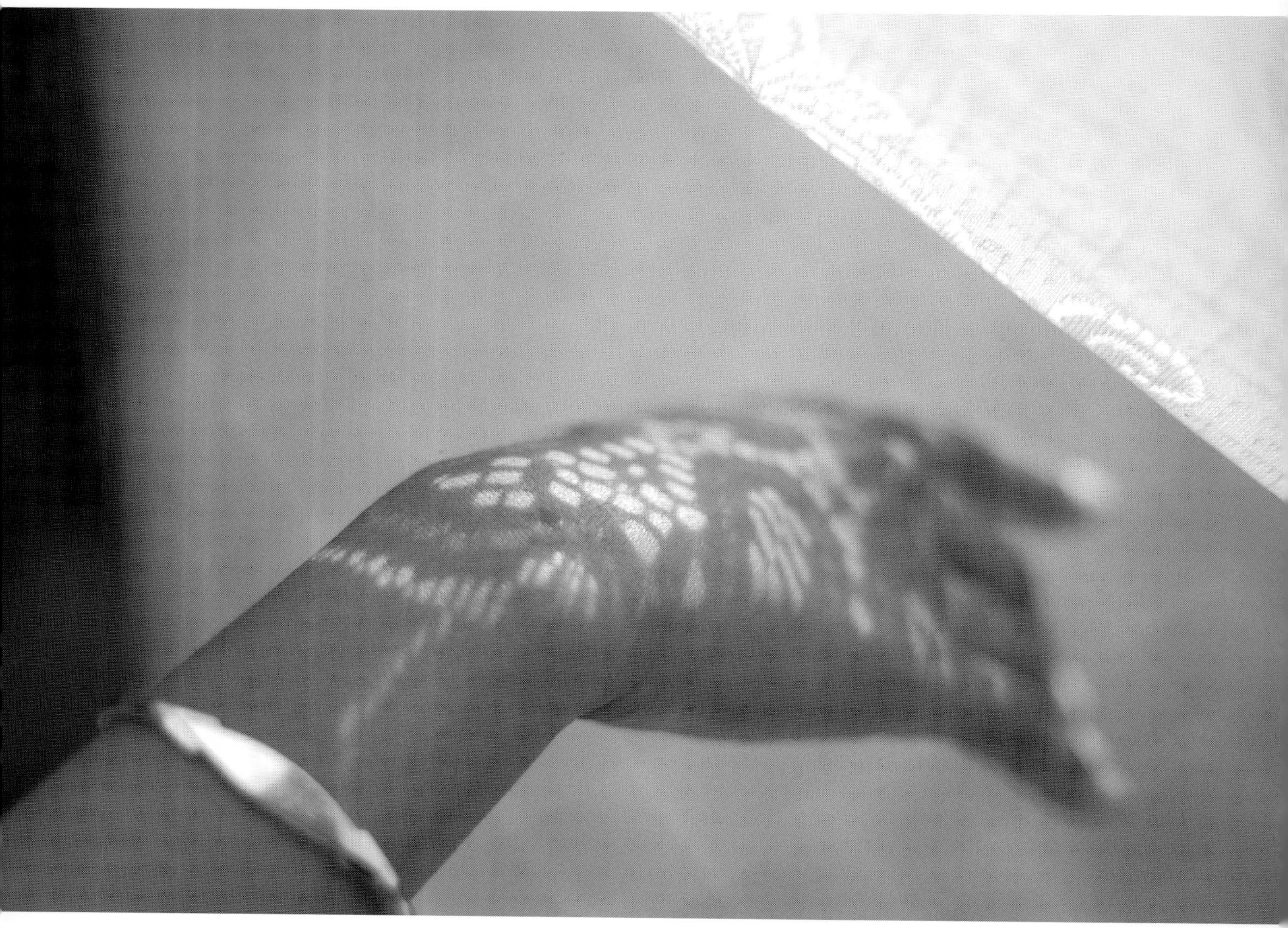

Humankind has not woven the web of life.
We are but one thread within it.
Whatever we do to the web,
we do to ourselves.
All things are bound together.
All things connect.

CHIEF SEATTLE
Native American leader
(1780-1866)

Adonis "Sporty" Jeralds | POINT GUARD

As a child, I was well acquainted with special people who worked selflessly to benefit others. There were my aunts and both grandmothers who served in the church, organizers of the youth programs that shaped me and my parents who were heavily involved in the community. Being of service to others had been a given in our household; yet when I went to college things changed. During those years, I was so into finding myself that I lost sight of childhood basics. And then in a flash, I was a young professional climbing the career ladder. It was not until I took a job in Charlotte that my life's work began.

Sporty Jeralds, my manager at the new job, became a mentor who showed me it is possible to achieve a balanced lifestyle even when working long, demanding hours at a sports arena. At Sporty's urging, I volunteered one summer for a youth reading program that he had started in the Dalton Village public housing project. Sporty used his own money and friends' donations to provide books and prizes for neighborhood children who were expected to read a book per week. Eager to please, the kids read like crazy all summer. Their reward was a highly anticipated trip to a local amusement park, orchestrated and financed by Sporty.

That summer Sporty made a difference in those kids' lives and mine too. He reminded me about my responsibility to serve others and stirred my interest to do more. He soon began recommending me for the boards of nonprofit agencies and all sorts of philanthropic work. I am forever grateful for his example and his game plan to increase my involvement. Now, when the juggling act of job duties and grown-up hassles throws me off balance, I am steadied by my labor of love in the community.

DIATRA FULLWOOD
Connection: *Former employee* ◆ Channel: *Member, Junior League* ◆ Cause: *Children, families and education*

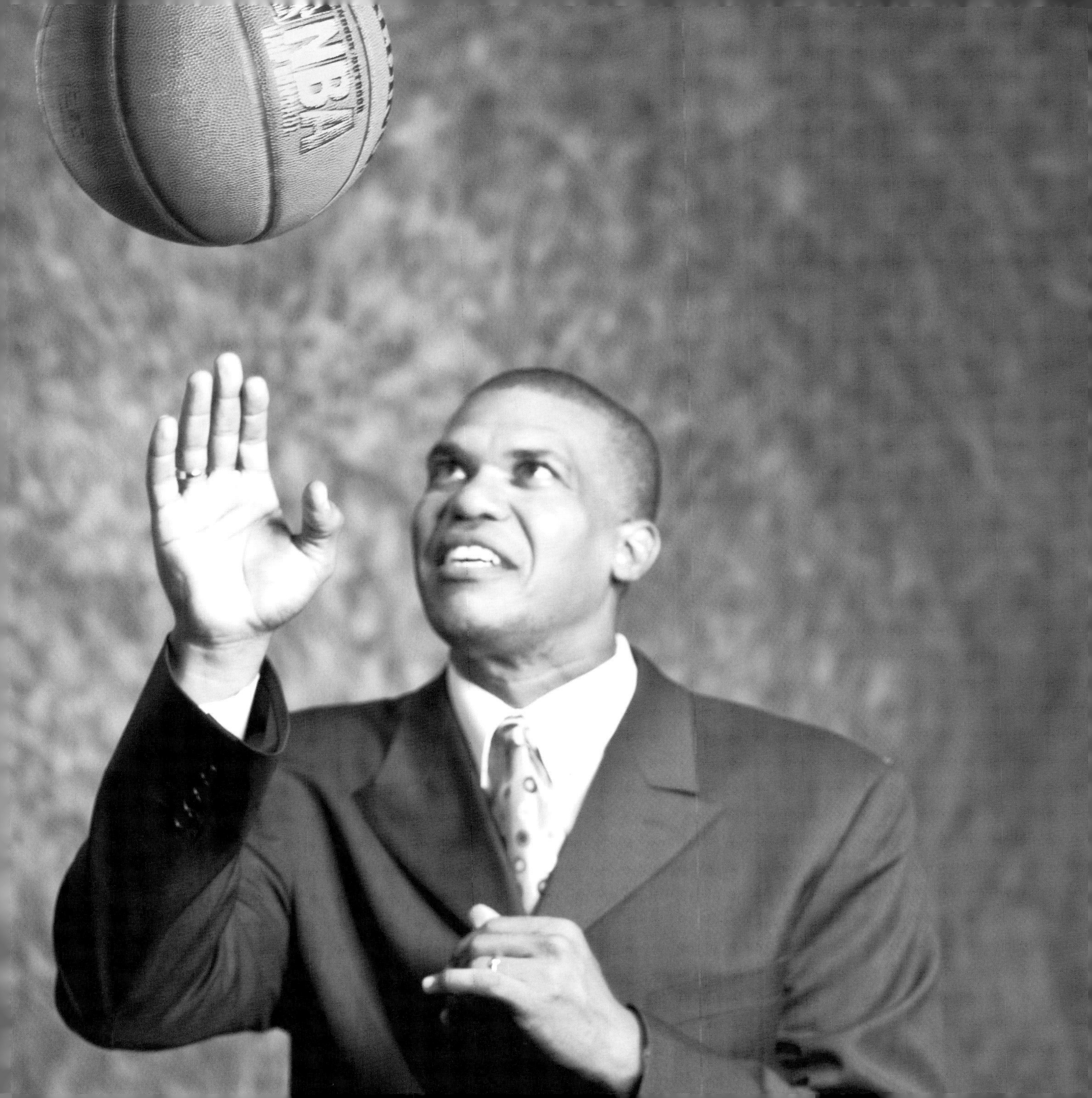
NBA

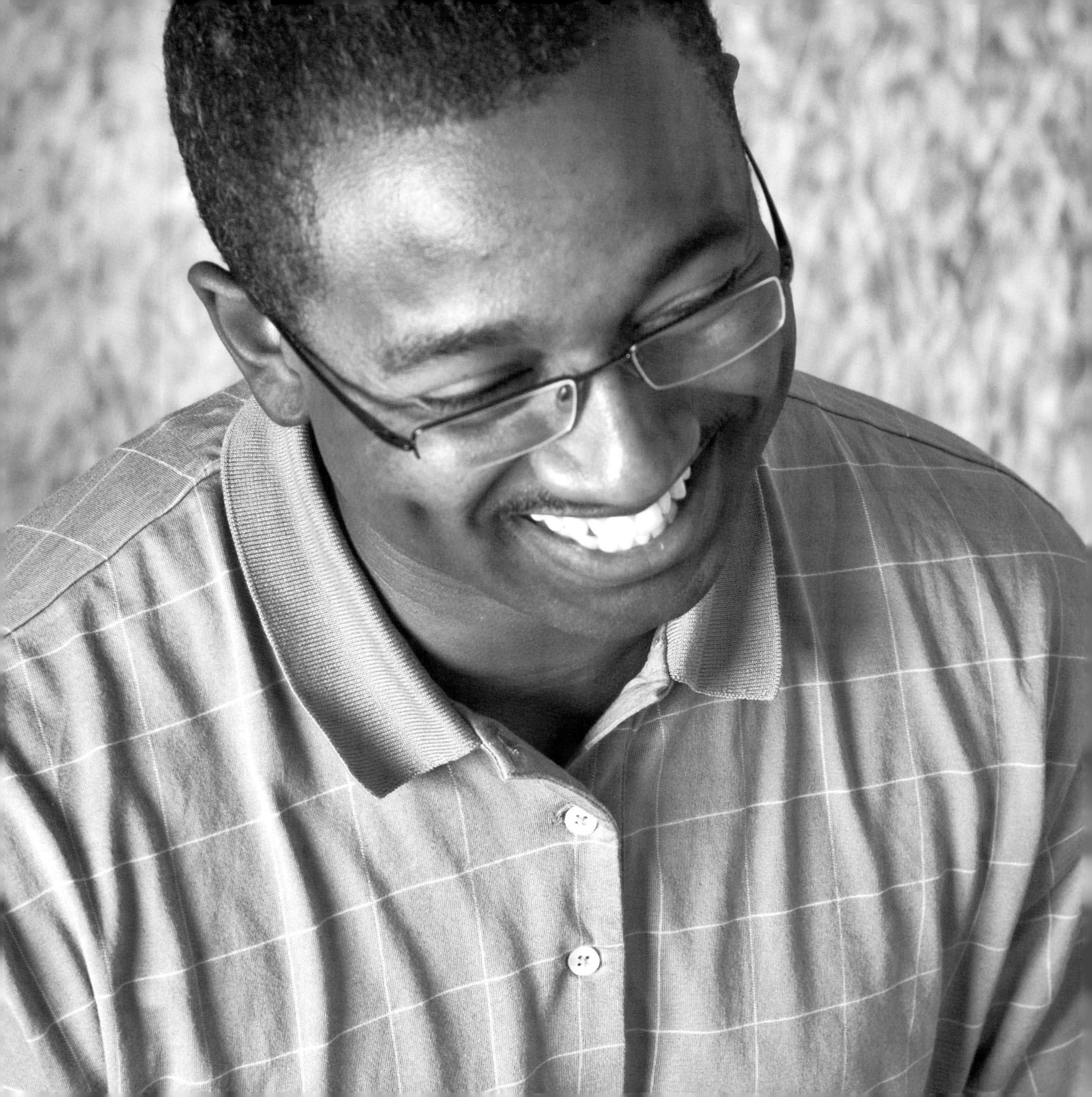

It's faith in something and
enthusiasm for something
that makes a life worth living.

OLIVER WENDELL HOLMES SR.
American physician, lecturer and author
(1809-94)

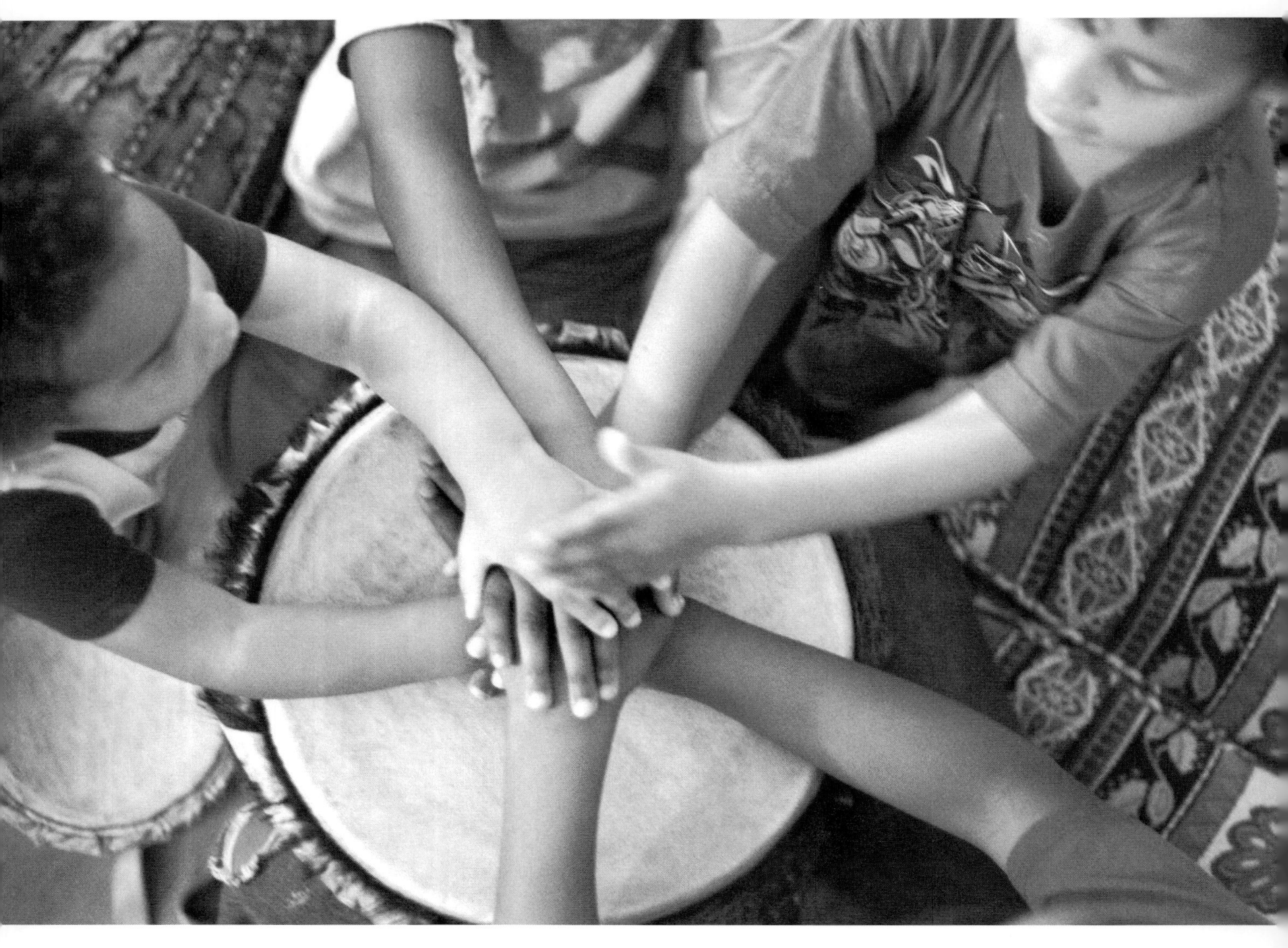

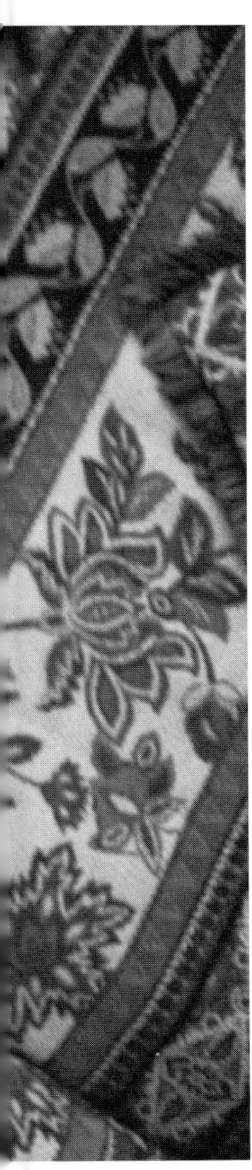

"OVER MY LIFE, I have given back in many ways. A few years ago, I was introduced to the concept of organized philanthropy. I have always been passionate about the power of collective action and its role in changing our society for the better throughout history. My personal conviction in philanthropy stems from the power of collective strategic giving, and the most powerful model I have been exposed to is giving circles.

"Being involved in the giving circle Birmingham Change Fund, I see firsthand the power that focused monetary investments can have in my community. I also see the effect of investing time and talent. I am a better-informed citizen and more engaged donor as a result of my giving circle work. A key to our community and country's future lies in people learning how to give collectively to tackle our society's inadequacies. Giving circles offer everyday citizens an opportunity to become a part of the solution as donors of time, talent and treasure to make a better tomorrow."

Charles E. Lewis
founding member of Birmingham Change Fund, founded in 2003 and
brother, Alpha Phi Alpha Fraternity, Inc., founded in 1906

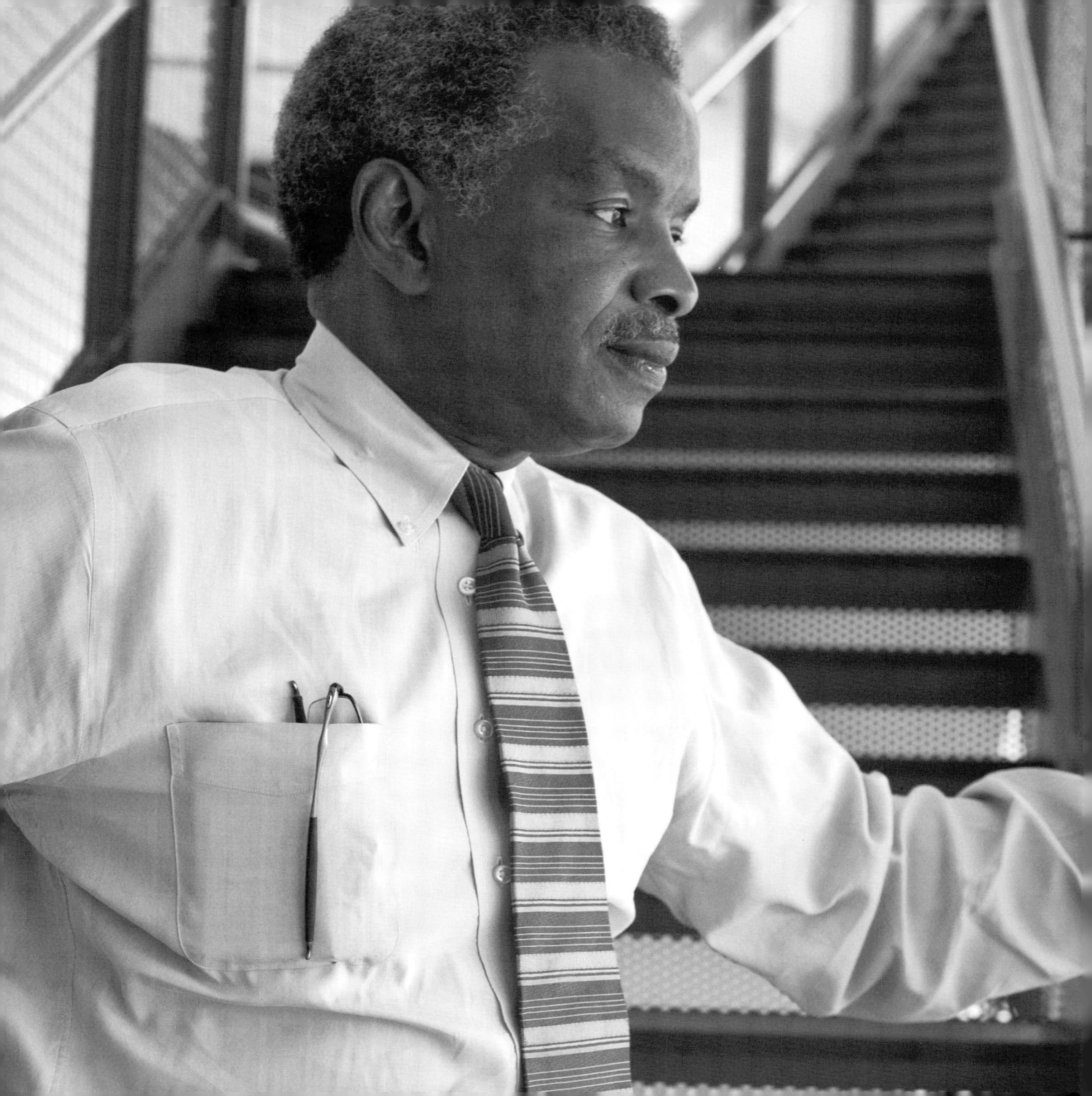

The progress of the world will call for the best that all of us have to give.

MARY MCLEOD BETHUNE
American educator and civil rights leader
(1875-1955)

Shirley Oliver Nelson | AN EXCELLENT EXAMPLE

Life in rural Alabama was far from easy for my mother's family. My grandmother suffered the loss of seven babies, before my mom became her only surviving child. Maybe it was overcoming such odds that fueled Mom's drive to fulfill her purpose and spur others to find theirs.

From the stories told, my mother was focused even as a child. Her resourcefulness and ambition paid dividends when she finally was able to leave home to attend Alabama A&M University. There, she excelled academically, pledged Delta Sigma Theta and blossomed socially—even voted Miss Alabama A&M. After graduation, she married my father and relocated to Northern Virginia, where I grew up.

Education stood chiefly important to my mom. "Only excellence is good enough" was her beloved motto. A fierce advocate of service and high achievement, she pushed not only me to strive for excellence but also my friends and nearly everyone who crossed her path. I was about twelve when her commitment to young people inspired the creation of the Chantilly Pyramid Minority Student Achievement Committee (CPMSAC). She founded CPMSAC to provide mentoring and tutoring support to students in order to close the achievement gap. Twenty-six years later, her nonprofit sustains its mission through various programs, including award ceremonies, honor-roll recognition and an MLK Jr. program. The number of program participants has mushroomed from twenty-five kids to more than three thousand a year.

My mother's sudden death five years ago shook my family and our community. How she lived, however, has had the greater impact. She was utterly dedicated to her philanthropic causes and was willing to work relentlessly to make good things happen for others. She modeled a purposeful life and guided me to define my own. Today, my friends and I are constantly reminded how not a month would go by without Mom asking: *What are you doing to serve?*

MEKA S. SALES

Connection: *Daughter* ◆ Channel: *Founder, Be A Blessing, Inc.* ◆ Cause: *Mentorship of young adults*

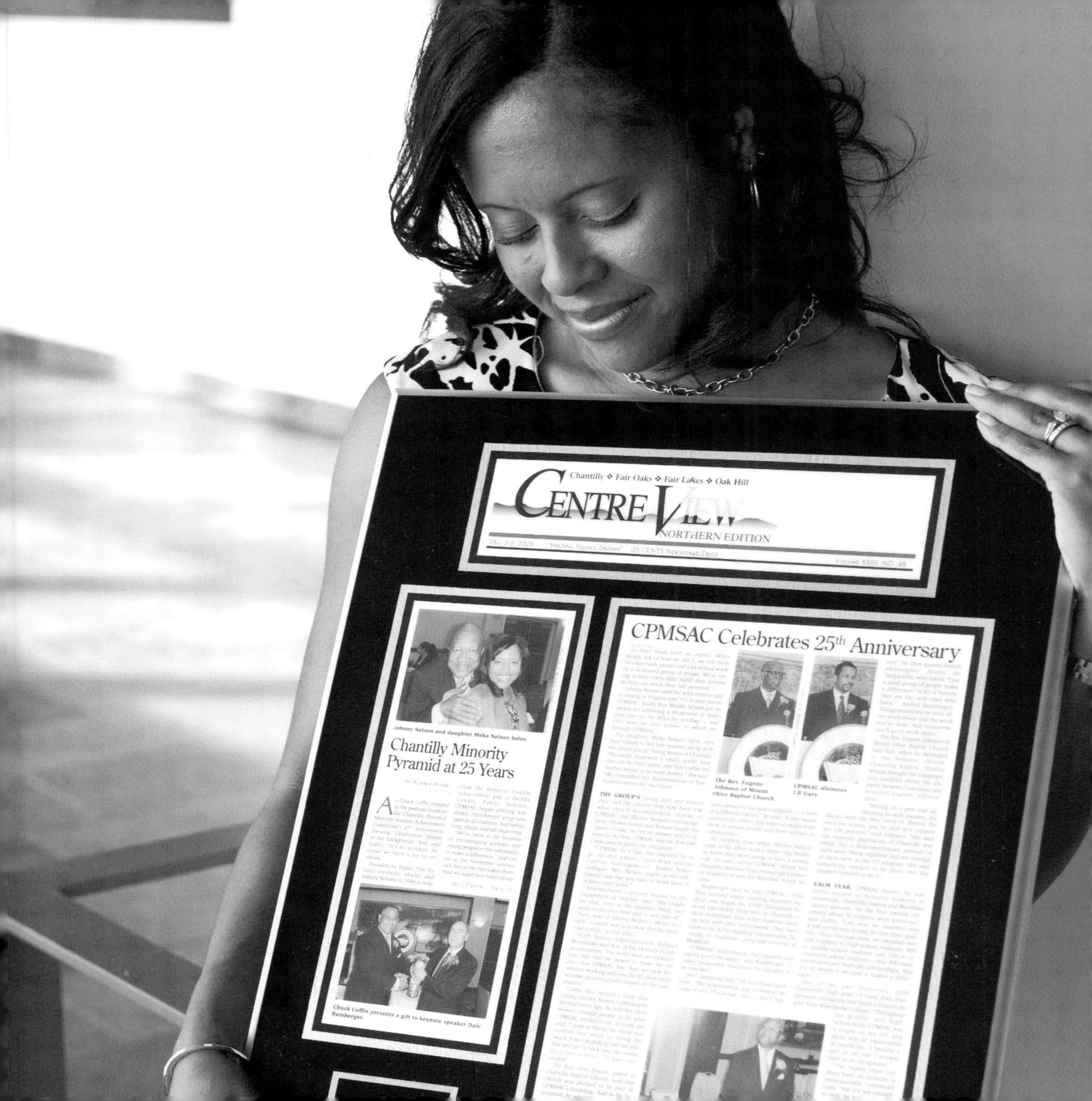

Chantilly ❖ Fair Oaks ❖ Fair Lakes ❖ Oak Hill
CENTRE VIEW
NORTHERN EDITION
CPMSAC Celebrates 25th Anniversary
Johnny Nelson and daughter Meka Nelson Sales.
Chantilly Minority Pyramid at 25 Years
The Rev. Eugene Johnson of Mount Olive Baptist Church.
CPMSAC alumnus J.P. Gary.
Chuck Coffin presents a gift to keynote speaker Dale Rumberger.

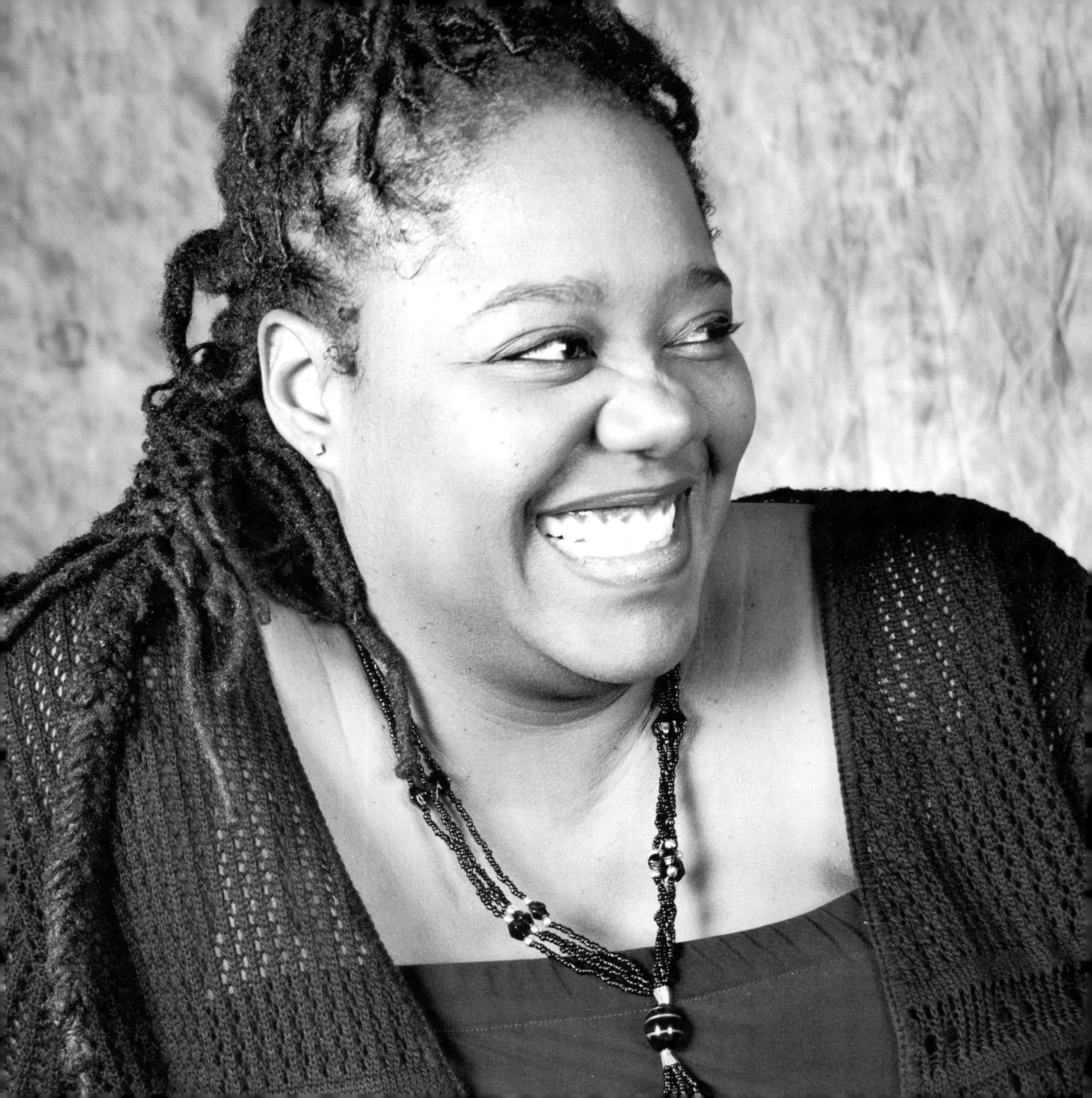

Kindness in word creates confidence.
Kindness in thinking creates profoundness.
Kindness in giving creates love.

LAO TZU
Chinese philosopher and founder of Taoism
(circa sixth century BC)

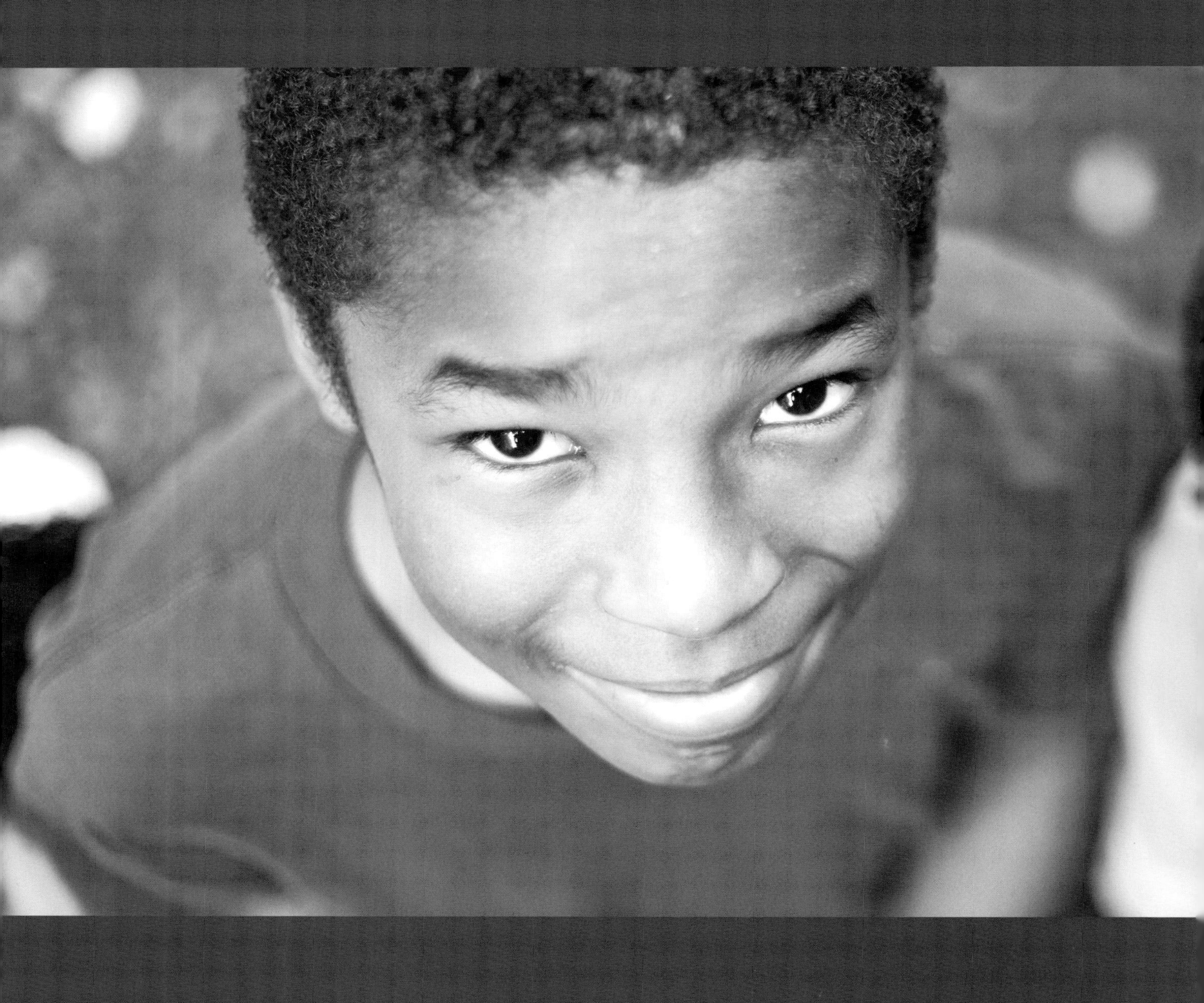

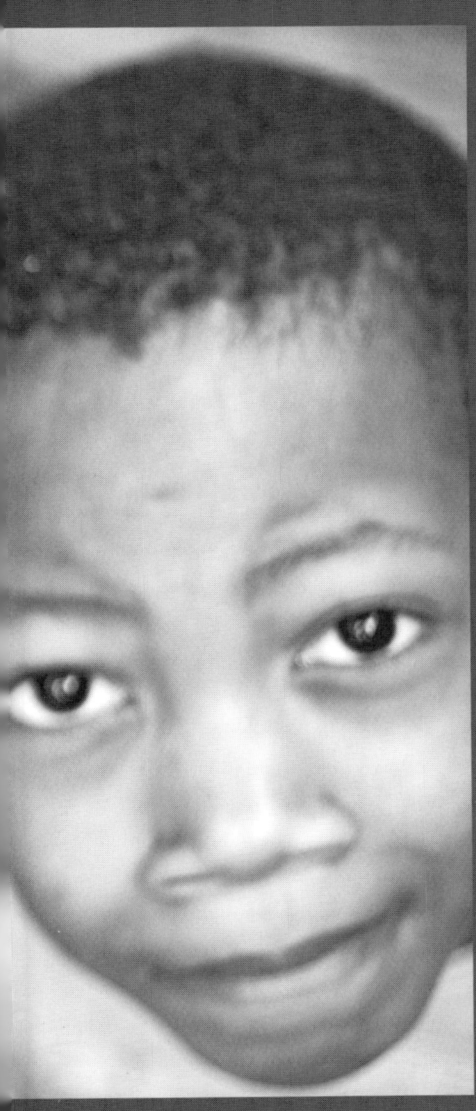

"IT TEARS ME UP to know a child is mistreated. I've been around some children who were needy. Helpless kids sometimes don't have parents or their parents are just too poor and can't do the things they should to take care of their children. That's why I'm always willing to give to any organization that helps children. If I got it, I'll do it. I feel an obligation to give regularly, just like I pay my bills every month."

James Mitchell
eighty-six-year-old retired trustee of St. Luke United Methodist Church

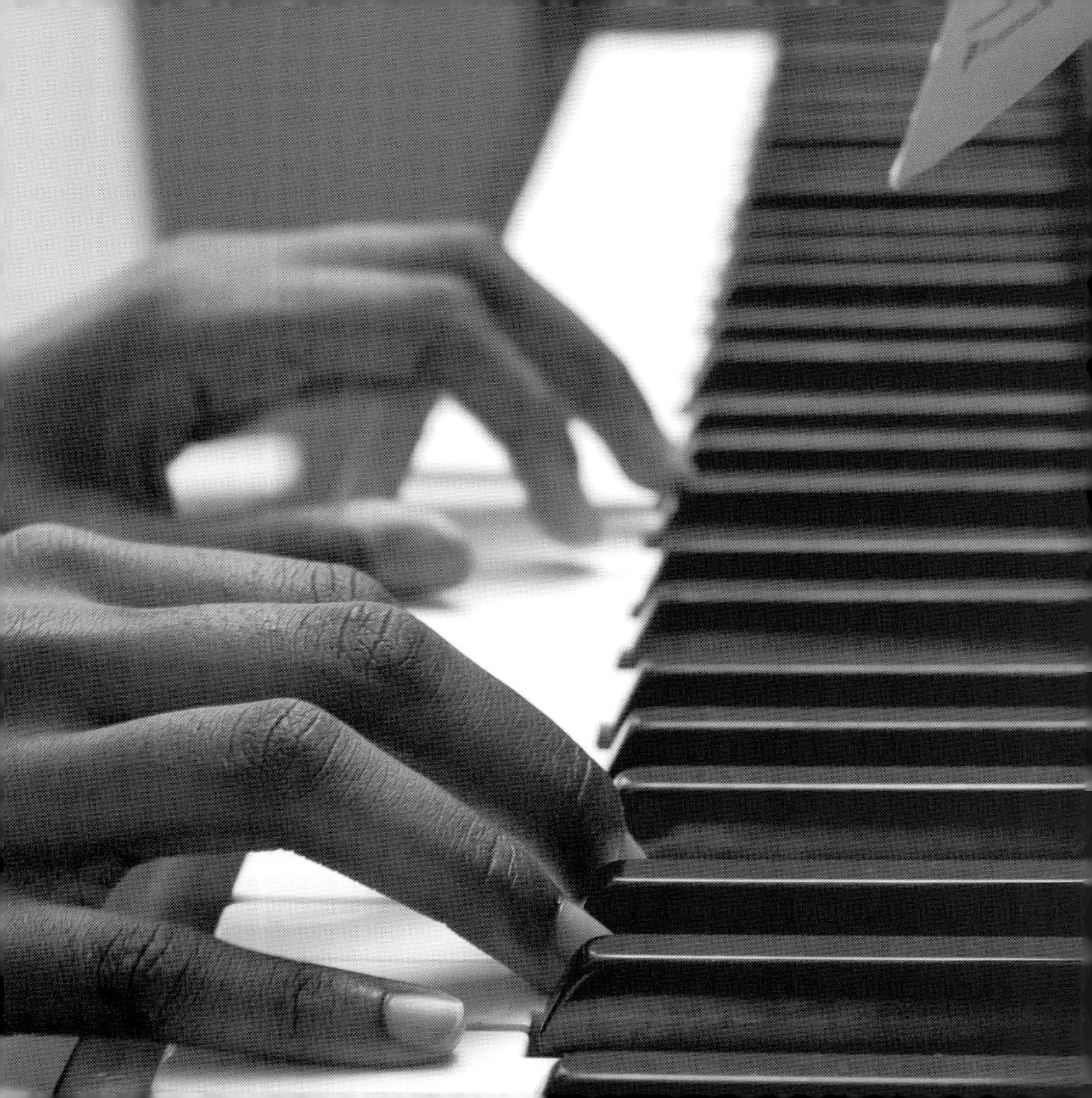

Rich relations give
Crust of bread and such
You can help yourself
But don't take too much
Mama may have, Papa may have
But God bless the child that's got his own.

BILLIE HOLIDAY & ARTHUR HERZOG JR.
American jazz musicians

From "God Bless the Child," 1939

Donna Murray Lacey | PICTURE OF HEALTH

Mostly I remember the diversity of people we would meet when I shadowed my mother at health fairs. Mom started Project HealthShare, a community health organization for people without a primary doctor or health insurance. At around ten, I began helping at weekend health screenings while she checked blood pressure and tested blood sugar levels. Volunteering those weekends, I learned that while everyone is not the same, you can find ways to interact despite the differences. I also learned to appreciate my blessings because good health and access to a doctor are not guaranteed.

I am grateful to my mother for those opportunities and lessons at such a young age. She is a hardworking woman who has been through a lot and who cares a lot. Sometimes it seems she cares more than her patients do about their own health. She constantly discourages bad habits and urges healthy eating and living. Operating a nonprofit free clinic is a testament to my mother's commitment to caring for people. She gives the love of a parent to every patient.

Now that finishing high school is a priority, I haven't been involved in health fairs lately, but I see giving back in my future. Attending Berklee College of Music is my next goal, and one day I'd like to start a program that provides music lessons for underprivileged children. Music will be my way of contributing to the health of the community.

RAHSAAN LACEY

Connection: *Teenage son* ◆ Channel: *Assistant camp counselor for children's museum*

Cause: *Using music to develop youth and build community*

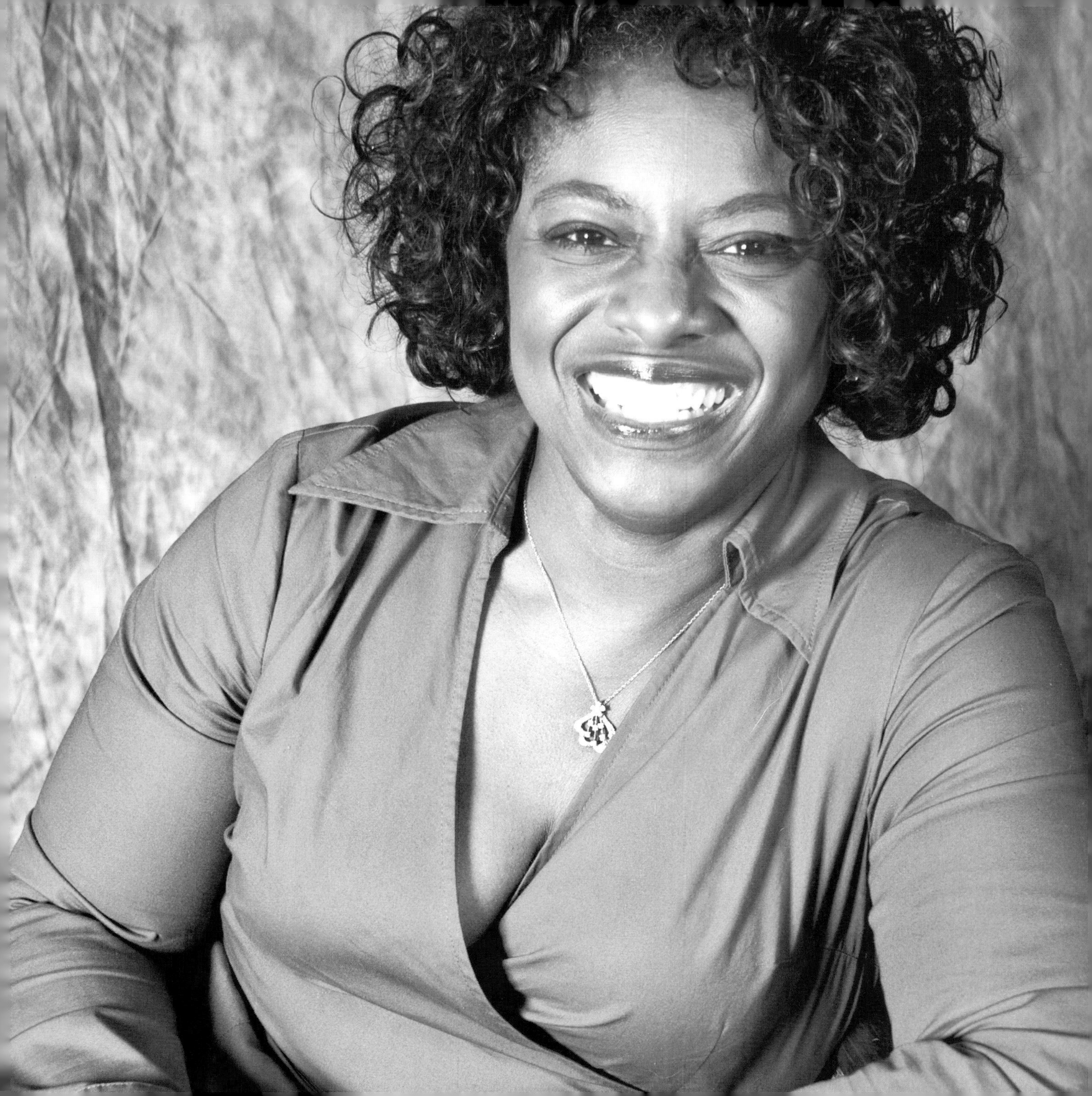

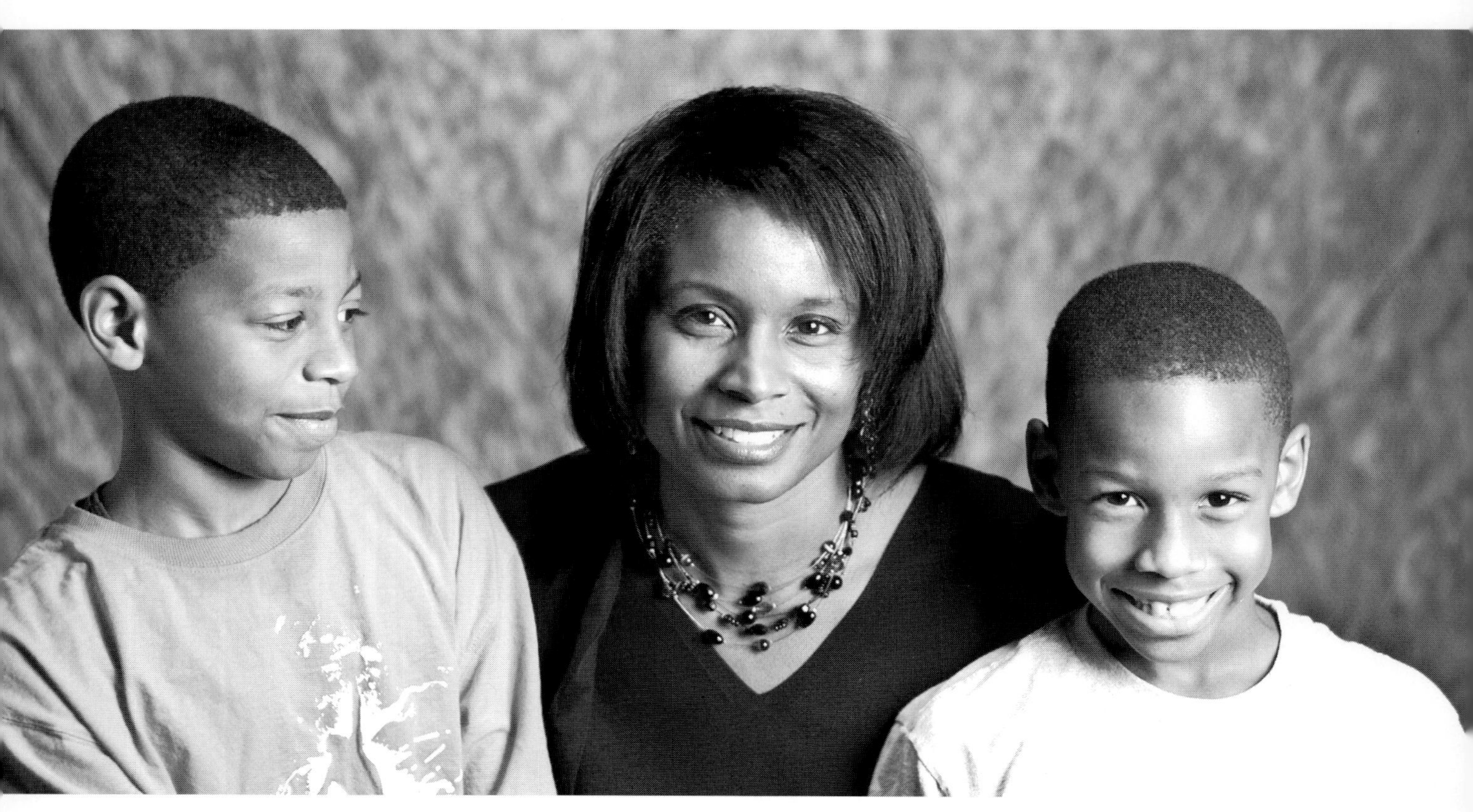

It is easier to build strong children than to repair broken men.

FREDERICK DOUGLASS
American orator, writer, statesman and social reformer
(1818-95)

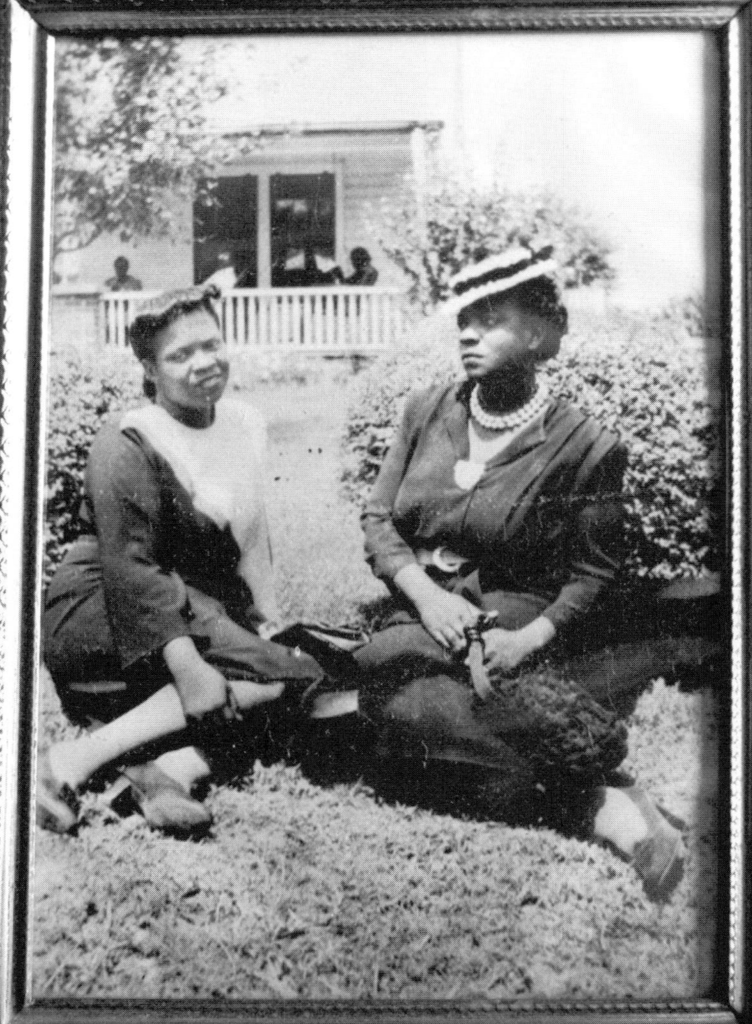

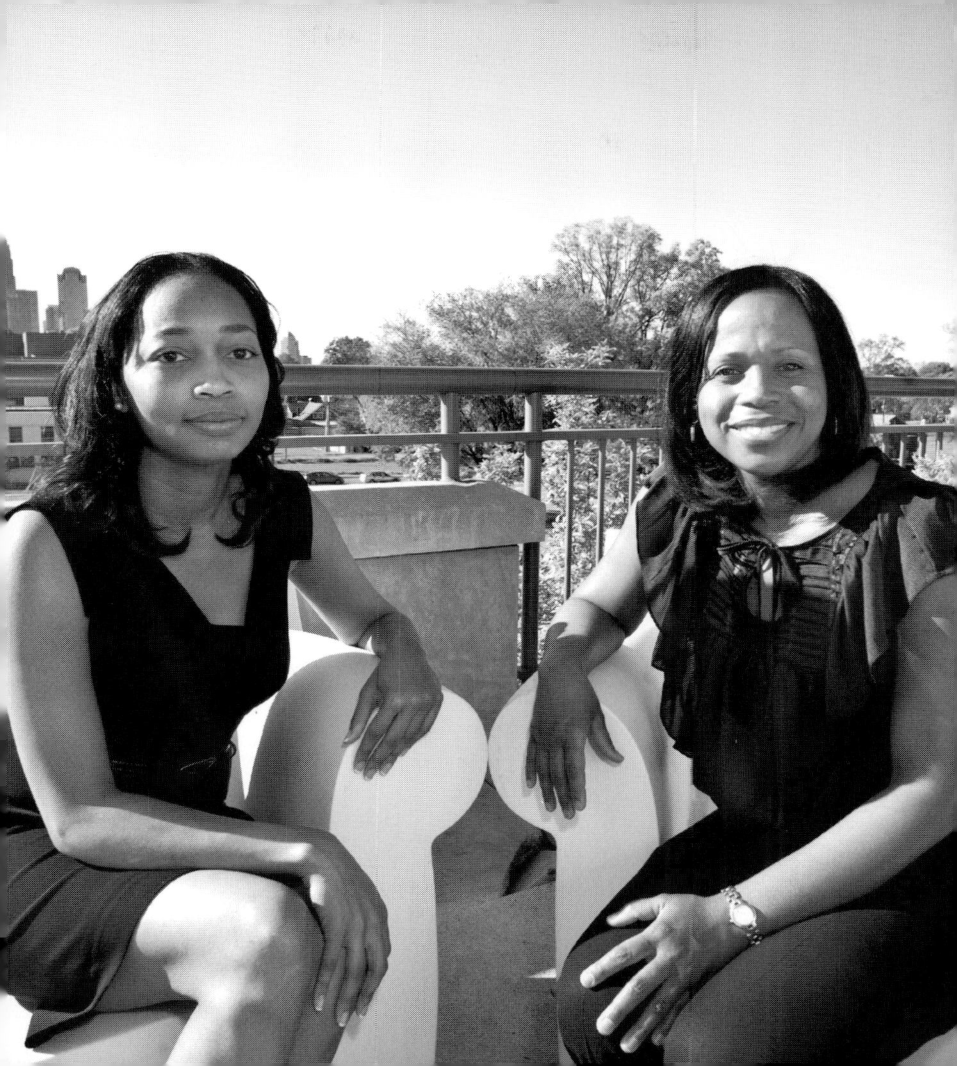

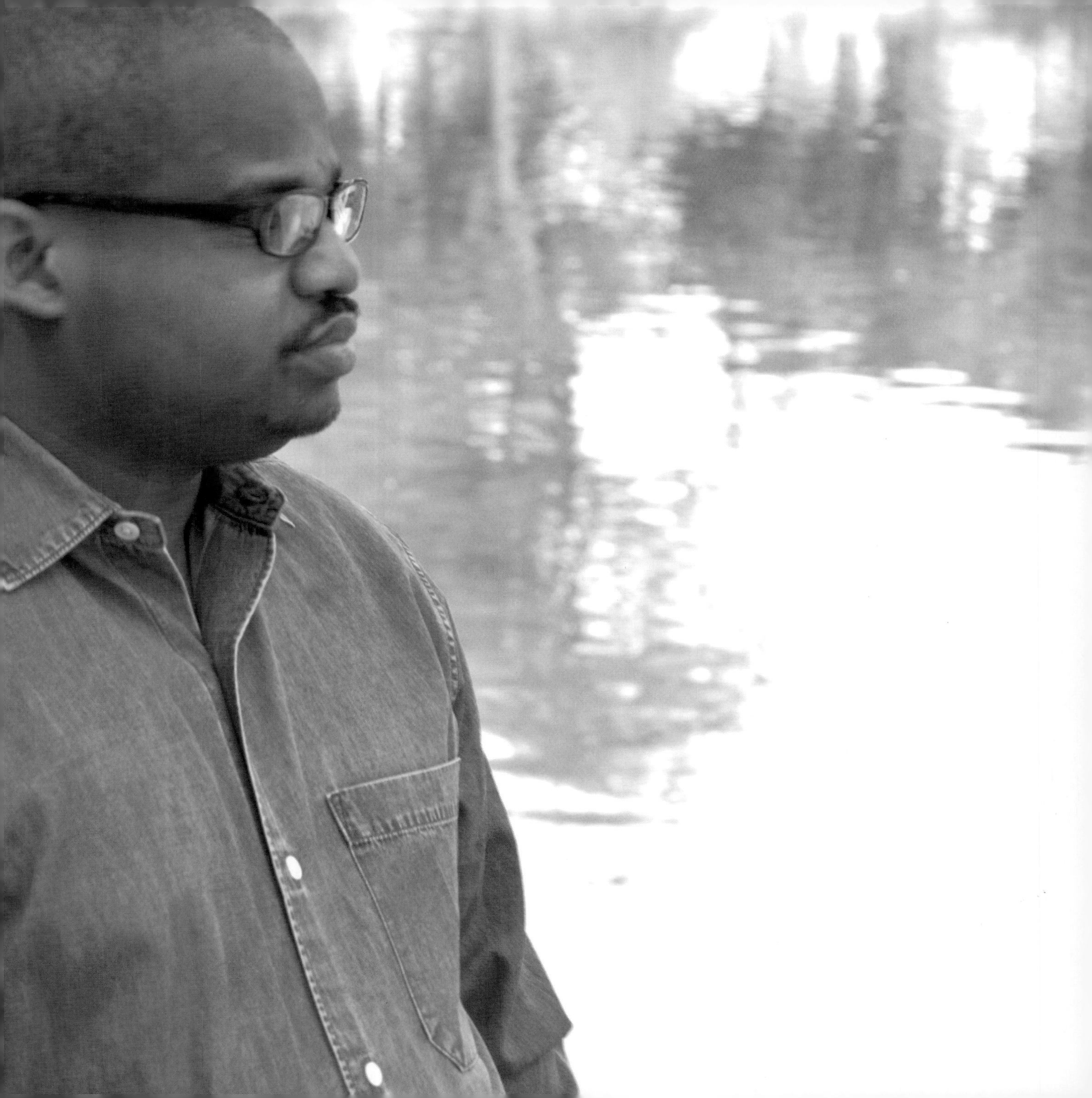

Help thy brother's boat across and lo! thine own has reached the shore.

HINDU PROVERB

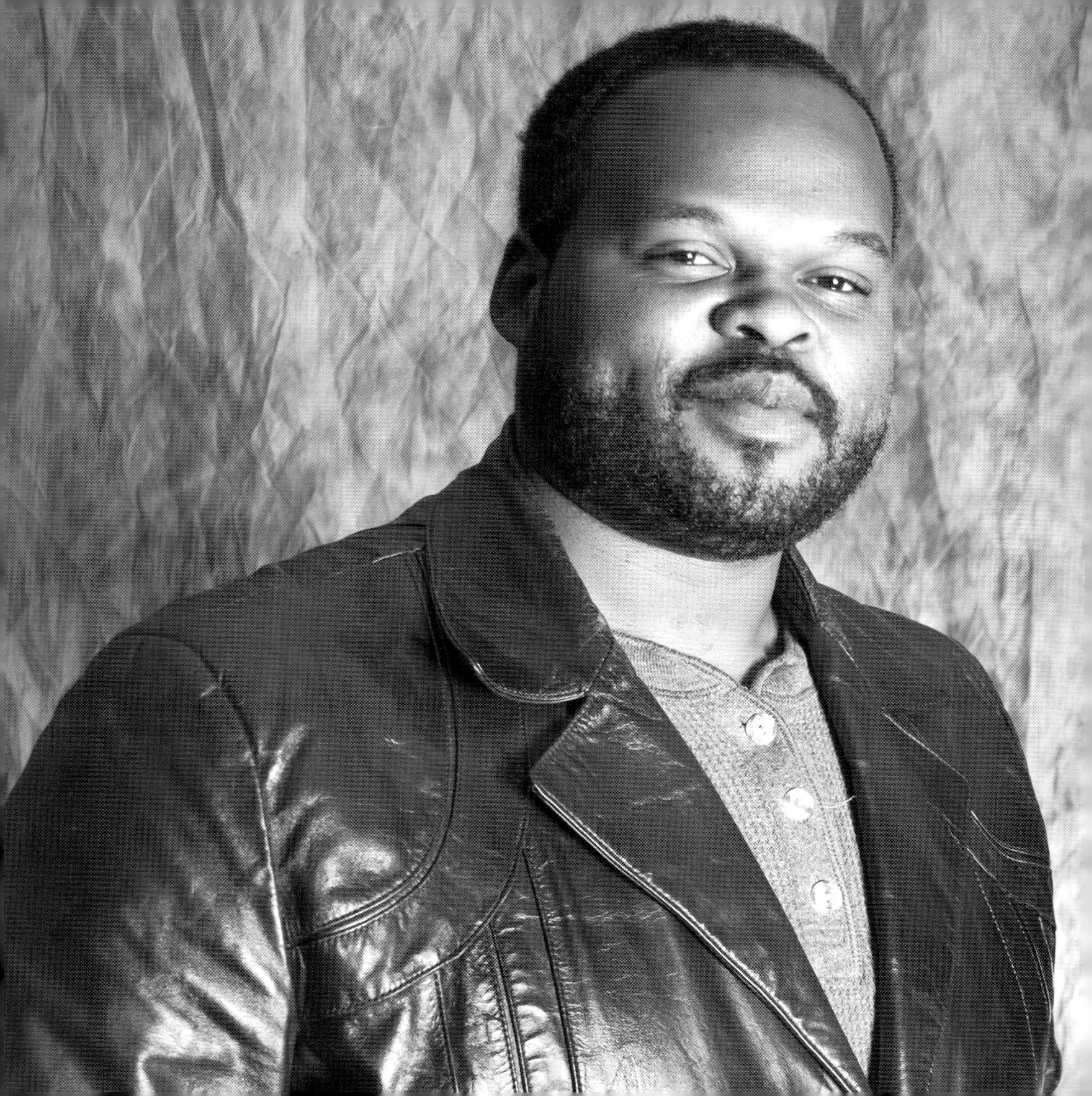

Lessons

What lesson about giving back do you wish you'd learned earlier?

There is no magical dollar value to give. It is important to give whatever you can. — *Jennifer Miles*

I wanted to be a voice for the voiceless, later I learned every one of us has a voice, we may just need help finding it. — *Endia Brabham*

How to be strategic in giving — *Ihsan Abdin*

I wish that I had learned that 'philanthropy' was not a big word for only Oprah Winfrey, Bill Gates and the financially wealthy of our world. Philanthropy, as love for humankind, lives inside each of us. It's expressed in our everyday uplifting and elevation of the individuals and the communities we love. — *Renee L. Bradford*

That you can be very targeted in your giving — *Christian Friend*

That in order to be a blessing to others, I needed to be a good steward of what I had been entrusted, whether that's financially, time-wise or other resources. — *Sherry Waters*

Make sure to do thorough research regarding the organizations you donate to — *Jeanene Thompson*

Giving back is a form of investing in the present and the future. Giving back is a bold statement of belief in the betterment of the current situation. Giving back acknowledges our deep connections with each other. — *Jennifer Henderson*

That a little is a starting point. It doesn't always have to be money; your time is very valuable! — *Belinda E. Alston*

I received a good foundation about giving back. More information about how one moves from relief giving to strategic and social-change giving would have been good. — *Darryl K. Lester*

Giving collectively has a greater impact not only on those in receipt of what was given, but also on those who gave, because of the bond that forms. — *Ohmar Land*

One of the lessons I wish I could have learned earlier is how personally rewarding it is to be able to help others in need. Giving back should be done with sincerity—not expecting anything back in return. — *Kimberly Parham*

Connecting with like-minded folks to leverage our giving can have a deeper impact on the recipients and the givers than doing it alone. — *LaDawn Sullivan*

That small gestures can make a big difference in the lives of others — *Britt Brewer Loudd*

To give through a social justice lens — *Edgar Villanueva*

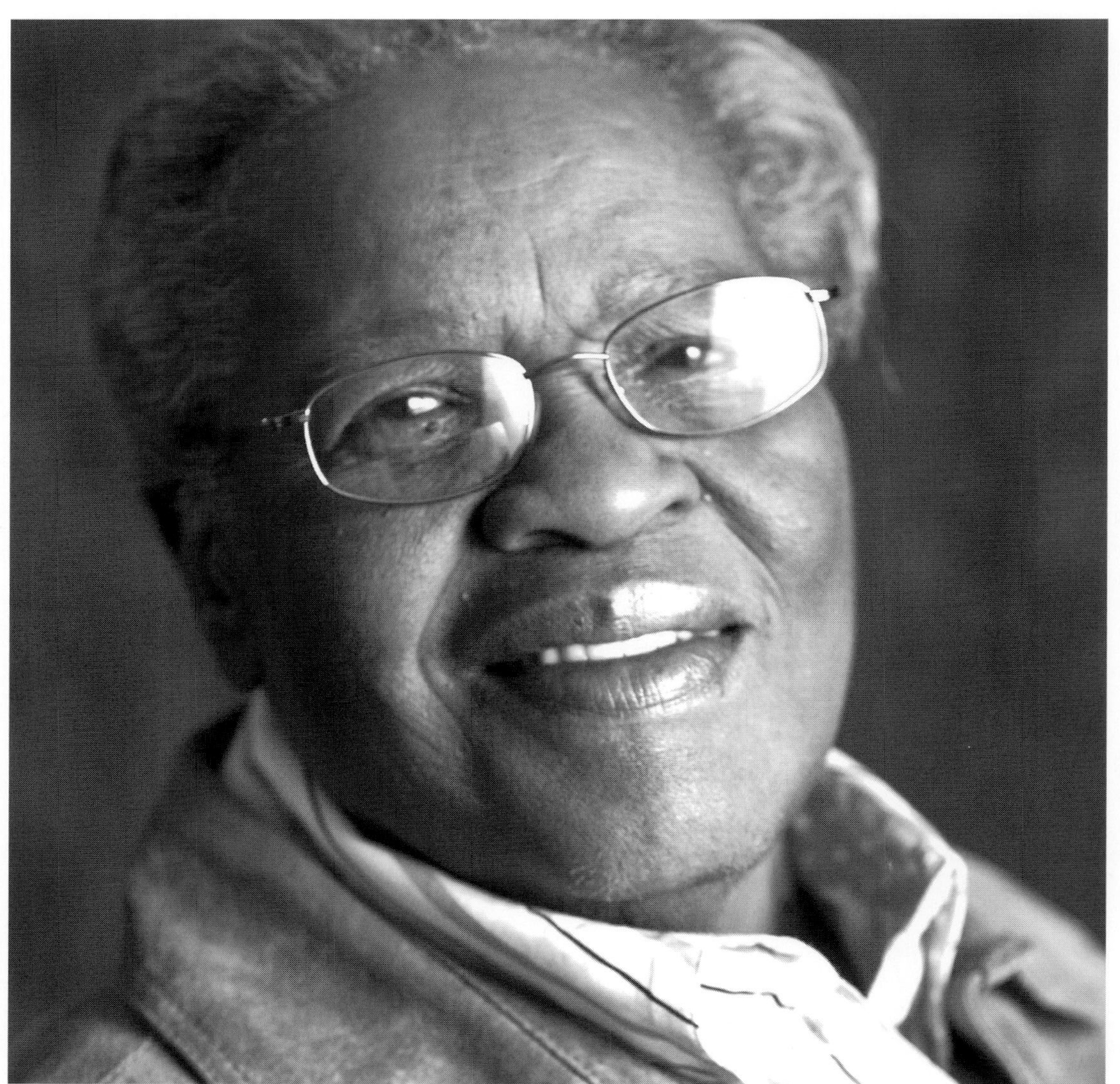

No one has ever become poor by giving.

ANNE FRANK
Jewish diarist and Holocaust victim
(1929 - 45)

Renee L. Bradford | PURSUER OF PURPOSE

If I had known then, what I know now. That thought seeded First Purse, the nonprofit program I created to teach girls about financial literacy and philanthropic giving. First Purse has a redeeming value to me. As a child, no one was talking about how to save, invest or give back. I was fully aware of what it was like to "get" but giving was something I had to learn as an adult.

My early experiences keep me sensitive to people who find themselves on the receiving side of philanthropy. I know that many have a desire to be givers too but struggle with how. To be taught how to give is a privilege. There was a time when I was captive to the belief that I could give only when my situation improved or my income reached a certain status. But once I learned to become a giver through the examples of everyday people, I discovered amazing freedom in the service of others.

When my daughter was around seven, I sensed an opportunity. She started asking questions about her money: *What should I do? Buy bubble gum? Save? Give to the church?* Looking back, I wished that at her age somebody had helped me find answers. It was then I began developing First Purse, as a means to provide her with something I never had.

Today, the program includes lots of daughters and mothers, and our connections are both local and global. First Purse brings full circle my lessons about philanthropy. I hope one day to see the girls as women teaching their young daughters about being a giver.

RENEE L. BRADFORD
Channel: *Founder, First Purse* • Cause: *Inclusive philanthropy*

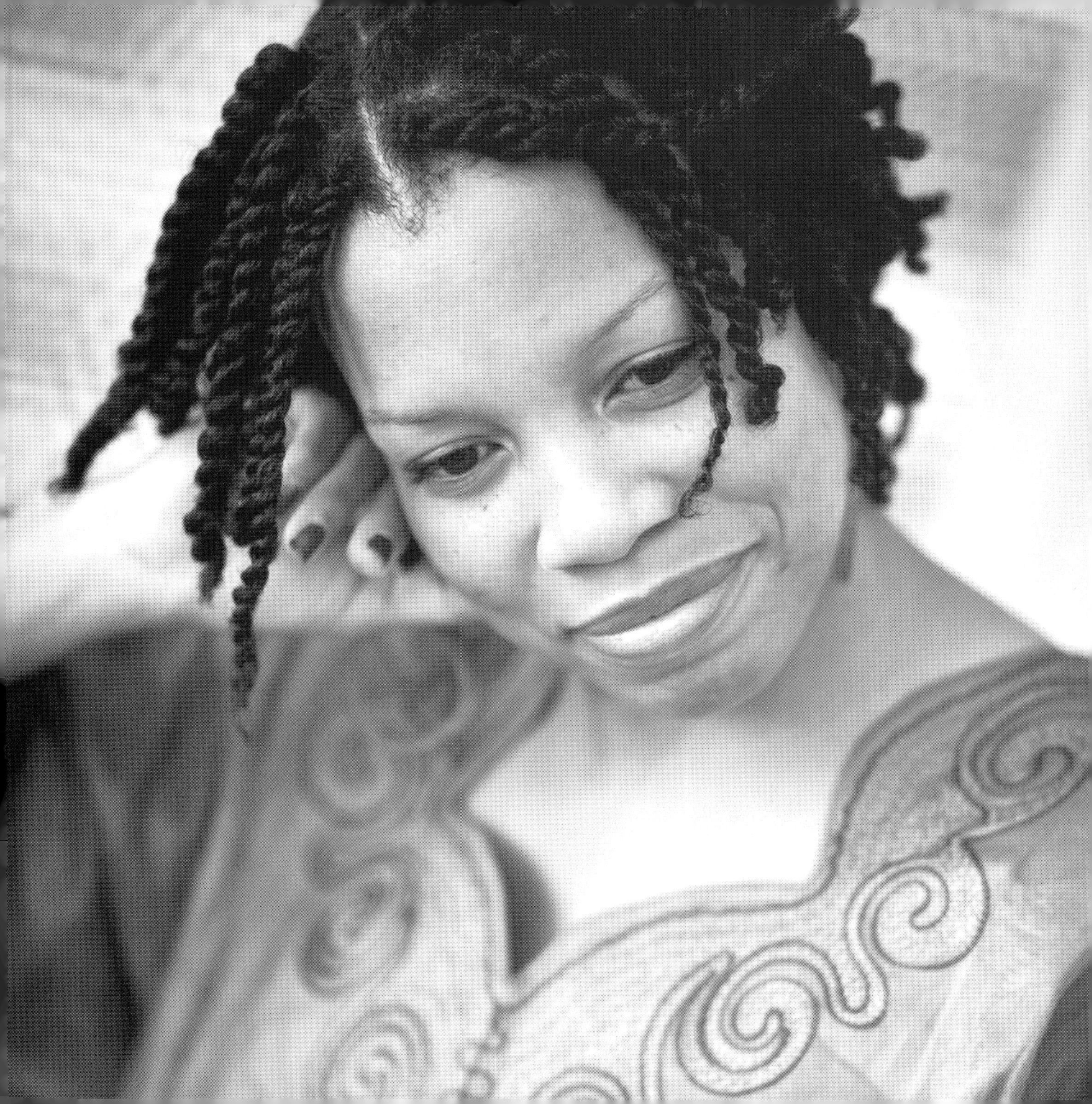

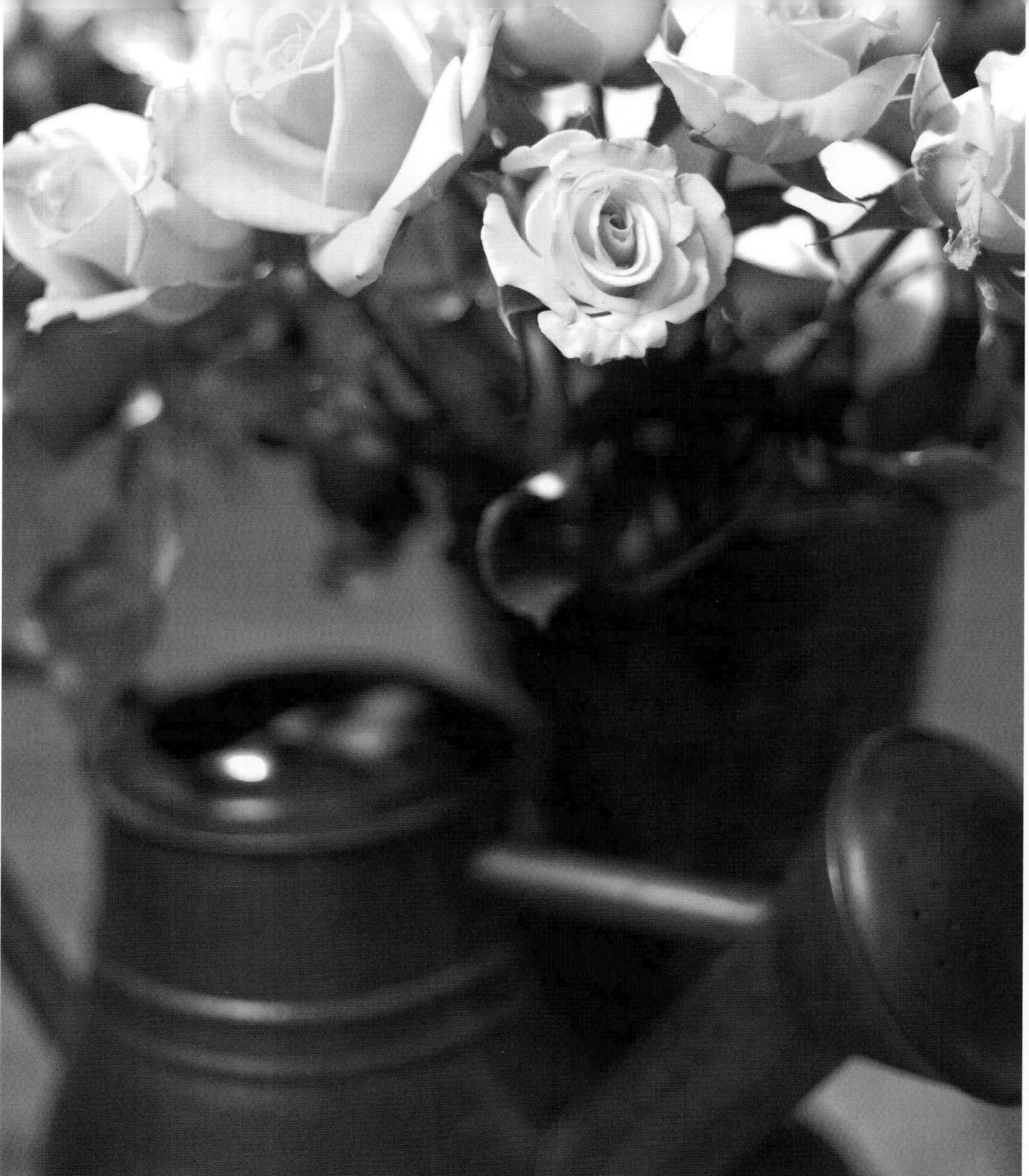

He who waters will himself be watered.

PROVERBS 11:25

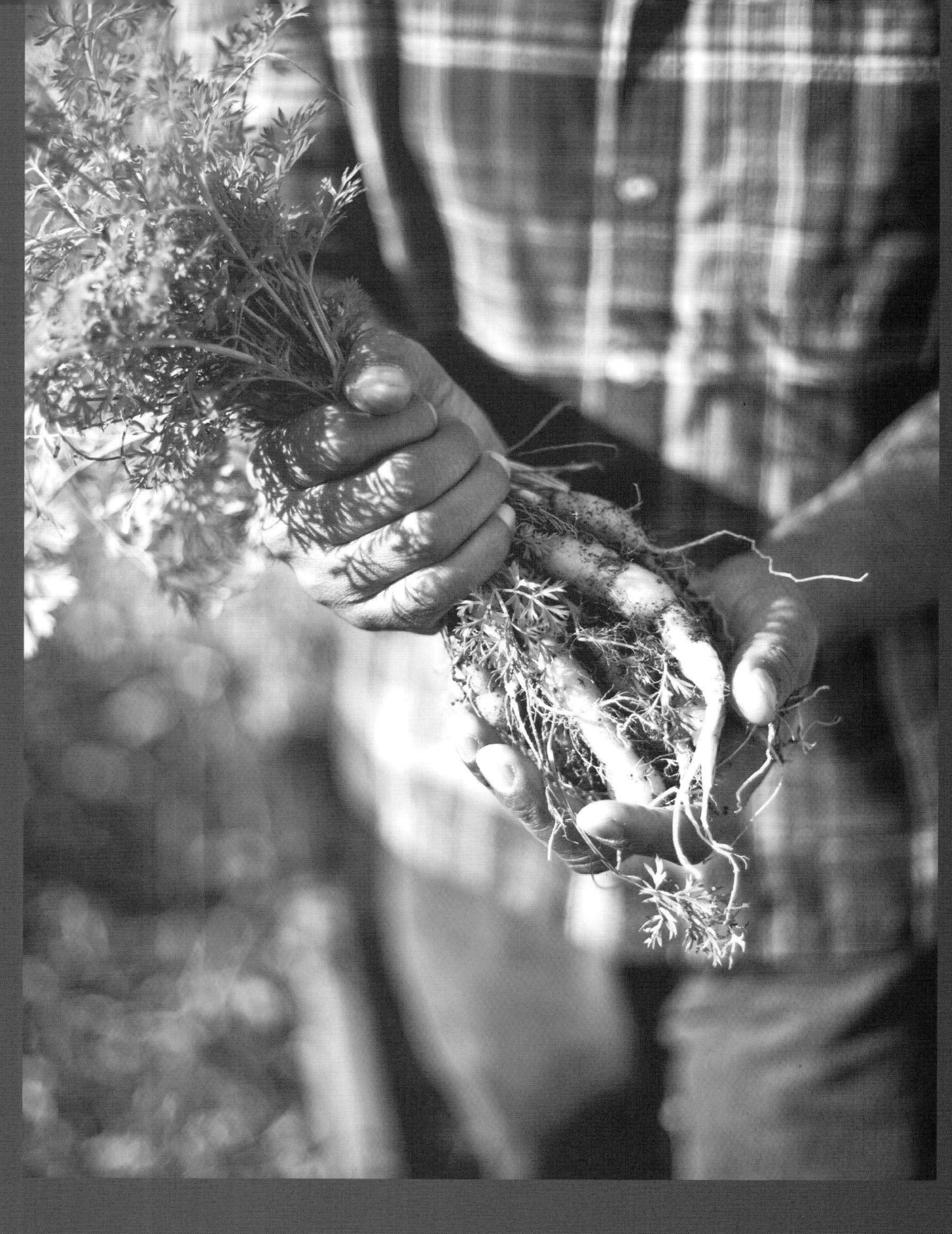

"DESPITE COMMON PERCEPTIONS, Black men have long been industrious. And evidently my grandfather Riley was as hardworking as men of any race come. I call him a Black entrepreneur, but back then *industrious* is the word people used.

"I archive and keep our family's history. I have scoured over family artifacts and census data. Some time in the mid-1800s on the McGimpsey farm in Burke County, North Carolina, a slave named Clarissa gave birth to a son she named Riley. While born into slavery, Riley eventually became a sharecropper who sold his part of the produce—corn, wheat, molasses and such. Documents I have come across show his products sold as far away as Mullins, South Carolina, which was hundreds of miles from the farmland of Fonta Flora. He even owned one of the county's few reaper-binders and loaned it out to others.

"Fondly remembered and respected by people all over the county, my grandfather prospered in farming and with various small enterprises. He grew well known for giving away fresh produce and all kinds of things to community people, regardless of color. Riley was born a slave, but died an entrepreneur and philanthropist. Don't let a meager start or scant resources limit what you do in life."

Nettie McGimpsey McIntosh
founding member of Burke County Historical Society and
board member of The History Museum of Burke County

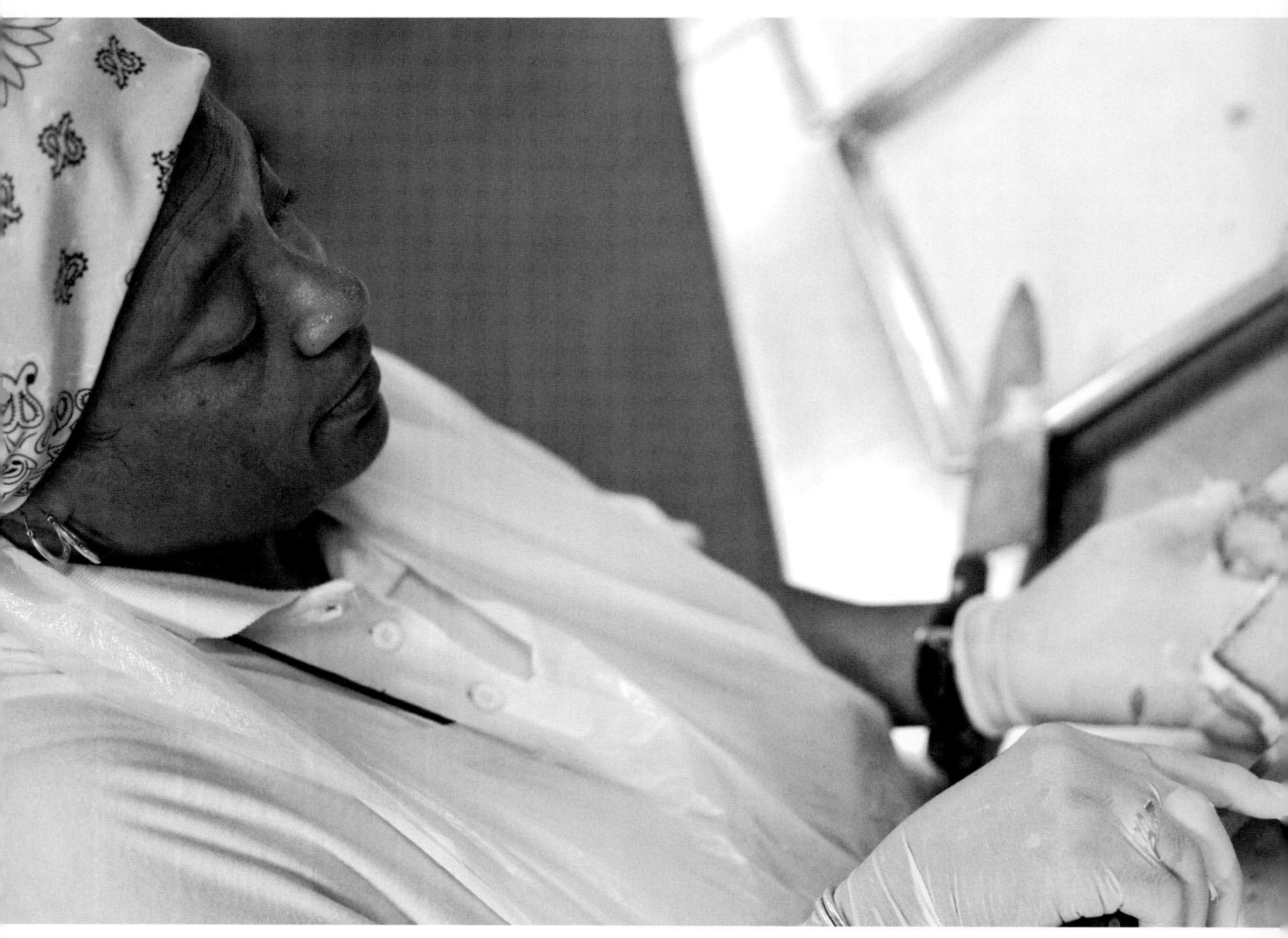

No act of kindness, however small, is ever wasted

AESOP
Fabulist of the ancient world
(circa sixth century BC)

Eric Shelton | GOOD SPORT

I never gave. Even with plenty of opportunities I passed on giving. Adults gathered for receptions, galas and suit-and-tie events in the name of charity were what I knew. Those functions seemed to be only about hobnobbing with celebrities and mingling among socialites and then writing a check. That kind of philanthropy left me unsatisfied and failed to move me to give.

One day, I helped out at a youth football camp. Most of the players were middle schoolers preparing for high school. After field scrimmage, I had an opportunity to speak to the kids, and their response surprised me. They listened and expressed excitement about a professional athlete spending time with their team. I felt good about having something to offer. Plus, their unfiltered questions were refreshing. *Did you make a million dollars? Do you drive a Lamborghini?* Kids are unpretentious and easier to have an influence on than adults.

That experience changed the game. I began seeing the benefits of giving and how it affects the lives of the recipient and the giver too. Youth development has become my primary interest and working with that team stirred a passion for mentoring young men. Teaching a kid about football and also about becoming a well-rounded and humble man is like watching a plant grow over time. This work requires putting yourself out there—your face, your time, your experiences, your knowledge and your testimony. It is way more than writing a check.

Since retiring from pro football, I have more time on my hands and give back even more. I am glad to know now that it does not matter who you are, where you came from or how you were raised, there is always time to make things right with God, yourself and your community. Back in Lexington, Kentucky, my mother raised me, yet I also benefited from positive men in my life, like my father, uncle and coaches. Now, it is my turn to encourage young men. Everything in nature is part of a cycle and giving back is one of life's circles.

ERIC SHELTON
Channel: *Volunteer & Donor, Amateur Athletic Union-AAU Team Charlotte* • Cause: *Youth*

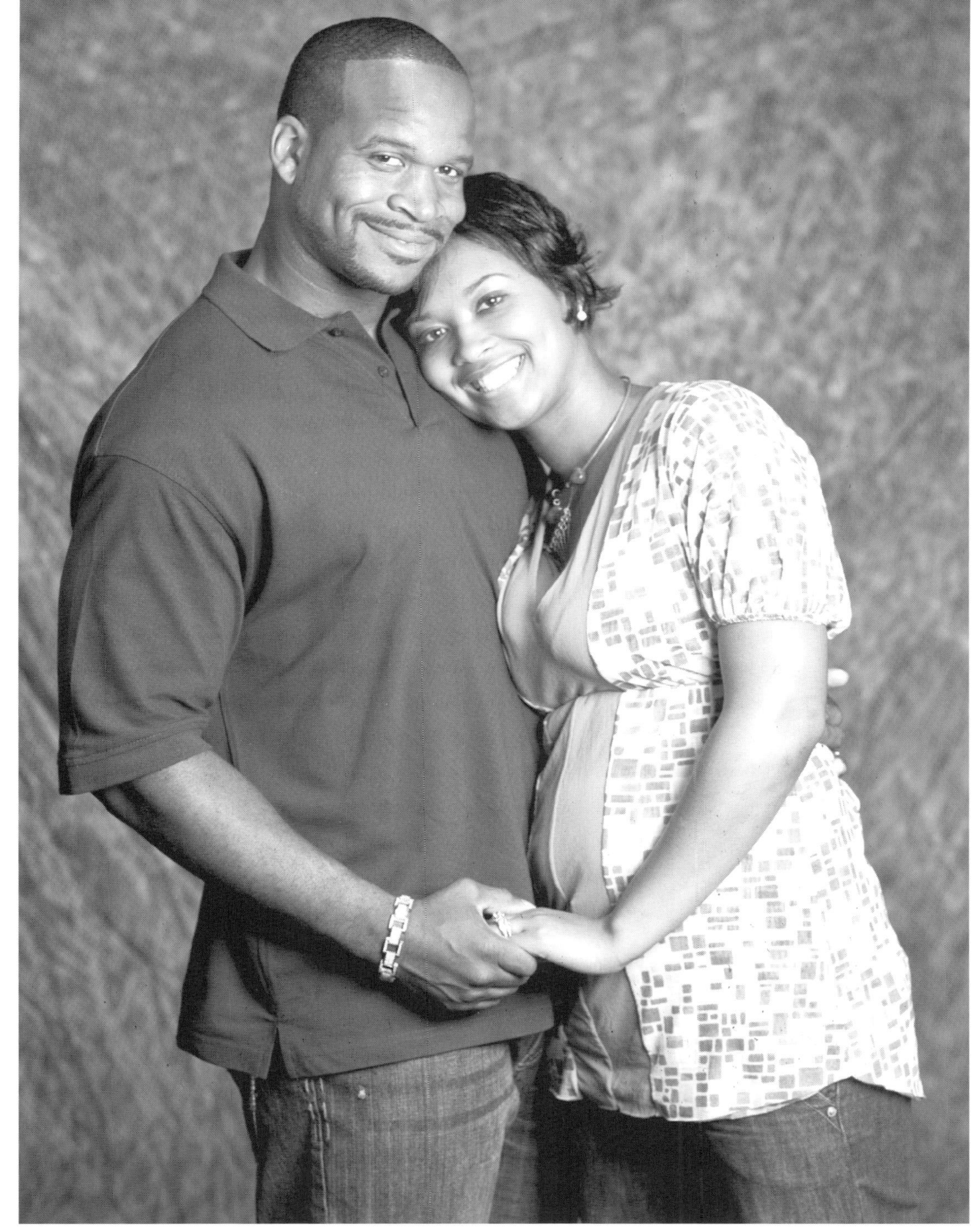

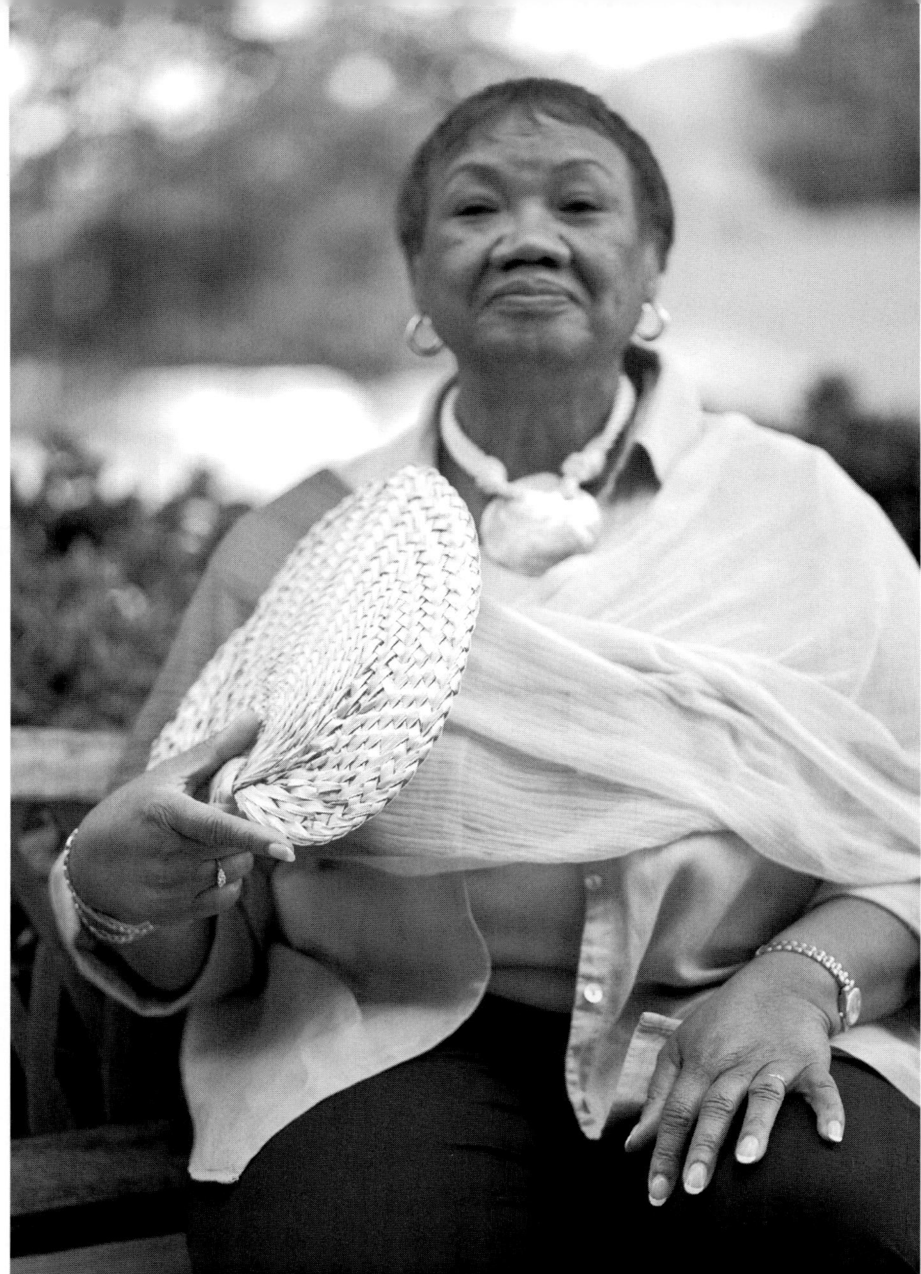

I have held many things in my hands, and I have lost them all; but whatever I have placed in God's hands, that I still possess.

MARTIN LUTHER
German priest and theologian
(1483-1546)

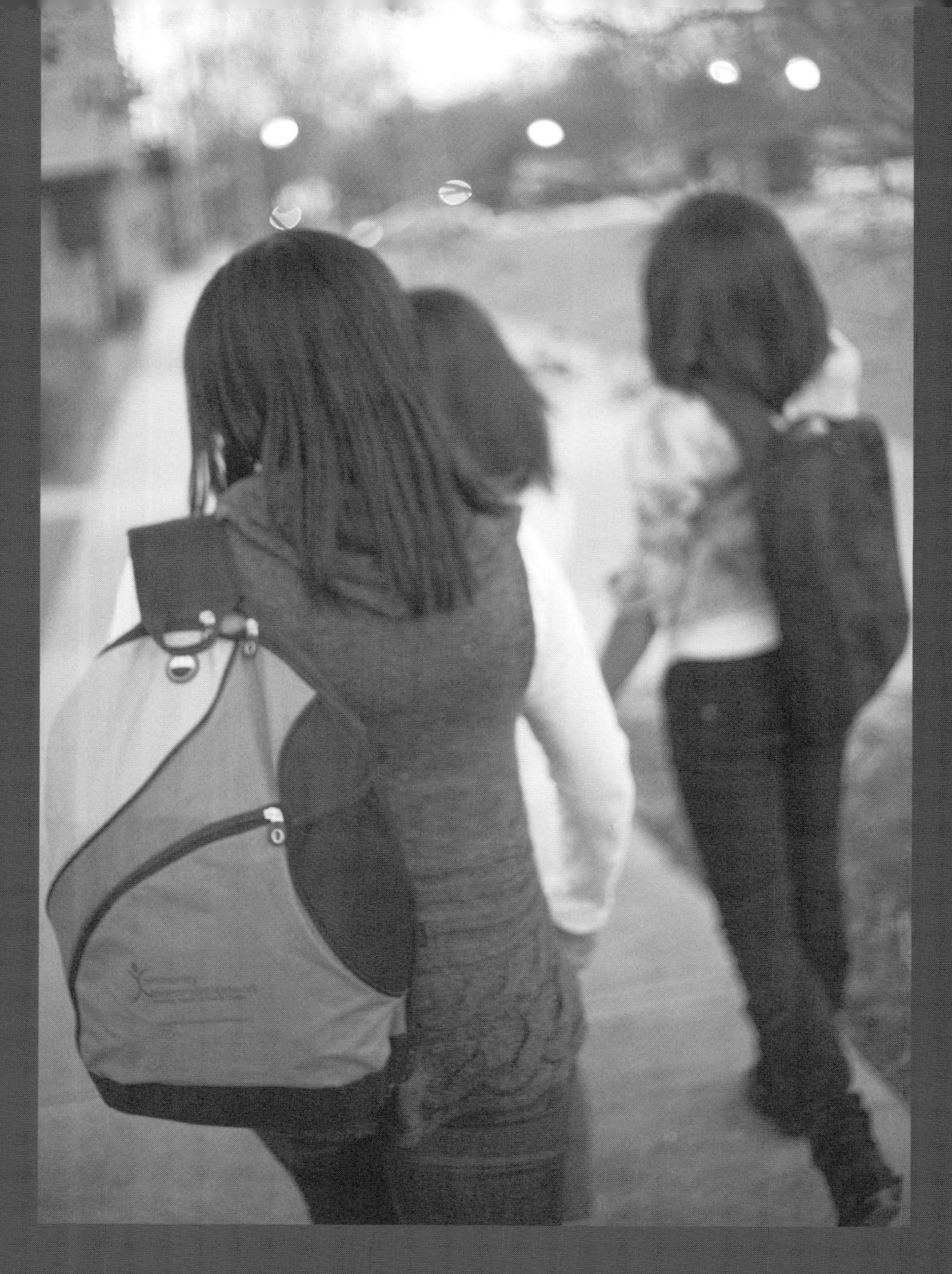

"TEN YEARS AFTER GRADUATING from Spelman College, I attended my first reunion. 'Forgo one new pair of shoes a year,' then-president Dr. Johnnetta Cole suggested to alumnae, 'and donate that one hundred dollars to Spelman.' Soon after returning home, I received a report outlining my cumulative giving; it was less than a thousand dollars.

"I was the first in my immediate family to graduate college and was only able to attend because of an academic scholarship. My opportunity had been funded by individuals who shared a philanthropic spirit. I was a well-paid professional and gave generously to family and friends, yet my sporadic gifts to my alma mater had been paltry. Humbled, I began then to support Spelman annually."

Bonita Buford
alumna of Spelman College, an HBCU founded in 1881 and board member of
The Charlotte Post Foundation, linked to a Black publication founded in 1878

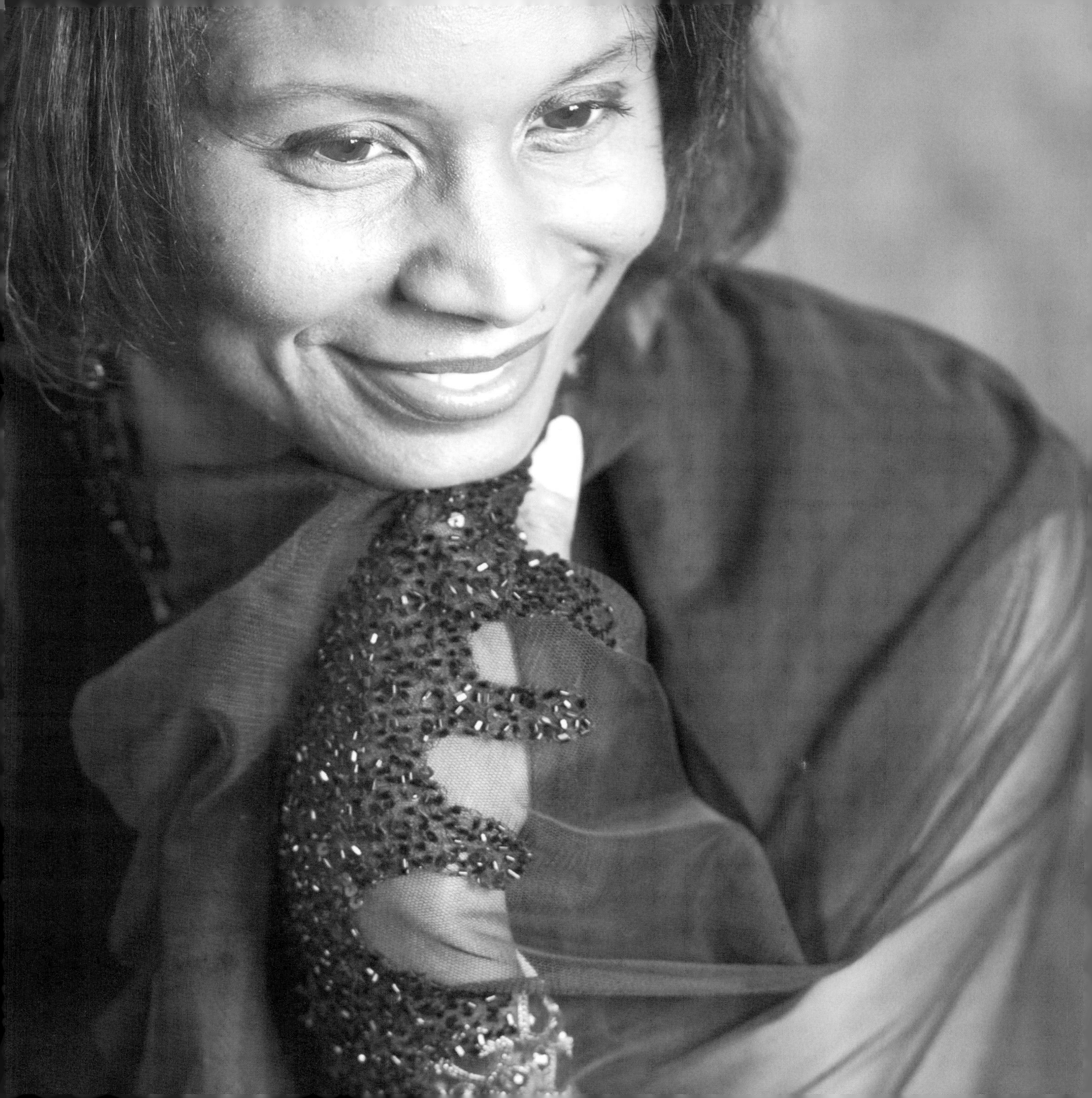

Whatever thy hand findeth to do, do it with all thy heart.

ECCLESIASTES 9:10

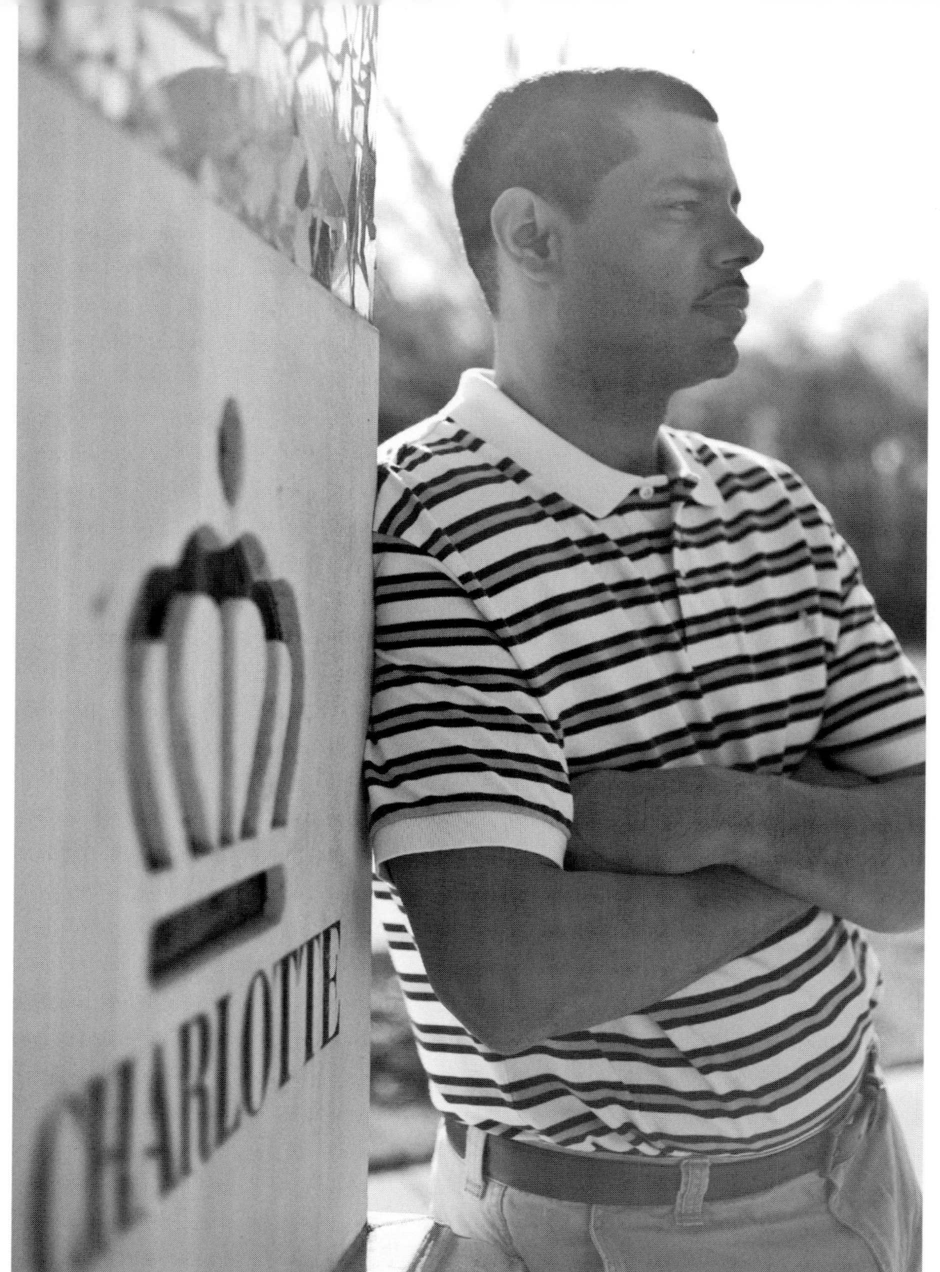
CHARLOTTE

That best portion of a good man's life; his little, nameless, unremembered acts of kindness and love.

WILLIAM WORDSWORTH
English poet
(1770-1850)

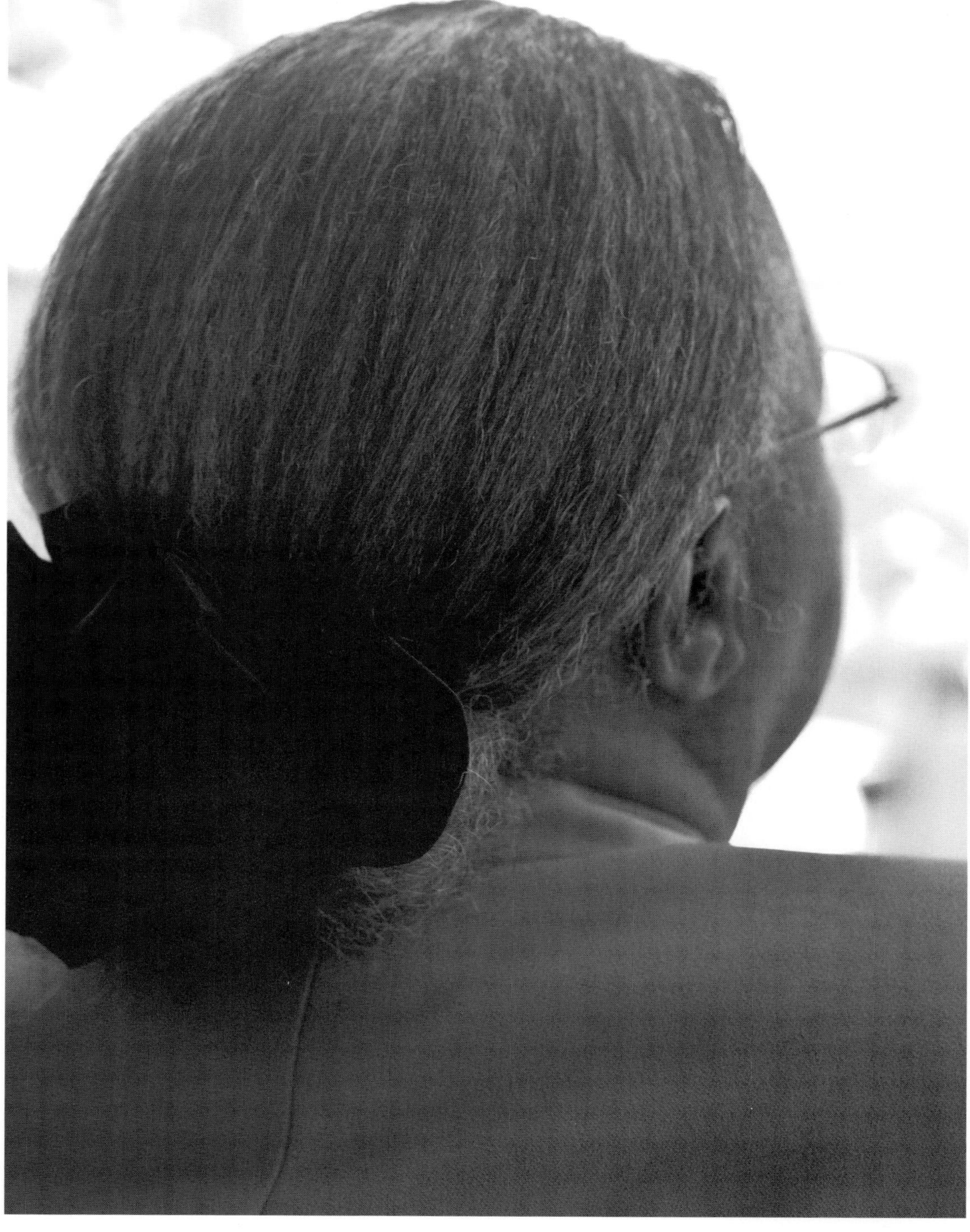

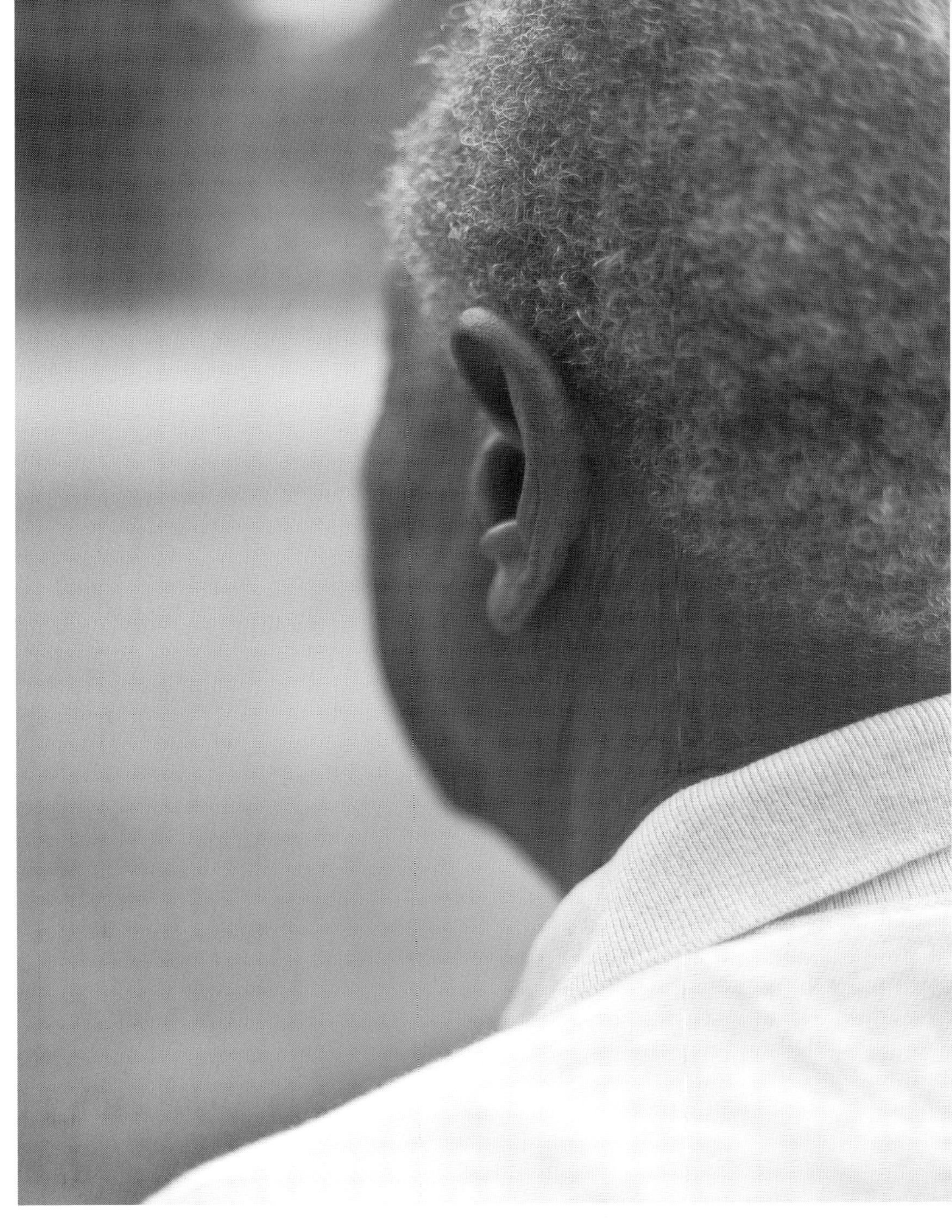

Never look down on anybody unless you're helping them up.

REV. JESSE JACKSON
American civil rights activist and minister
(b. 1941)

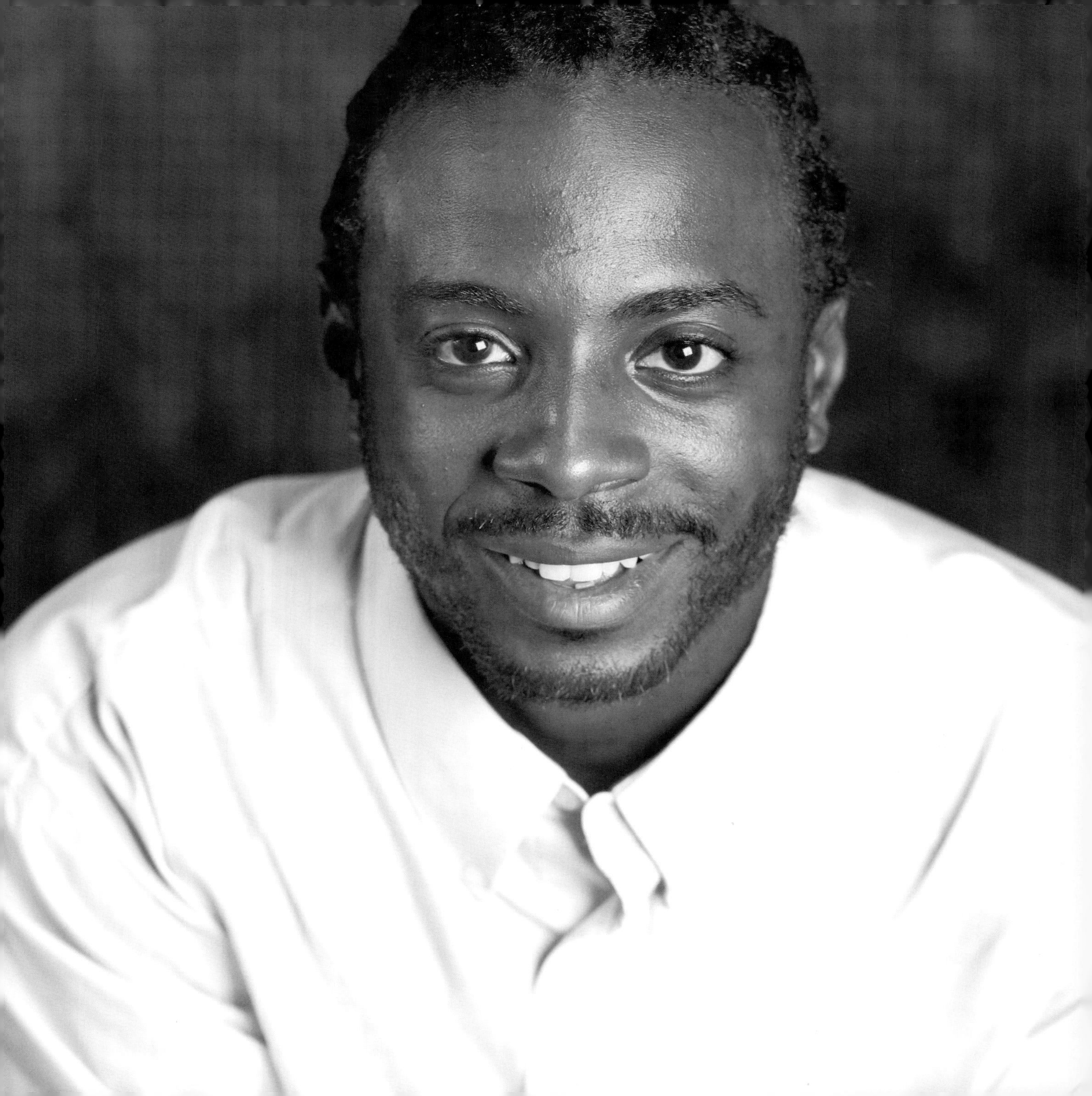

HOPES

What's one thing you hope to see more African American philanthropists do?

Continue to stress the concept of self-reliance and 'paying for your own freedom.' — *Reggie Singleton*

Be more supportive of arts organizations, beyond buying tickets. — *John Moore*

Make donations outside of the church. — *Jeanene Thompson*

Share their experiences with folks who do not necessarily hear the message. We tend to talk to those at church, in our community groups, within our own circles. We need to do a better job of getting the message out in non-traditional places and circles. — *Britt Brewer Loudd*

Contribute to smaller grassroots organizations in our community and nationwide. — *Donna Murray Lacey*

First, stop attributing philanthropy to White folks and then be more strategic in the giving that they are engaged in. — *Darryl K. Lester*

Come together and collectively leverage charitable resources to impact issues facing our community. — *LaDawn Sullivan*

To simply give more, give often, give together but continue to give. — *Ohmar Land*

Share the 'good news' of giving—not by bragging but by describing the incredible impact of every philanthropic act of kindness. Philanthropists should feel compelled to recruit others to this opportunity to serve. — *Jennifer Henderson*

Partner with other agencies to address specific needs. — *Christian Friend*

Understand the institutional side of philanthropy. — *Linsey Mills*

Share with others and especially young people on how to give. — *Belinda E. Alston*

Get others on board. — *Edgar Villanueva*

Follow through. — *Joy Webb*

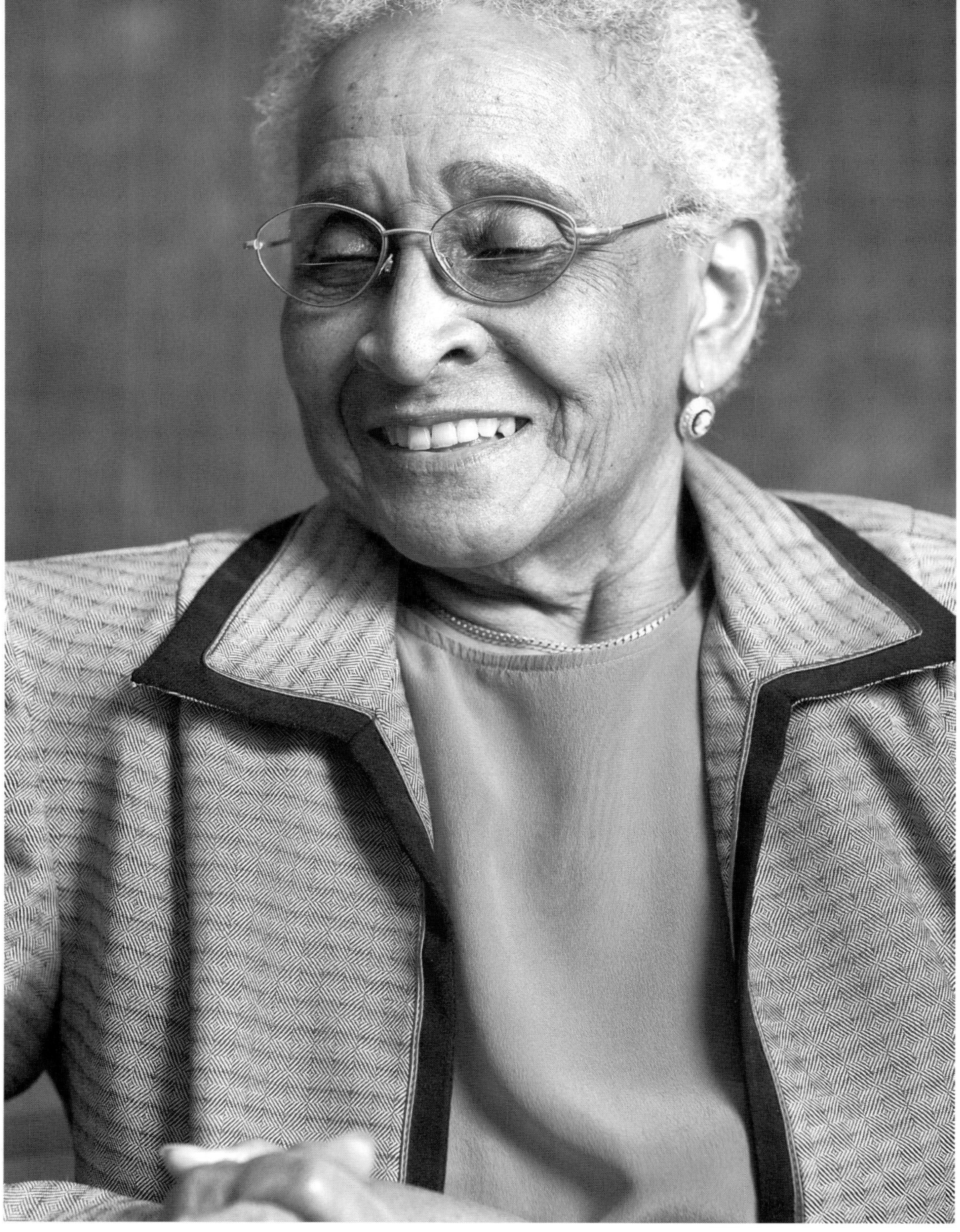

We must use time wisely and forever realize that the time is always ripe to do right.

NELSON MANDELA
Former President of South Africa
(b. 1918)

Mary Harper, Ph.D. | CULTURAL CATALYST

Archbishop Desmond Tutu once called it a "jewel" in the Queen City's crown. Now known as the Harvey B. Gantt Center for African-American Arts + Culture, Charlotte's treasured community gem is a product of the dynamism of Dr. Mary Harper and co-founder Dr. Bertha Maxwell Roddey over thirty-five years ago.

The Black Power movement, war protests and student demonstrations marked the early Seventies when Mary Harper, an assistant professor of English at the University of North Carolina at Charlotte, was pursuing her doctorate. Mary's doctoral research had illuminated the absence of organized efforts to preserve local landmarks and places of cultural significance to African Americans. She questioned the rationale and tactics of civic initiatives such as "urban renewal" that continually dismissed and demolished Black neighborhoods, enterprises and historic sites. When Mary's coursework required a project demonstrating societal change, she had an idea.

At the time of Mary's academic work, Bertha was director of the university's Black Studies Program. Bertha was known for advocating cultural awareness and urging students to give back. So when Mary revealed her vision—a communitywide cultural and service center—Bertha was immediately an ally. The dynamic duo began investing intellectual and social capital to create a place to learn about African American heritage.

Mary and Bertha's campaign culminated in an outdoor festival in Marshall Park on August 31, 1974, the founding date of what would evolve to become the Gantt Center. Informed and unwavering, Mary triggered a chain of events that transformed student research to a grassroots project, a project to a fledgling nonprofit and a startup to an esteemed community institution. As one of the founding mothers of a historic organization whose sole mission is the preservation and celebration of African American art, history and culture, Mary Harper embodies the maxim about being the change you wish to see.

DAVID R. TAYLOR

Connection: *Grateful admirer* ◆ Channel: *President & CEO, Harvey B. Gantt Center for African-American Arts + Culture* ◆ Cause: *Preservation of African American art, history and culture*

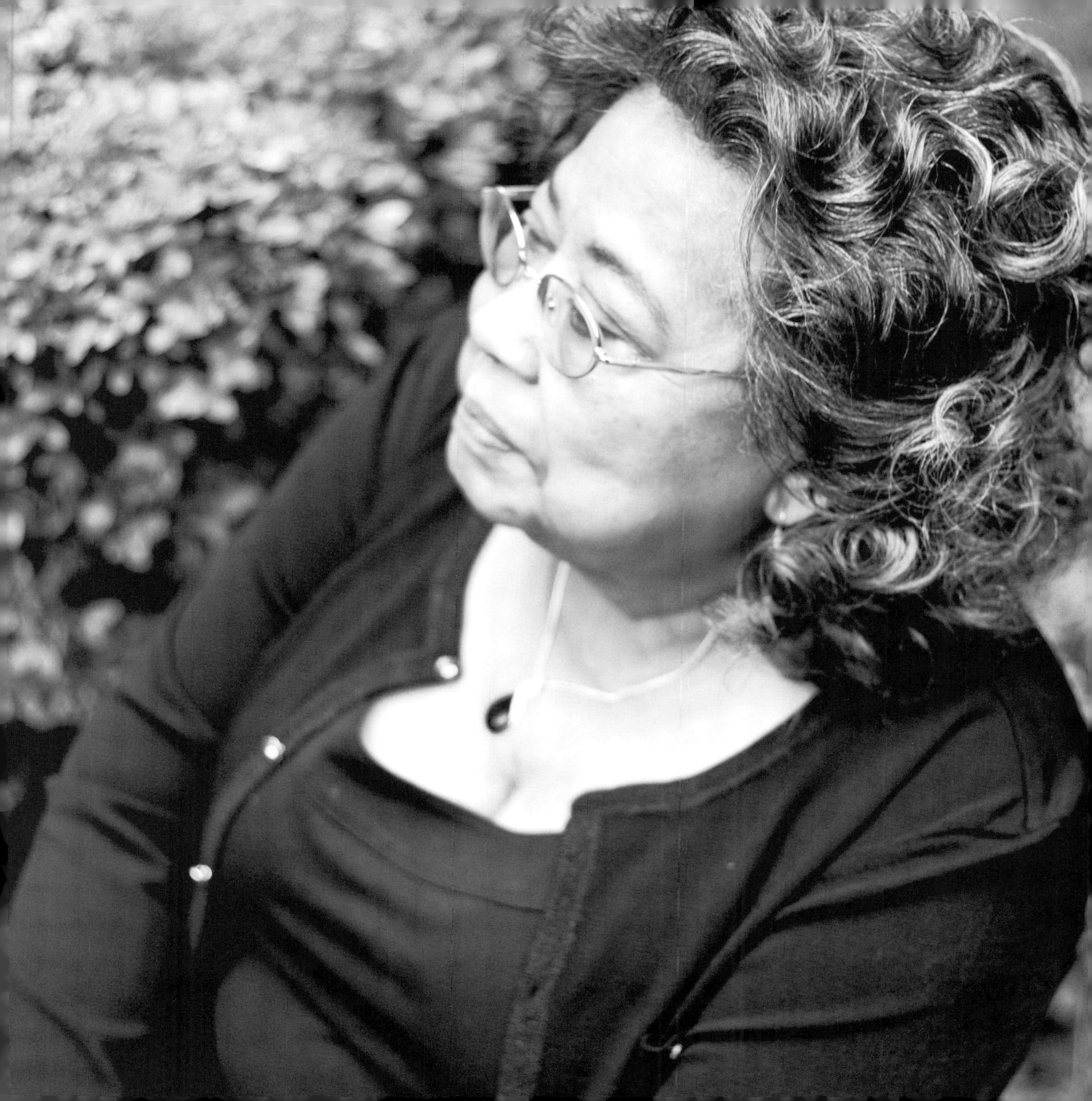

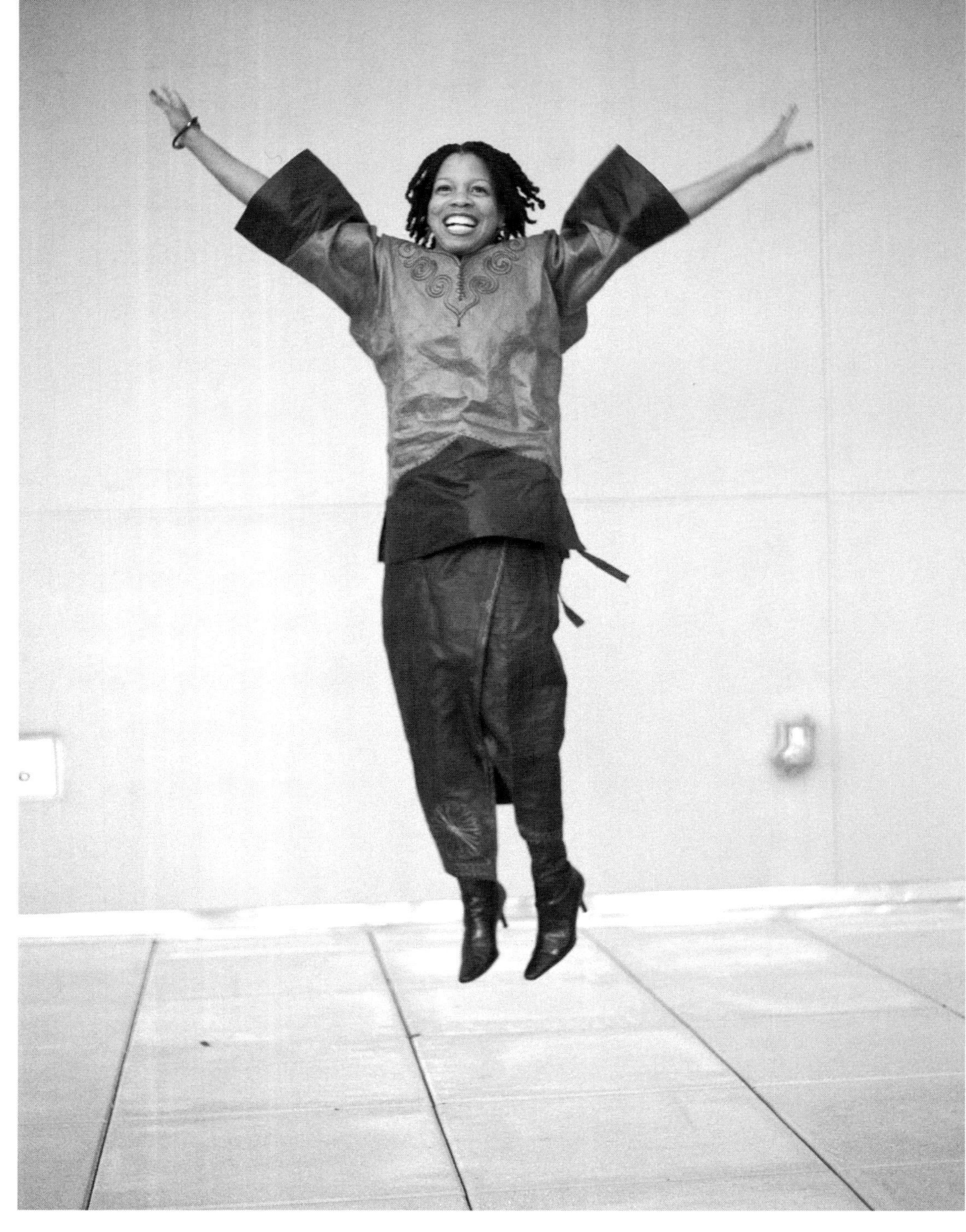

Every great dream begins with a dreamer.
Always remember, you have within you the strength, the patience,
and the passion to reach for the stars to change the world.

HARRIET TUBMAN
American abolitionist and humanitarian
(1822-1913)

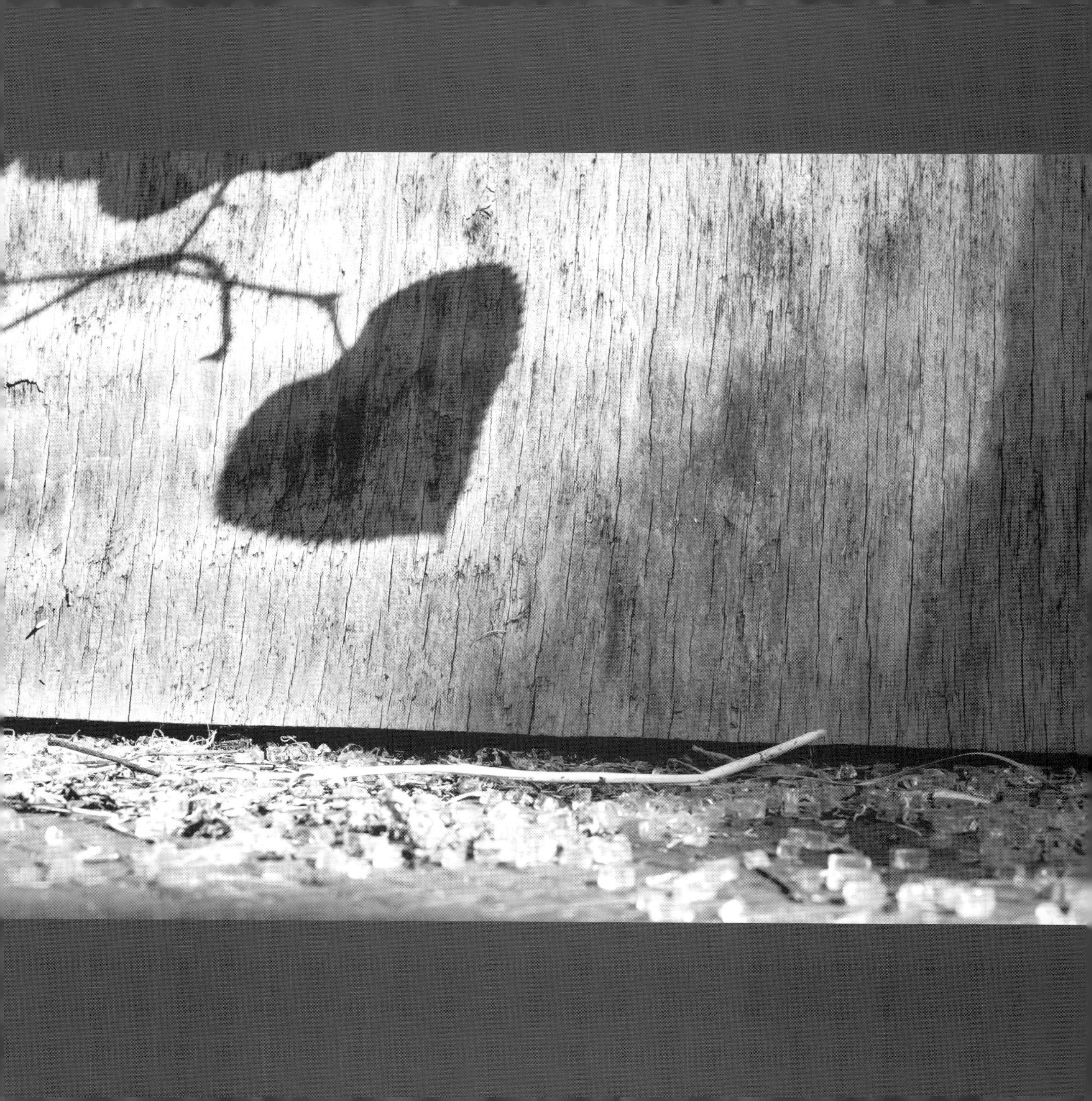

"SOMETIMES GIVING BACK MEANS taking back your neighborhood. Kids didn't have anywhere to go except in the streets. People were afraid to sit on their porch because it was infested with drug dealers. Me and a preacher in the neighborhood began to change things. We established a community policing program. We worked in partnership with others. Citizens began to take notice and rallied around us.

"A leader can't do it by himself. Without community, a leader can't do it. You need to rally around an issue. Today, we have a community center, a neighborhood park, houses redeveloped, new homes . . . people are moving back. Senior citizens are coming back out."

Wallace Pruitt
president of Seversville Neighborhood Organization & resident of Seversville for 50-some years

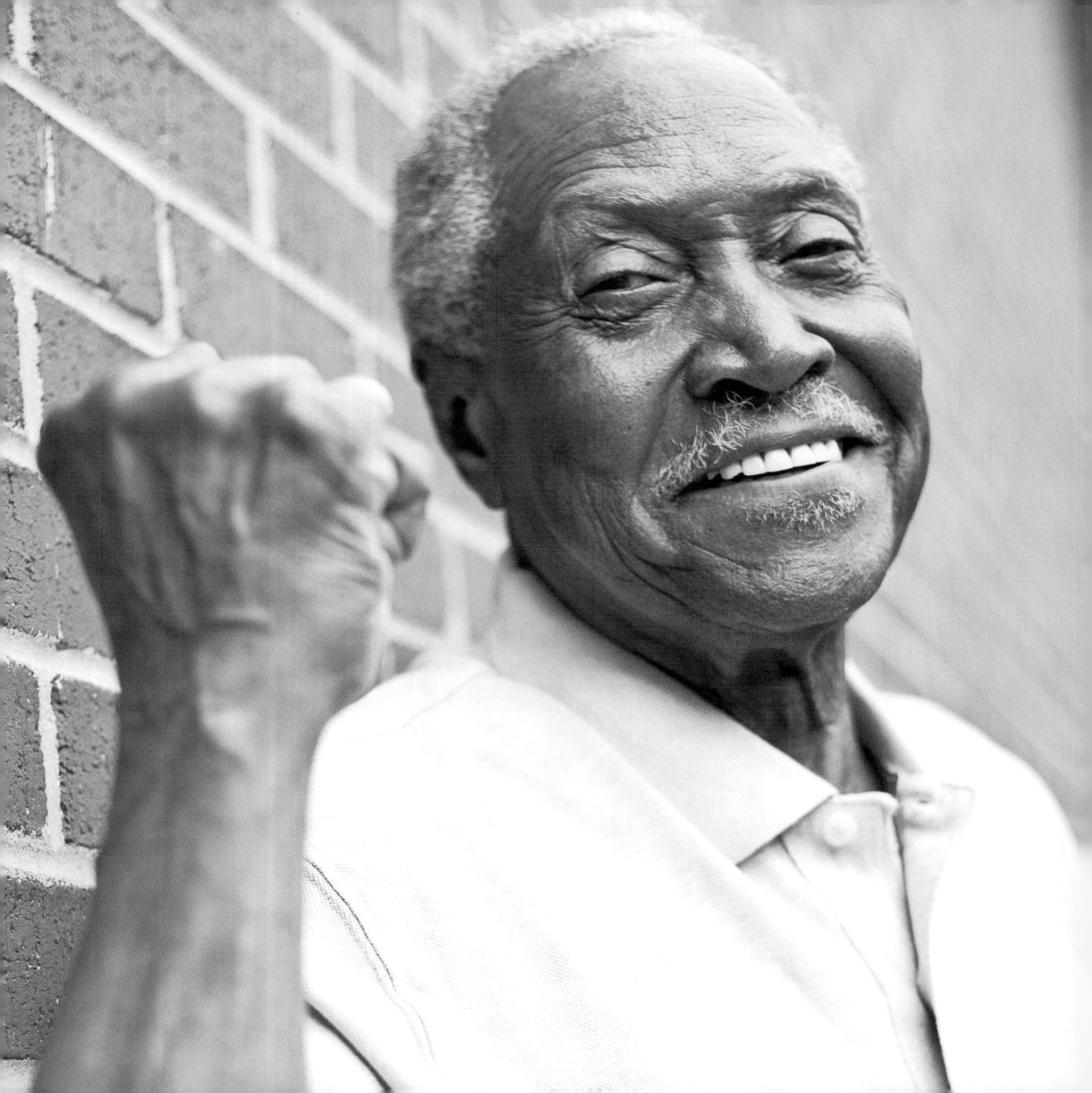

If there is no struggle, there is no progress.
Those who profess to favor freedom, and yet depreciate agitation, are men
who want crops without plowing up the ground. They want rain without thunder
and lightning. They want the ocean without the awful roar of its many waters.
This struggle may be a moral one; or it may be a physical one;
or it may be both moral and physical;
but it must be a struggle.

FREDERICK DOUGLASS
American orator, writer, statesman and social reformer
(1818-95)

William Pretty Jr. | TRUE GRIT

The example my father set is a pivotal force in every aspect of my life. Bill Pretty, nicknamed "Grit" by friends, was a devoted family man who loved people and was driven to pursue excellence. I have always admired how he overcame obstacles to blaze trails in business and eventually become the Raleigh region's first African American owner and operator of McDonald's franchises. While my father made an indelible mark in business, his servant spirit in giving defines his legacy.

A memory I still hold about the man my father was comes from when I was about seven years old. It was late fall and Dad was driving the family to my grandfather's restaurant when a flat tire halted the ride. I got out of the car to help change the tire. When Dad opened the trunk, my eyes brightened with surprise to see it filled with toys. I promptly learned these were not for my brother and me but instead were Christmas gifts that our father had bought for children whose families were unable to buy them.

Giving back was Dad's life mission. He believed there was no higher calling. If he learned of someone in need, he always lent a hand. I recall an instance when he literally gave another man the shirt off his back. My mother, Mildred, shared his commitment and helped found the Ronald McDonald House in Durham. Together, they made a great team that embraced philanthropy and social responsibility. They groomed my brother and me to follow suit as selfless and respectful givers.

My parents met while attending Shaw University, which, established in 1865, has the distinction of being the oldest HBCU in the South. My dad loved that school and worked tirelessly on university boards and in support of education. When he passed away in 2003, our family established The William Pretty Jr. Foundation at Shaw to honor his legacy. The foundation has raised over $120,000 to award scholarships to deserving business students who demonstrate academic excellence and a high level of commitment to the community.

I share my dad's commitment to education that empowers young people to dream bigger and to become trailblazers by "experiencing school" instead of just going to school. I may never know the impact of my efforts, but I can be a catalyst.

REGINALD F. PRETTY

Connection: *Son* • Channel: *Member, Victory Christian Center* • Cause: *Christian-based knowledge and education to improve lives*

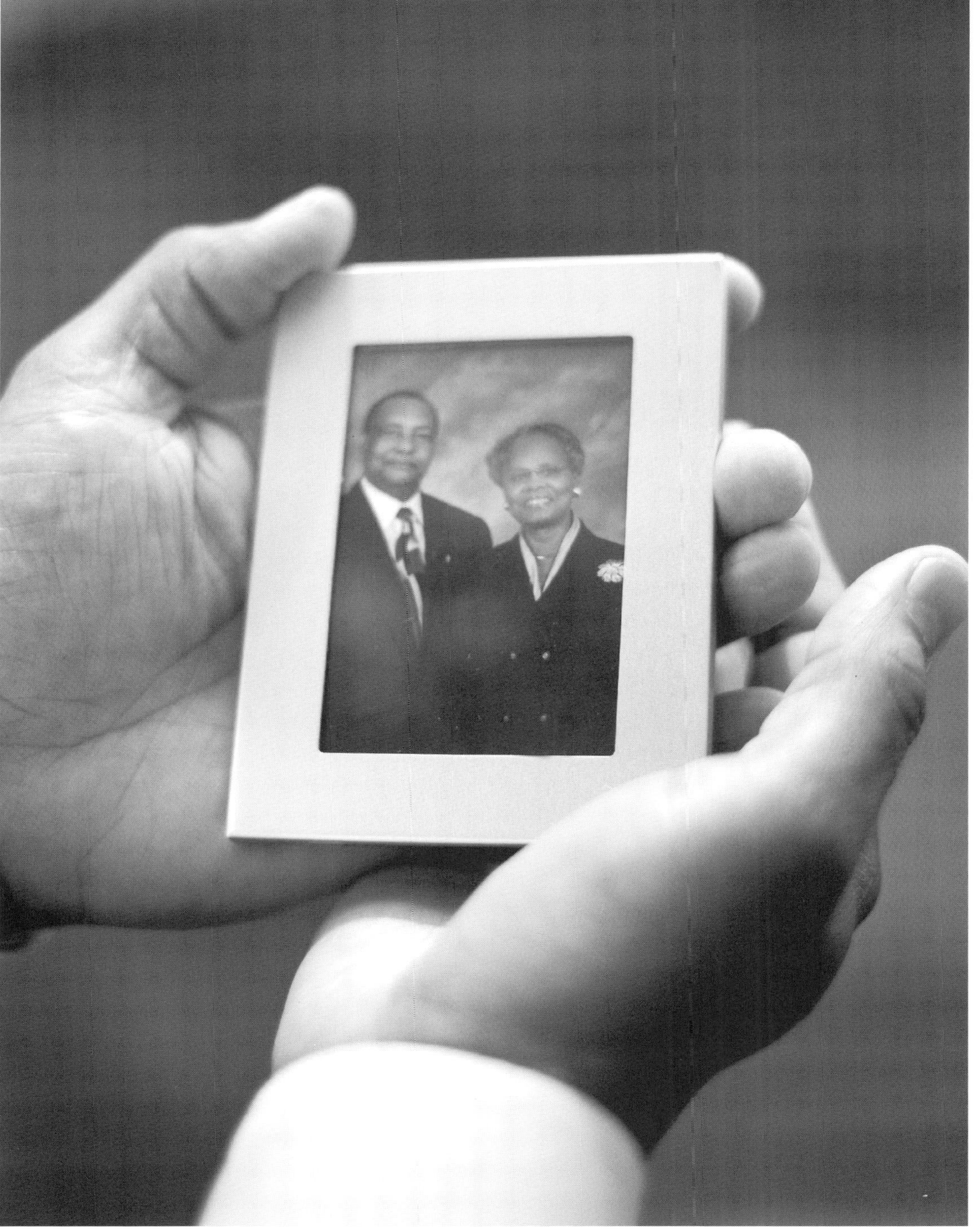

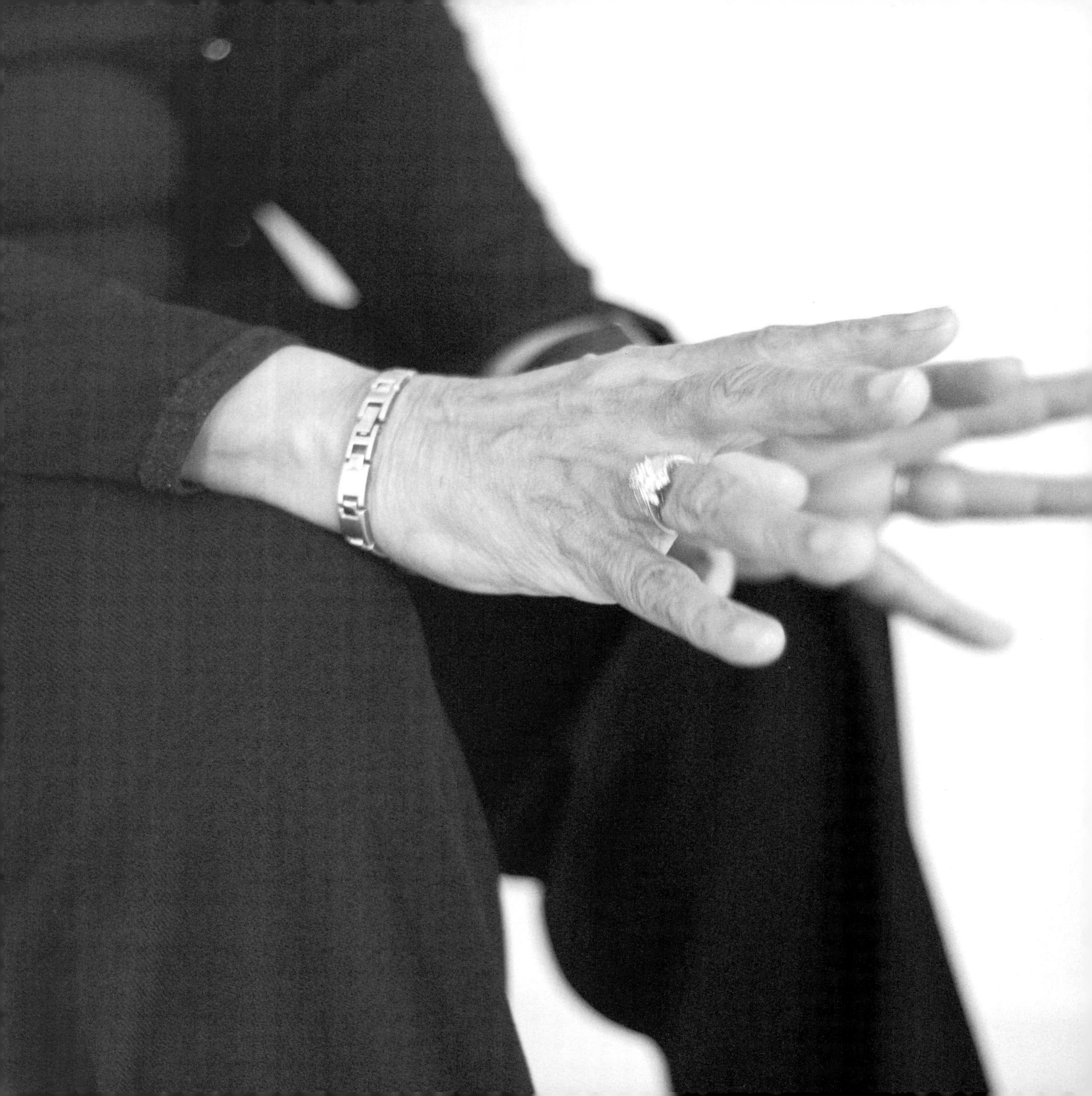

Giving back involves a certain amount of giving up.

COLIN POWELL
American statesman and former four-star Army general
(b. 1937)

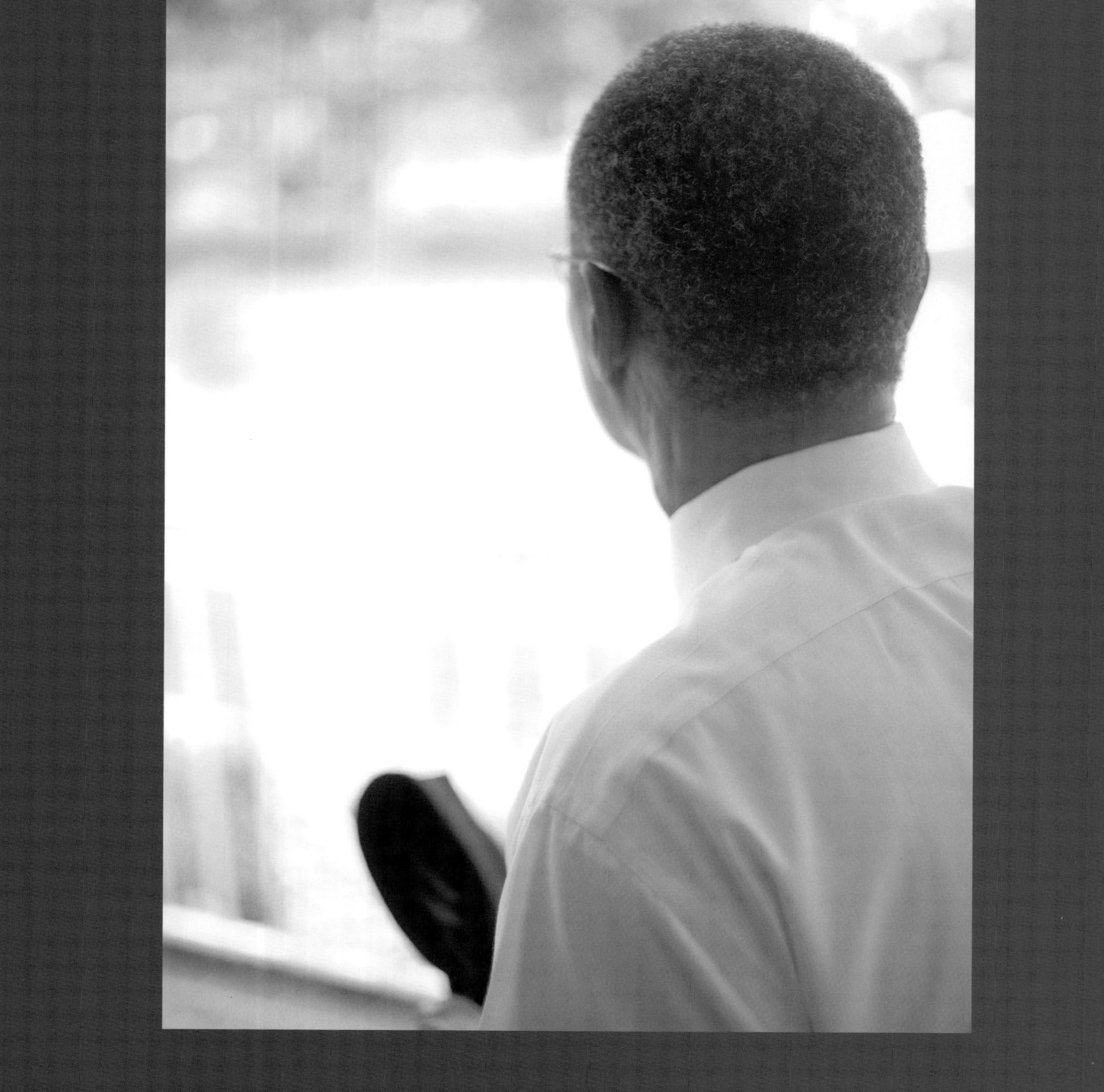

We lived simply, so that we could give money away. People say, "How can you afford it?" Well, how can people afford new cars and boats? Instead of those, we deliberately kept our standard of living down below our means.

THOMAS CANNON

Retired postal worker and Richmond, Virginia's self-described 'poor man's philanthropist'

(1925-2005)

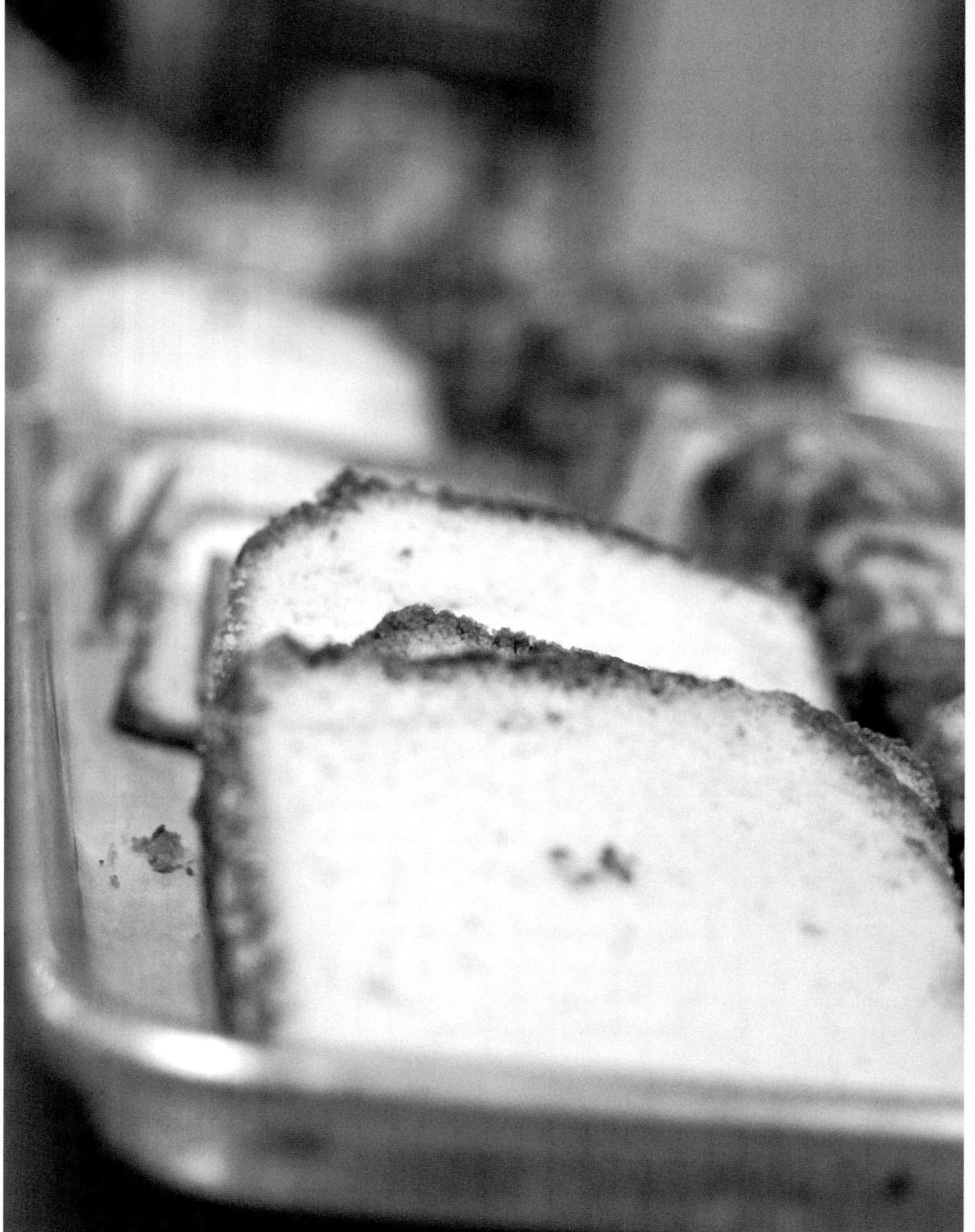

It is an unfortunate human failing that a full pocketbook often groans more loudly than an empty stomach.

FRANKLIN D. ROOSEVELT
32nd President of the United States
(1882-1945)

Elizabeth Ross Dargan | THE BENEVOLENT BENEFACTOR

You didn't dare say no to Aunt Lib. Dad's youngest sister, Elizabeth, was known for being determined and a bit stubborn. Our family comes from Polkton in Anson County, North Carolina, and soon after graduating high school in 1941, Aunt Lib left to make her mark on the world.

With a sense of adventure combined with strong-mindedness, Aunt Lib enjoyed a full life that comprised a career in education, around-the-world travel, dedication to her AKA sisterhood, and service to a litany of nonprofits and institutions—the Urban League, American Red Cross, Mount Carmel Baptist Church, Carolinas Healthcare System, Fayetteville State University, Johnson C. Smith University and Habitat for Humanity. Giving underscored her living.

Aunt Lib was resolute about service to others. Her faith sealed it. She used to say that when things happened in her life, she got through them only because there always was help. She would tell us, "You have to help the next person." Two defining experiences shaped her pay-it-forward beliefs about giving, and she often recounted those stories.

Once when Aunt Lib was young, recently widowed and worried about making ends meet as a beautician, she stumbled upon an employment ad seeking a dorm mother at Fayetteville State. She drove an hour to apply for the job and was dejected when a woman on campus told her she was too young and unqualified. Seeing hints of desperation and determination on Aunt Lib's face, the women enrolled her at the college.

The other story took place soon after her graduation. The college president had generously referred her for a job, and Aunt Lib was ecstatic. En route to the out-of-town interview, she felt her high hopes deflate when her car died suddenly, leaving her stranded roadside. She trudged to a service station only to find it closed, but a note gave a number to dial for help. Soon after her call, a mechanic arrived. She fretted openly about her impending appointment, so he worked quickly. When he revived the car, Aunt Lib voiced her deep gratitude. The mechanic's single request was that she help someone else.

Aunt Lib remarried, taught for decades, traveled everywhere and forever remembered turning points when people aided her progress. In return, she gave. Systematically. Broadly. Generously. She gave. In fact, you could honestly say Aunt Lib gave back till the day she died and even afterward. At age 83, she passed on. Only then did the family learn she had bequeathed a quarter of a million dollars to the organizations she served faithfully in life. Not surprising, Aunt Lib had the last say, again.

ESTHER WITHERSPOON

Connection: *Niece and executor of estate* • Channel: *Donor, Levine Children's Hospital and UNCF* • Cause: *Healthcare and education*

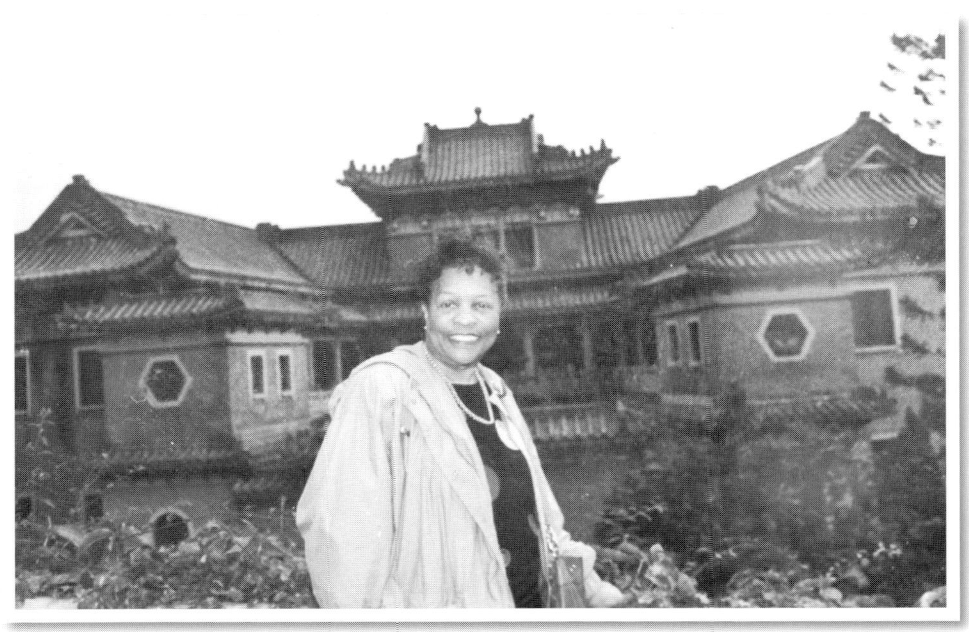

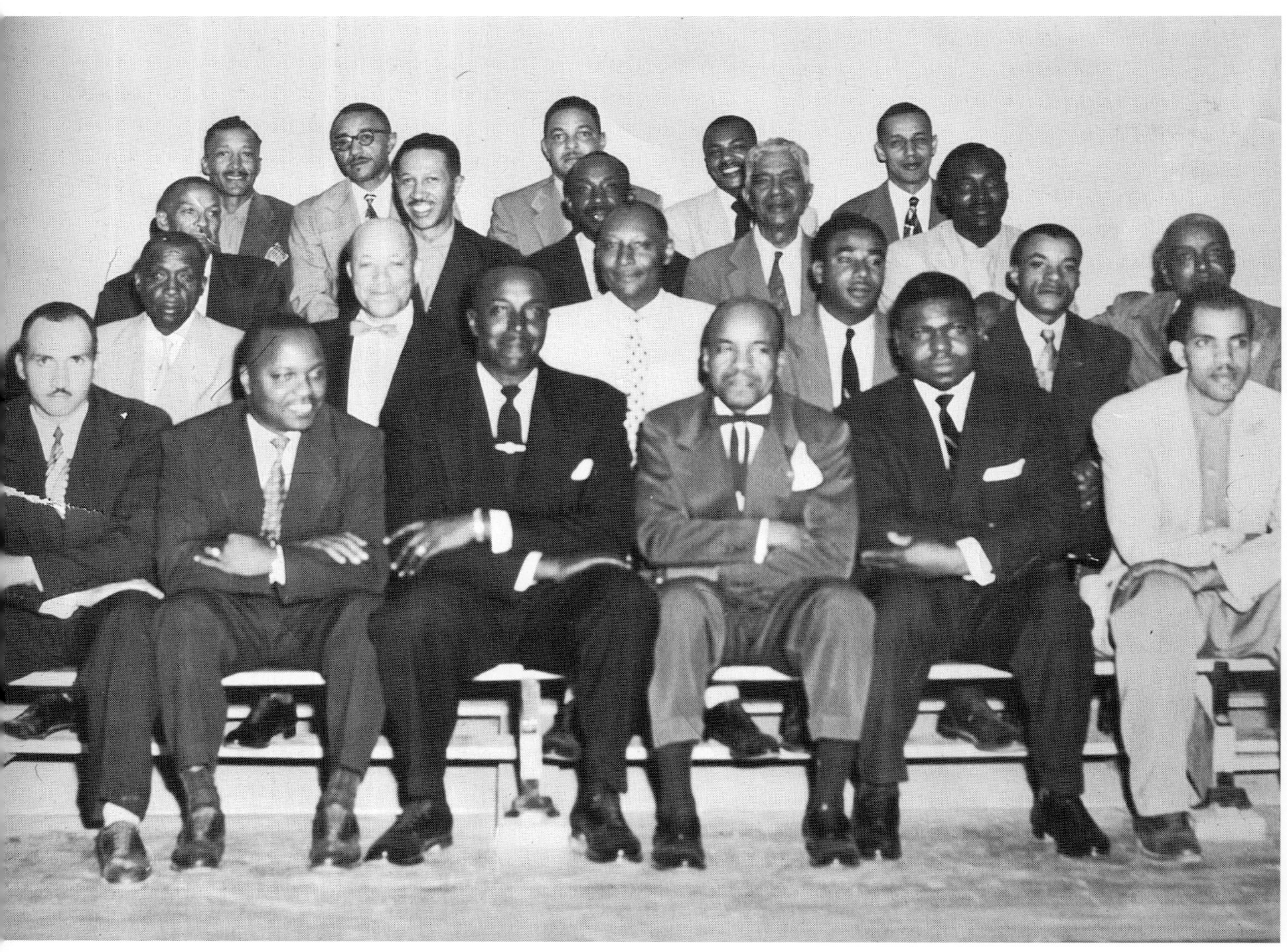

No man is an island, entire of itself;
every man is a piece of the continent.

JOHN DONNE
English poet and satirist
(1572-1631)

I choose to rise up out of that storm and see that in moments of desperation, fear, and helplessness, each of us can be a rainbow of hope, doing what we can to extend ourselves in kindness and grace to one another. And I know for sure that there is no them . . . there's only us.

OPRAH WINFREY
American television host and producer
(b. 1954)

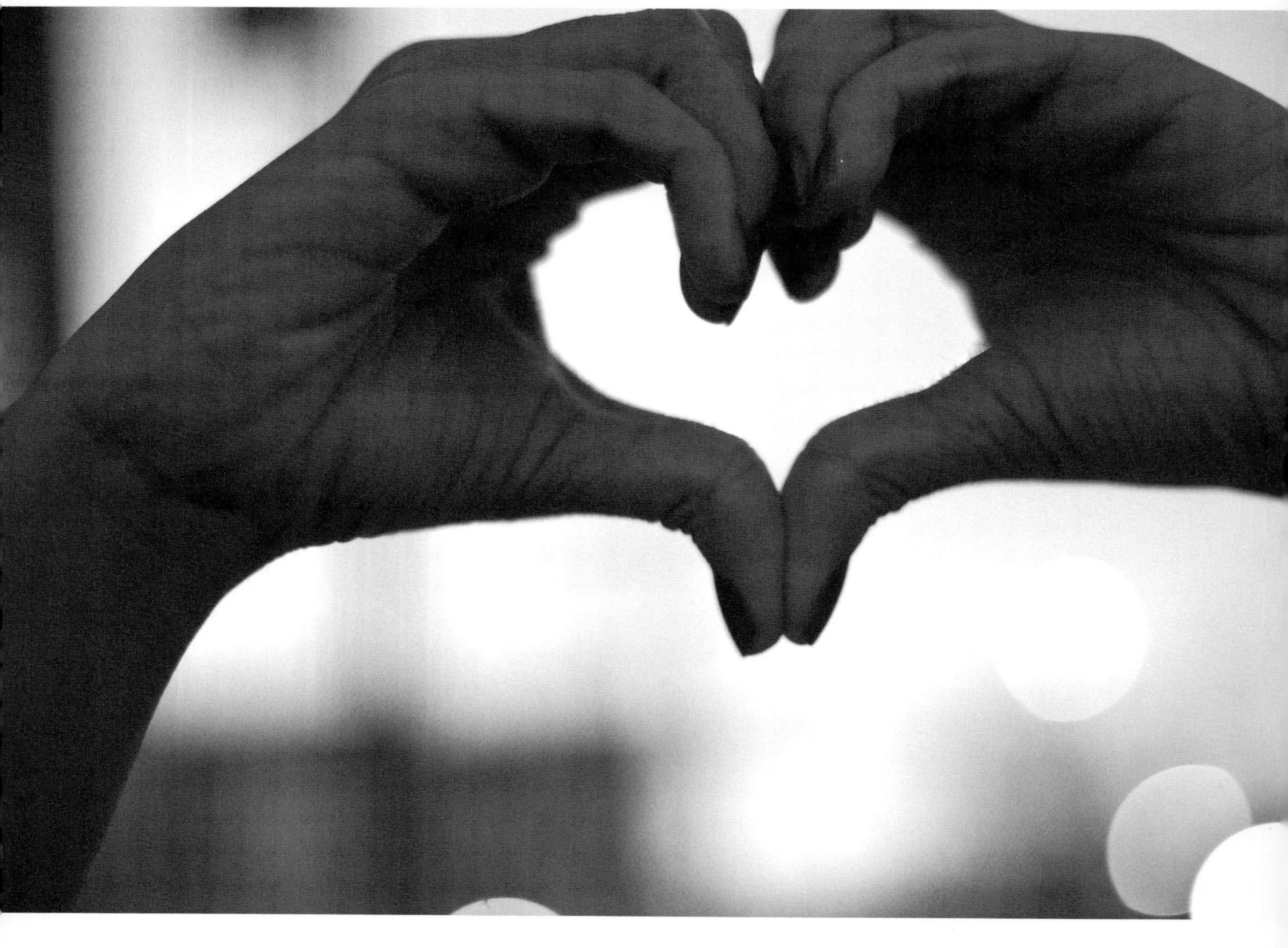

"NO ONE EVER TOLD ME to give. I learned it. My parents, grandparents, extended family members and ancestors are all givers. Watching someone give back is very powerful. It creates a giving imprint that can last for years and across generations. So it's important to show our youth of today how we make a difference. That's one reason why I created The Black Benefactors Fund—not only to support organizations in our community, but to leave a fund for them as a vehicle to give back and effect change."

Tracey Webb
founder, The Black Benefactors, a giving circle established in 2005, and BlackGivesBack.com, a popular blog

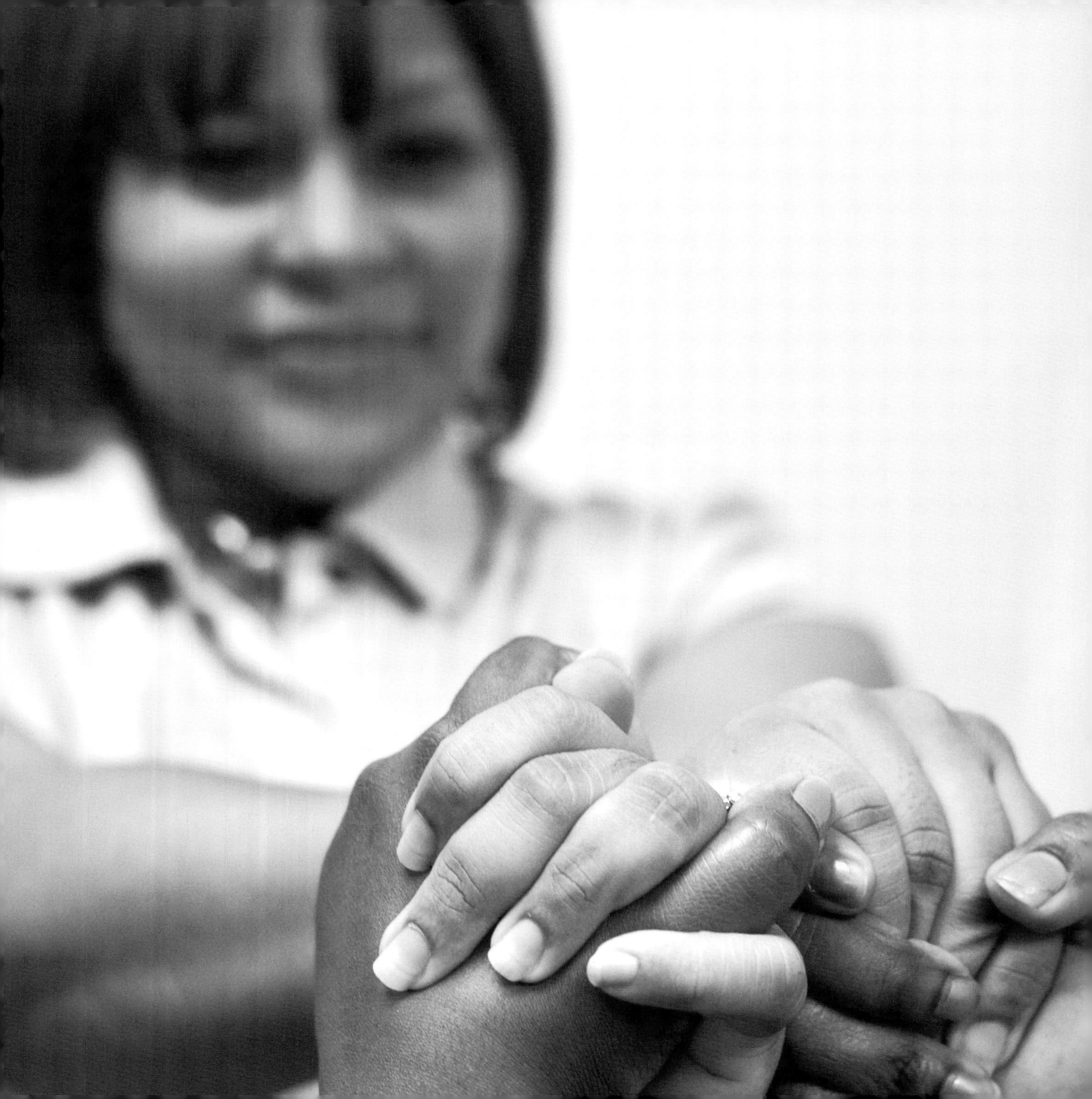

There are two ways of exerting one's strength:
one is pushing down, the other is pulling up.

BOOKER T. WASHINGTON
American educator, orator and political leader
(1856-1915)

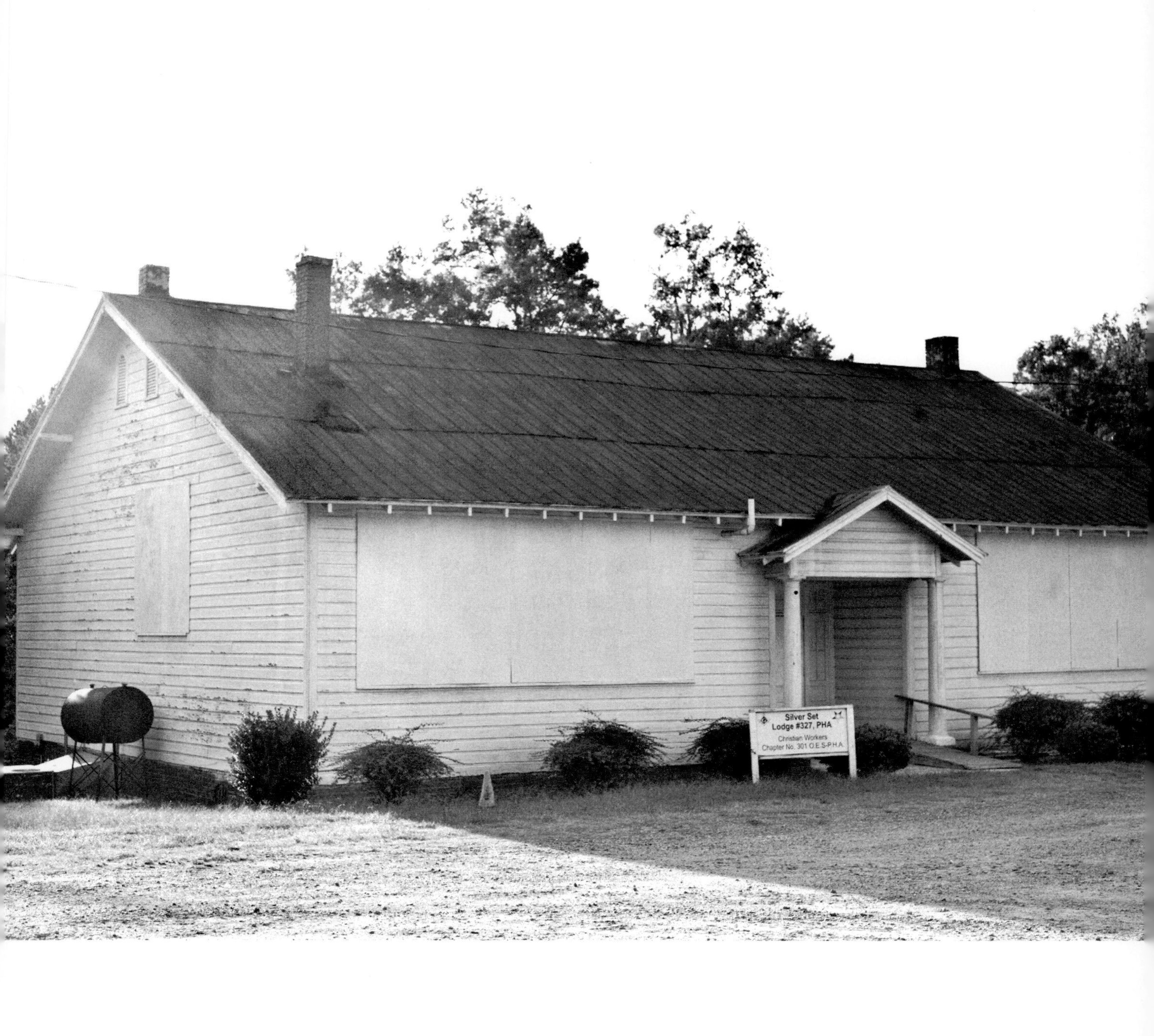
Silver Set
Lodge #327, PHA
Christian Workers
Chapter No. 301 O.E.S-P.H.A.

Do not be fooled into believing that because a man is rich he is necessarily smart. There is ample proof to the contrary.

JULIUS ROSENWALD

American clothier and donor who matched funds to establish "Rosenwald schools" for African Americans in the South

(1862-1932)

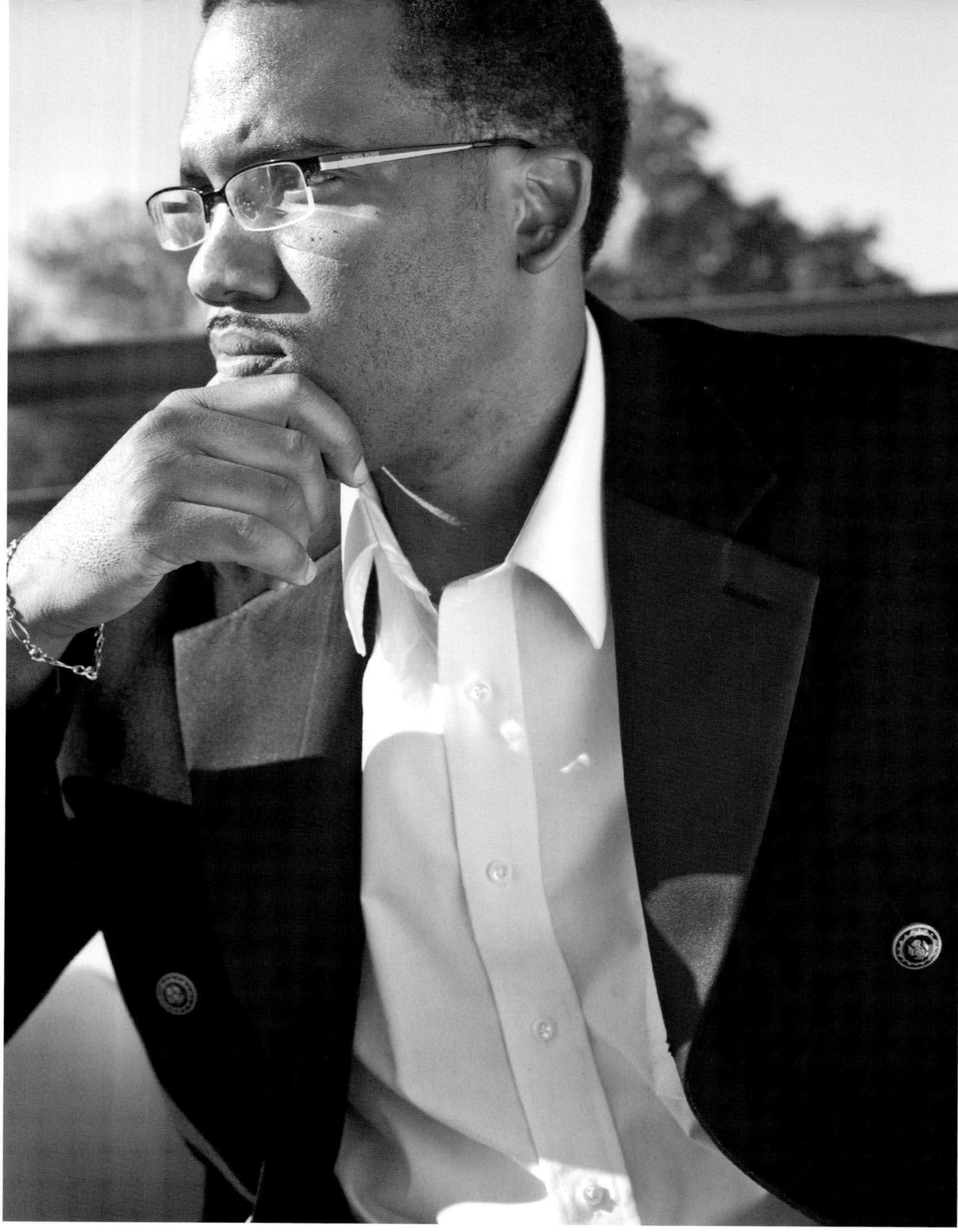

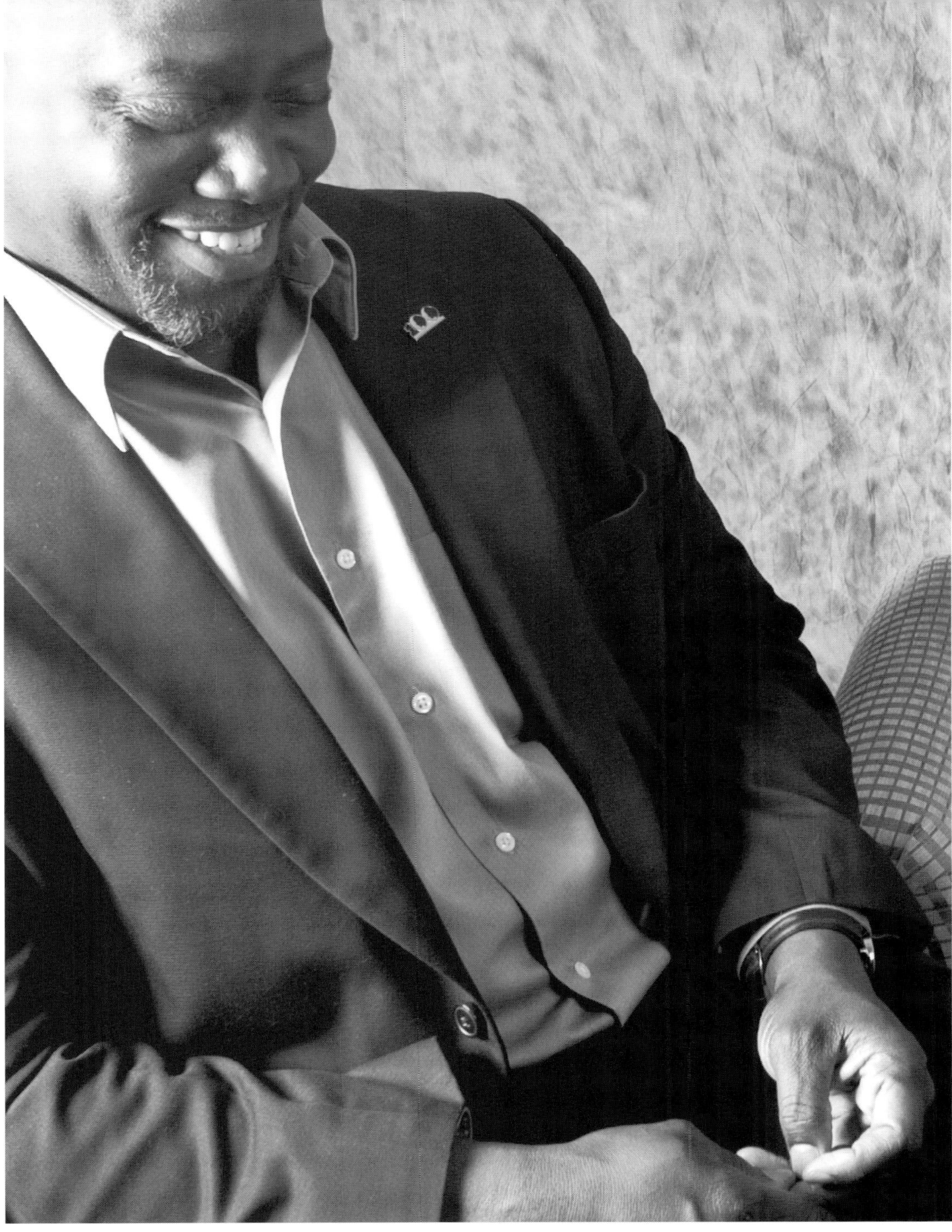

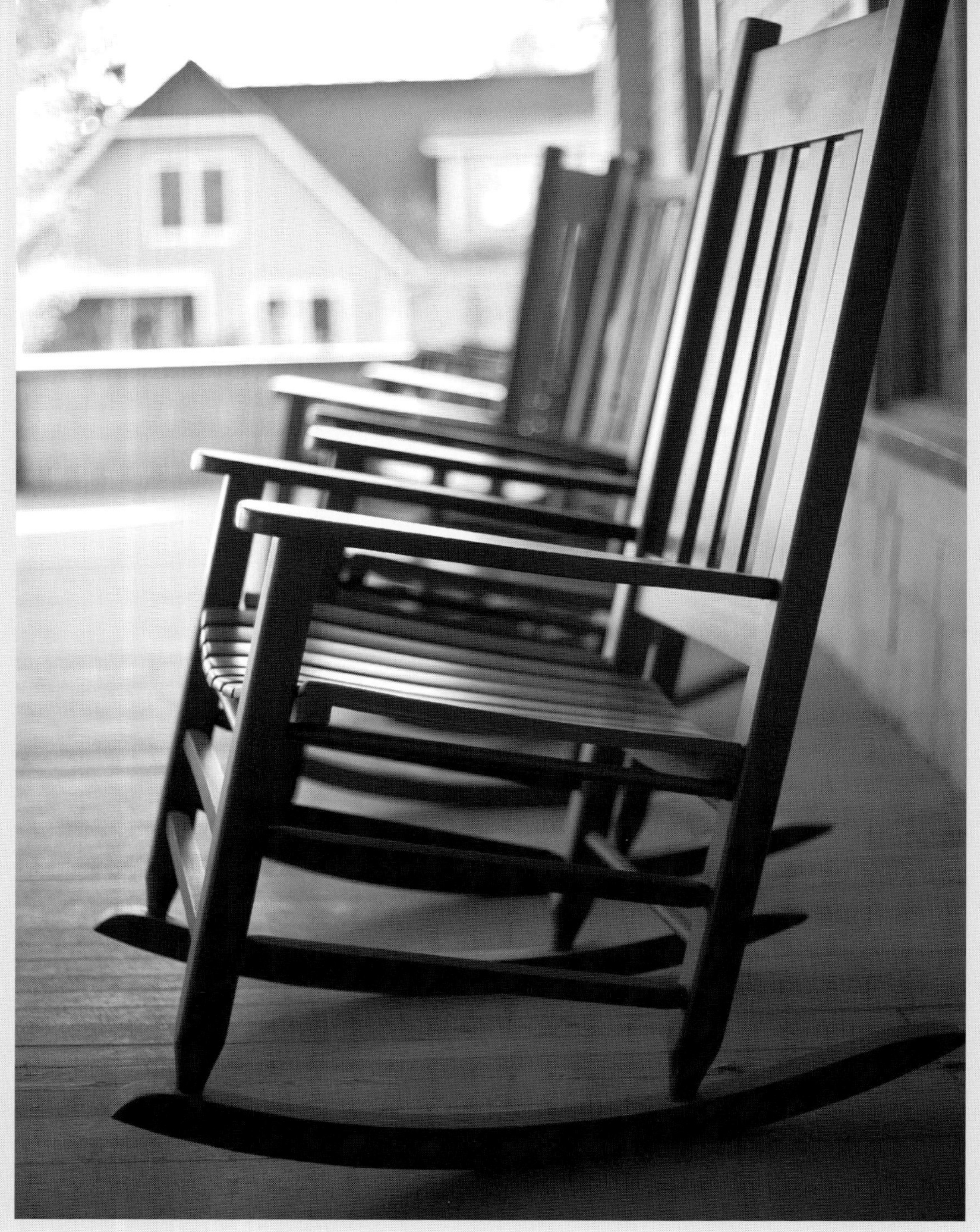

Don't sit down and wait for the opportunities to come; you have to get up and make them.

MADAM C.J. WALKER
Entrepreneur and first self-made American woman millionaire
(1867-1919)

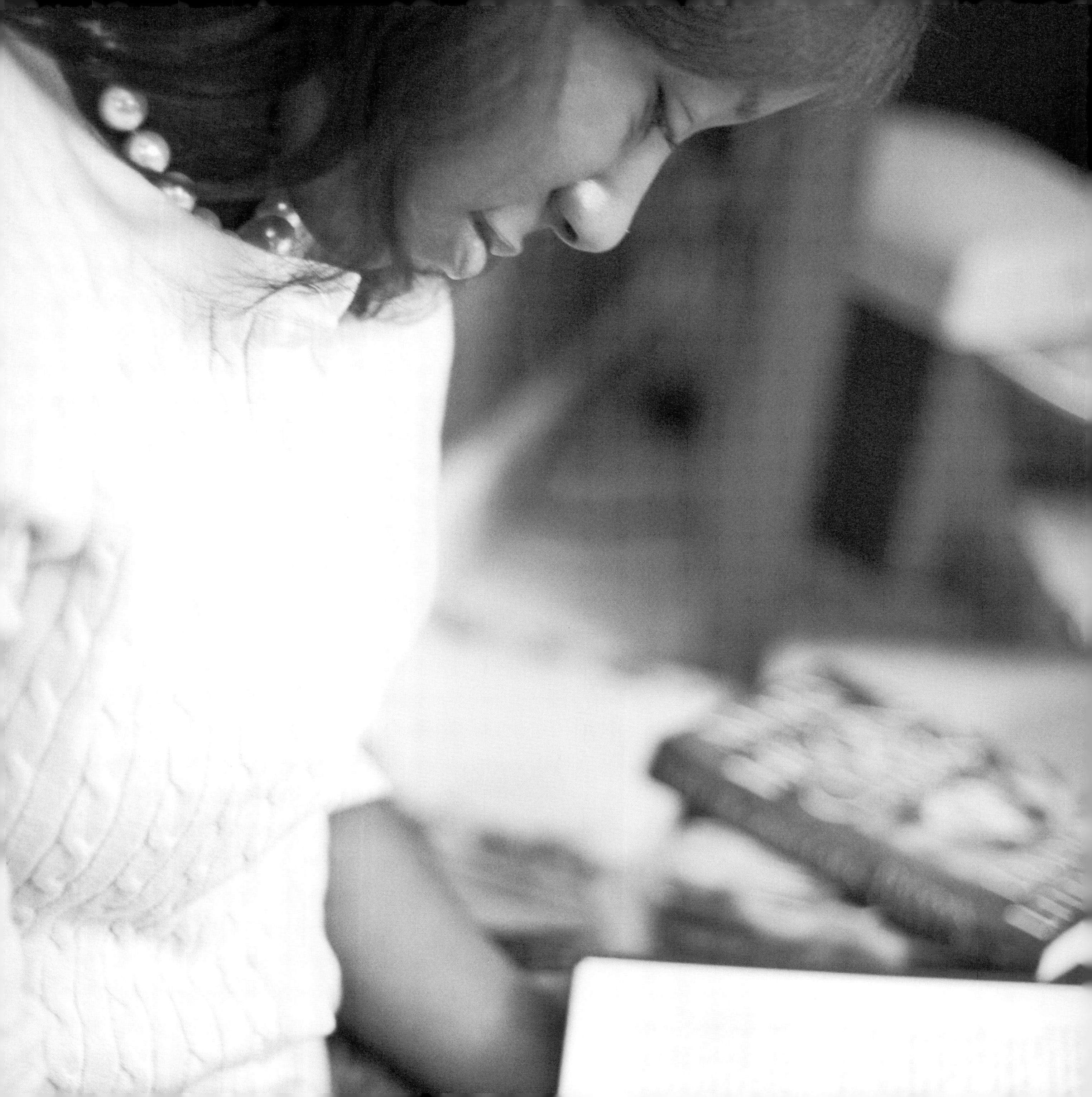

Knowledge

What do you wish more philanthropists knew?

I wish that more philanthropists knew that there are a number of ways to give back outside of giving money. There are organizations and causes that need hands to assist with everyday activities and operations to help them be effective to the people they serve. — *Qiana White*

Money is not the only thing that you can give to help others or to further a cause and that whatever is given however big or small makes a world of a difference. — *Ohmar Land*

You don't have to be a millionaire to give. — *Melandee Jones*

Remember that time and talent are just as valuable as monetary gifts. — *Diatra Fullwood*

The joy of giving! . . . Humans who interact with each other in these ways actually live more joyful and longer lives. — *Jennifer Henderson*

A little goes a long way. — *Joy Webb*

I wish more philanthropists knew that a 'small' investment can create big ripples of change in our communities. — *Darryl K. Lester*

I wish more givers knew three things my aunt taught me. One, there is more pleasure in giving than receiving. Two, the spirit in which one gives, not the amount, determines a gift's value. And three, great confidence and peace come with giving that's based on Biblical teachings and faith. — *Cathy Peterson*

More data on the specific needs of our communities — *Christian Friend*

Every gift, any amount can make a difference. — *Jeanene Thompson*

That while any support is welcome, leveraging that support with encouraged collaboration and strong community partnership can triple their initial investment. — *LaDawn Sullivan*

Which organizations will bring the best results from your investment — *Charles Smith*

To be strategic and purposeful in giving — *Ihsan Abdin*

That, when it really comes down to it, they truly serve an audience of one: God. — *Sherry Waters*

I wish more philanthropists knew that philanthropy is more than just money. The meaning of philanthropy is 'love of mankind.' Giving money is not the same as caring about someone else's quality of life. . . . Giving out of care of the well being of a fellow human being is the most powerful reason to give. Money does not inspire people. People inspire people. To be a philanthropist you have to give yourself. — *Lyord Watson Jr.*

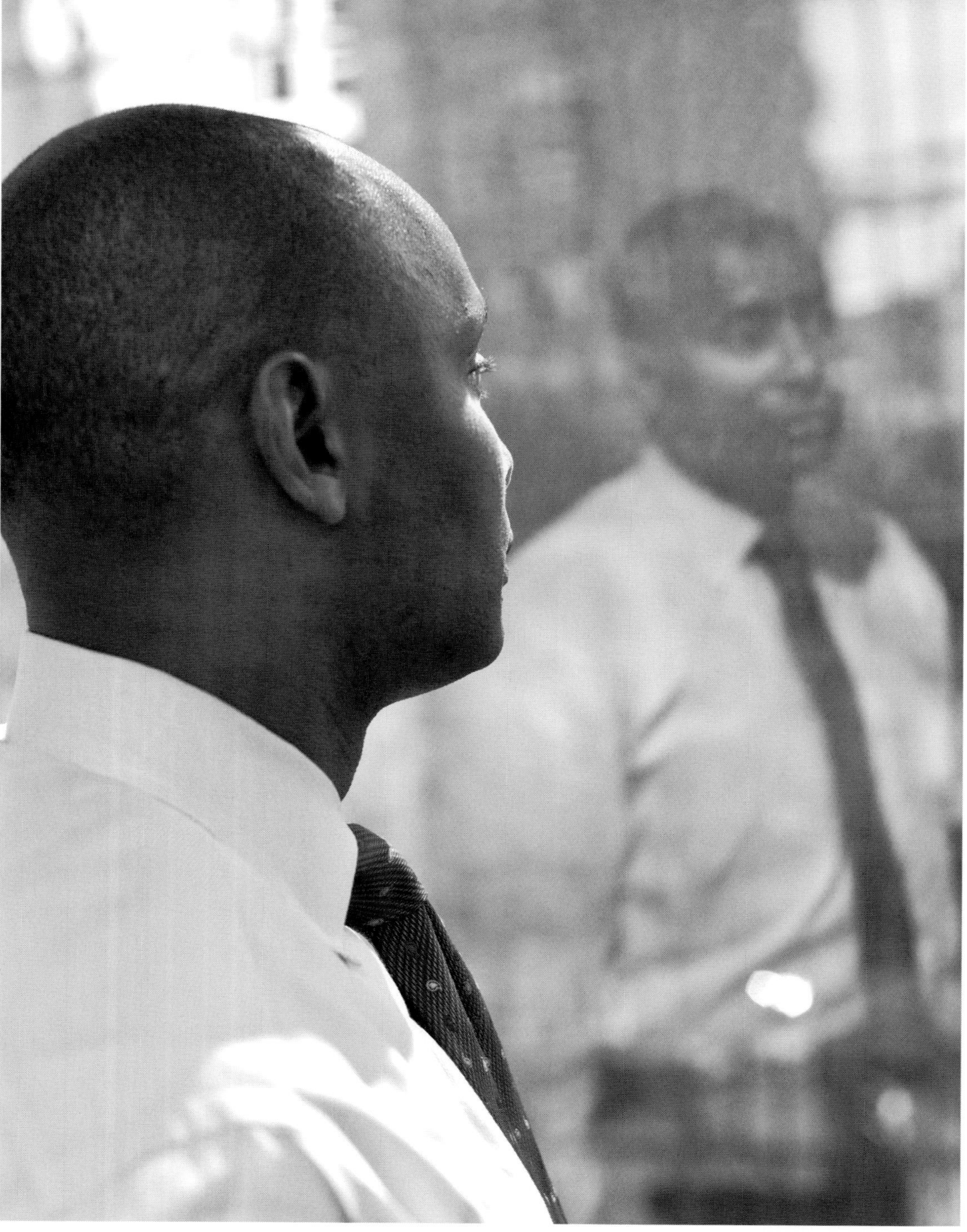

Everyone thinks of changing the world,
but no one thinks of changing himself.

LEO TOLSTOY
Russian mystic and novelist
(1828-1910)

Willette Chambers | CHEERFUL GIVER

Everyone who knew my dad's older sister, Willette, has a story. Some tales about her could make you cry laughing, but most, by far, reveal her giving spirit. Aunt Willette always gave willingly, whether it was a little bit of money, something to eat, her co-signature for a loan or just an empathetic ear. And, if she didn't have what you needed, she would call around until she found someone who did. She would hand over her last five dollars to anyone in need, thanks to a generosity and confidence firmly rooted in faith.

The last time we sat together at church, Aunt Willette reached deep into her big Sunday pocketbook, focusing a minute to be sure to gather every dollar and loose cent for the offering plate. Though many might be inclined to say, "I need to keep some of my money, just in case," Aunt Willette instead gave it all. Her nature reminds me of the widow's offering in the Gospel of Mark. In a crowd putting money into the temple treasury, rich people tossed in large amounts, but a poor widow approached and laid down two tiny copper coins. Seeing this, Jesus told his disciples that while others gave out of wealth, the widow, in poverty, put in everything and thereby placed more into the treasury than all the others.

The widow's sacrifice and my Aunt Willette's example remind me that the spirit of a gift, not the amount, determines its value. Every day I strive to become a joyful and trusting giver.

CATHY PETERSON

Connection: *Niece* • Channel: *Member, National Association of Negro Business and Professional Women's Clubs, formed in 1935* • Cause: *The homeless*

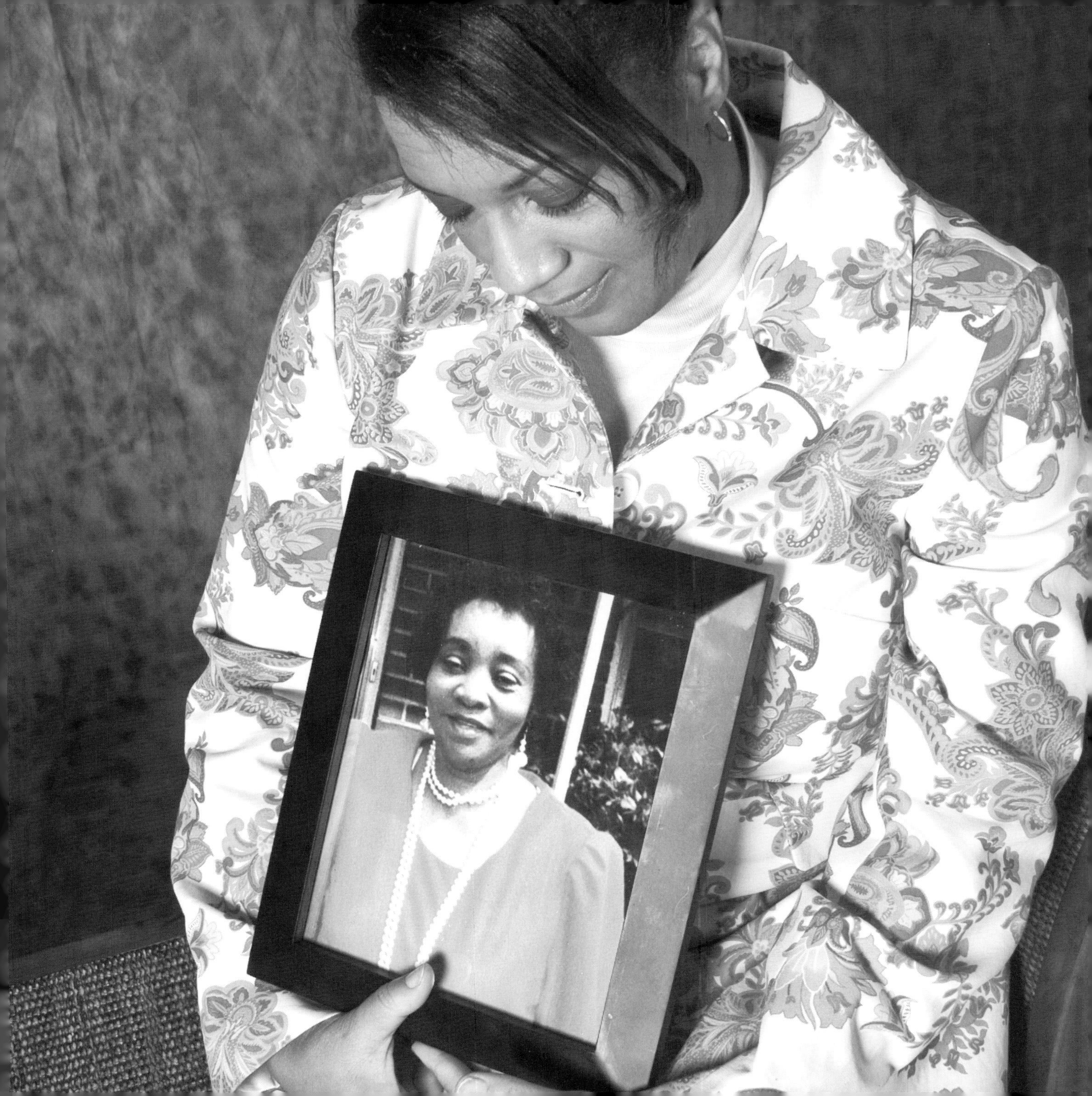

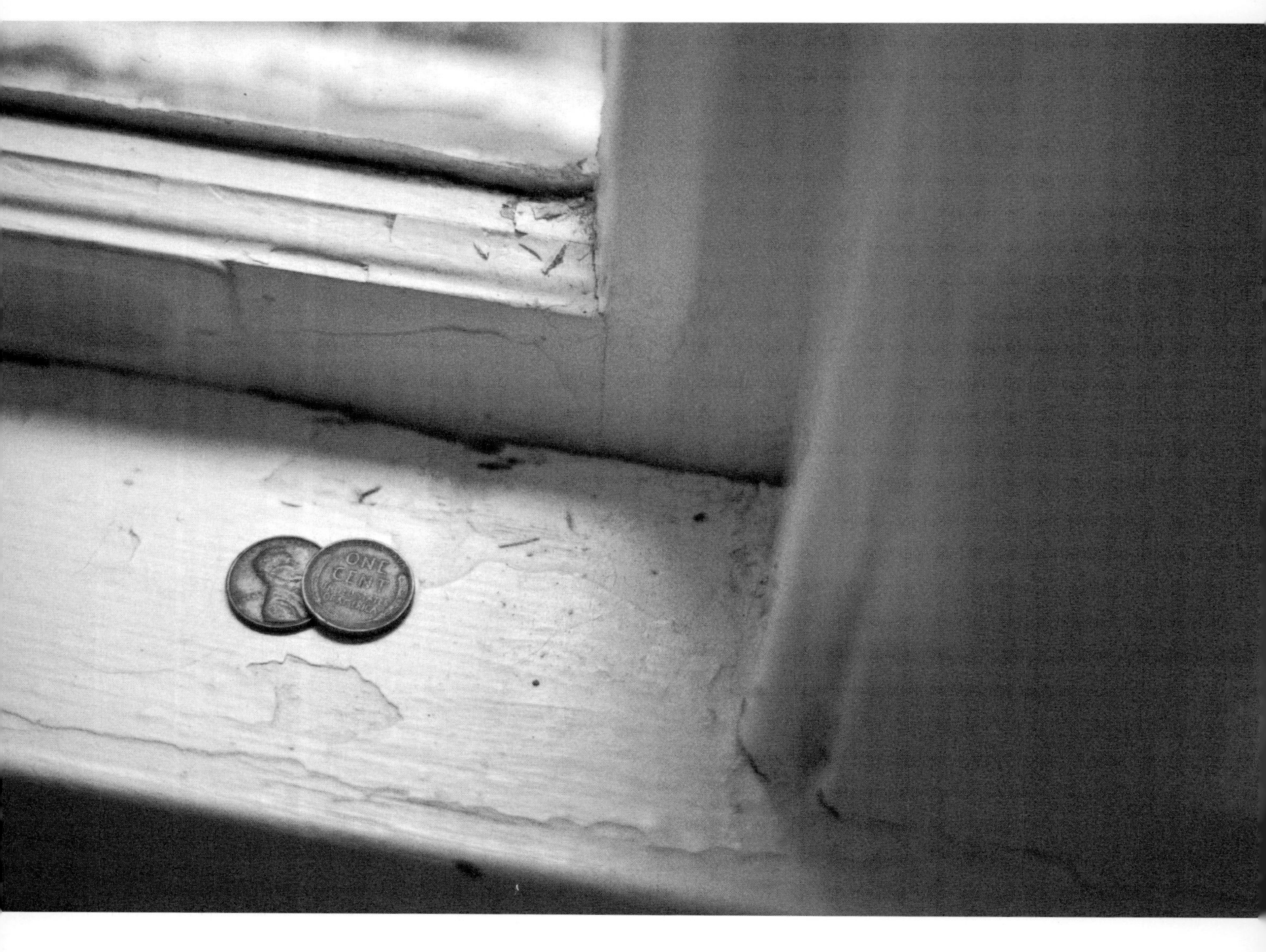
ONE CENT

Everything is a gift from you, and we have only given back what is yours already.

1 CHRONICLES 29:13-14

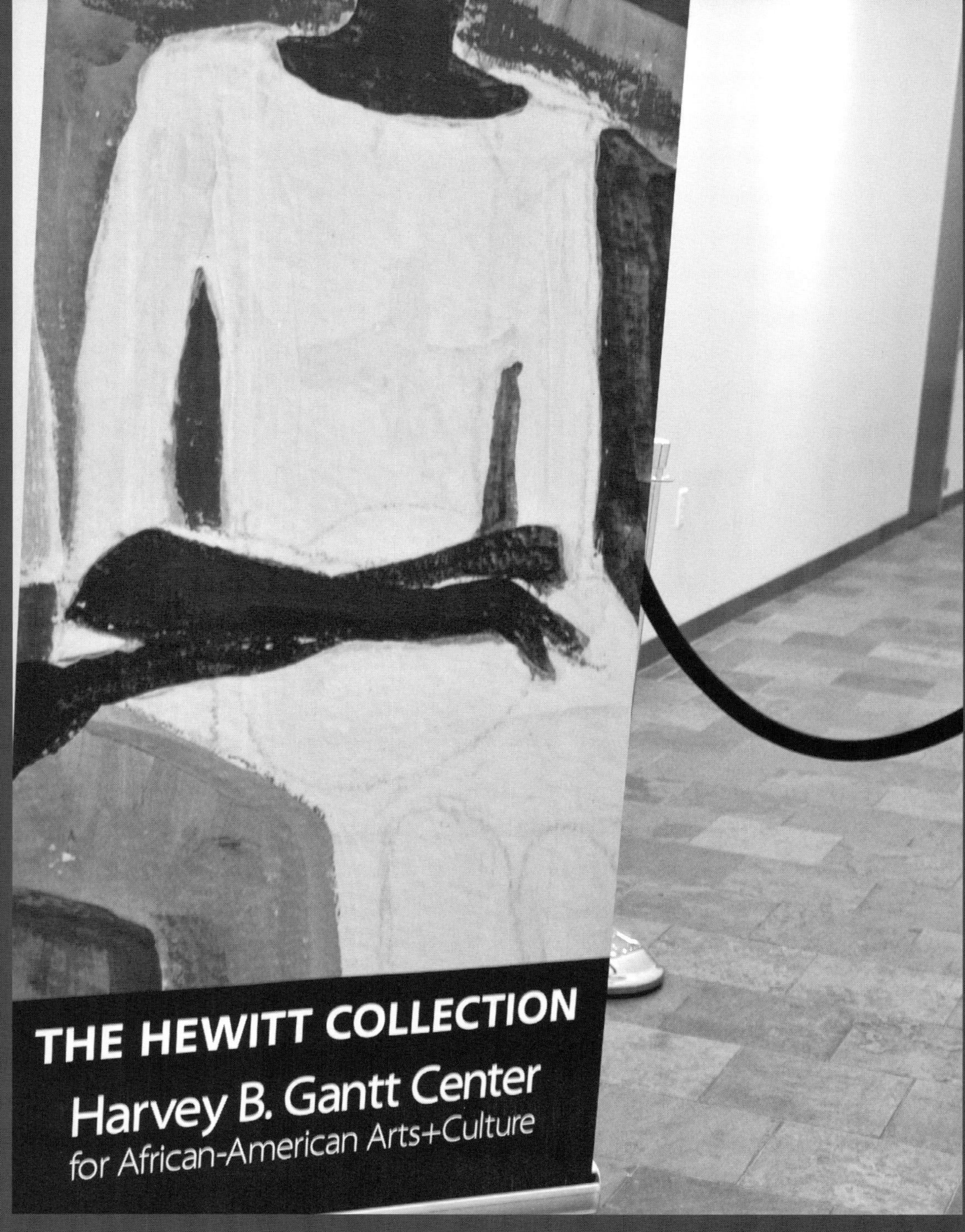
THE HEWITT COLLECTION
Harvey B. Gantt Center
for African-American Arts+Culture

"RECENTLY, I ACCEPTED AN INVITATION to join the board of directors of the Bechtler Museum of Modern Art. Consideration of this opportunity required great thought, as this museum reflects the story of a European family that befriended artists during the tumultuous World War II era. My decision solidified when I reflected on another family—an American family that held the same values and befriended African American artists in much the same way. Joining the Bechtler's board had everything to do with the Hewitts.

"While serving as president of NationsBank Foundation, now Bank of America, I received an inquiry about whether the bank would be interested in purchasing a collection of African American art held by Vivian and John Hewitt. After conferring with the bank's leadership and getting to know the Hewitt family, my colleagues and I decided that this acquisition offered a wonderful opportunity to express our corporate enlightened self-interest and to engage communities across the country. Now, the legacies of two visionary families that supported a cultural industry during troubled times will encourage and teach humanity for years to come."

Laura Foxx
patron of the arts and board member of the Bechtler Museum of Modern Art

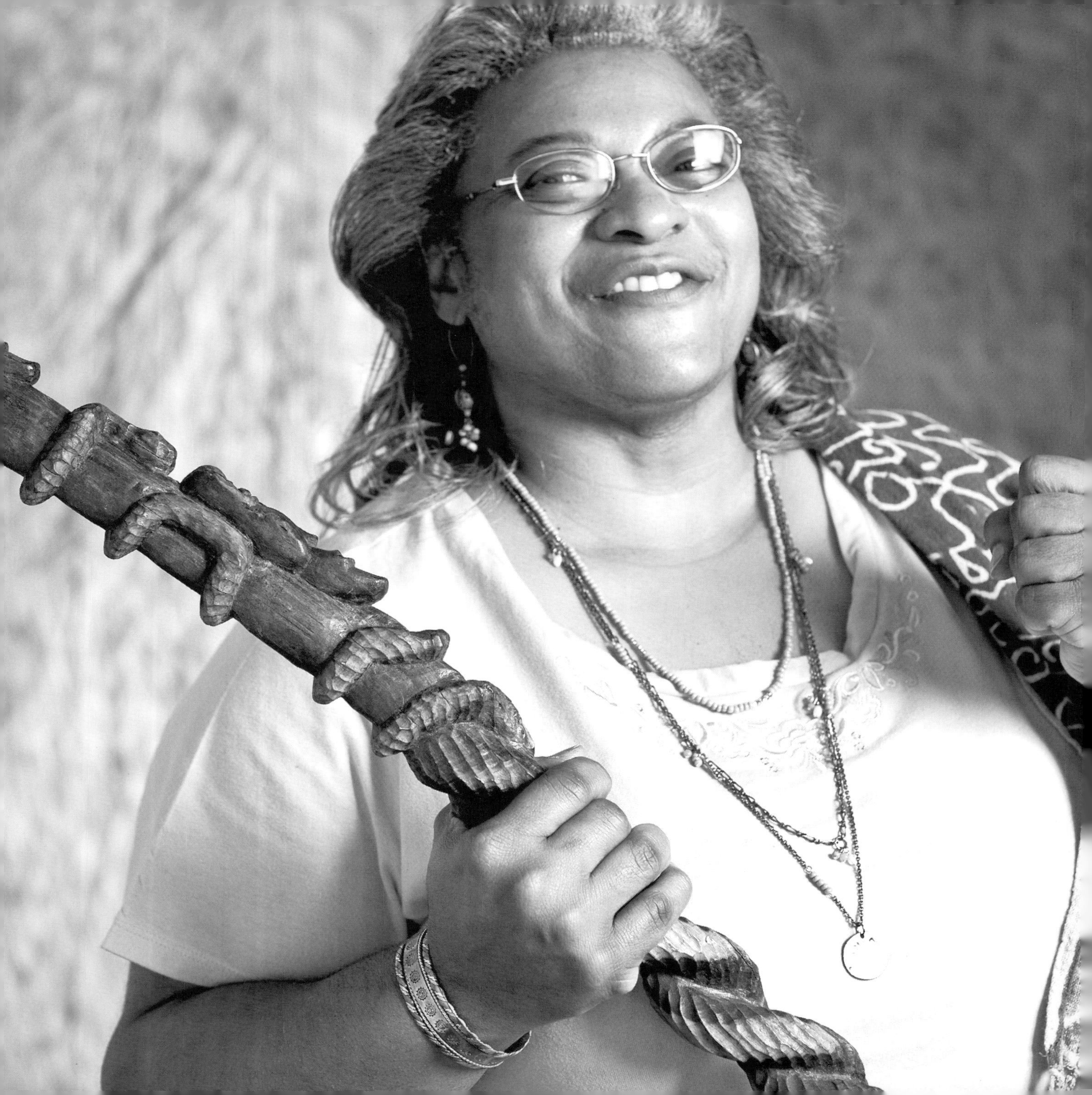

I used to want the words "She tried" on my tombstone. Now I want "She did it."

KATHERINE DUNHAM
American dancer, choreographer, author and activist
(1909-2006)

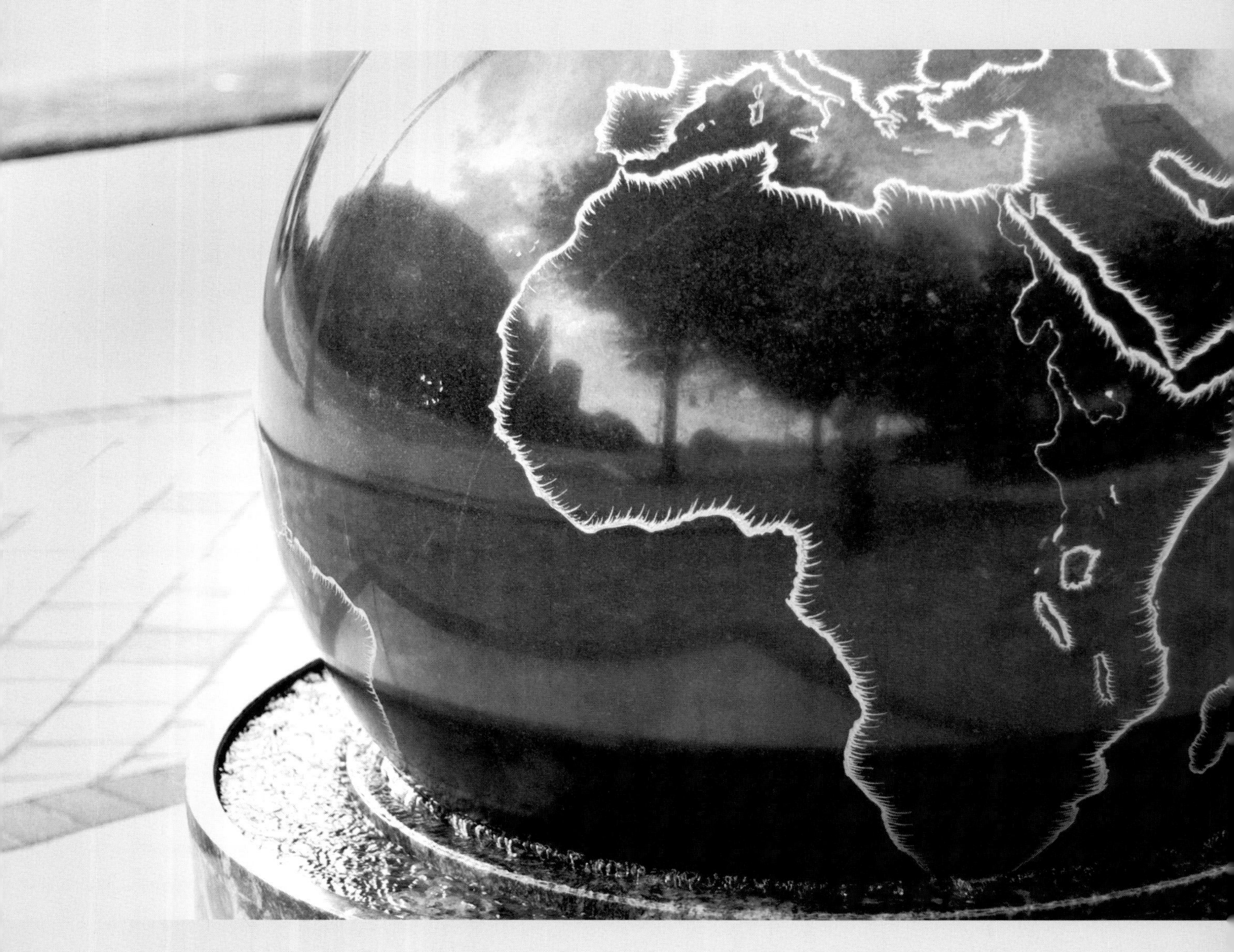

Determination and perseverance move the world;
thinking that others will do it for you is a sure way to fail.

MARVA COLLINS
American educator and school founder
(b. 1936)

Emmanuel Ohonme | SOUL OF THE SAMARITAN

By happenstance, I crossed paths with Manny's wife, Tracy, at the mall before I met him. When she learned I too was Nigerian, she eagerly told me about her husband. Just hearing about him, I loved his heart.

After coming to know Manny, I found inspiration in his story. He grew up in Nigeria without shoes. Then, at age nine, he received his first pair from an American visiting his village. Manny never forgot the stranger's generosity that forever changed his life.

Exceptional intellect and athleticism were Manny's passports to a U.S. college. After graduating, he was doing well in the information technology industry when he surprised his boss with news he was leaving and starting a ministry. Manny soon founded Samaritan's Feet, a nonprofit organization that provides socks and shoes to children around the globe. Everyday he works to give children the things he lacked as a child. It astounds me how my friend took one blessing and multiplied it exponentially to change the lives of thousands and thousands of people.

Presently, Manny is on a quest to give new shoes to ten million children in a decade. When my wife and I make a return visit to our home country this year, we will do our part to accomplish the goal. Manny has provided one hundred and fifty pairs of shoes for us to take to kids in a village that he does not know. The ultimate purpose of his giving is to share God's love.

Through our friendship, I have seen that there is more to living than getting whatever you can grab for yourself. I have also learned that givers inevitably receive far more than they give. It is a beautiful paradox of life.

DIMEJI ONAFUWA
Connection: *Compatriot & friend* • Channel: *Board member, Belmont Community Development Corporation* • Cause: *Sharing God's love*

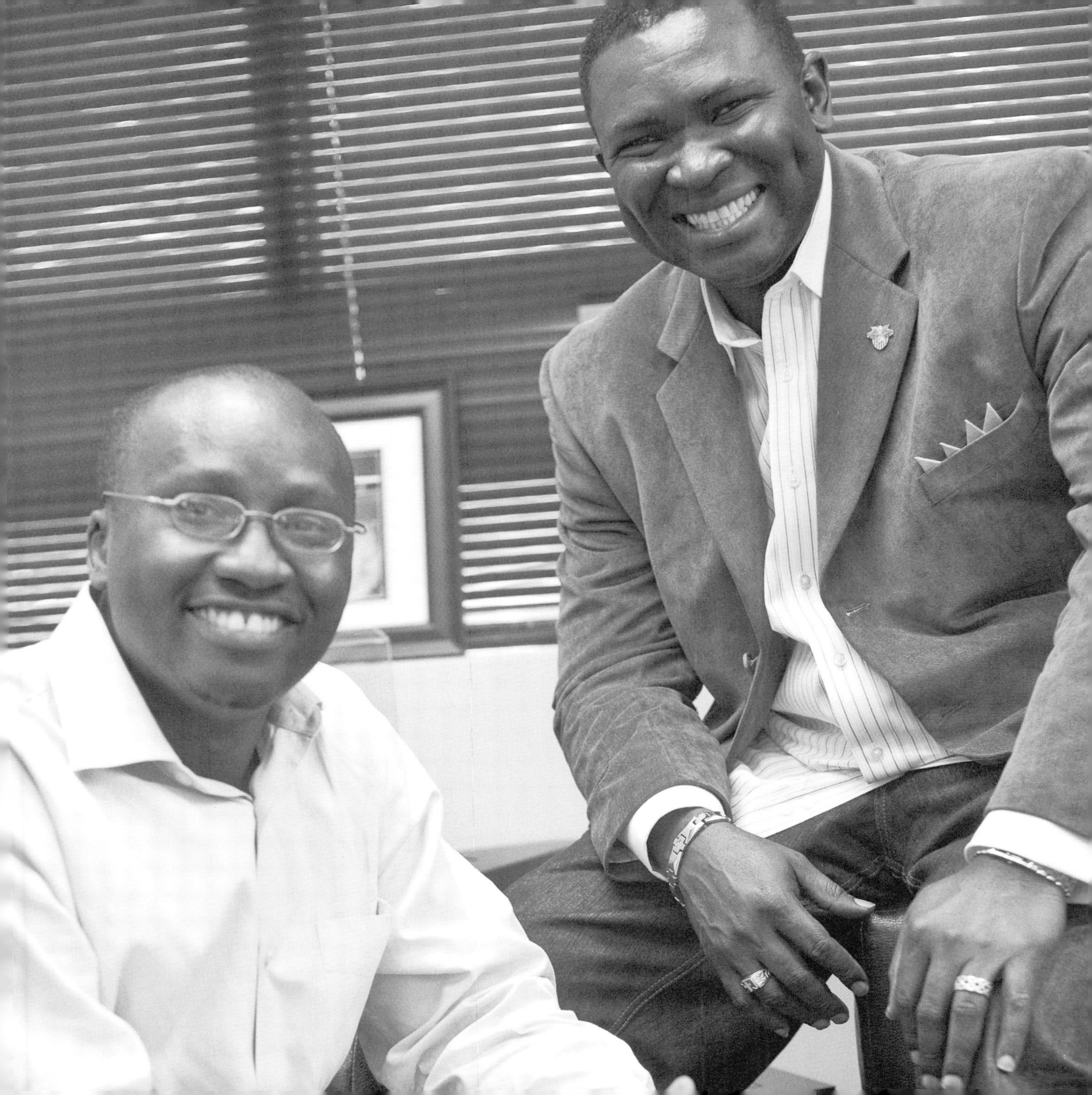

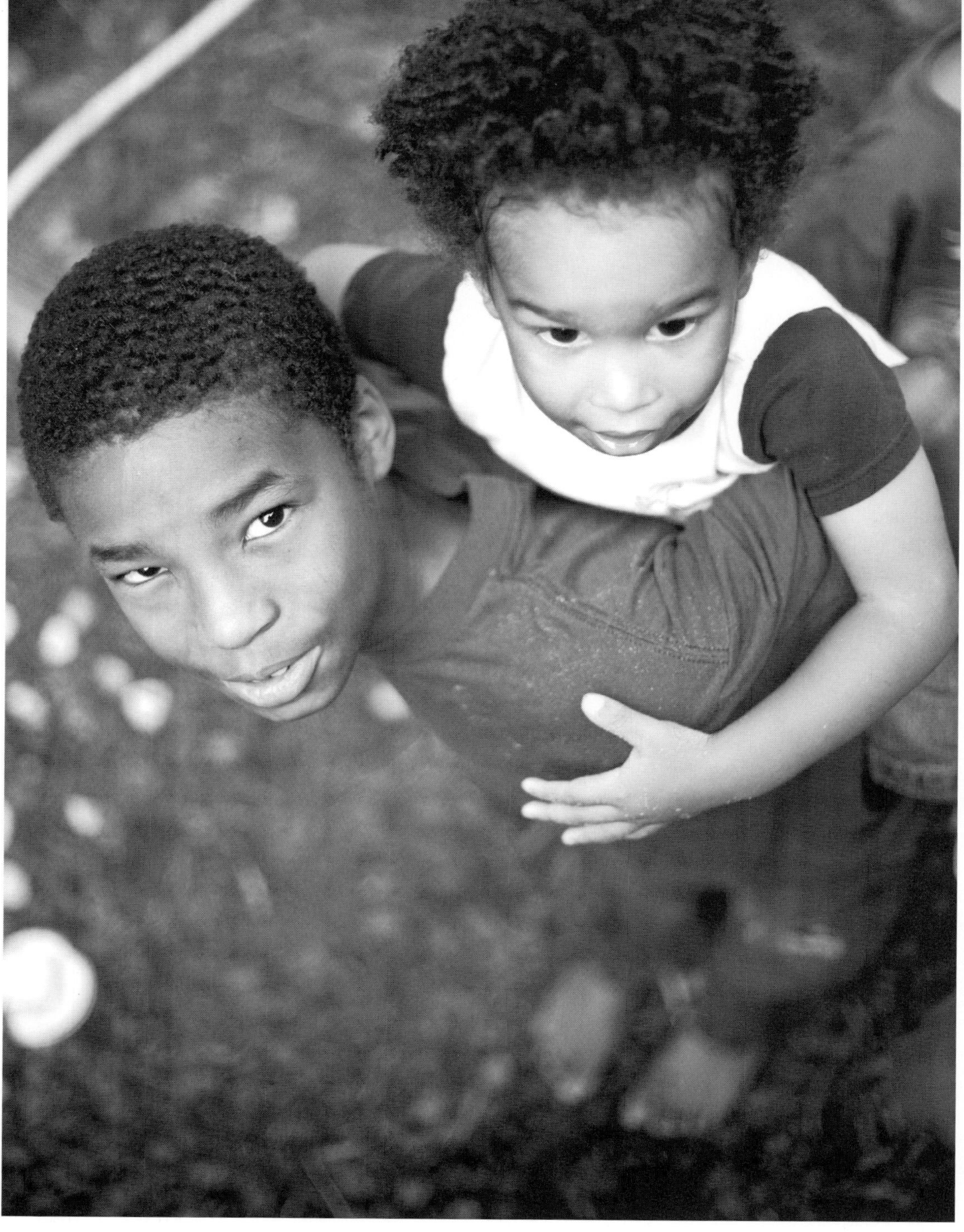

A man's feet must be planted in his country, but his eyes should survey the world.

GEORGE SANTAYANA
Spanish-American writer and philosopher
(1863-1952)

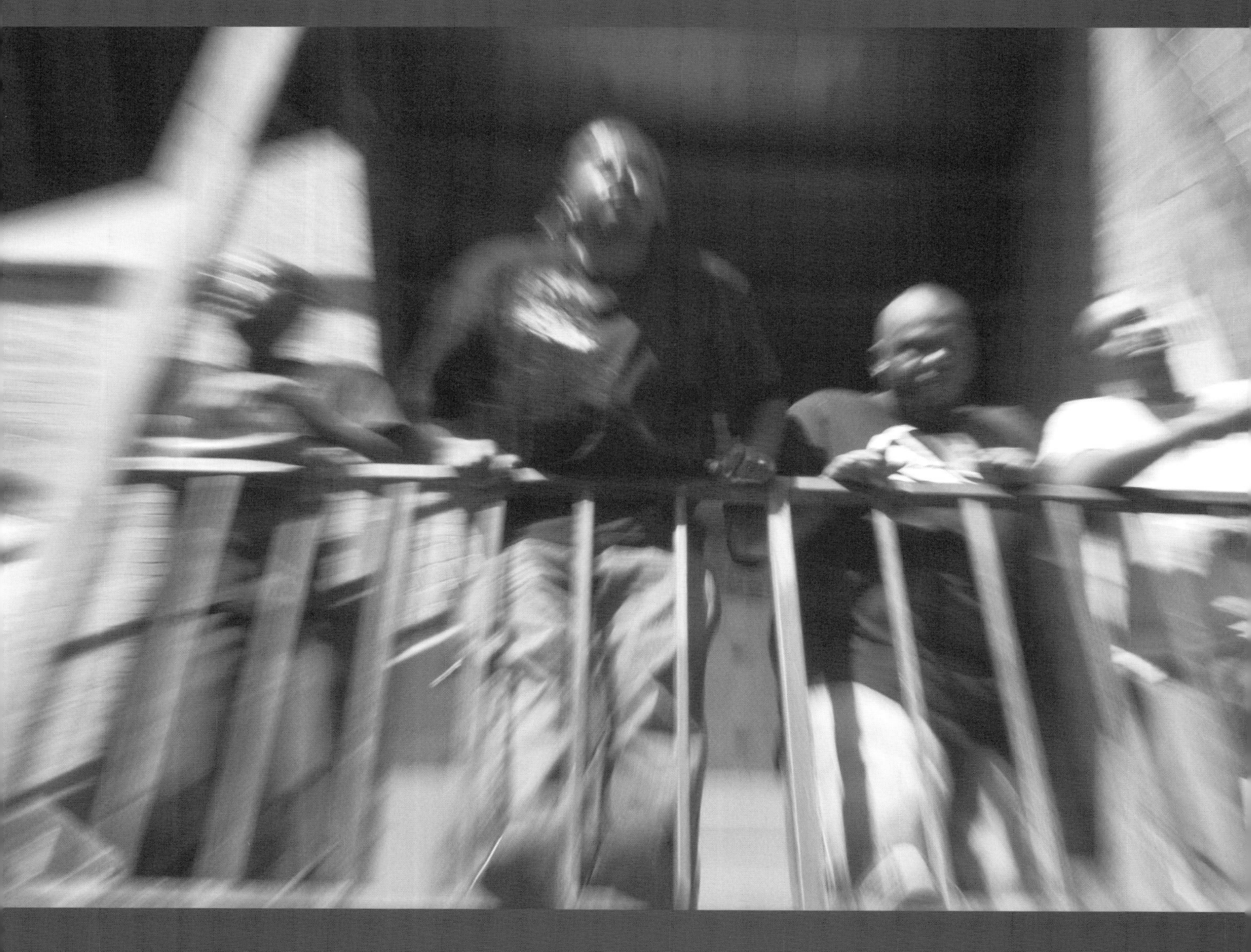

"ONE OF MY MOST rewarding philanthropic experiences occurred nearly a decade after I had established several college scholarships at my Chicago, inner-city public high school. As a requirement of the program, scholarship recipients are required to write a short letter describing their college aspirations. I was surprised and pleased to learn in reading one such letter that the student was the son of a close high school classmate of mine who I had not seen since our own graduation. Giving back pays forward and the circle is completed in unexpected ways."

Emmett D. Carson, Ph.D.
CEO and president of the Silicon Valley Community Foundation

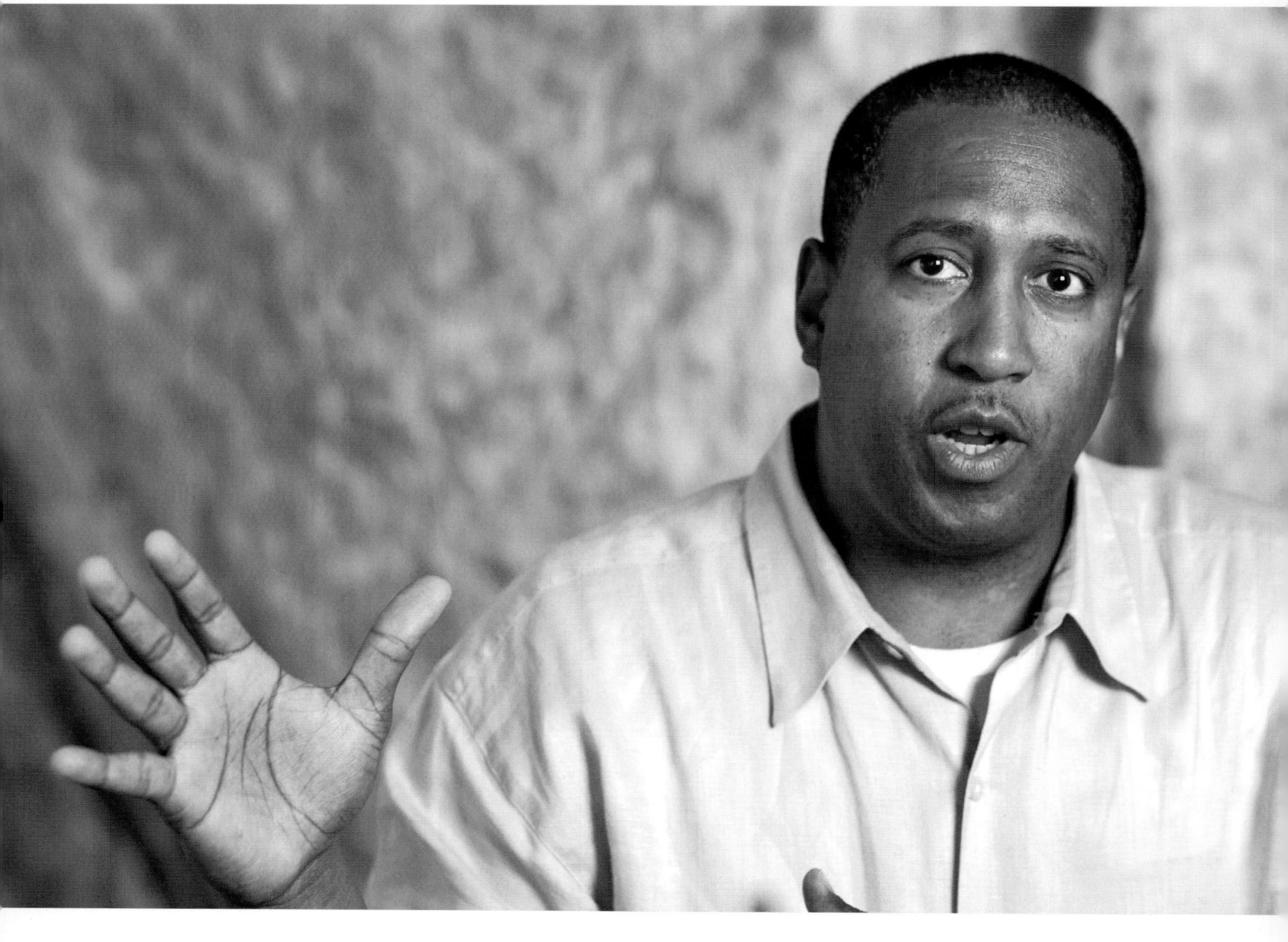

To give away money is an easy matter . . . and in any man's power. But to decide to whom to give it, and how large and when, for what purpose and how, is neither in every man's power nor an easy matter. Hence it is that such excellence is rare, praiseworthy and noble.

ARISTOTLE
Greek philosopher
(384 BC-322 BC)

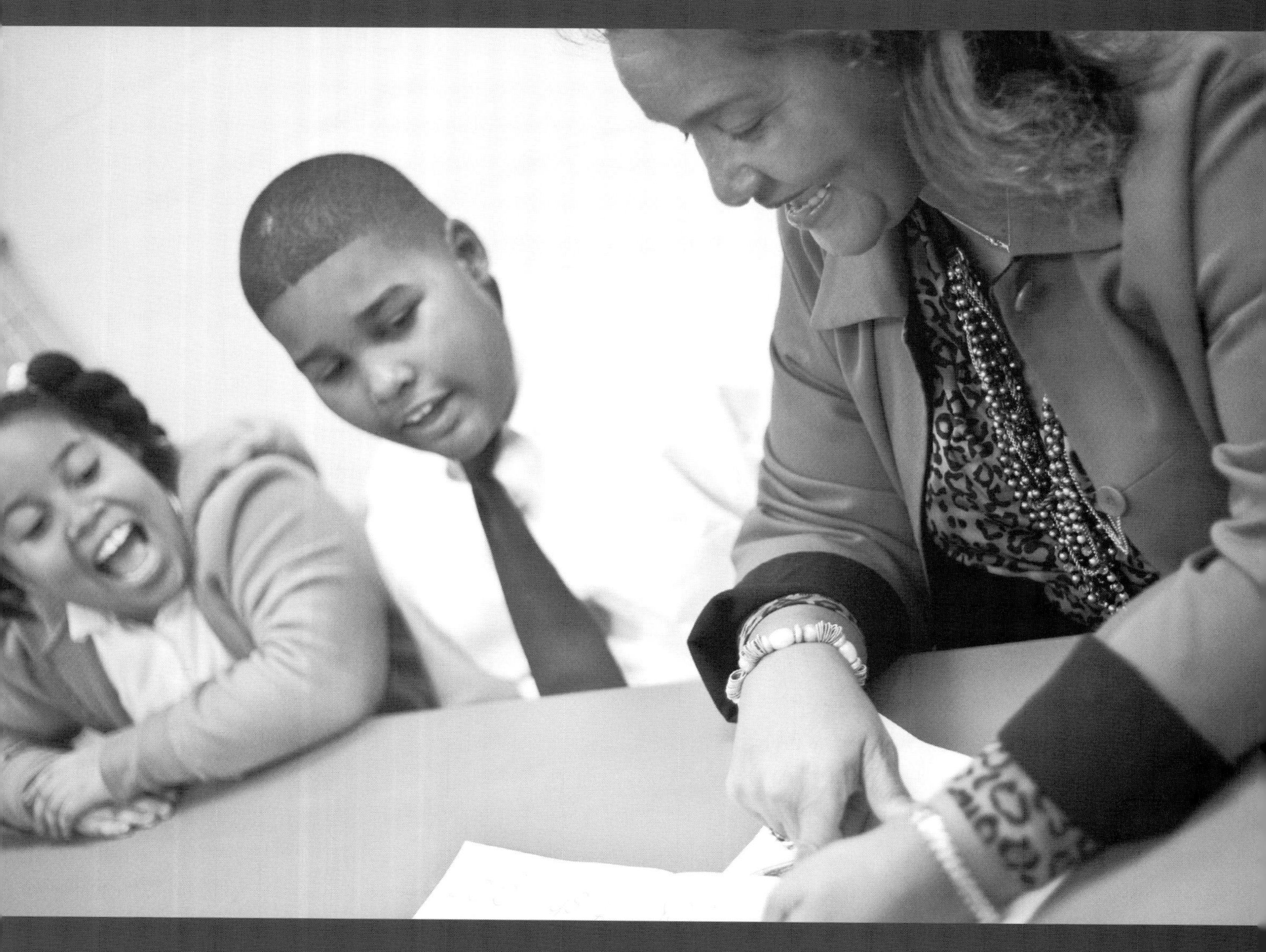

"THE WIT AND WISDOM of my grandmother lends a saying about *reasonable service* that I often use to encourage others in their philanthropy. Edith Lindsay reminded her grandchildren that whenever we are seeking to serve others we should always do that which is reasonable to the receiver and for the giver. She counseled that when others are in need, take appropriate action to meet their needs, without creating dependency or an undue load. Too often in our efforts to serve we don't act in a manner that restores dignity and too often we neglect taking care of ourselves. Rekindling another's dignity without burning out our own is doing one's reasonable service."

Athan Lindsay
founder of the Lindsay Legacy Fund, a family charitable fund

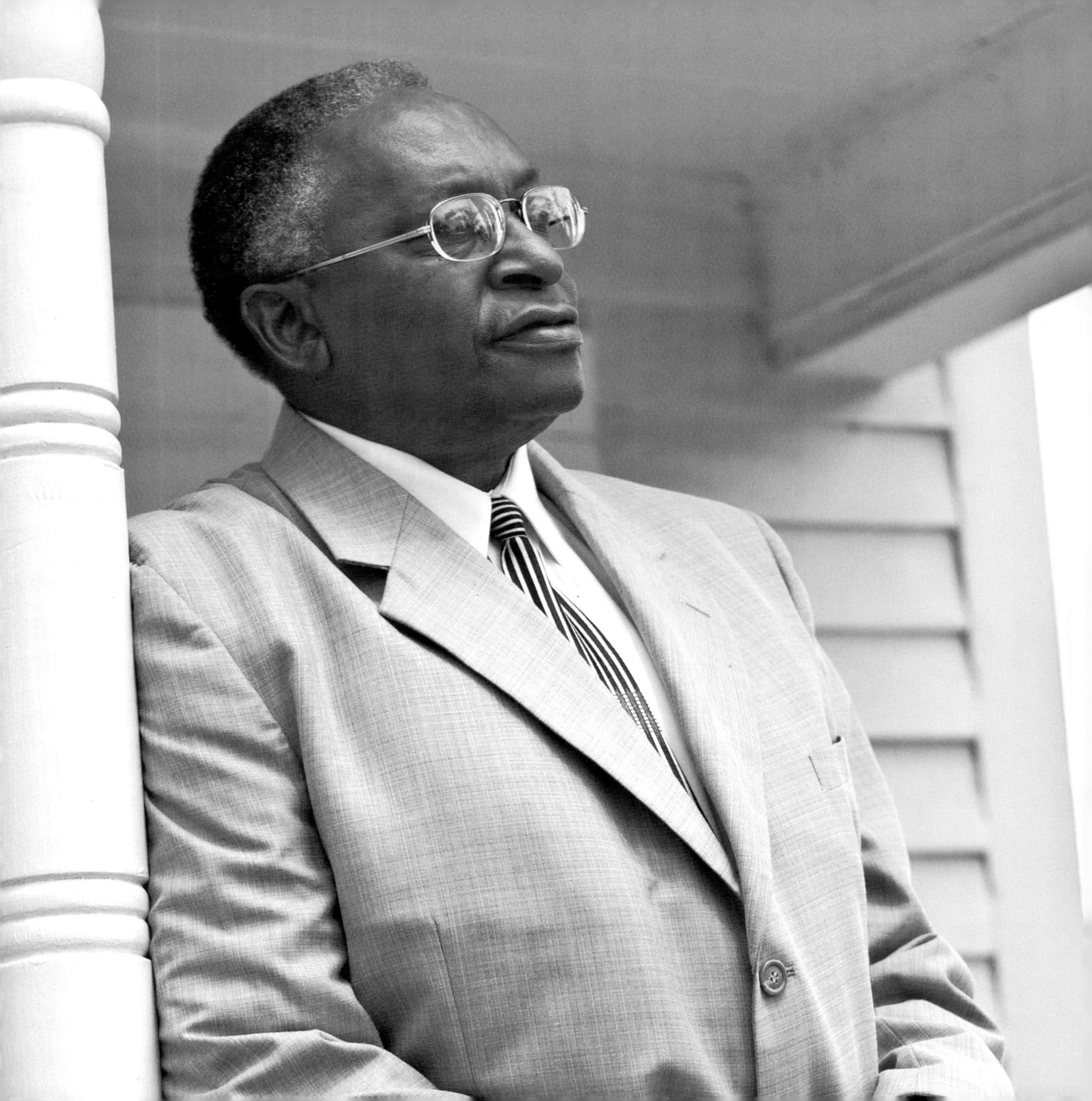

If you want to lift yourself up, lift someone else up.

BOOKER T. WASHINGTON
American educator, orator and political leader
(1856-1915)

Carlotta & Johnnie Jones | UNCOMMON COMMON PEOPLE

Dad is a one of those outgoing types who talks to every shopper in the grocery line. Mom is on the quiet side and more apt to relish a good book. While my parents' personalities are yards apart, their values are tightly aligned.

Sweethearts since high school, Mom and Dad grew up in the small, rural town of Enfield, North Carolina. Rooted in a place where the dirt is richer than most people, their families instilled strong beliefs about looking out for neighbors. In turn, my parents gifted those values to my sister Roslyn and me while raising us in Durham. We began serving our community so early and often that it became a natural part of life. I remember as kids we would make goodie bags and dole them out at Oxford Children's Home, nursing homes and among friends who could use them.

Roslyn and I have branched away from Durham, and yet our parents' concern for others still grounds us. Dedicated to Pilgrim Baptist Church, they tithe as well as donate to charities, faithfully every month. Multiple sclerosis has only strengthened my mother's resolve to champion the underdog and care for the elderly. With grown daughters, Dad now mentors impressionable boys on becoming impressive men. As our parents' ways of giving have expanded, so too has their ability to give. Described working class for a time, they are blessed with far more financial security today.

A huge full-circle moment occurred recently that affirmed our family's values. While in Baltimore for a funeral, we caused a flash reunion of people with roots in Enfield who had heard the Joneses were in town. Men and women I had never met flocked around my parents and grandmother to express gratitude for how our family helped their relatives generations prior. Middle-aged folks gushed about kind deeds from their childhood like they had occurred yesterday. For the first time I heard stories about how my people gave produce from the family farm to feed kids at the school, took in others' relatives and seemed always to cook enough for anybody who was hungry. The sacrifice and creativity shown by my kin when they too were surely struggling struck me most.

When Roslyn and I were little, we used to wonder whether all the things our parents had us do would ever make a difference. On that visit to Baltimore, I got a glimpse of what having a generational impact on lives looks like.

MELANDEE JONES

Connection: *Daughter* • Channel: *Coach and Volunteer, Special Olympics* • Cause: *Equal access to opportunities for minorities, women, children and the elderly*

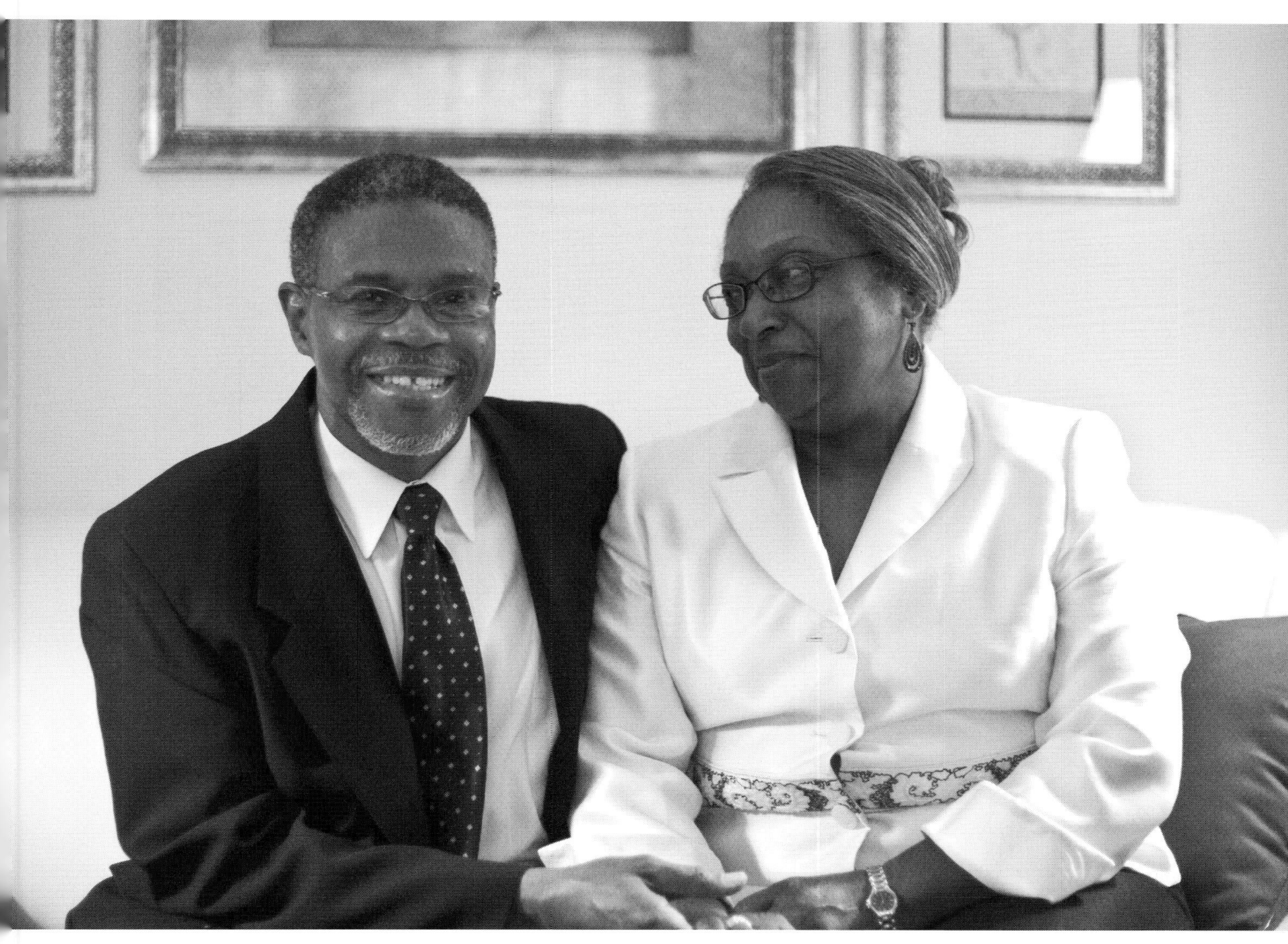

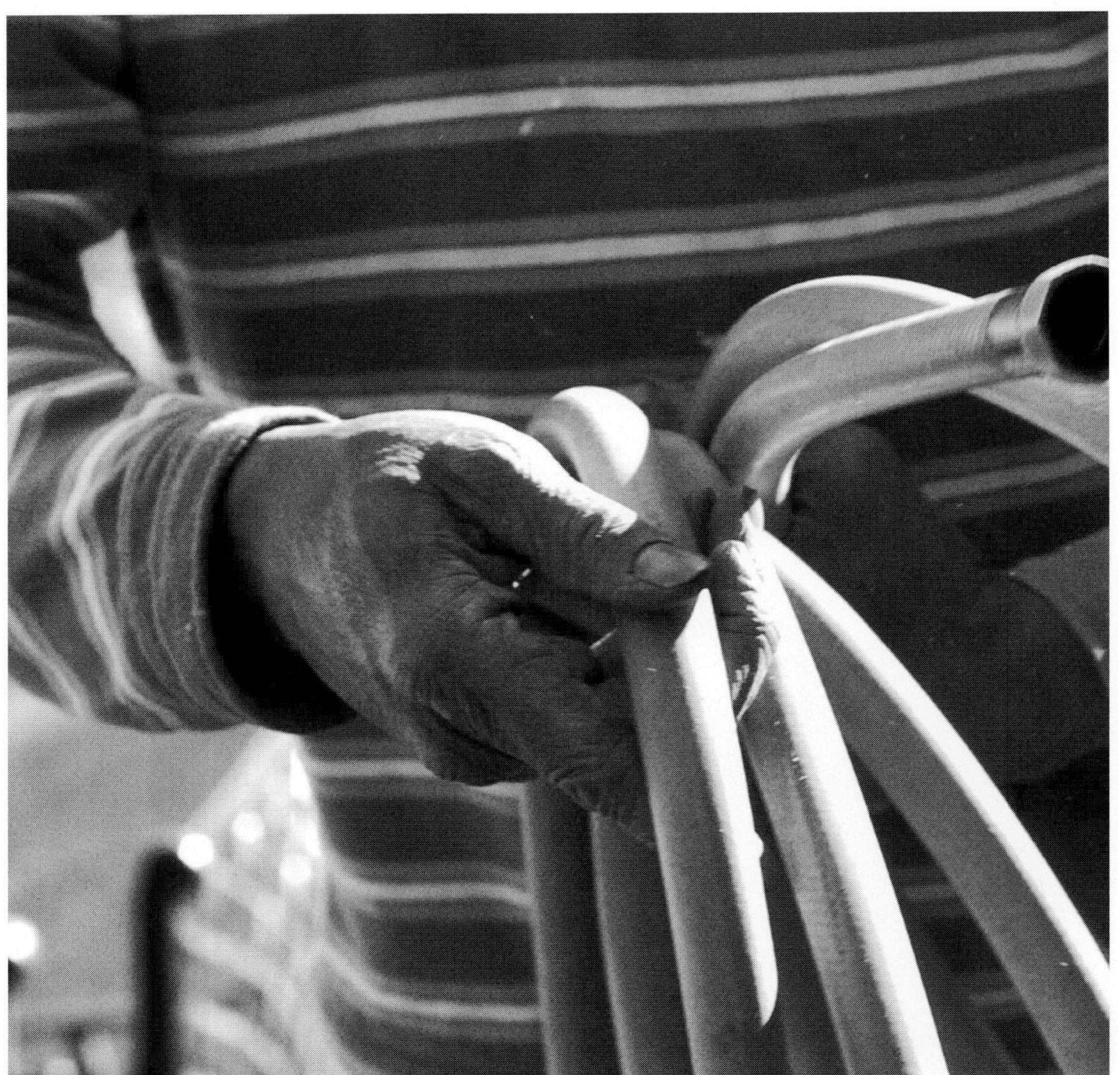

You must judge a man by the work of his hands.

AFRICAN PROVERB

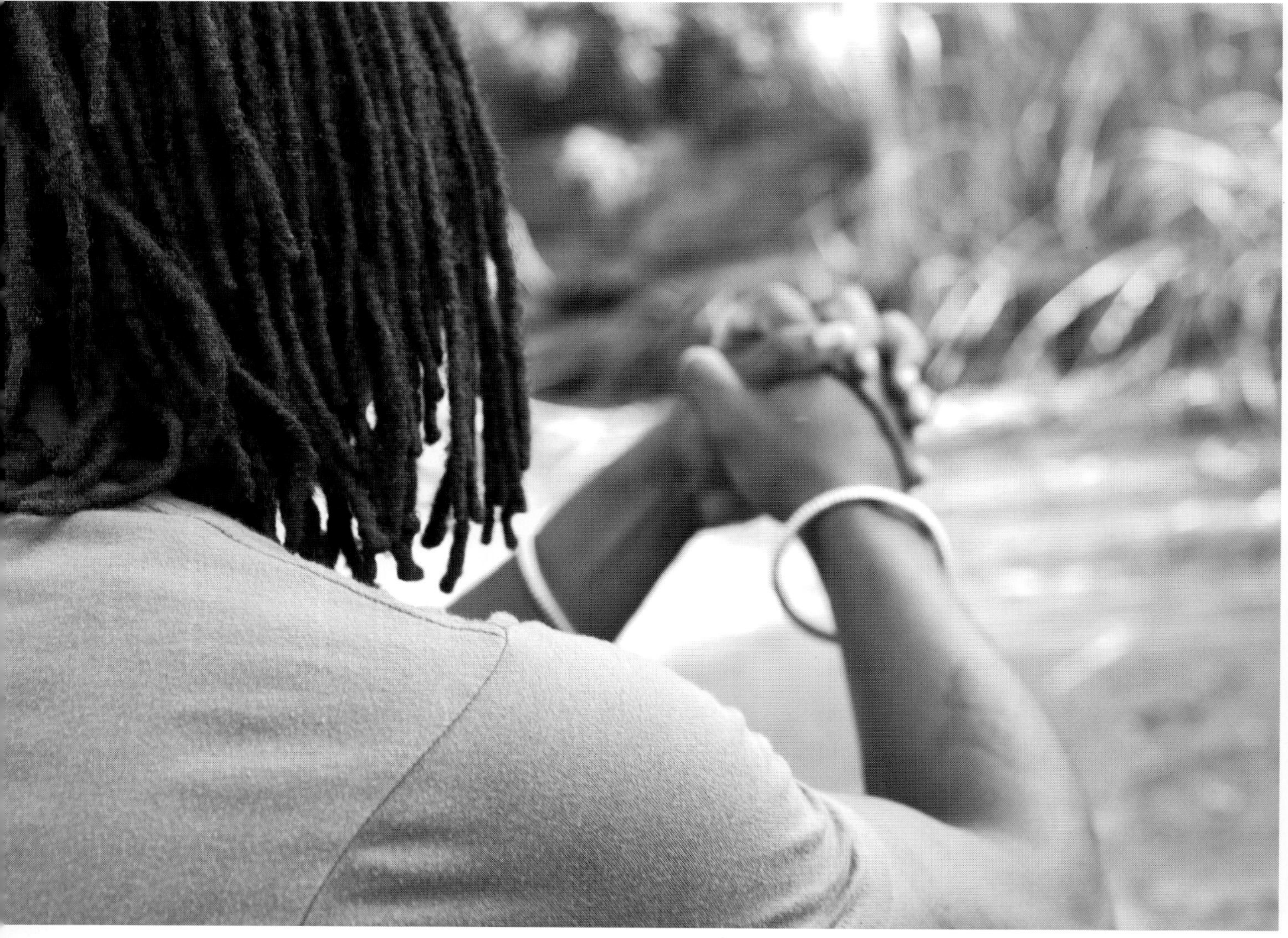

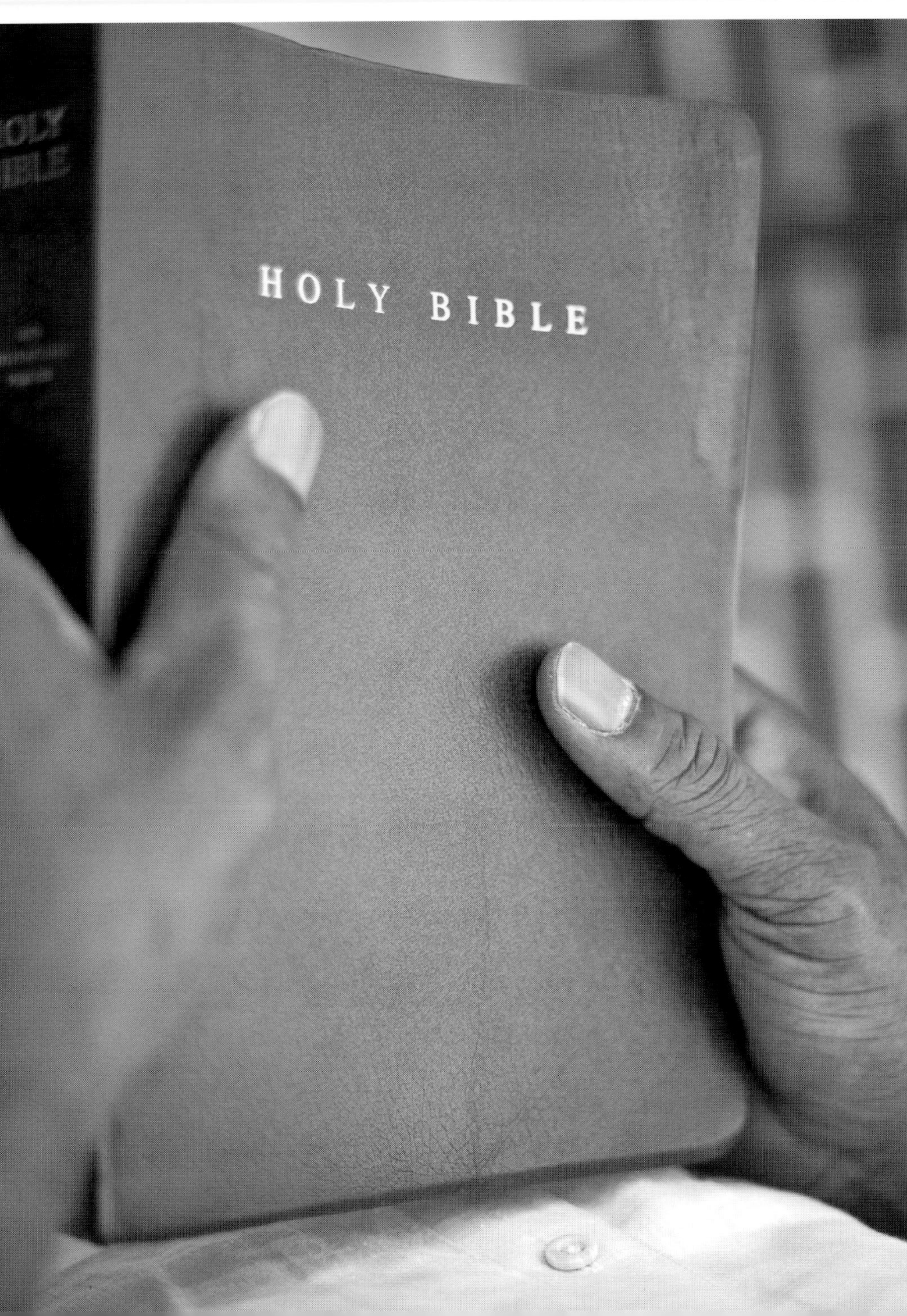
HOLY BIBLE
HOLY BIBLE

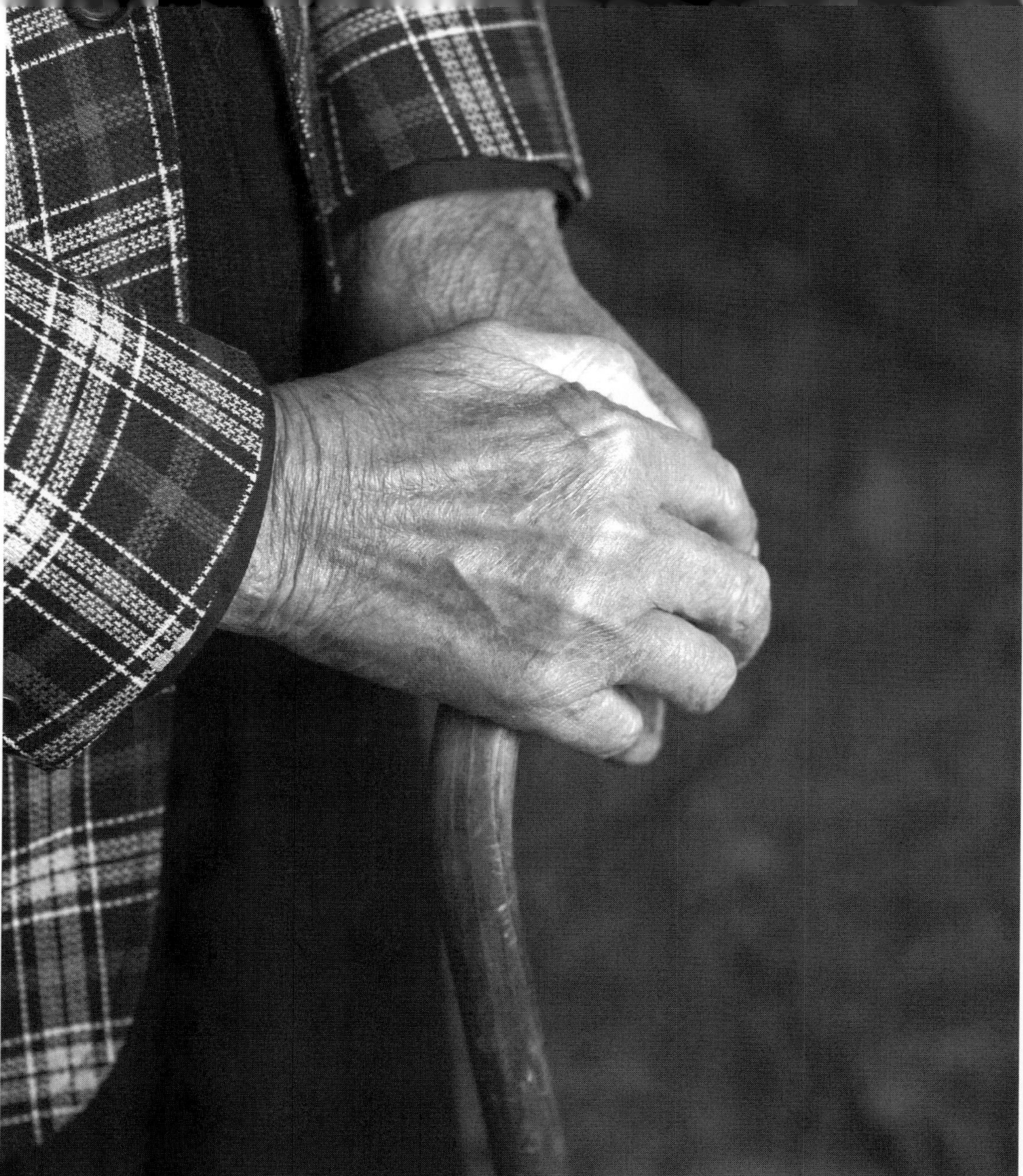

The past is a ghost, the future a dream. All we ever have is now.

BILL COSBY
American entertainer and author
(b. 1937)

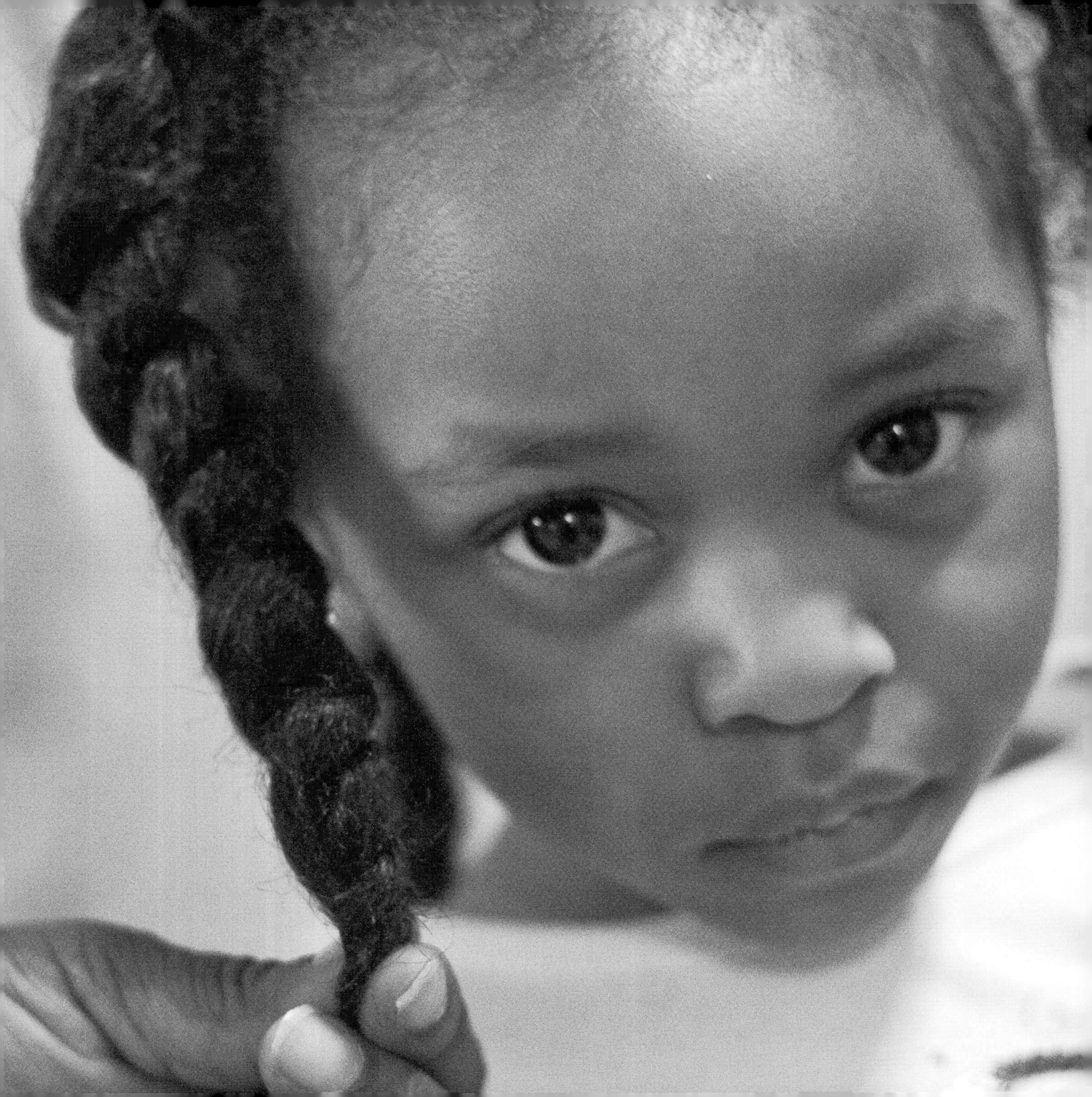

MESSAGES

What message would you offer to up-and-coming generations of givers?

First, giving back comes in all different forms . . . not just monetary. Second, there's no such thing as not having much to give. If you take what you have to offer and give back in a strategic manner, it will produce bigger results than you would imagine. Third, don't be afraid to let others know what you're doing, it may bring inspiration to them. — *Patricia Martelly*

African Americans should incorporate philanthropy into their mindset and treat giving like tithes and getting their hair done. — *Daryl Parham*

Philanthropy has always been a part of our history. — *Ihsan Abdin*

Get started early and make it a daily part of your life. — *Jeanene Thompson*

I am my brother's and sister's keeper. If I do not give, others can't be expected to give. — *Harvey Boyd*

I would encourage young people to look to their past to seek encouragement and motivation. We don't need popular figures or famous people to gain inspiration. Rely on your family for your road map and your path will present itself clearly, with reward, and in great abundance. — *Britt Brewer Loudd*

Giving is a gift that gives back. It's a blessing to be able to have something to give so why not share because someone gave to you. — *Ohmar Land*

To work together, transparently, to effect positive change in our community — *LaDawn Sullivan*

Giving involves more than your money. The blessings you get from giving are mutual to the giver and receiver. — *Denise Rowson*

No amount is ever too small. Whether it's your time or money, what you give to the community will come back to you tenfold. — *LaWana Mayfield*

Follow your passion! Find a cause or an issue that makes your spirit soar. Work with others to use philanthropy to support and advance this cause or issue. — *Jennifer Henderson*

Know the importance of our history and the contributions of African American philanthropists who simply used the 'village' approach . . . how we built churches with our gifts, talents and little funds. — *Mattie Marshall*

Think harder. — *Ed Fields*

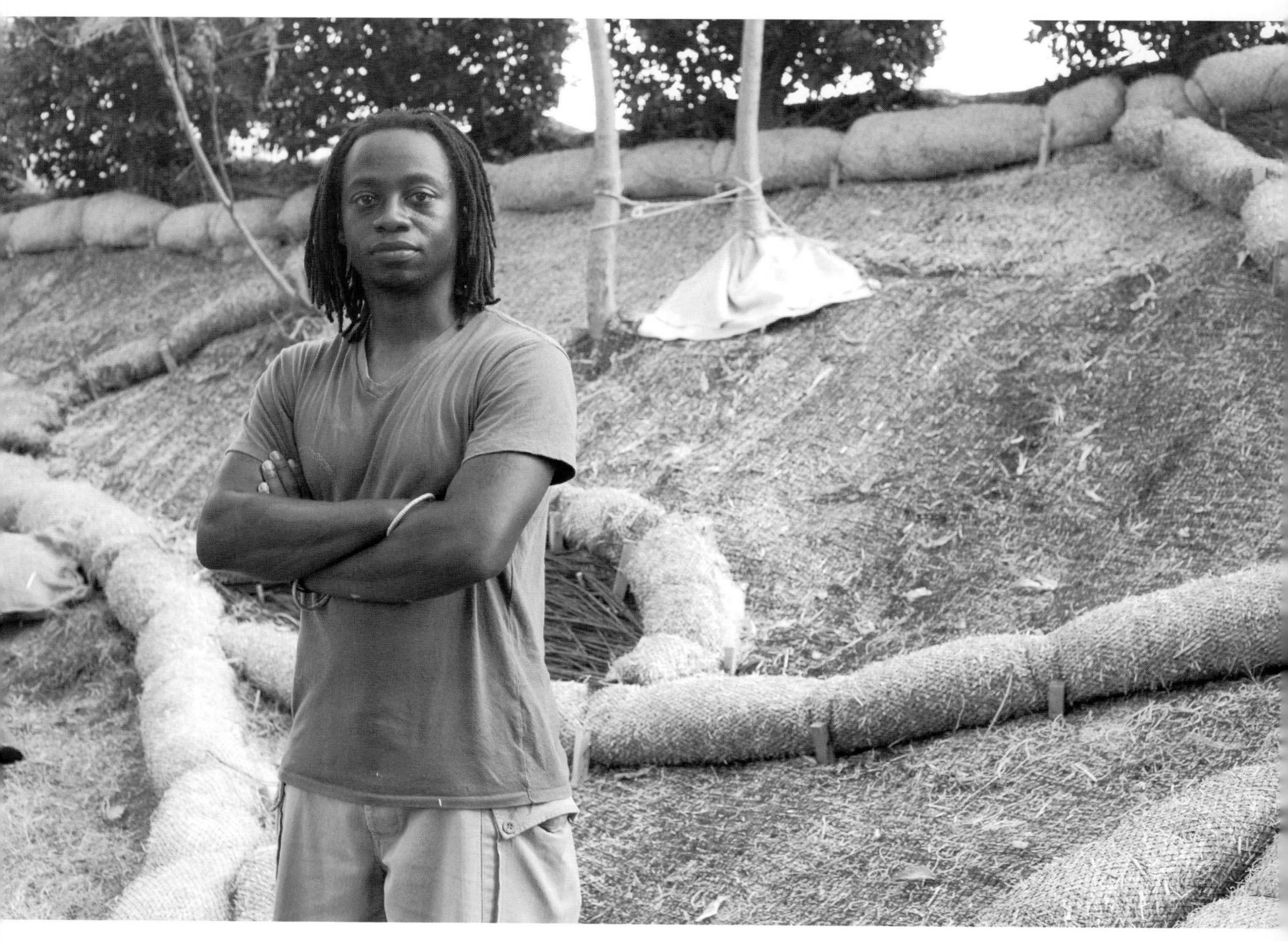

Throughout history it has been the inaction of those who could have acted, the indifference of those who should have known better, the silence of the voice of justice when it mattered most, that has made it possible for evil to triumph.

HAILE SELASSIE
Former Emperor of Ethiopia
(1892-1975)

Jelani Haskins | YOUNG, BLACK AND GIFTED

When teenage boys participate in The Males Place, the aim is to instill a sense of manhood, pride and culture and to impart knowledge about living a healthy and productive lifestyle. It is rare that a participant brings as much to the program as he takes away. Jelani is one of those extraordinary young men.

I met Jelani at J.T. Williams Middle School where he was an eighth-grade student. He appeared to be a kid who could benefit from our weekly program focused on manhood and leadership. Since enrolling in The Males Place, Jelani has revealed his bright light. He possesses strong leadership qualities and a genuine commitment to giving back. Acknowledging his talents and humility, the other program participants voted him president.

Even though volunteering is perceived un-cool by a lot of his peers, those attitudes fail to dissuade Jelani. He is hands-on with our community garden and our other service projects. On days when school is out, he visits and reads scripture to the elderly at Loving Touch Adult Day Health Care Center, where clients are "adopted grandparents" to our teens. Jelani has even shared his thoughts about various matters in a letter to the White House, and he received a response from President Obama.

Mighty and *powerful* are translations of the East African name Jelani. From the origin of his name to his promise as a servant leader, Jelani Haskins embodies the warrior spirit and values our program promotes. At fifteen years old, he has raised the bar for all of us.

REGGIE SINGLETON
Connection: *Program Elder* ◆ Channel: *Director, The Males Place* ◆ Cause: *Positively guiding youth through direct services and advocacy*

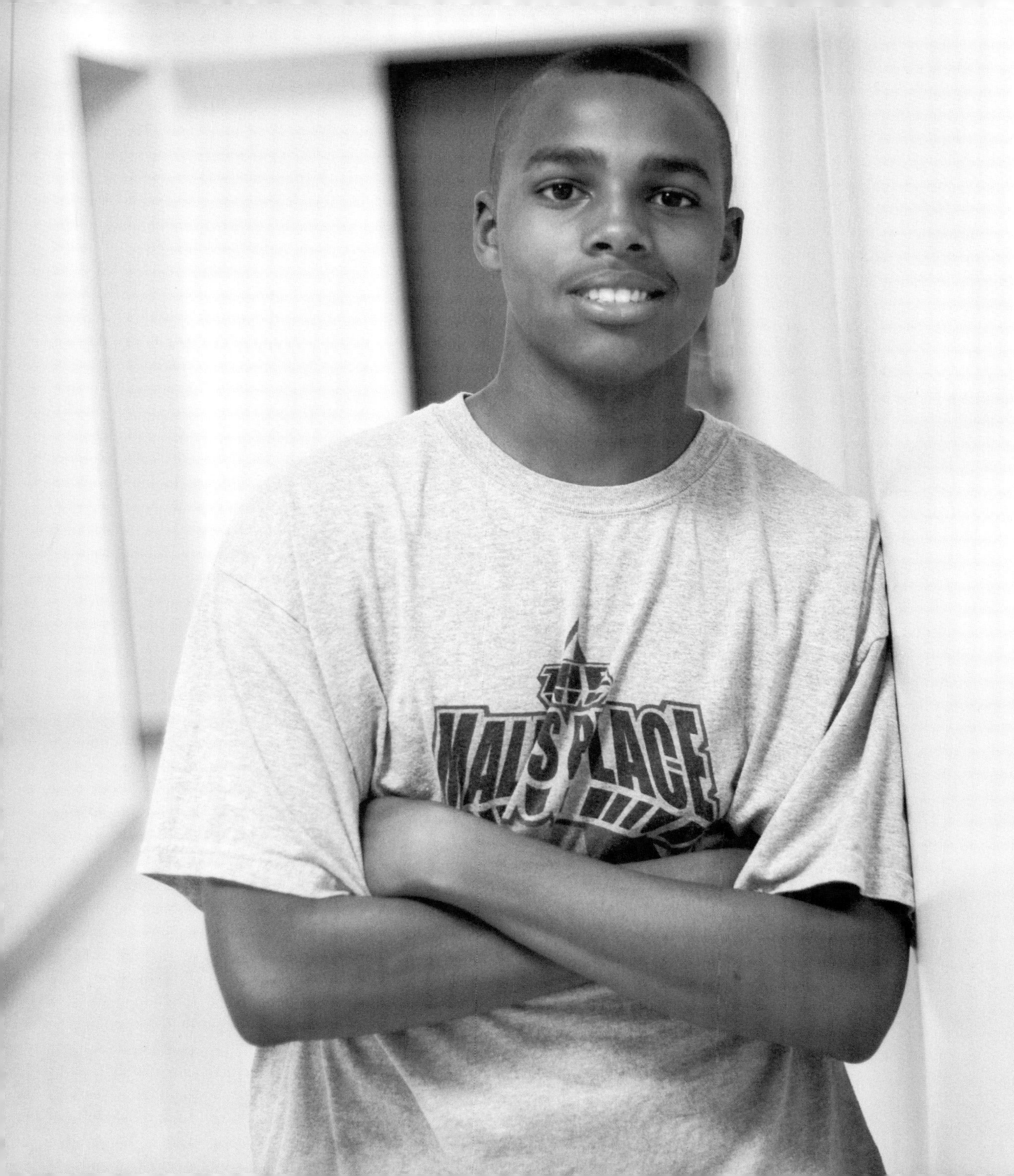

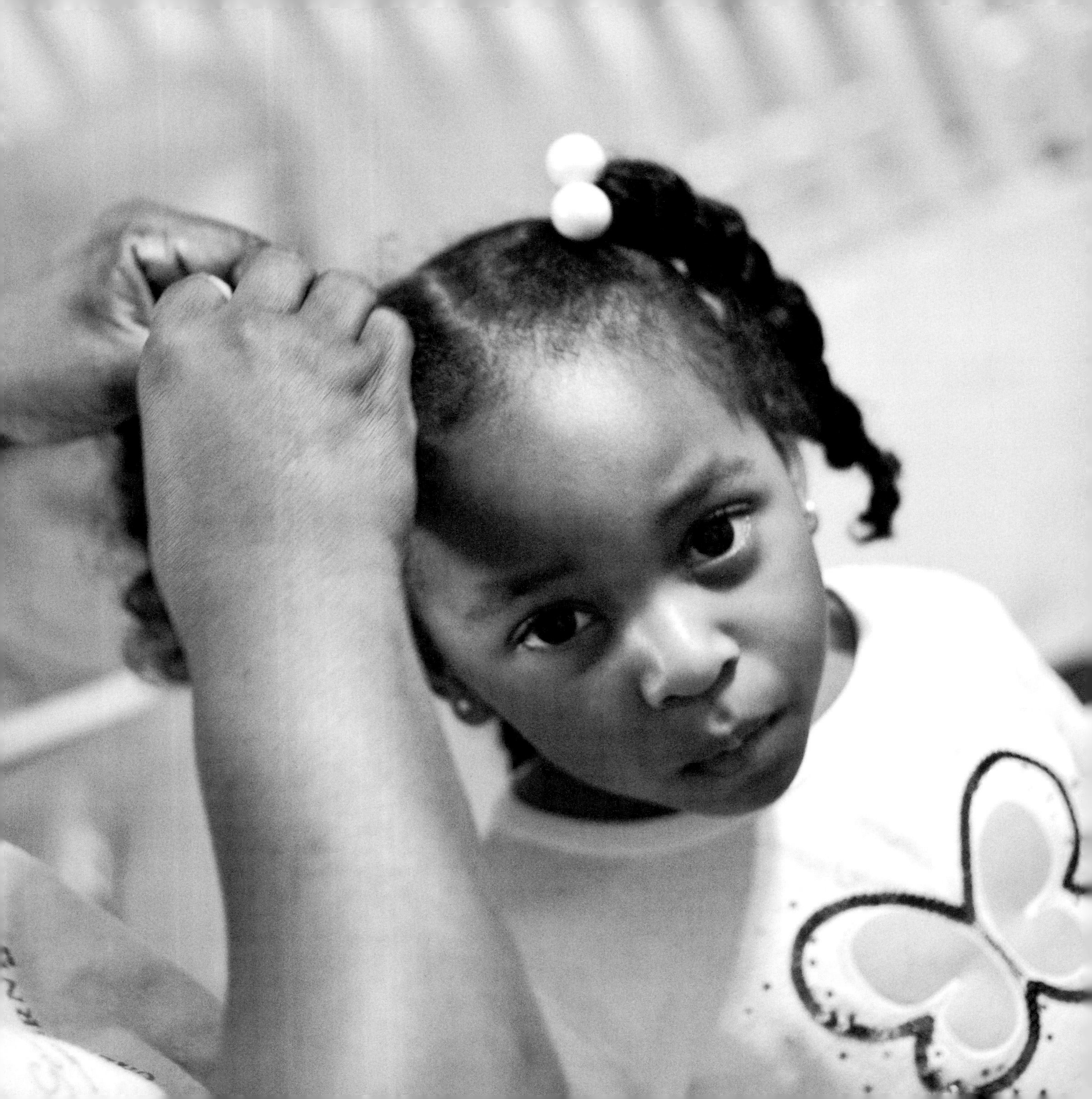

May the favor of the Lord our God rest upon us; establish the work of our hands for us—yes, establish the work of our hands.

PSALM 90:17

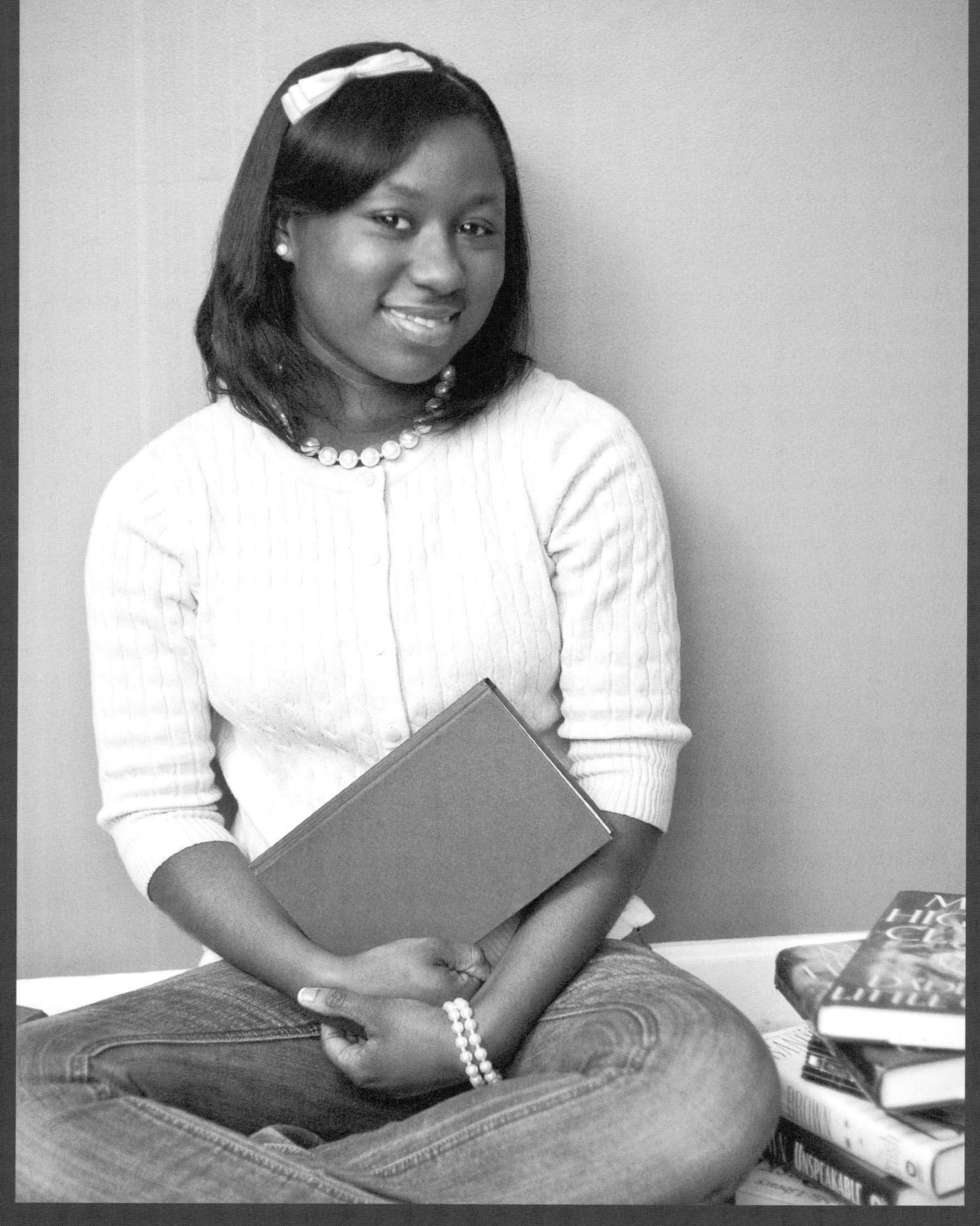

"A CHRISTMAS CELEBRATION for children of incarcerated parents takes place at my church every year. We present a program followed by dinner and gifts. I wanted to do something special, more than just a Christmas celebration. We had seen the kids for almost five years and didn't really know each other. I wanted to make a difference and so came the idea of PEN Pals Book Club. It is designed as a literacy-based organization. The children attend plays, social functions, sporting events and perform community service projects. I wanted them to know success even in their present situation."

Olivia Stinson, 16
founder of PEN Pals Book Club and
Support Group for Children of Incarcerated Parents

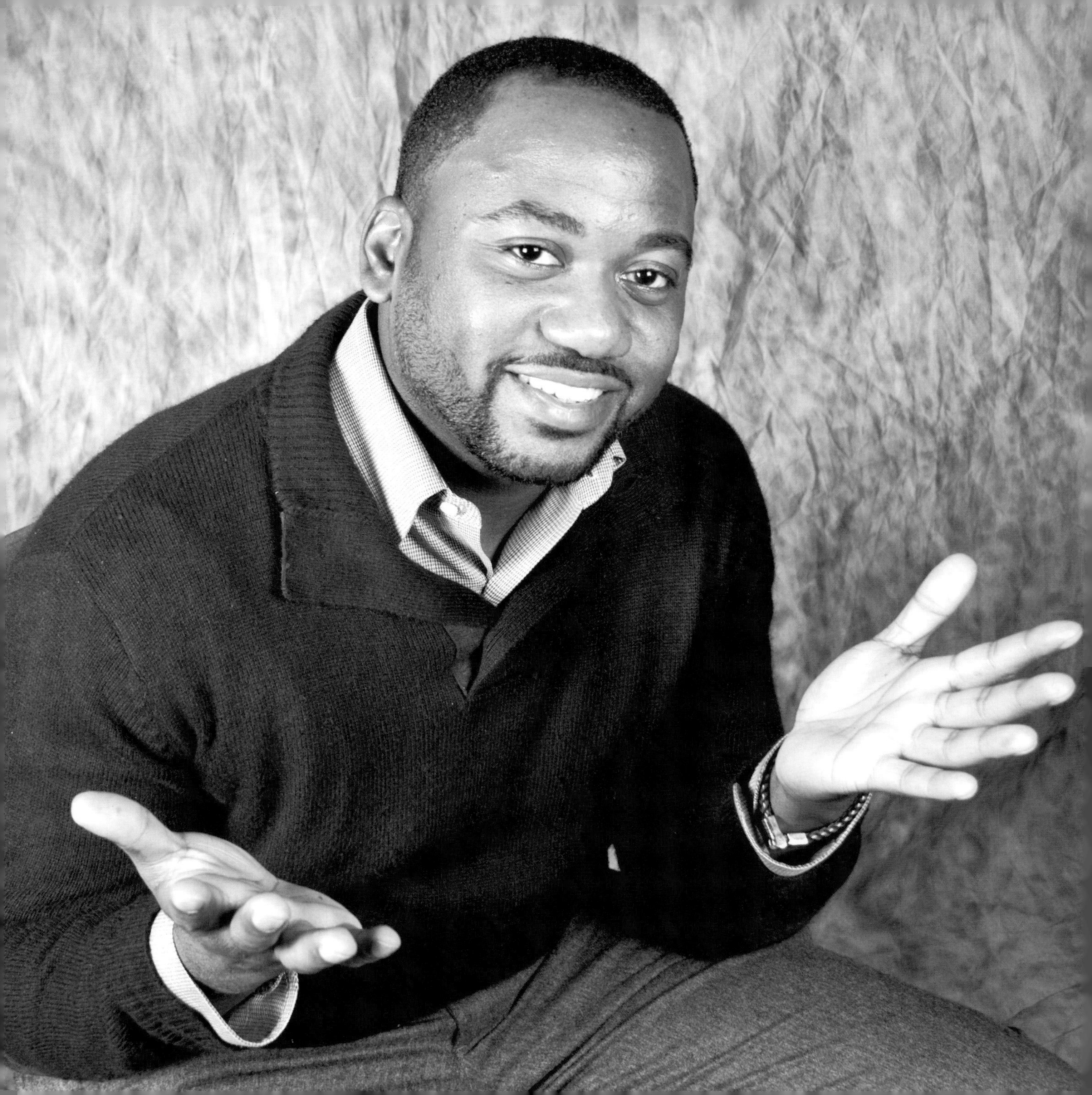

Do what you can,
with what you have,
where you are.

THEODORE ROOSEVELT
26th President of the United States
(1858-1919)

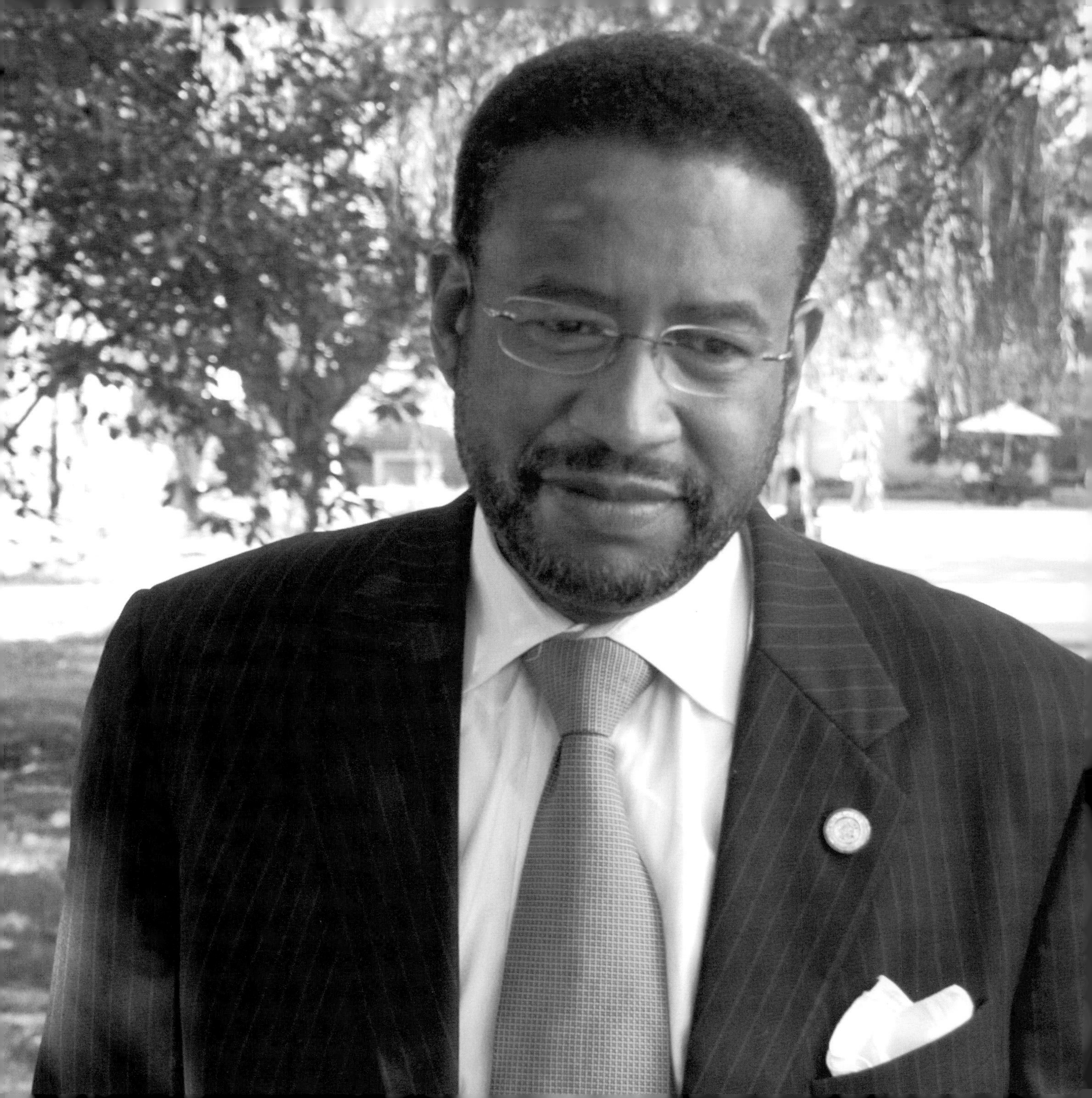

A man's true wealth is the good he does in this world.

MOHAMMED
Founder of Islam
(circa 570-632)

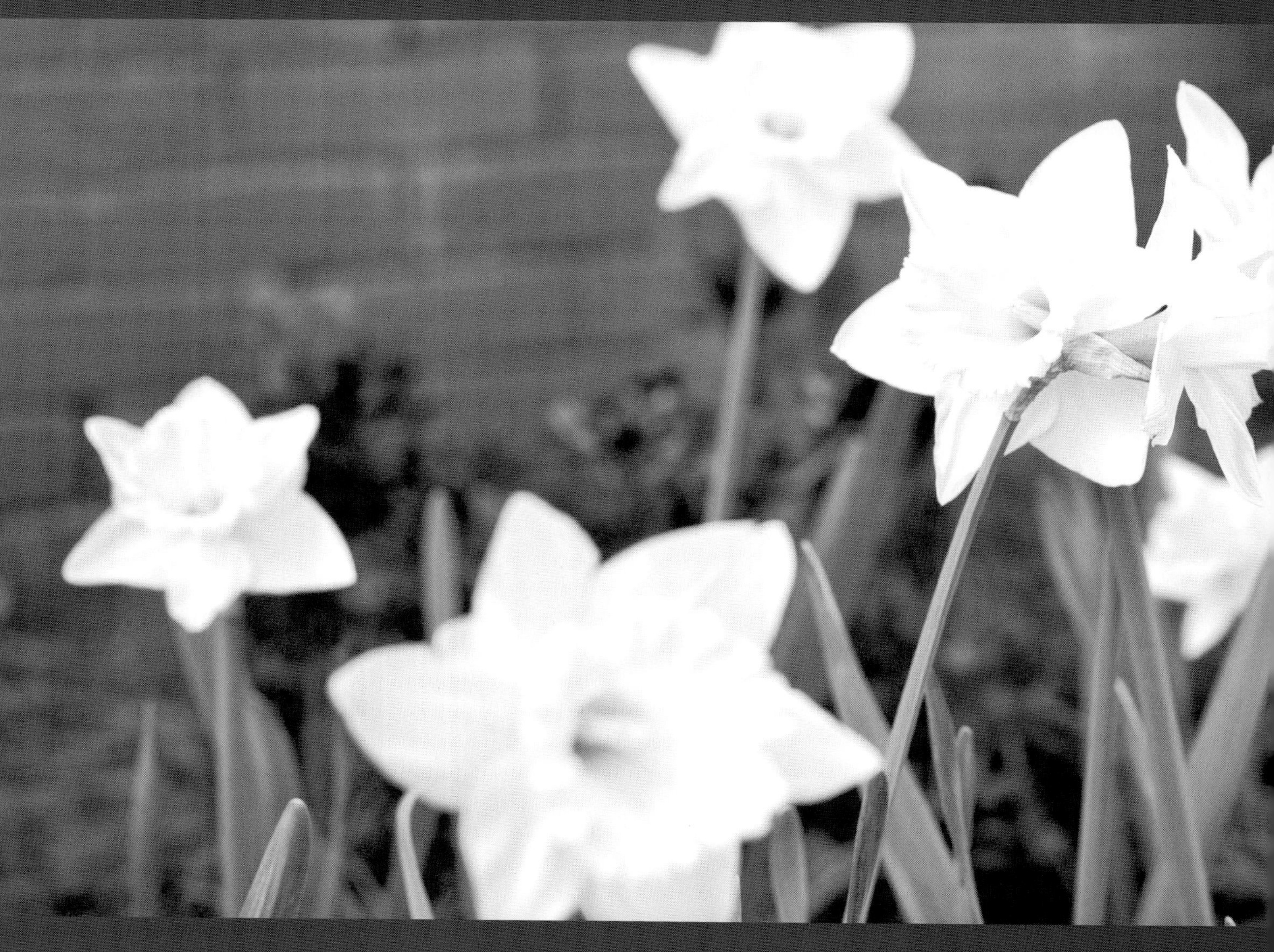

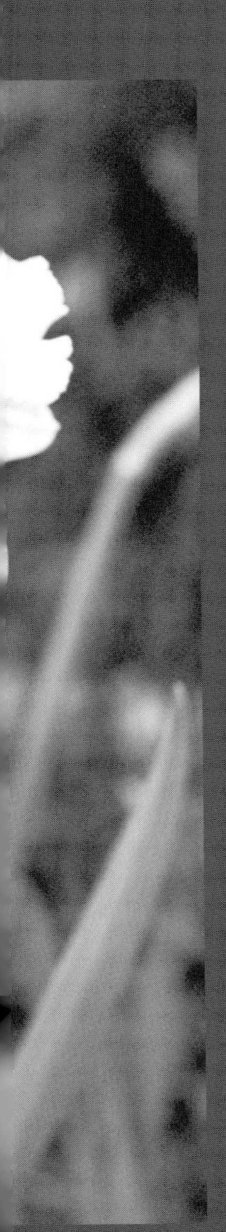

"THERE WERE SIX OF US, and I give because of what my parents taught us. My mother and father did just day work because they were not high school graduates. We're all high school graduates. They told us we had a responsibility and how you should be responsible and accountable.

"We are here for a purpose, and we should find that purpose and fulfill it. It blossoms when you know you're here for a purpose. We have a responsibility to answer that call."

Thereasea C. Elder
eighty-three-year-old founder of the Greenville Community Historical Society Inc.

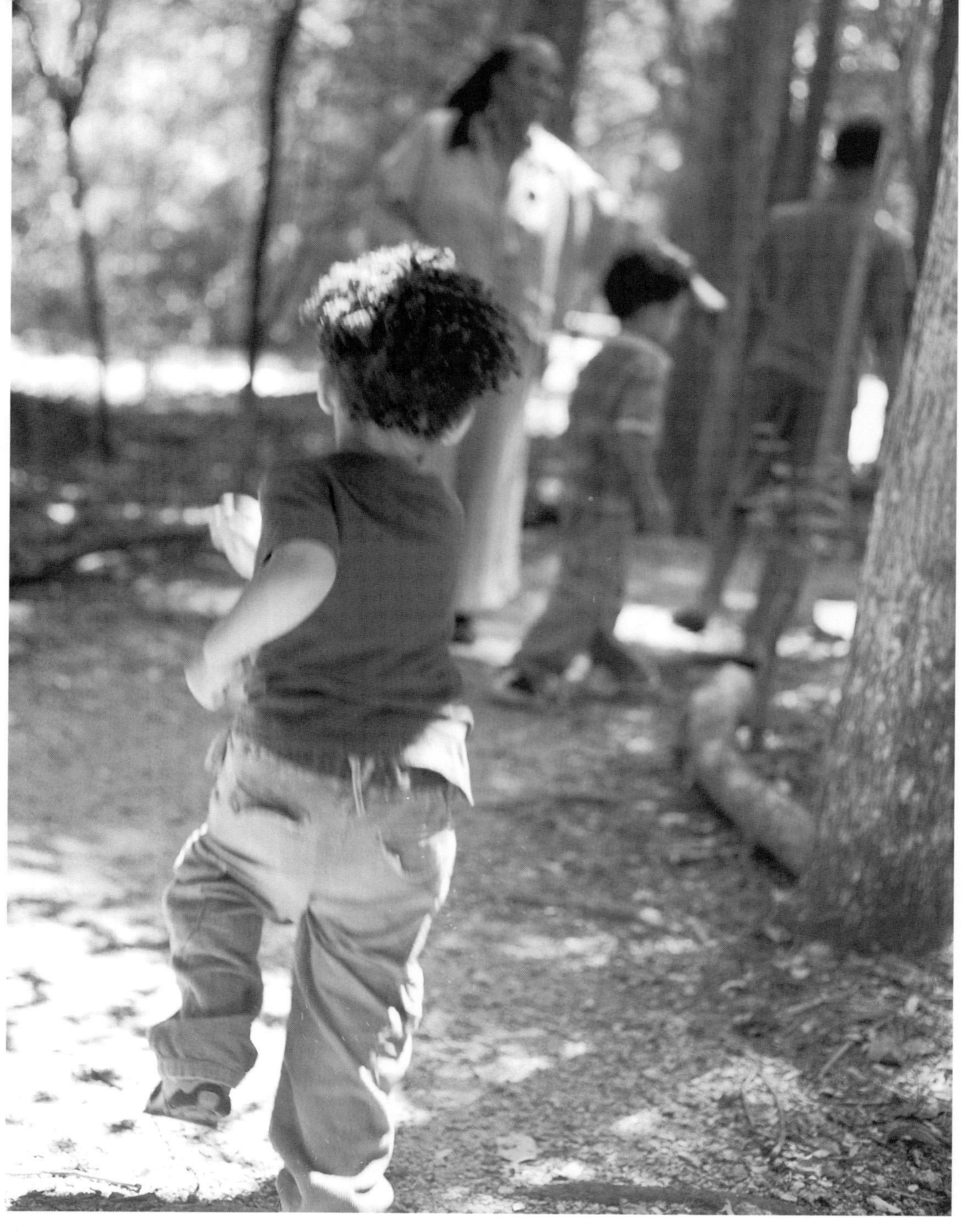

How far you go in life depends on you being tender with the young, compassionate with the aged, sympathetic with the striving and tolerant of the weak and the strong. Because someday in life you will have been all of these.

GEORGE WASHINGTON CARVER
American scientist, educator and inventor
(1864-1943)

Saundra Porter Thomas | GENEROUS SPIRIT

Most would say the odds were against Saundra Porter Thomas, but she decided early in life not to be defined by circumstances. Instead, she used her circumstances to propel her into a fulfilling life. She was a teenager when she dropped out of high school to become a wife and mother—my mother. The marriage ended, but the bond between my mother and me is unshakable. As her only child, I relish our closeness and have been inspired by her decision to have me and to mother me unconditionally.

During my childhood, we lived in an apartment complex in the Grier Heights neighborhood. Years after we had moved from Grier Heights, my mother returned to the same set of apartments, now as the property manager. *A coincidence?* Not hardly. She seized the opportunity to give back to a community that had given us so much. Most of the residents received public assistance, and understanding their struggles, she went far beyond her job duties to be supportive.

I recall how she stepped up to design and run a successful after-school program for neighborhood kids and their parents. She would help residents with rides to work, résumé writing and spiritual advice. She would stand in at a PTA meeting when a parent was unable to go. And sometimes she would even pay residents' rent without them knowing it. My mother gave from the heart, again unconditionally, and supported others to reclaim their power to pursue full lives. I learned to become an advocate by how she stood up for people during the times they couldn't do it alone.

Growing older and becoming a father, I now comprehend the significance of her generosity towards so many people. I am particularly grateful for the less-than-easy choices she made to benefit me. Insight into her sacrifices and values is gained by sharing the fact that my first day at work after graduating from Duke University was her very first day of college.

CHARLES W. THOMAS JR.

Connection: *Son* ◆ Channel: *Board vice chair, Community Charter School* ◆ Cause: *Child-centered education and fostering social enterprises*

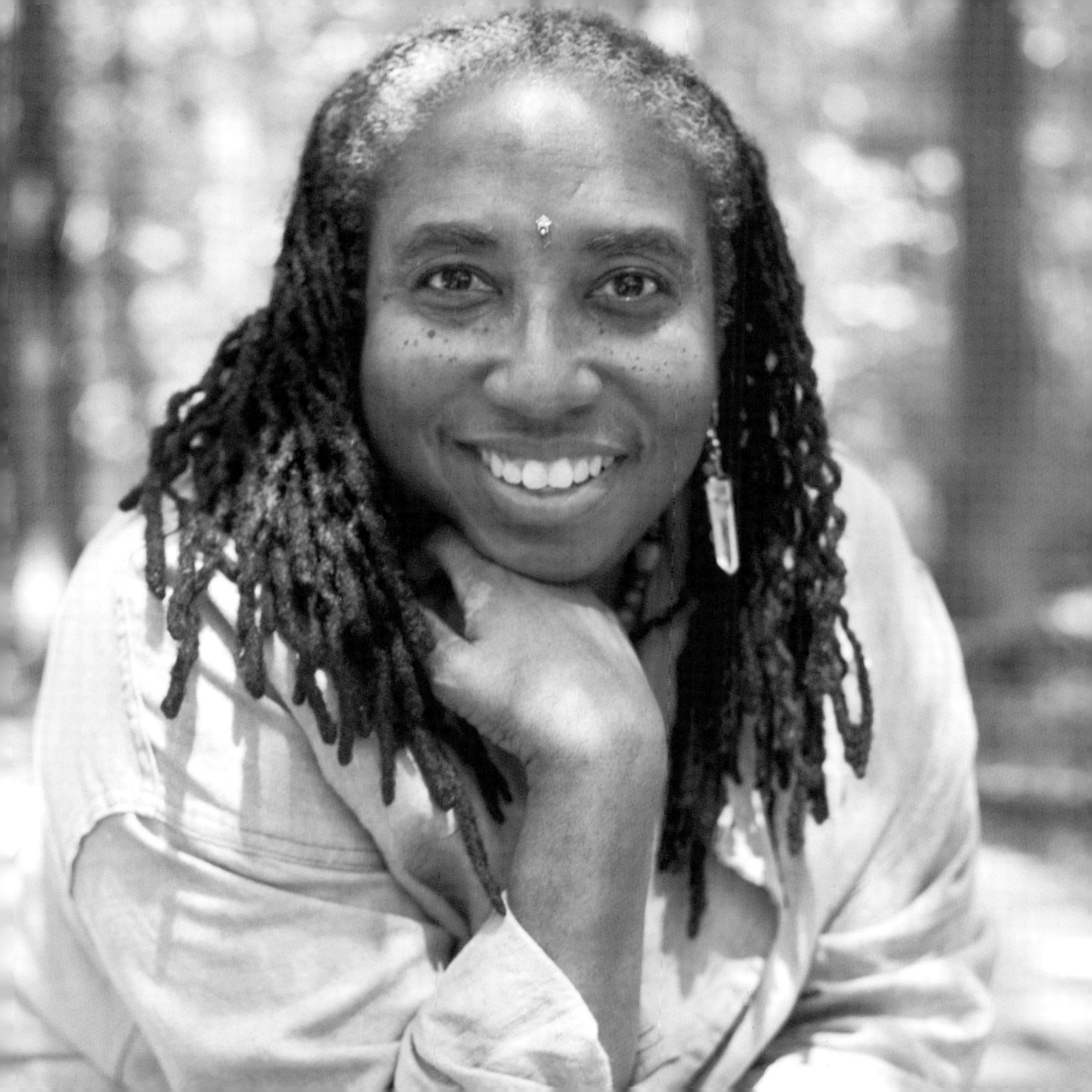

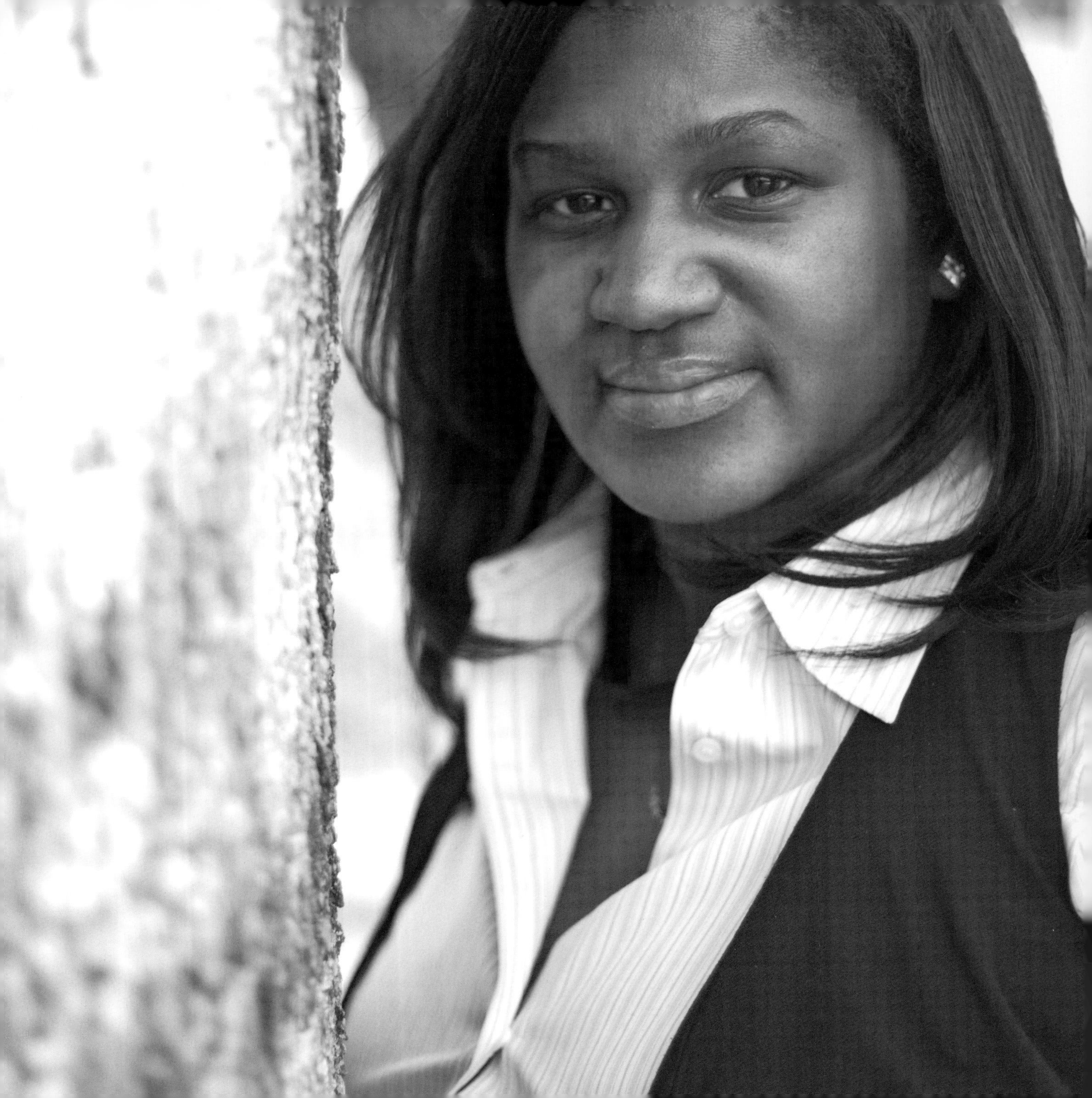

A people without the knowledge of their past history, origin and culture is like a tree without roots.

MARCUS GARVEY
Jamaican orator, publisher and leader of Pan-African movement
(1887-1940)

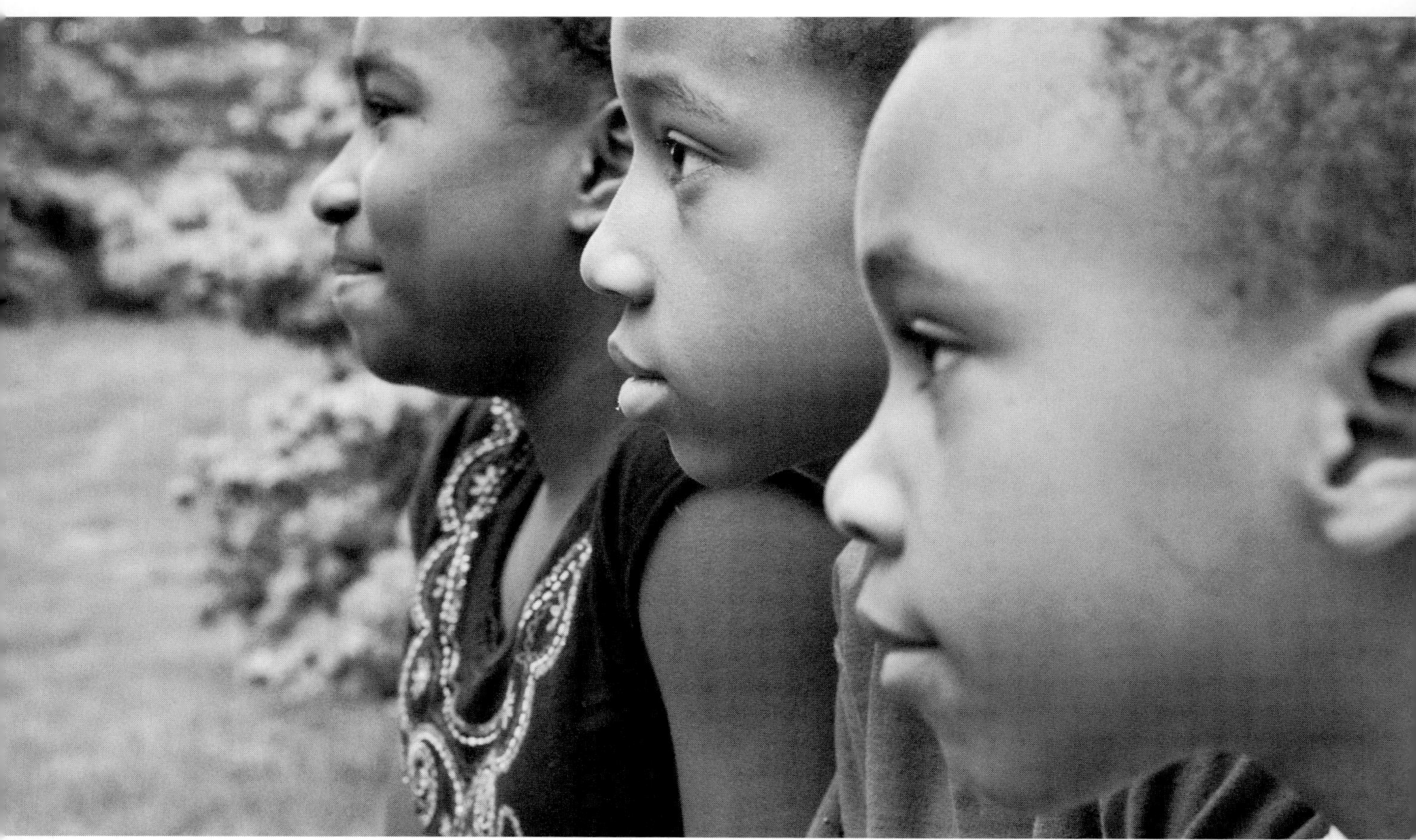

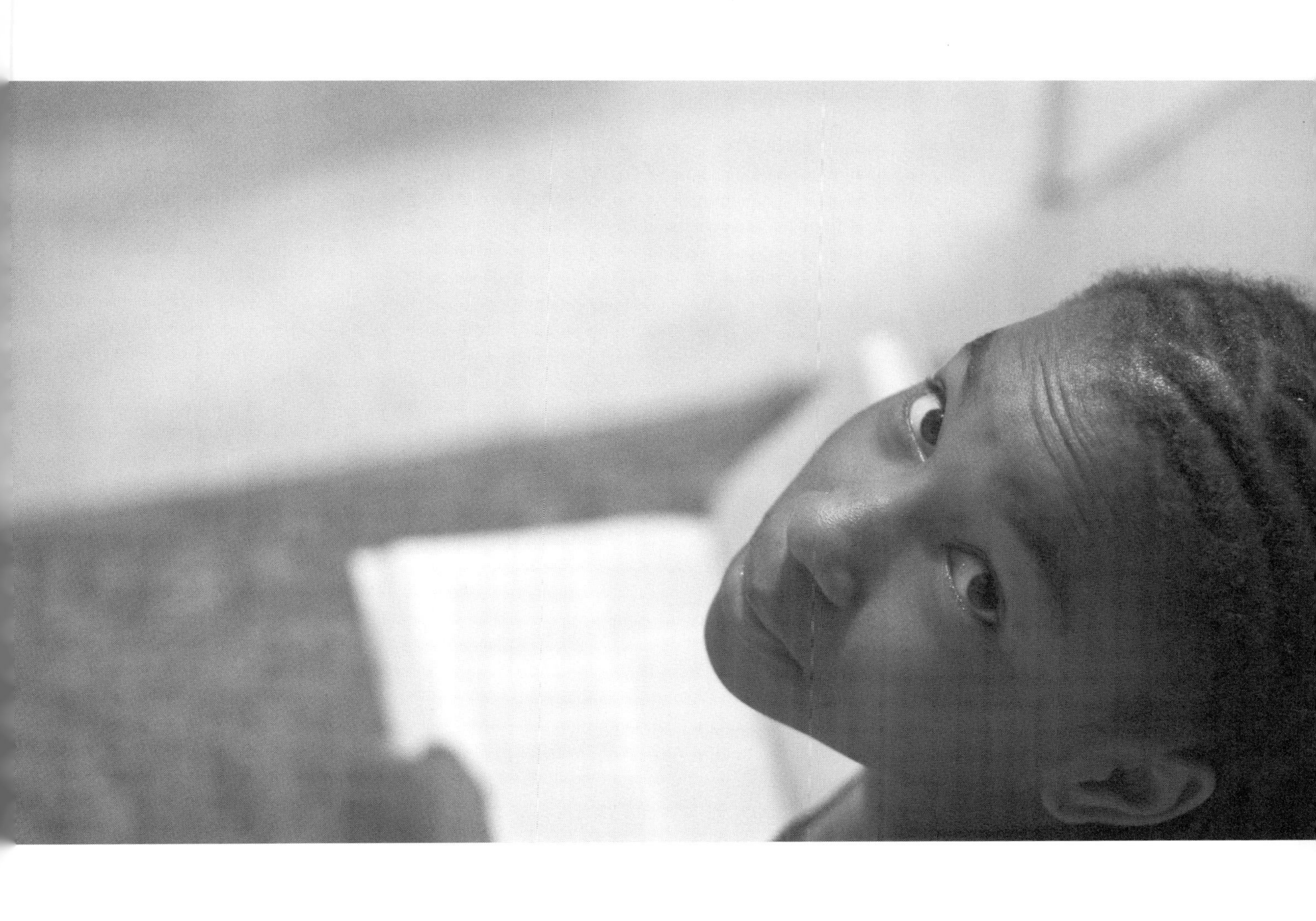

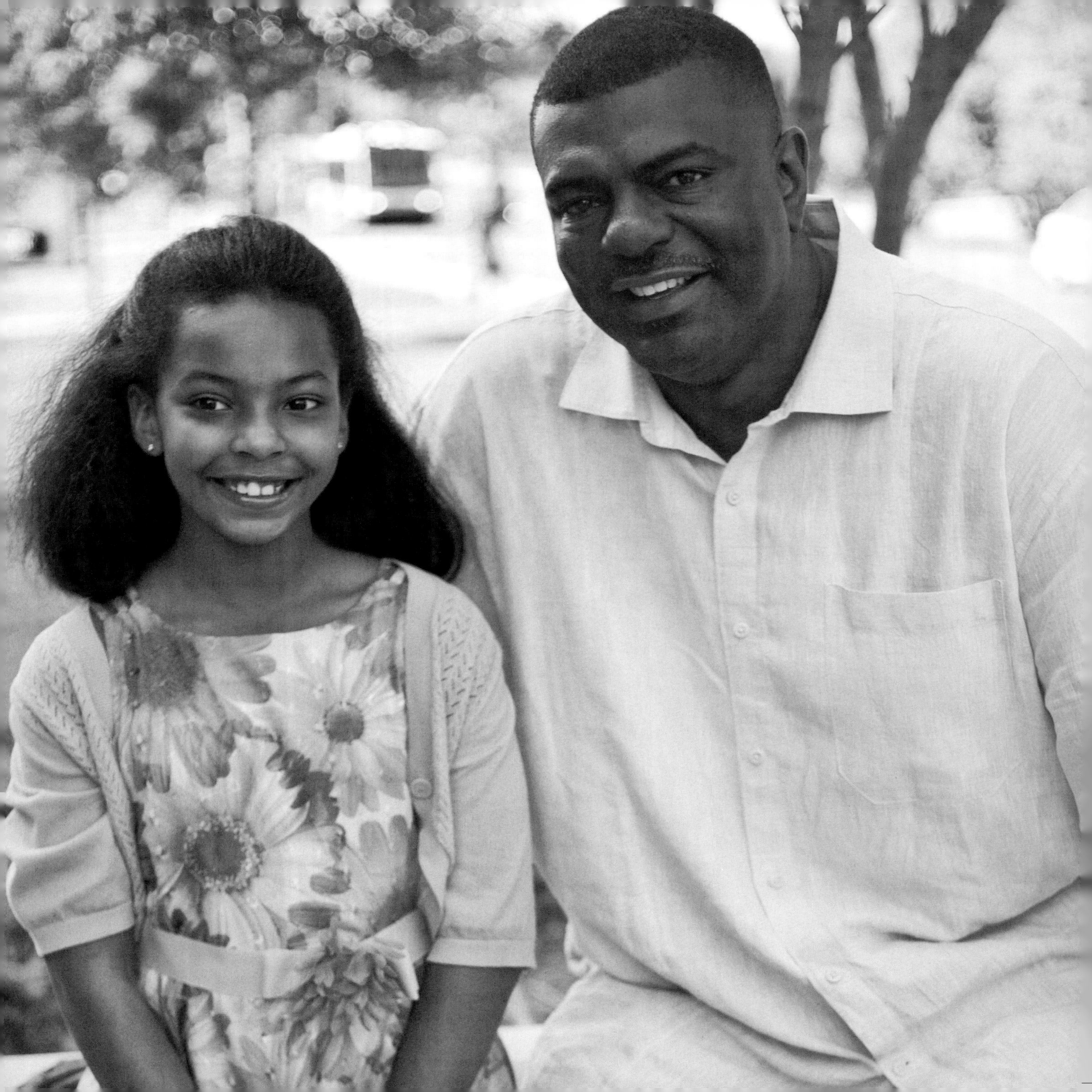

Children must early learn the beauty of generosity.
They are taught to give what they prize most that
they may taste the happiness of giving.

OHIYESA
Native American physician, writer and social reformer
(1858-1939)

FaJhenee: Philanthropy is giving back.

Seth: My parents are big givers. They do a lot of stuff.

Skip: We donate to Goodwill.

FaJhenee: My mom helps the girls in our community and helps them make good decisions about their money.

Seth: She helps Girls on the Run.
They run around the track and stuff.

FaJhenee: I'm doing 26 hours of community service. I help with my mom's nonprofit First Purse and also at my church. They give the homeless a place to sleep at night and feed them. My friends Kimoney, Morgan and Elena, we help out at church.

Seth: Sometimes I donate to homeless people.

Siblings
FaJhenee, *10 ½*
Skip, *9*
Seth, *6*

"GRANDMA ELLA, IN GARY, Indiana, is a big giver. Every month, she sends me money. A lot of time she sends a box full of candy and stuff. In her basement, she has a family that lost their house. She's had people in her backyard in tents and stuff. She helps people who need it. I want to be just like her when I grow up. She's eighty-six."

Lovell "Skip" Bradford Jr.
nine-year-old student

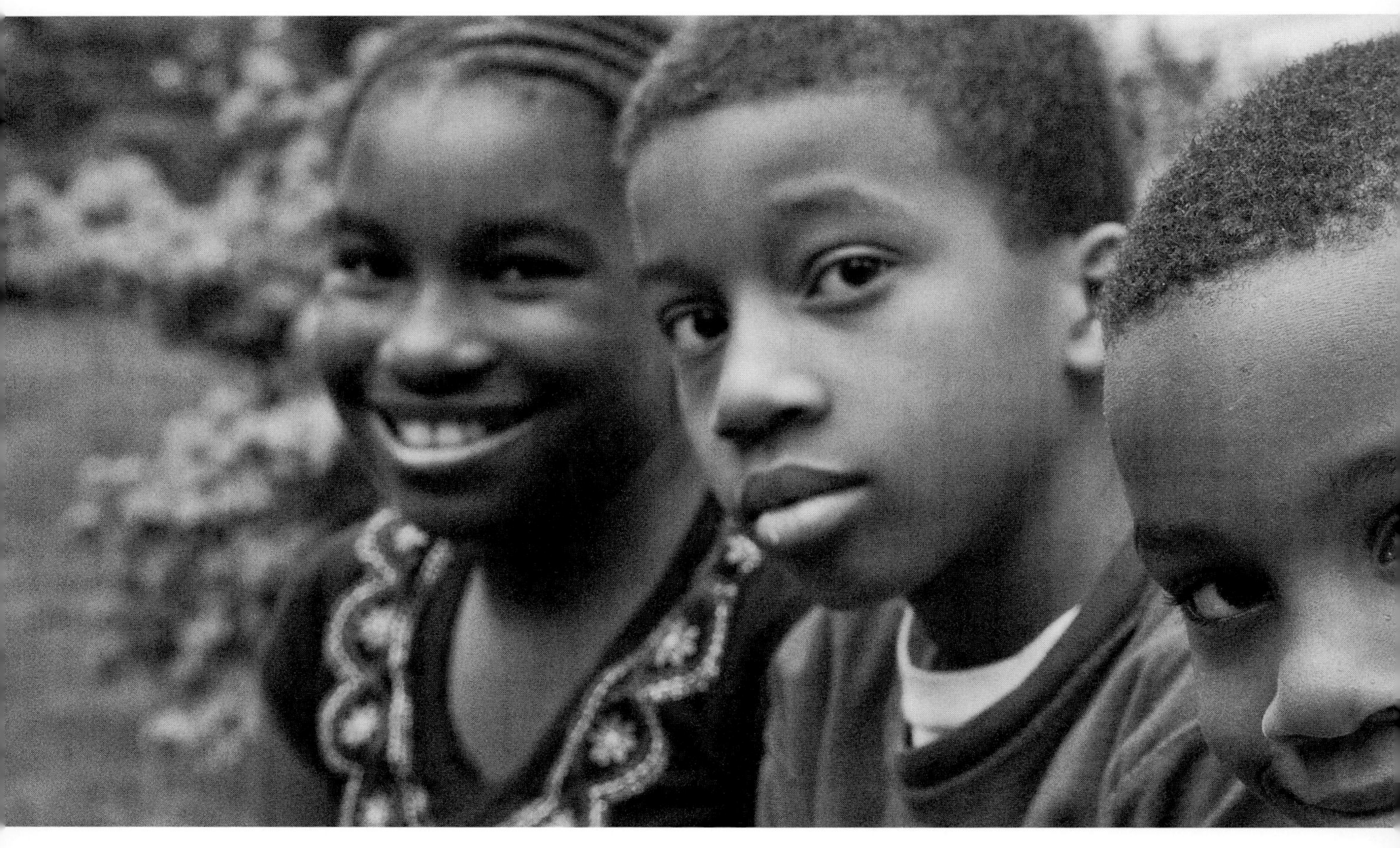

Each generation must, out of relative obscurity, discover its mission, and fulfill it or betray it.

FRANTZ FANON
Martinquen psychiatrist, philosopher and revolutionary
(1925-61)

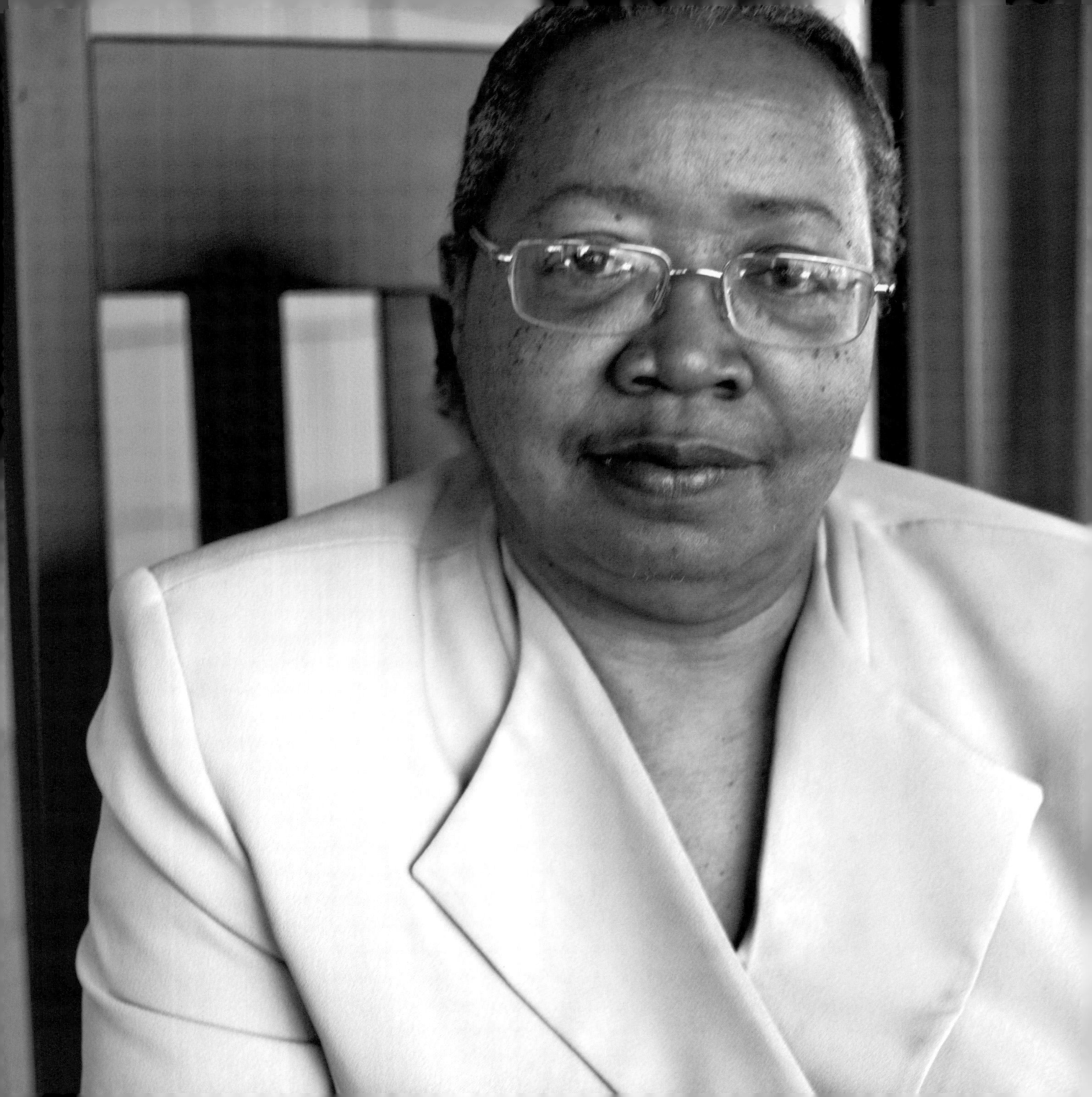

FRAMES OF MIND

What’s on your mind about philanthropy?

As the commercial influence of wealth alters the ways we think about each other, I choose to believe that our greater power of giving will prevail. — *Mildred Dwiggins Swift*

When philanthropists approach the jail environment, it is always refreshing to see people dedicated to the long-term success of the inmates. They allow their resources to be part of the solution . . . by beginning programs inside of the jail so that the people may return to the community better. — *Keith Cradle*

I'm thinking about strategic partnerships with other funders, government and the philanthropic sector—how we maximize impact. — *Edgar Villanueva*

With all that has already been done, there are so many more ways that philanthropy can be utilized. I would love to see more innovation and creativity in the ways we express philanthropy. It is our destiny to continue to interpret philanthropy in a way that speaks to the current needs. — *Jennifer Henderson*

I'm focused on how we move more folks to the supply side of philanthropy so that we begin to change the narrative that African Americans are only recipients of others' largesse. — *Darryl K. Lester*

Now is the time to make a major shift. The attention is on the Black community in a way that it has not been for decades. Folks are motivated, charged up and ready to act. Let's not let the opportunity slip away. — *Britt Brewer Loudd*

Everyone plays a role: Give your time, dollars and thoughts, at any level. Be thoughtful in giving: Research organizations and focus. Be an example to the next generation: Encourage your children. Know that your job and work-life are just a means to an end. We are all blessed to be a blessing to others. — *RoShawn Ross-Hampton*

How can we create lasting collaborations and partnerships with both public and private entities to make philanthropy more targeted and effective? — *Christian Friend*

Philanthropy is a big word but giving can be achieved in small ways that add up over time. Give your time as a friend, role model and service provider. Give financially, strategically and consistently, so that your donations add up over time with a deeper impact. — *Charles W. Thomas Jr.*

It's become a lifestyle for me to give my time, talent and treasure to make my community a better place. — *Ohmar Land*

Giving is love . . . and fruit of the heart. — *Mattie Marshall*

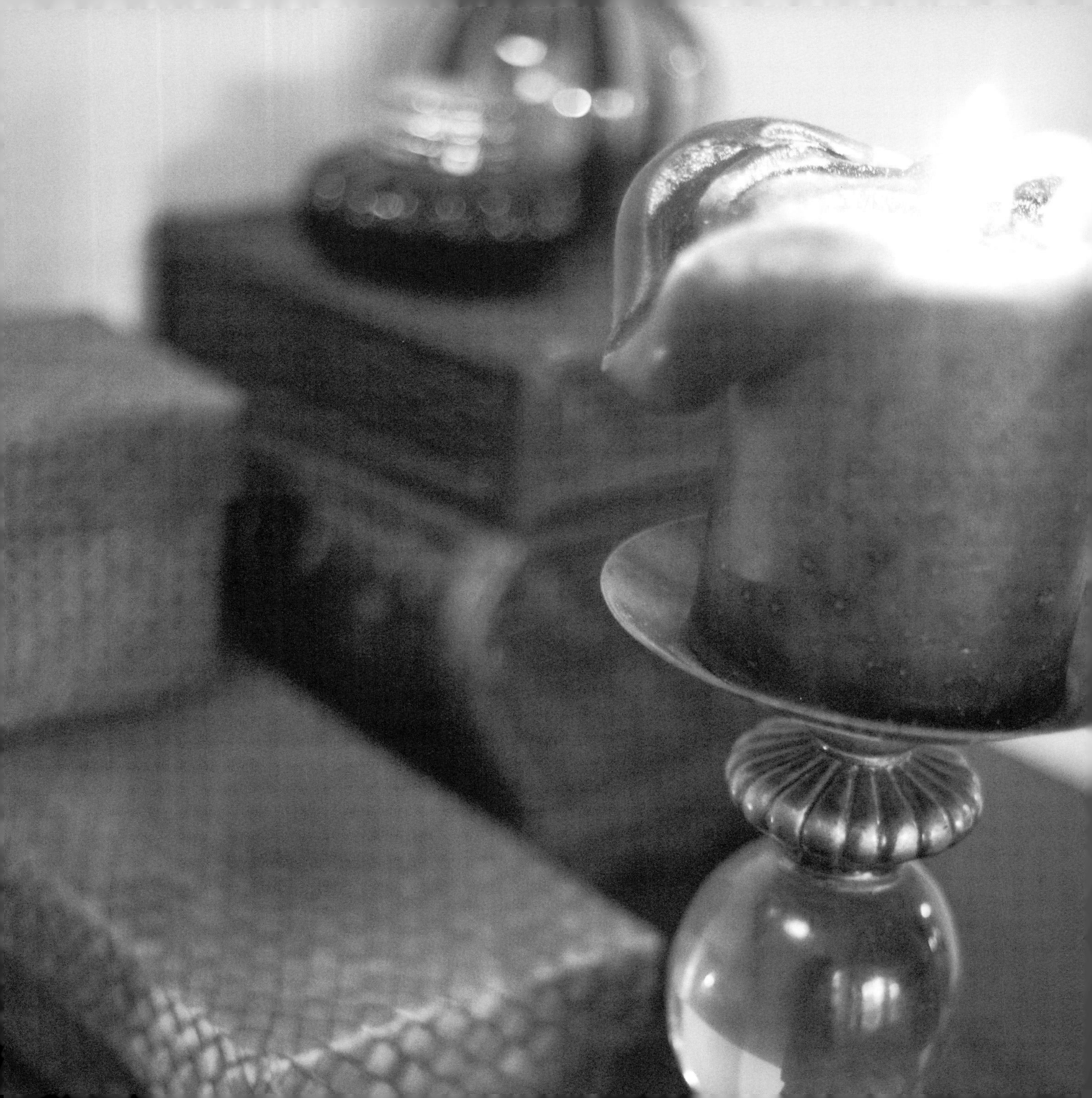

Better to light one small candle than to curse the darkness.

CHINESE PROVERB

Nancy Moore | WISDOM WHISPERER

Everything that I do or even try to do, Grandma Nancy supports me. She is the quintessential grandmother. Strong. Wise. Caring. She's attentive as a listener, and I can talk to her about almost anything. And of course, she is a great cook.

My grandparents have five children, twelve grandchildren and four great-grandchildren. After fifty years of marriage, they lead a laid-back life built around family, flea markets and fishing. Family includes their church family at Shiloh AME, where my grandmother sings in the choir. Retired from nursing, Grandma has a quiet strength that she exercises over the whole family.

Grandma encourages my passions for music, cooking and volunteering, and she influences how I give back. She has taught me to stick to whatever I choose to do, and I do a lot in the community. At school, I participate on the student leadership council, which leads food drives for Brenner Children's Hospital. I sometimes serve at a soup kitchen with First Baptist—the oldest African American church in Winston-Salem. The biggest part of my community involvement is the Boy Scouts. I became a Scout at five and am always looking for ways to apply our values to improve my community.

In these and other activities, my grandmother's message to me is clear: Stay involved. *You will do something great and help uplift a lot of other people,* she is always telling me. I have learned to believe that if you stay at it, your work will eventually have an impact.

ALEXANDRÉ BAILAND BOHANNON

Connection: *Teenage grandson* • Channel: *Senior Patrol Leader, Boy Scout Troop 718* • Cause: *Children and youth*

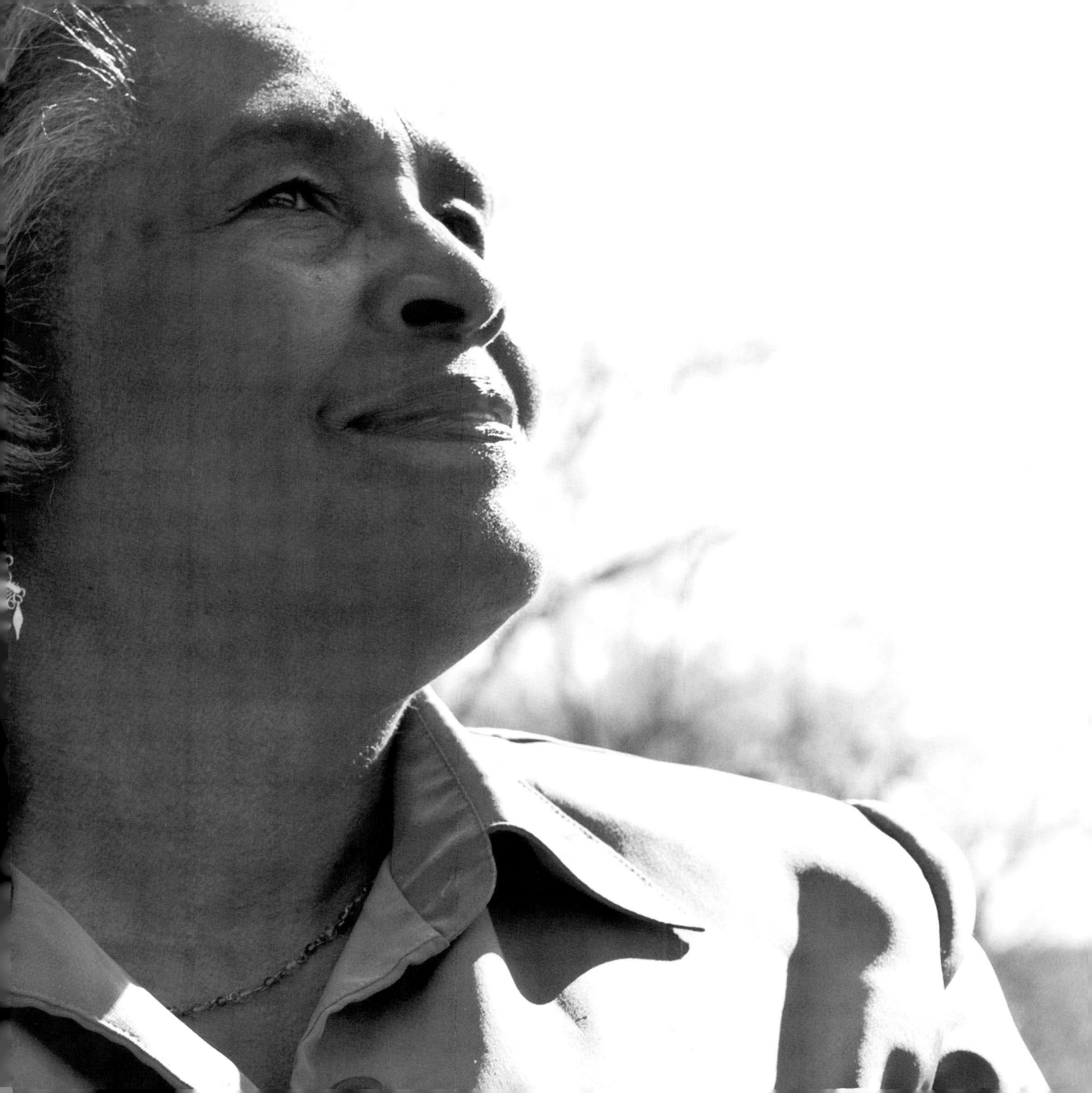

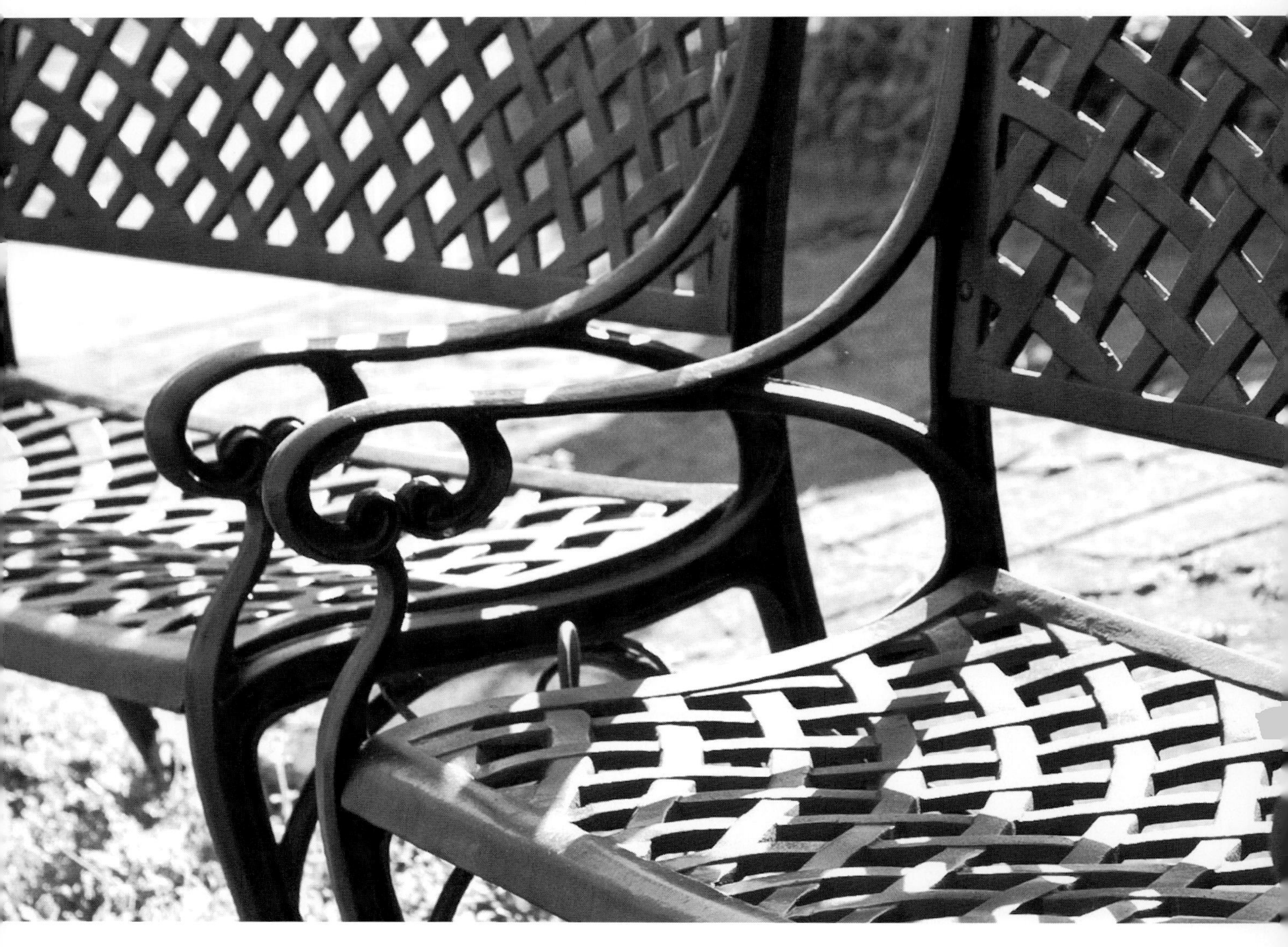

It is not only for what we do that we are held responsible,
but also for what we do not do.

MOLIÈRE
French playwright and actor
(1622-73)

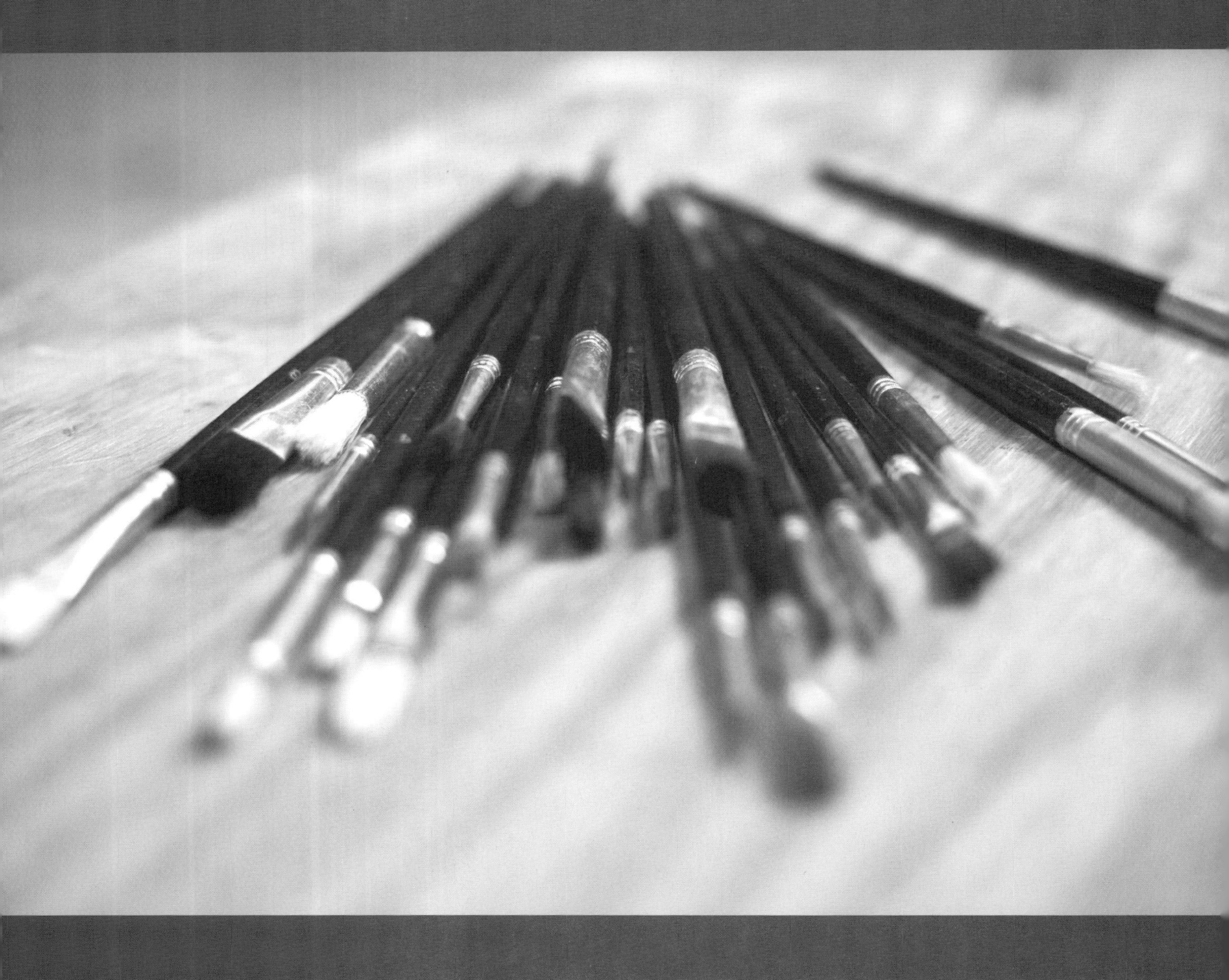

"THE FIRST TIME WE MET, it was weird finding other Black men living in Charlotte who were on the same wavelength about the same things—art, music, comics and politics. We had known of each other indirectly, but when we all came together the connection just happened.

"God City started as a support system for ourselves as artists. We began creating the art shows and music events that we had always wanted to see in Charlotte. Our first show was called *The Art of Hip Hop*. Originally, there were four of us: Marcus Kiser, Wolly Vinyl, John Hairston and me. We have grown to about eight members since the beginning. Our manifesto is 'to educate, assist, entertain and enlighten the people through artistic expression.'

"Black people seldom see themselves represented in visual arts. Our work is a representation of who we are and reveals images and experiences from our community. We give workshops at schools, where we draw with kids and talk to them about life. So many kids have a limited view of what Black people can do. Our presence says, 'You can be an artist.' A cool thing I have noticed is that, since we are in our twenties and thirties, we are a bridge between generations. We can take the message of parents and teachers and relay it in ways that teenagers can understand.

"Members of the collective help each other and other underground artists. It's a family thing. There are advantages to working together."

Antoine Williams
founding member of God City art collective, established in 2005

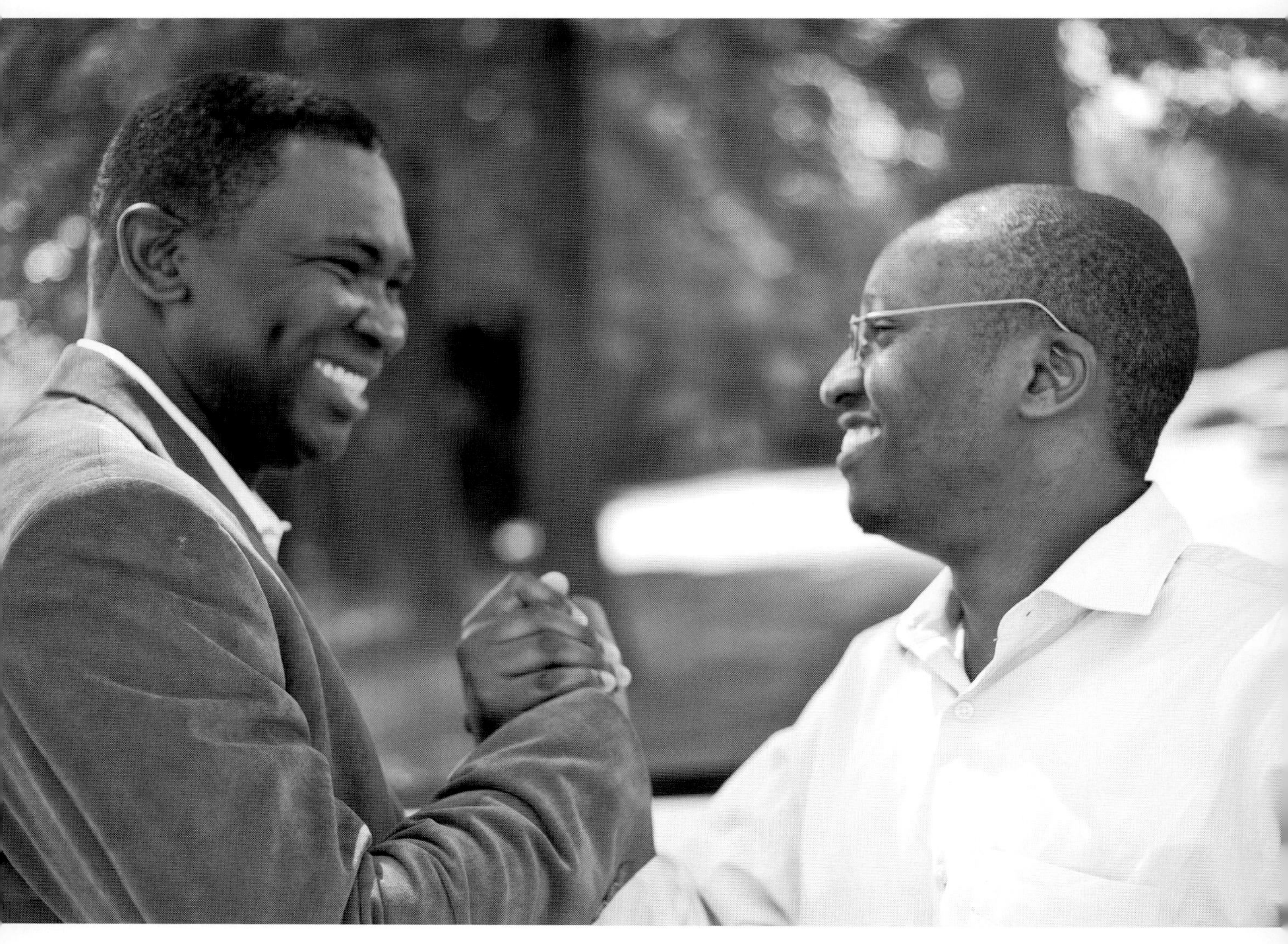

It is one of the most beautiful compensations of this life that no man can sincerely try to help another without helping himself.

RALPH WALDO EMERSON
American philosopher and poet
(1803-82)

Byron A. Smith Sr. | REAL POWER BROKER

It was 1999 when I met Byron Smith, a dynamic instructor of the Real Estate Associate Program at Clark Atlanta University. I had enrolled in Project REAP shortly after graduating from Auburn because it focused on increasing diversity in the commercial real-estate industry, where at management levels, minorities make up less than 1 percent. Unbelievably, there are fewer than a thousand people of color in an industry with over one hundred and twenty-five thousand professionals. Byron, however, is a trailblazer. He has helped a lot of Blacks, Latinos, women and others from minority groups advance in their careers.

Byron and I became friends instantly through Project REAP. I learned of his Cuban roots and years growing up in Florida. He shared stories about his experiences in real estate and described the challenges he had faced while trying to break into the industry. Byron was actually one of the first people in real estate to listen to my career aspirations. He not only heard me, he referred me to programs and matched me with people who could get me where I wanted to go.

I call Byron's style of guidance and mentoring of young professionals *giving back*. After experiencing barriers, he was intentional about removing obstacles for others. He didn't just talk about helping me succeed; instead, he made sure I gained essential skills and resources for finding success. He even urged me to make giving back a core business practice.

Byron is kind and genuine and he also expects excellence. I admire that. He is a heavy influence on why I strive to put my best foot forward every day and to lend a helping hand wherever I can.

RASHAD DAVIS

Connection: *Protégé* • Channel: *Founding member, New Generation of African American Philanthropists, a giving circle established in 2006* • Cause: *Land*

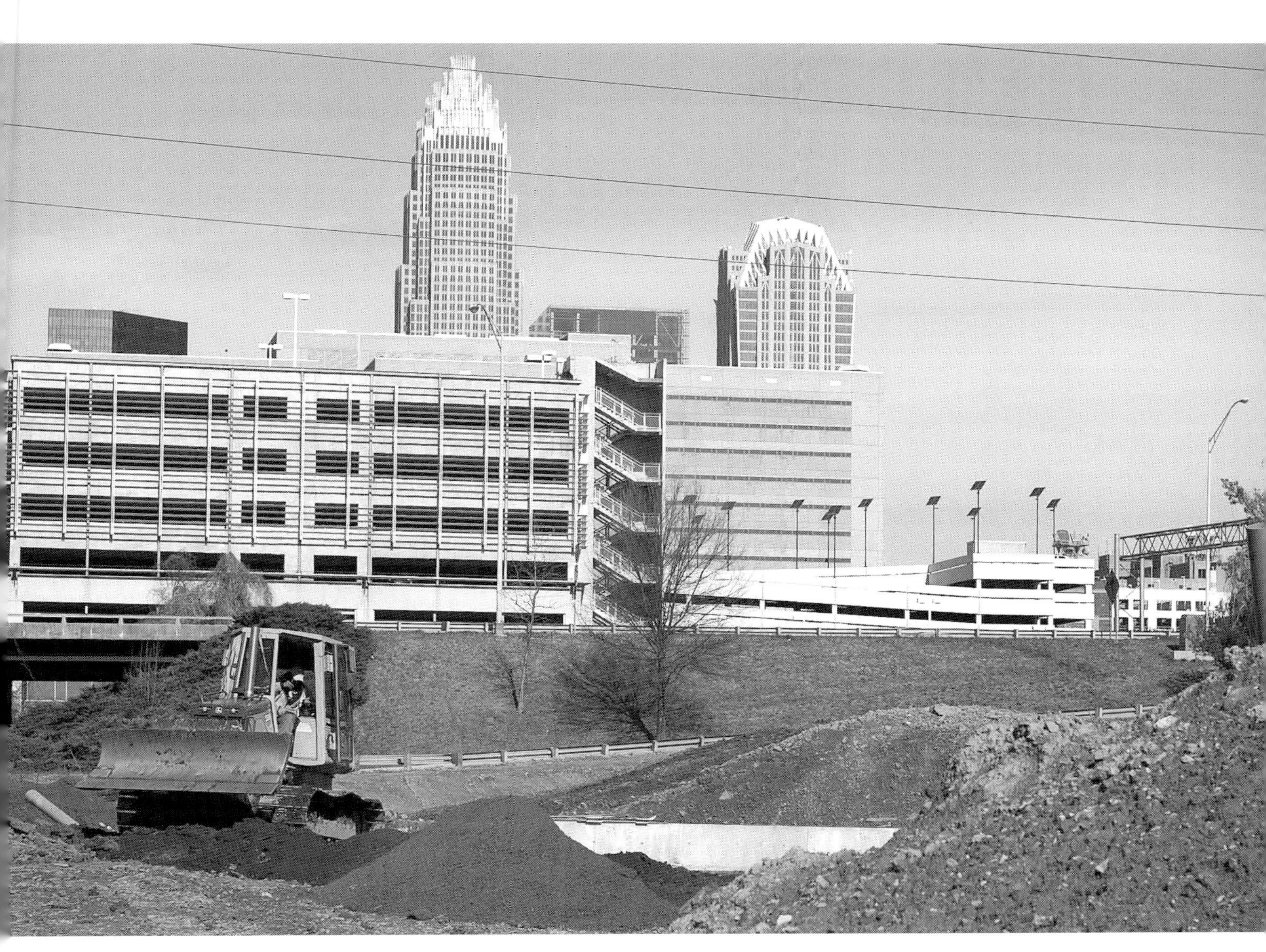

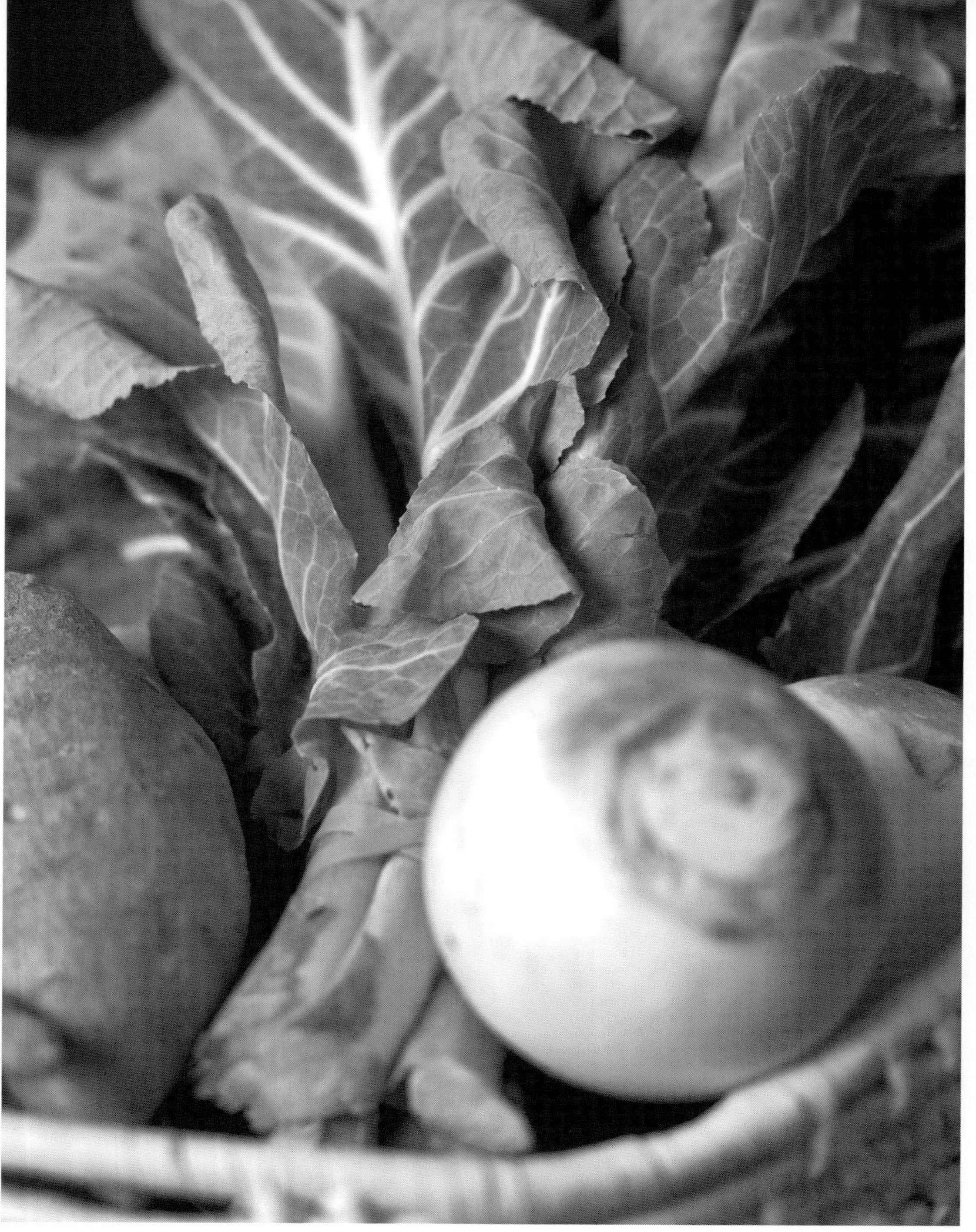

We are each other's harvest; we are each other's business;
we are each other's magnitude and bond.

GWENDOLYN BROOKS
Pulitzer Prize–winning American poet
(1917-2000)

Lucille Erwin Scott | NEIGHBOR'S KEEPER

Jonesboro bears the name of my great-grandfather Jones Erwin. It is a close-knit neighborhood where my mother's mother, Lucille Scott, spent her entire life and where my best memories are rooted. My parents lived with Granny Cille when I was little, and as her first grandchild, naturally she spoiled me rotten.

Petite with a graying little Afro, Granny Cille channeled what is best described as nervous energy into serving her community as the undisputed go-to person of Jonesboro. If a nearby family needed a ride across the hill, she'd drive them. If neighborhood folks needed to get their papers in order, she'd help them. When one of Jonesboro's colorful characters had had one too many drinks, she'd heat up food and black coffee, and she would steady them.

Then, there were instances when Granny cared for elderly neighbors. I remember specifically how as age and ailments slowed Miss Louise, Granny Cille saw to it that her utilities were paid and that she got to doctors' appointments. When Miss Louise could no longer live at home, my grandmother helped get her into a nursing home and visited regularly until her death.

Thinking back, I would guarantee Granny did something for every household in the neighborhood and likely each person too. She never turned anyone away. It's funny, but until now I failed to recognize just how much I put into practice lessons from Jonesboro about helping a neighbor, whether right next door or clear across town. Without setting out to teach, she taught me what matters about giving.

CORON JORDAN
Connection: *Granddaughter* ◆ Channel: *High school teacher* ◆ Cause: *Educating young people about character and citizenship*

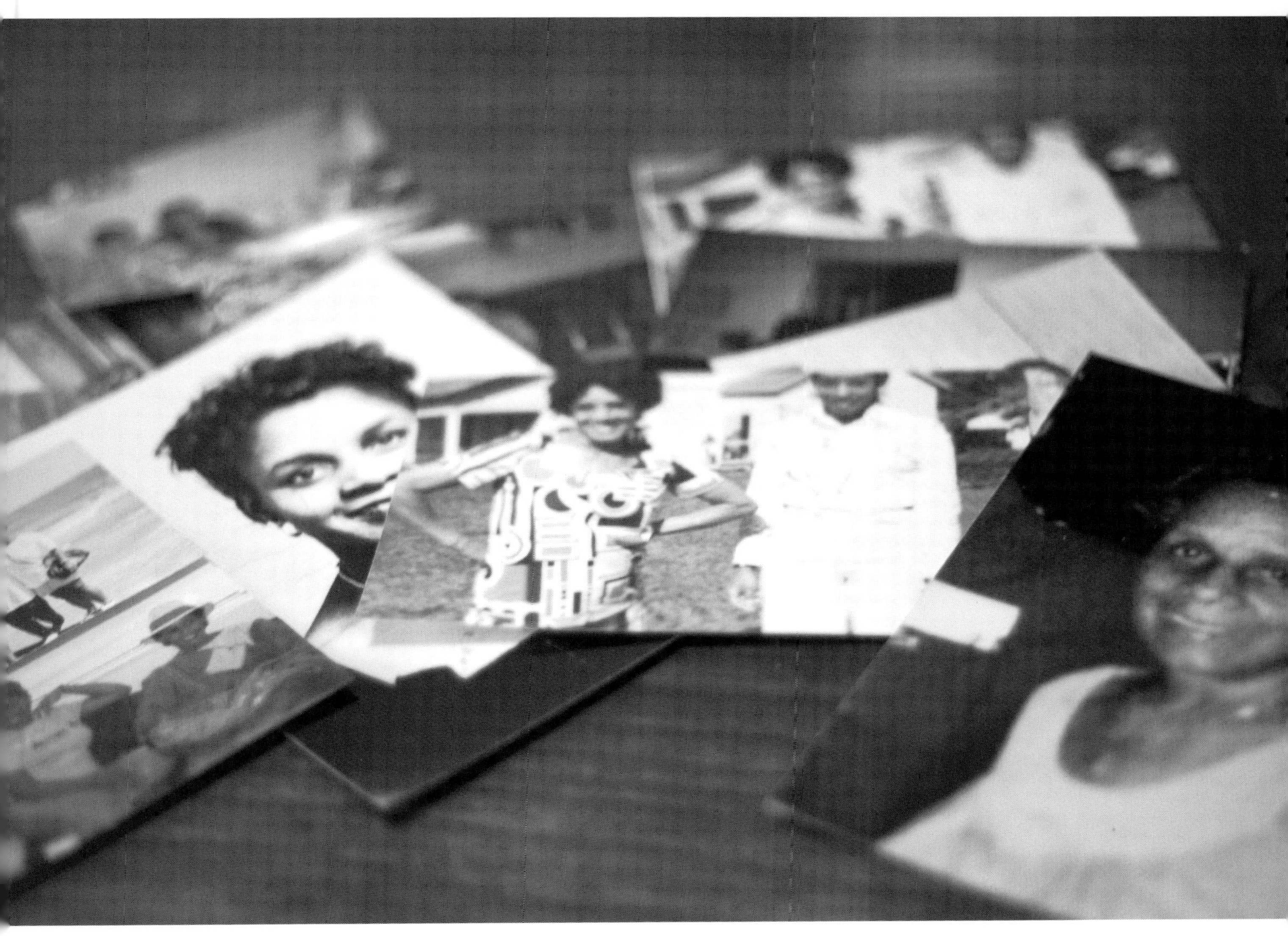

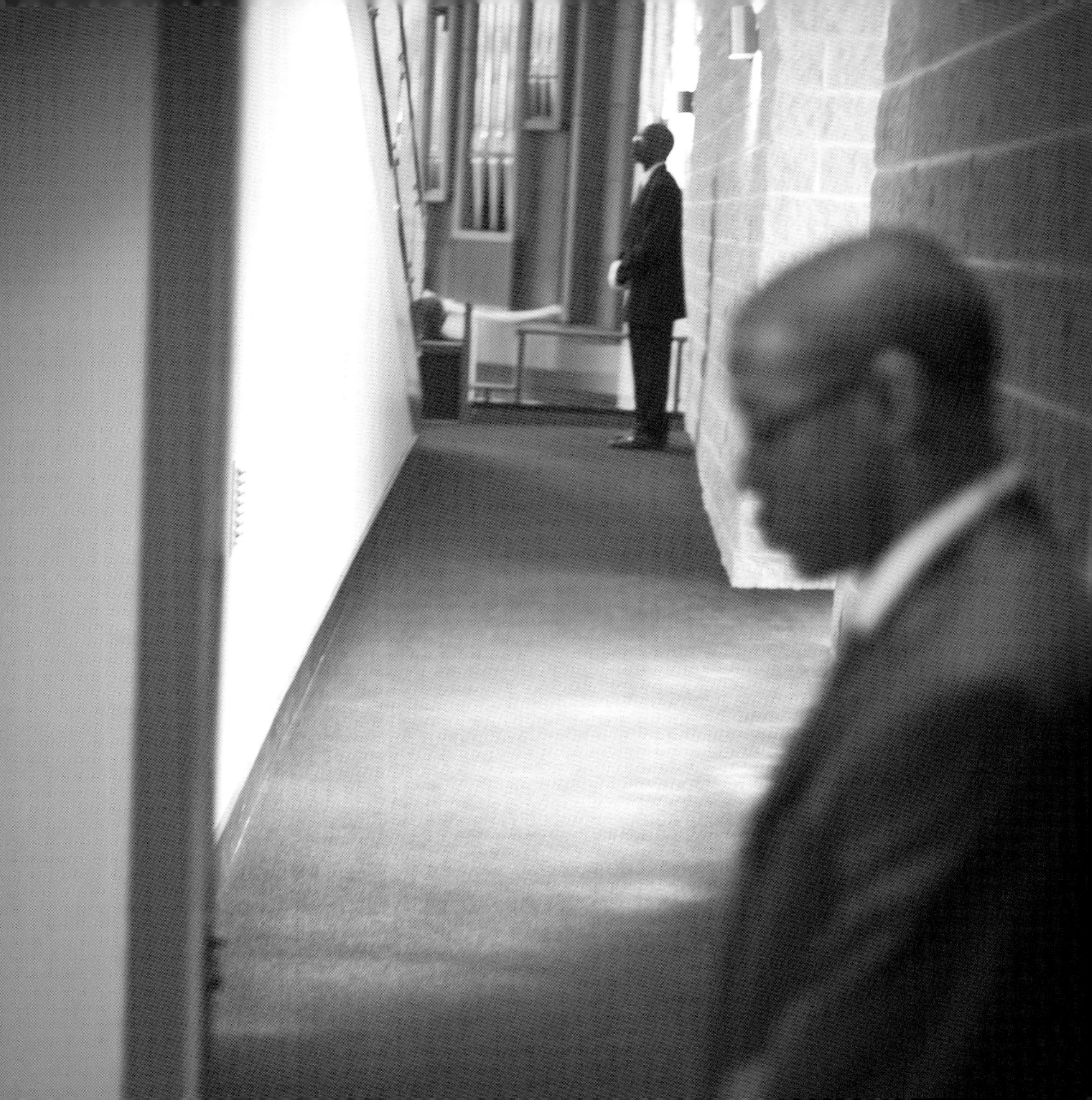

A gift opens the way for the giver and ushers him into the presence of the great.

PROVERBS 18:16

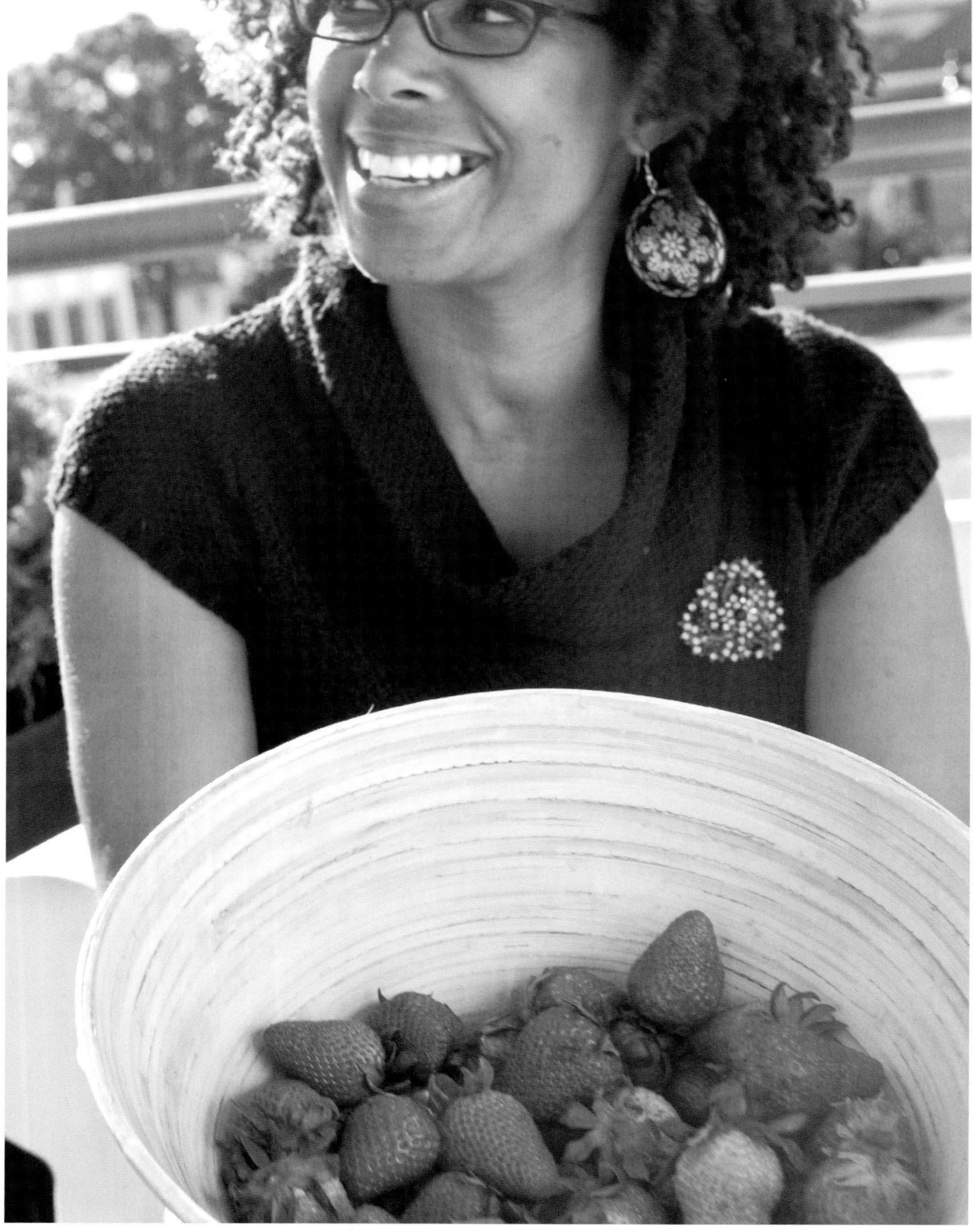

Love is a fruit in season at all time, and in reach of every hand.

MOTHER TERESA
Humanitarian
(1910-97)

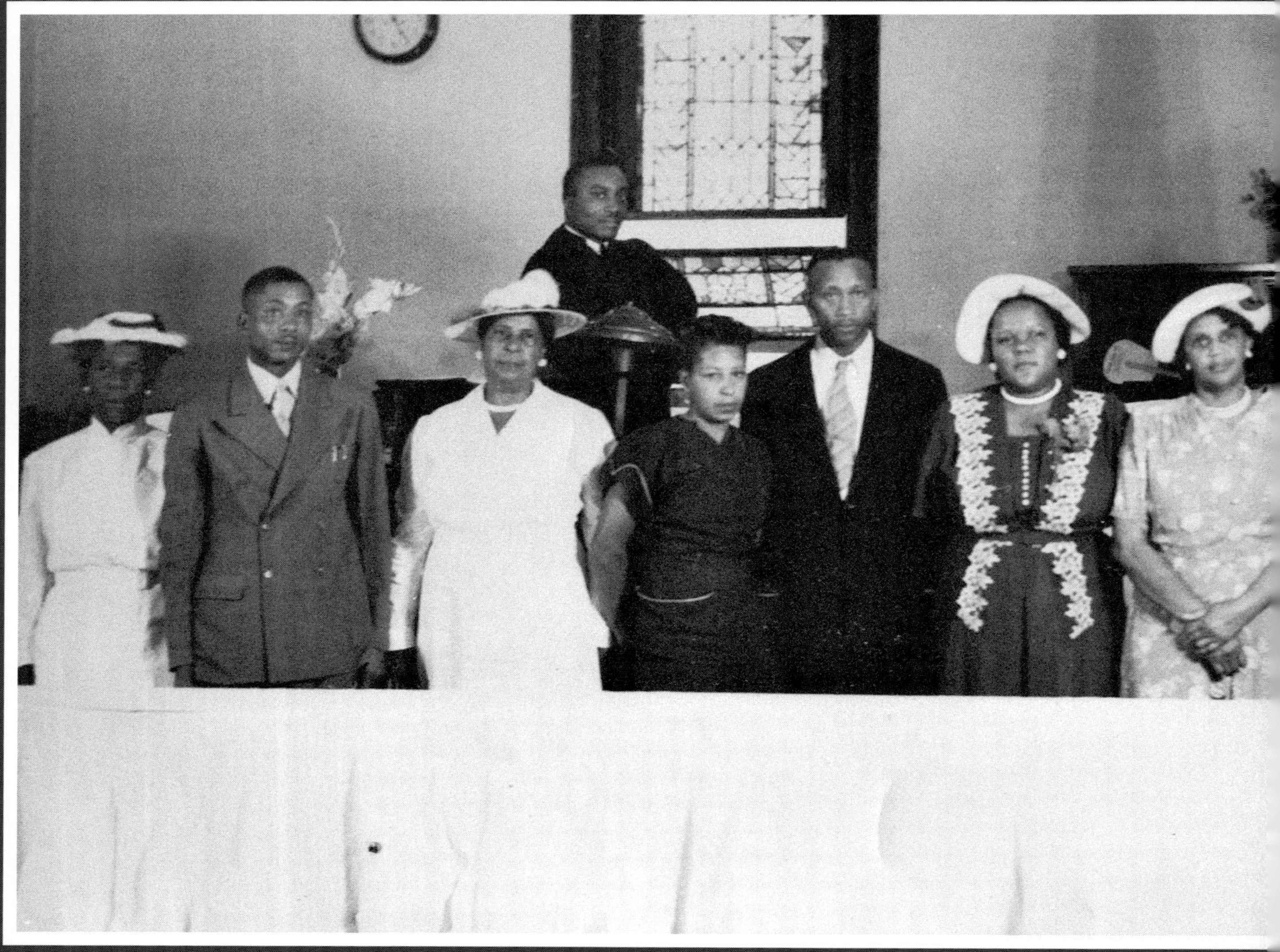

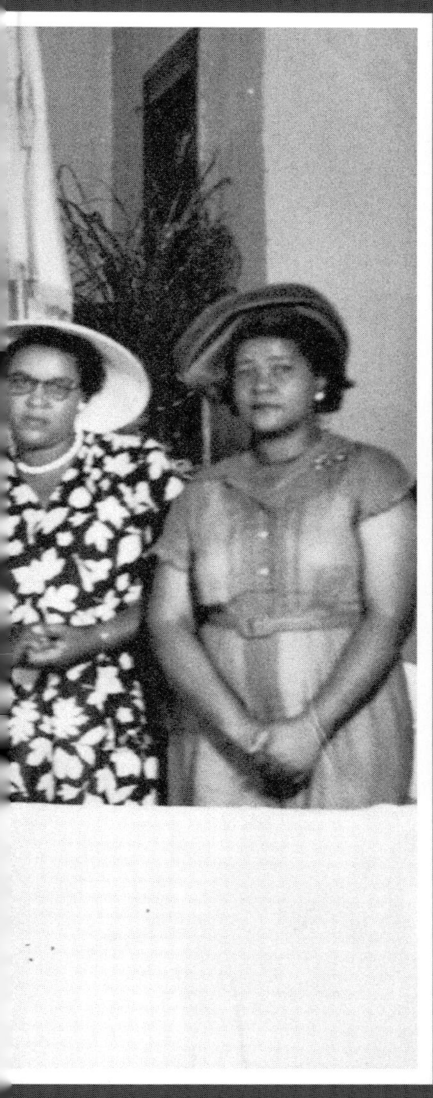

"PHILANTHROPY IS and has always been in the Black community, especially in the Black church. Many times when Black people think about philanthropy, they think about a business executive who gives a lot of money to various causes. However, what the Black church has done in the community is the same thing that any other nonprofit has done. The disconnect is in the language, which is why it's on my mind. As a preacher and a philanthropist, I want to talk about the semantics between the Black church and philanthropy. Language is very important. Language leads to understanding; understanding affects perspective; perspectives change actions; and actions repair communities."

Lyord Watson Jr.
divinity school student & founding member of Birmingham Change Fund, a CIN giving circle

Philanthropy

Mastery of language affords remarkable power.

FRANTZ FANON
Martinquen psychiatrist, philosopher and revolutionary
(1925-61)

Cleon C. Arrington, Ph.D. | LEGACY LEAVER

We chose to honor my dad by creating the Dr. Cleon C. Arrington Scholarship For The Sciences when he passed away on February 19, 2010. Much earlier in 1998, he lost a leg to vascular disease and spent months in the hospital, where friends, family and his colleagues in academia showered him with flowers. It was an embarrassment of riches back then to carry home armfuls of lovely bouquets from the hospital and throw away some to make room for the newest arrivals.

When Dad's long health battle turned its bleakest, I faced the inevitable and began thinking about how to honor his legacy. A scientist, educator and administrator, my father was well known for his passions around working at Georgia State University, Atlanta University and Morehouse College, teaching chemistry to African American students and giving back in the community. I approached my mother about creating a memorial scholarship through donations in lieu of flowers. After a meeting with the Georgia State University Foundation, we submitted paperwork and committed to donate $25,000, over five years, to establish an endowed scholarship fund.

Friends, family and his colleagues again showed enormous support once Dad made his transition. Three months after his death, close to a hundred people had made donations, ranging from five dollars to one thousand dollars. I now know the power of collective giving with purpose. While flowers are lovely, they last only days. Scholarships, on the other hand, will sustain his legacy and benefit his beloved institution and students forever.

MICHELLE ARRINGTON

Connection: *Daughter* • Channel: *Major donor, Georgia State University* • Cause: *Health, fitness and education*

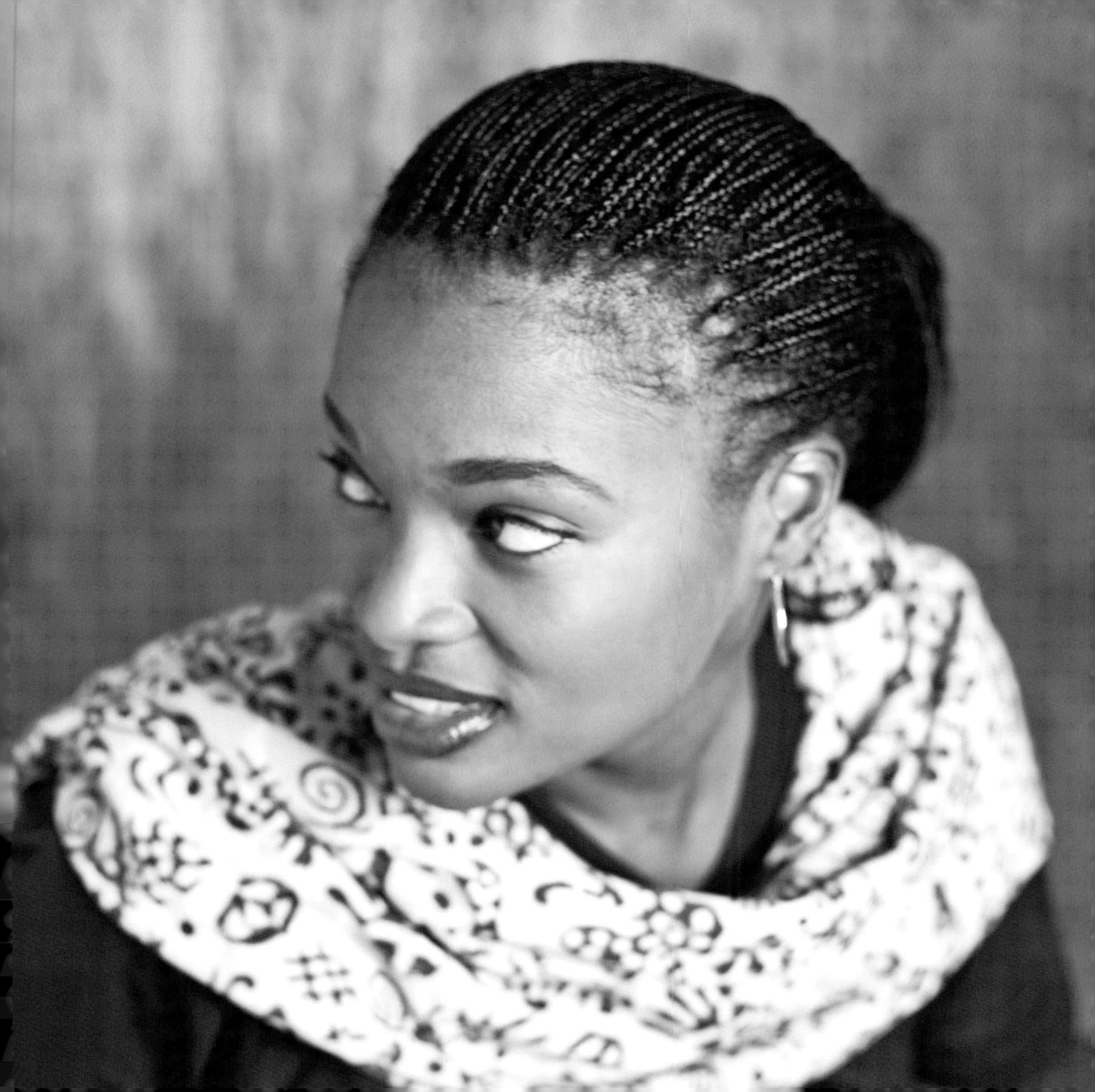

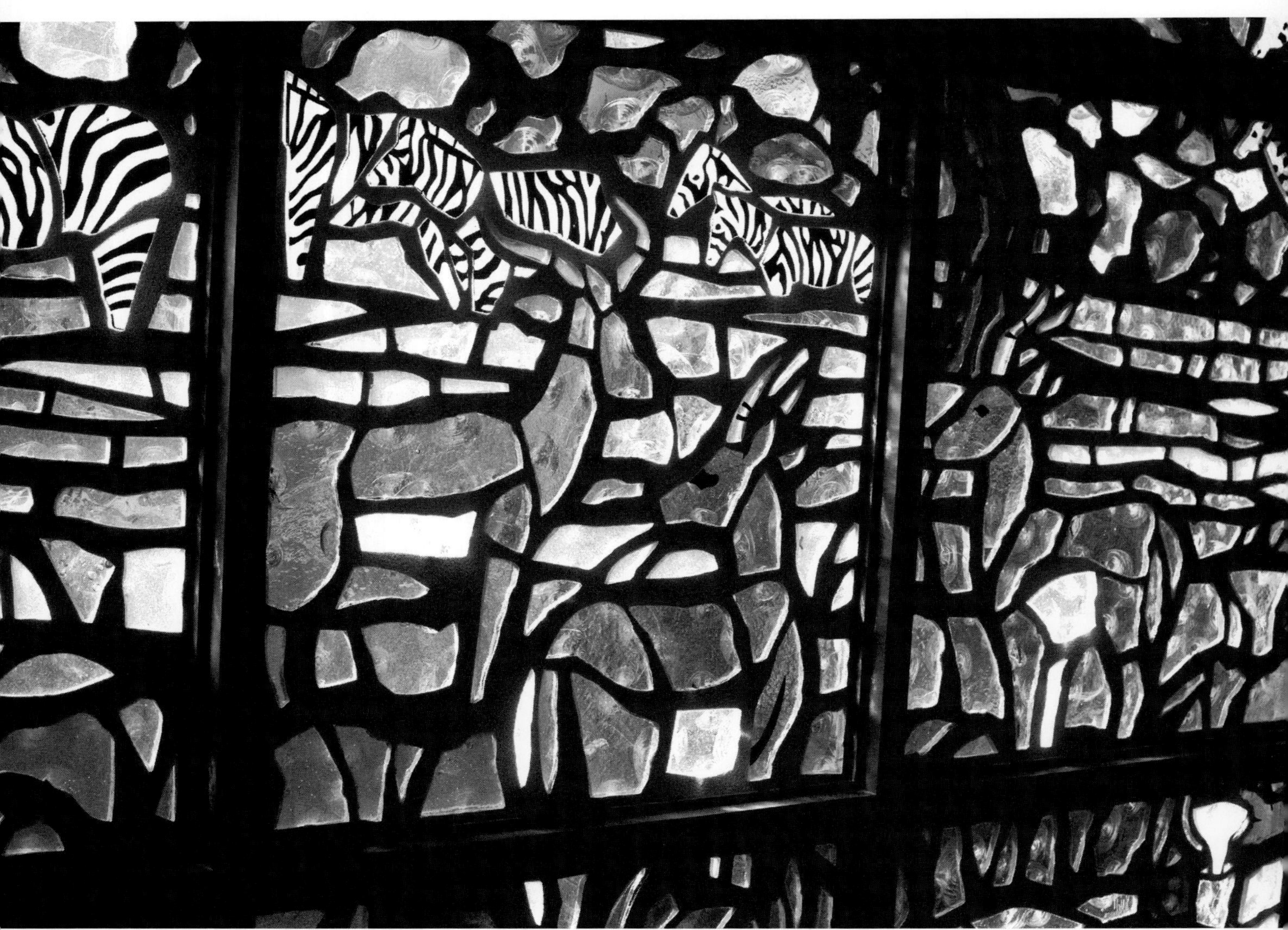

In the long history of humankind (and animal kind, too) those who learned to collaborate and improvise most effectively have prevailed.

CHARLES DARWIN
English naturalist
(1809-82)

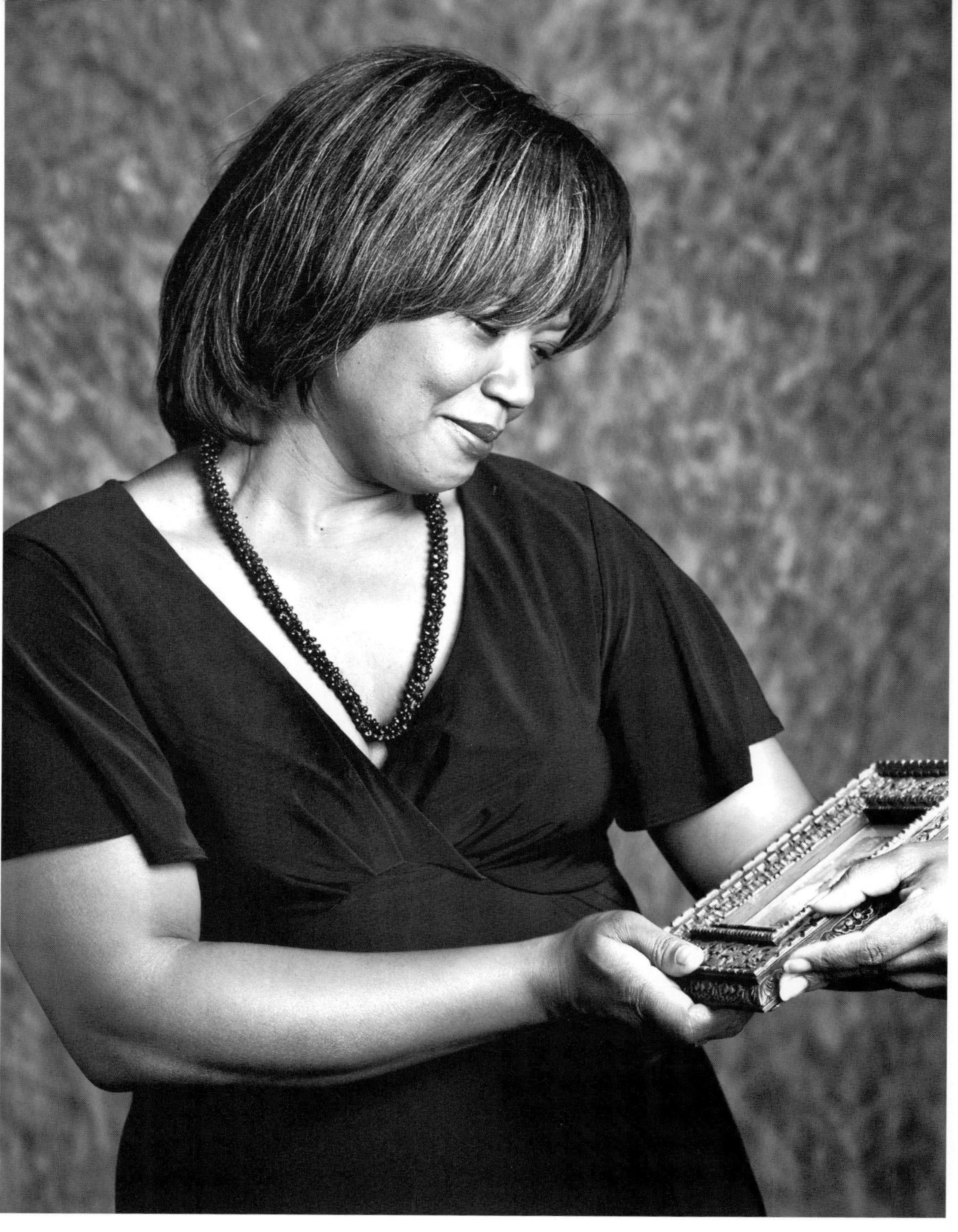

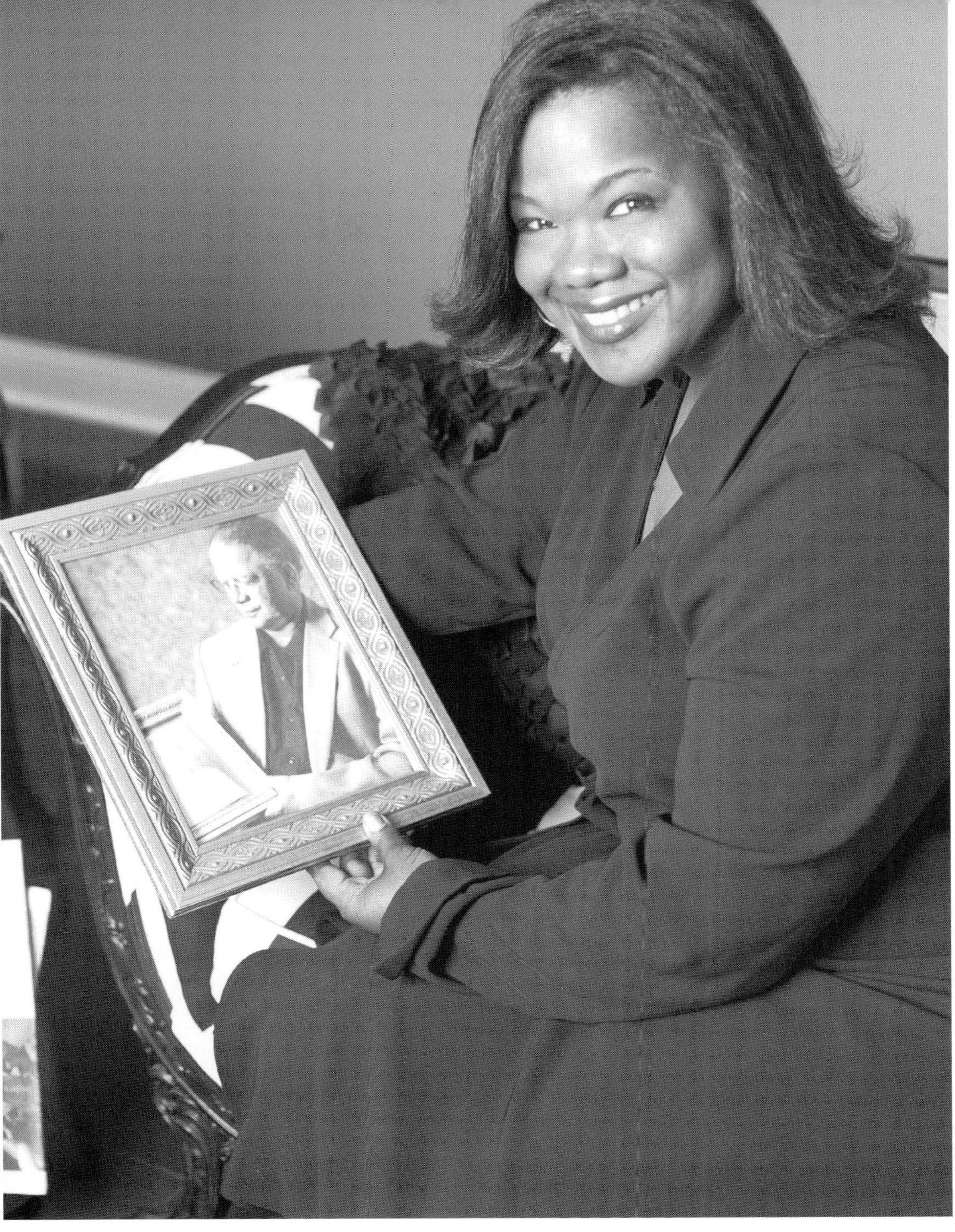

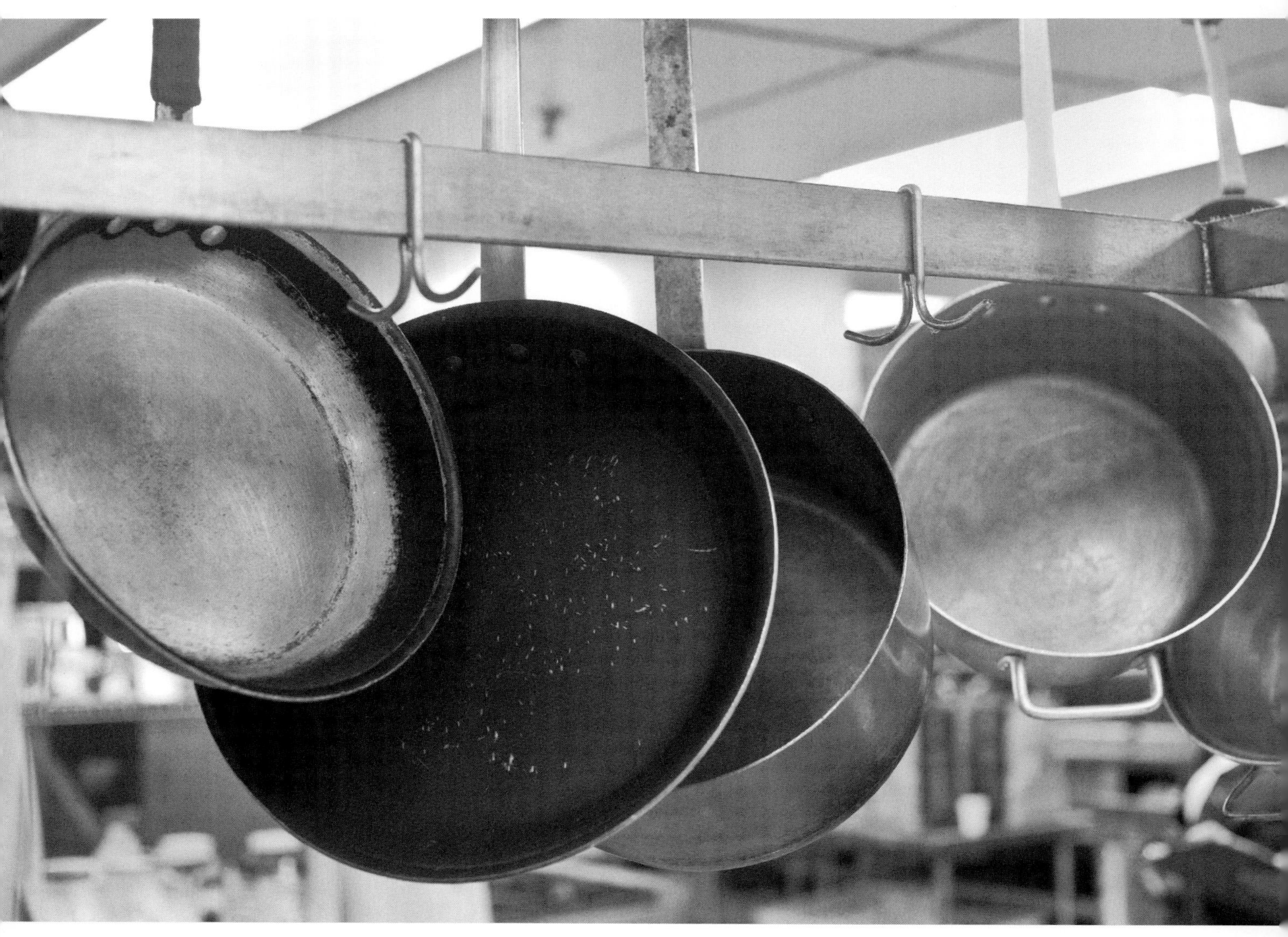

If you knew what I know about the power of giving,
you would not let a single meal pass
without sharing it in some way.

BUDDHA
Eastern spiritual leader and founder of Buddhism
(circa 563 BC-483 BC)

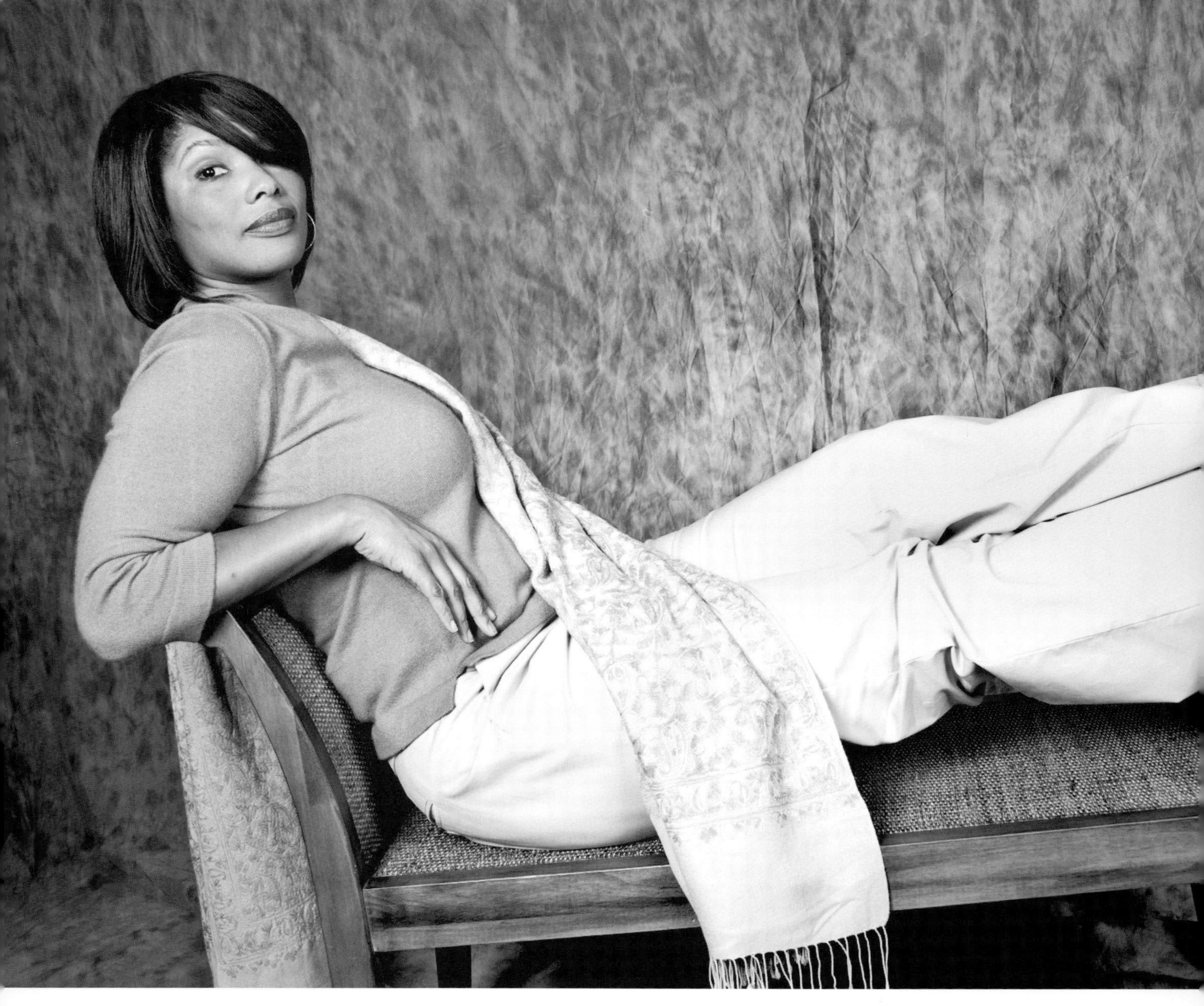

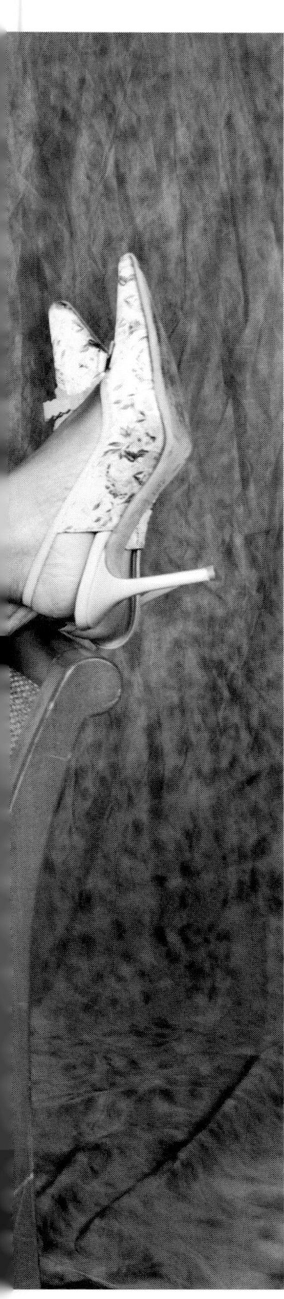

This is the one true joy in life, the being used for a purpose recognized by yourself as a mighty one; the being a force of nature instead of a feverish, selfish little clod of ailments and grievances, complaining that the world will not devote itself to making you happy.

I am of the opinion that my life belongs to the whole community and as long as I live it is my privilege to do for it whatever I can.

I want to be thoroughly used up when I die, for the harder I work, the more I live. I rejoice in life for its own sake. Life is no "brief candle" to me. It is a sort of splendid torch which I have got hold of for the moment, and I want to make it burn as brightly as possible before handing it on to future generations.

GEORGE BERNARD SHAW
Irish playwright and political activist
(1856-1950)

Full Circle

this is work in progress
a new generation
paying homage

this is full circle
to who
came before us

giving back like ancestors
gave back to community

For philanthropy is weighed
in different ways,
than those of the European
kind of standard.

this seed was planted
before landing
on these shores

this is custom
tradition
culture preserved

Now the next generation
will continue the legacy
of creating our own support system
with the intention of being my brother's keeper.

we are soul
giving the mind
time for family

we have always cared
for one another
by using our hands

Creating opportunities
for the love of humankind
for giving back takes
treasure talent and time.

we are the spirit
of black folk
dipped in tradition

so listen to the ancestors
so the future will
know the correct story

they/we/us
are the root

reclaiming the truth
spreading generosity
toward the future

led by example
in turn our work
comes full circle.

Quentin "Q" Talley
poet

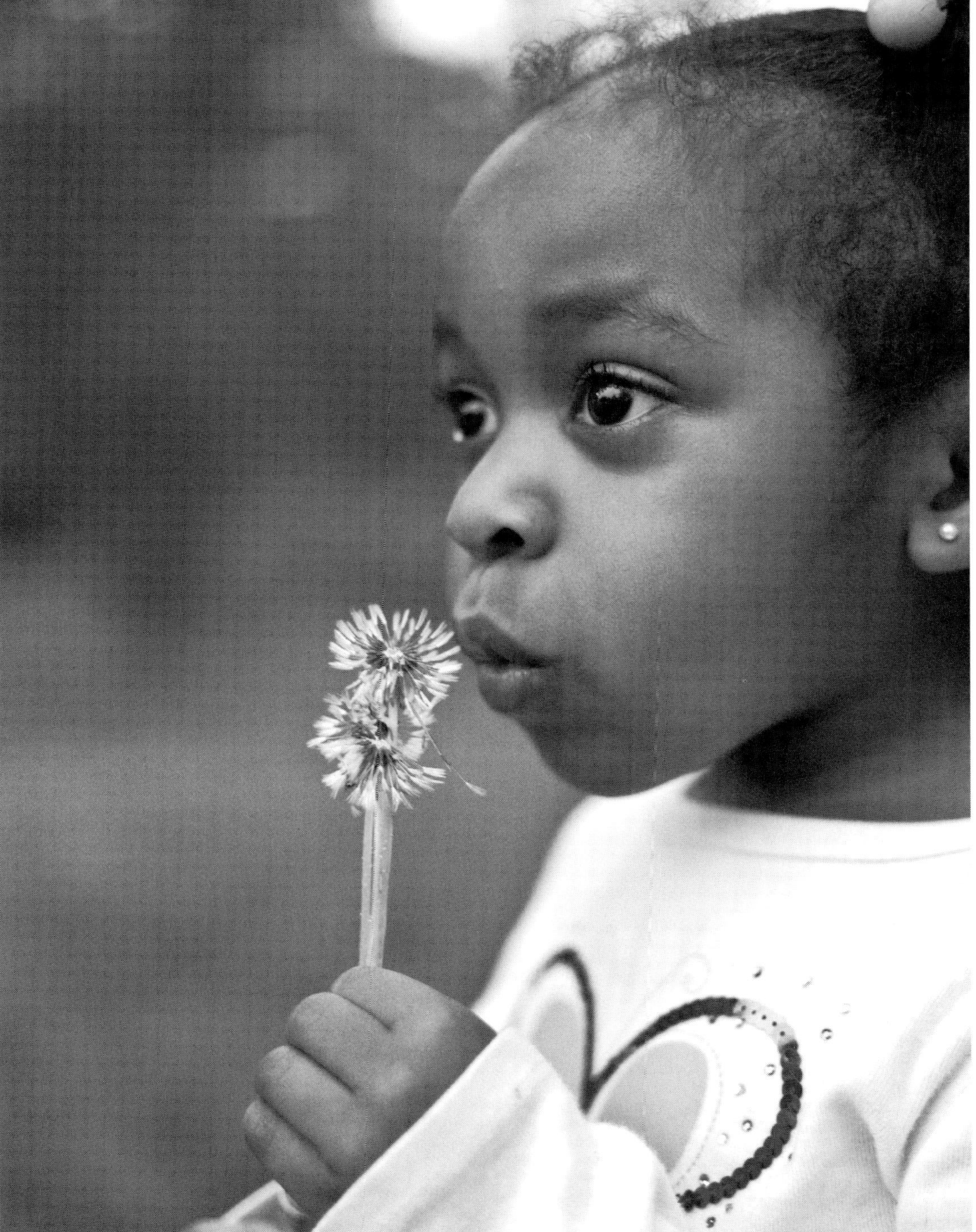

Author's Notes

Grace is a gift always welcome. And I was showered with grace while developing *Giving Back*. When I first conceived of the idea, zeal and naivety blinded me to its magnitude. I thought it would take a year to develop the book; instead it led me on a four-and-a-half-year odyssey that proved torturous and joyous.

At times, doubts would swarm with stinging questions about whether the vision was attainable. I questioned whether I was up to the sacrifices and risks that seeing it through seemed to require of me. People I spoke with believed in the project; they saw the significance of documenting authentic stories and producing a socially relevant book. This helped fend off some of my fears. Even with dispiriting episodes, I could never suppress for long the call of these stories.

Interviewing people was a privilege and extraordinarily gratifying; yet the gravity of the undertaking weighed heavily on me too. Each set of interview notes seemed so delicate. I gained deeper recognition of how precious each story was and how potent it could become if I possessed the wherewithal to craft a compelling body of work and get it in front of readers.

I felt like a surrogate entrusted to carry not one but scores of seeds, each exceptional, fragile and bundling possibilities. Humbled and often daunted, I knew I had to take care in crafting each story with due reverence. Demanding equal finesse was clearing an uncertain path to bring the book's narrative and photographic content out of the obscurity of our families, our communities and my laptop into the light of the wider world. Guidance, often from unexpected people and places, came at each crossroad.

Always brightening the journey were the hopes and confidence expressed by family, friends and giving circle members. I remember the excitement of Ohmar, Renee and Rashad when they first heard my idea while on a road trip to a Black philanthropy conference. I think about Aunt Dora's smile upon learning she inspired the book. I recall early conversations with Charles about my vision and the alignment of our artistic aspirations. Collaboration with Charles has been a God-sent steadying force, from his initial blind faith in the project to his ease, professionalism and quiet generosity.

The most beautiful gift while writing this book was being immersed in its content. I couldn't help but become re-inspired when each day required me to delve into literally hundreds of narratives and photographs meant to inspire and motivate —I call it *chicken and dumplings for the giver's soul*. Gratitude bubbles over when I look back on the gracious acts that brought *Giving Back* into being. Without a doubt God's grace is greatest, but grace granted by the people around me was wonderfully sweet too.

If there's a book you really want to read, but it hasn't been written yet, then you must write it.

— Toni Morrison, Nobel Prize and Pulitzer Prize–winning American writer

Photographer's Lens

When Valaida first approached me in 2008 and talked with me about becoming the photographer for the Giving Back Project, I was on the verge of putting my camera on the shelf. I was ready to give up on being an artist and business owner after eight years of being a professional photographer.

At the time, I felt that I was no longer being true to my mission of serving the community as an artist. I was tired and ready to focus on achieving my goals through nonprofit administration and education. But then Valaida, a dreamer, visionary and strategist, asked me to join her in reframing the story of philanthropy in the African American community. I was so thrilled about the opportunity to hear stories from our community and about the privilege of sharing, visually, how "we" give that I quickly said yes and forgot about giving up my art. I immediately thanked the universe for hearing my prayers about using my gifts for community building and service.

I am grateful to Valaida, NGAAP-Charlotte and our funders for having the vision and desire to explore the meaning of philanthropy. I appreciate Valaida's insight and understanding of how we all make too little of our abilities to give because we think we are somehow lacking. I had wrongly believed that my gifts were not enough to sustain me and to provide for my family and community.

The Giving Back Project showed me the many ways we can give, both big and small. More importantly, the project unveiled the magic that exists in the act of giving. We all must acknowledge what we have to share and how we can contribute and then *choose* to give back rather than give up. My experiences on the project have left me feeling emboldened about how my life and talents are indeed enough and in fact gifts from God meant to benefit the community. But this deeper awareness set in only when I was willing to step into and trust my power to make a difference.

The subject matter is so much more important than the photographer.

— Gordon Parks, groundbreaking and celebrated American photojournalist

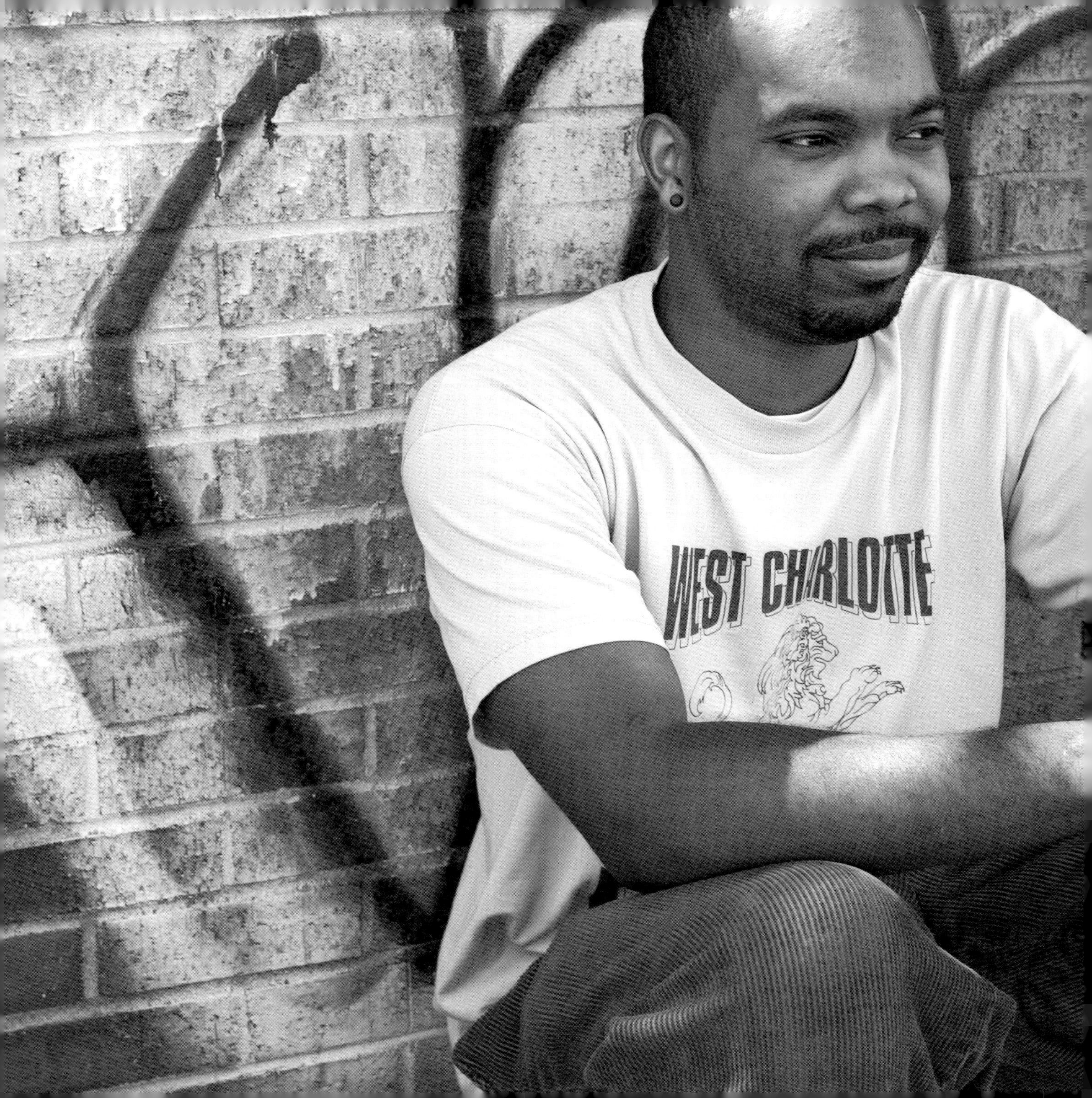
WEST CHARLOTTE

ACKNOWLEDGMENTS

Giving Props

About New Generation of African American Philanthropists

New Generation of African American Philanthropists (NGAAP-Charlotte) is a giving circle based in Charlotte, North Carolina. Much like a book club, a giving circle is made up of people who have common interests and values. Members of our giving circle share values around philanthropy and have decided to pool our charitable dollars to give back to the community. NGAAP-Charlotte uses its funds to make grants to nonprofit organizations having a positive impact on African American children, families and neighborhoods.

Founded in 2006 by a group of nearly twenty member-donors, NGAAP-Charlotte envisions "a healthy, safe and prosperous community for African American families to live, work and flourish." Our mission is "to promote philanthropy—the giving of time, talent and treasure—among African Americans in the Charlotte region, with the goal of enhancing the quality of life within our communities."

Through the Giving Back Project's book development and community engagement campaign, members of NGAAP-Charlotte are reframing portraits of philanthropy. The circle ventures to reclaim the root meaning of philanthropy—*love of humankind*—by celebrating African American history and traditions. As a group, we explore new as well as time-honored ways of giving and embrace a definition of philanthropy that encompasses gifts of not only money, but also time, energy and intellect.

Proceeds from the book *Giving Back* benefit the grantmaking and civic engagement initiatives of NGAAP-Charlotte. An artistic expression of our cultural heritage, *Giving Back* is a vehicle for sharing our collective stories and promoting inclusive and responsive philanthropy. We want it to become a springboard for deeper conversations and more mindful giving.

SOUL | *who we are*	a giving circle that gives back
MIND | *what we envision*	a healthy, safe and prosperous community for African American families to live, work and flourish
HEART | *why we care*	inextricable ties to past, present and future generations
HANDS | *how we work*	promoting philanthropy—the giving of time, talent and treasure among African Americans in the Charlotte region, with the goal of enhancing the quality of life within our communities

MEMBER-DONORS

Men Tchaas Ari

Renee L. Bradford

Heather Carty Ward

Deborah Charles

Rashad Davis

Tonya Edwards

Dawn Fisher

Ed Franklin

Diatra Fullwood

Valaida Fullwood

Melandee Jones

Ohmar Land

Eric Law

Tameka Lester

Patricia Martelly

Fontella McKyer

Jennifer Miles

Vernetta Mitchell

Cathy Peterson

Meka S. Sales

Jenene Seymour

Jehan Shamsid-Deen

Annette Taylor

A small body of determined spirits fired by an unquenchable faith in their mission can alter the course of history.

— Mahatma Gandhi, Indian civil rights leader

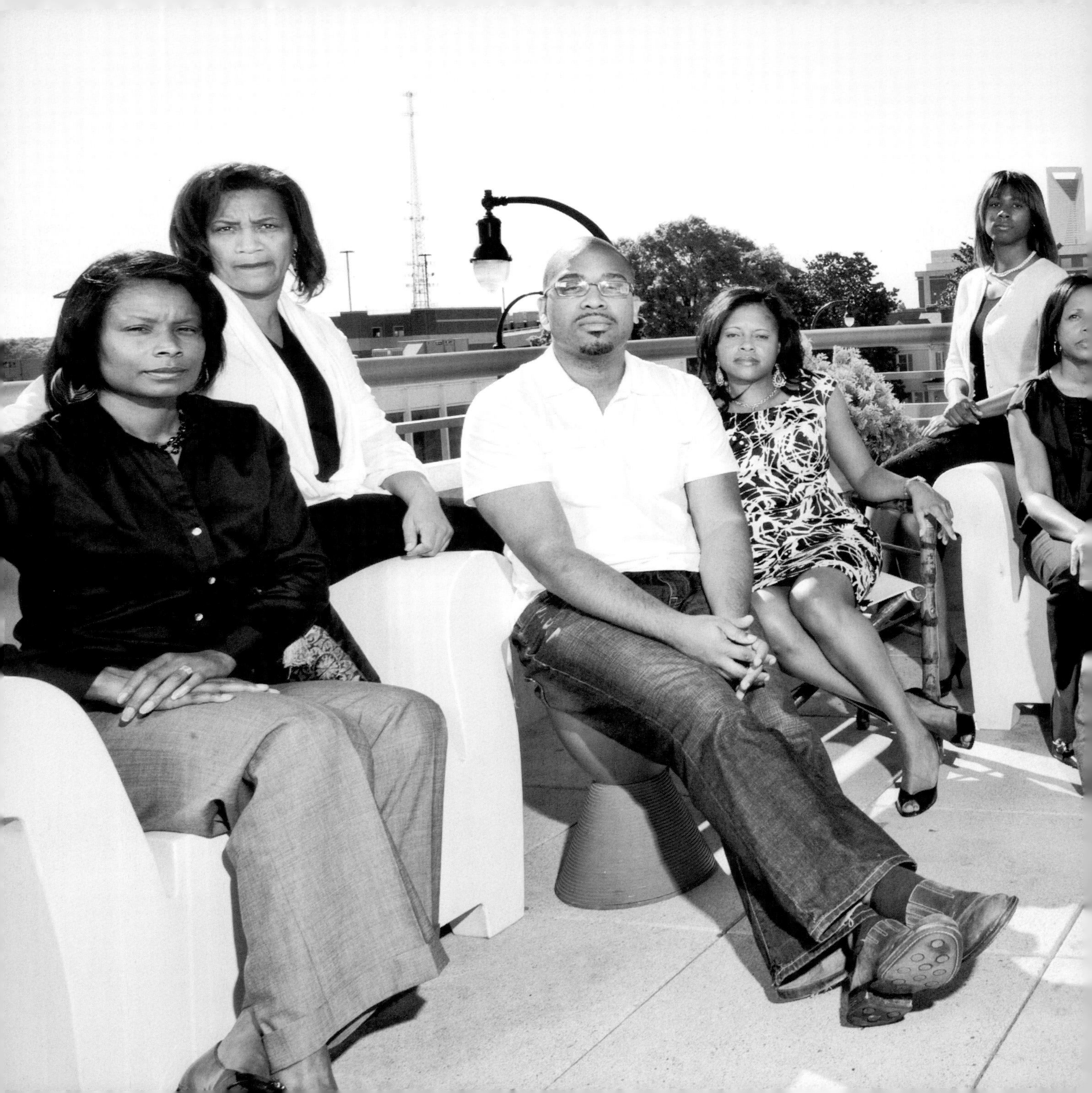

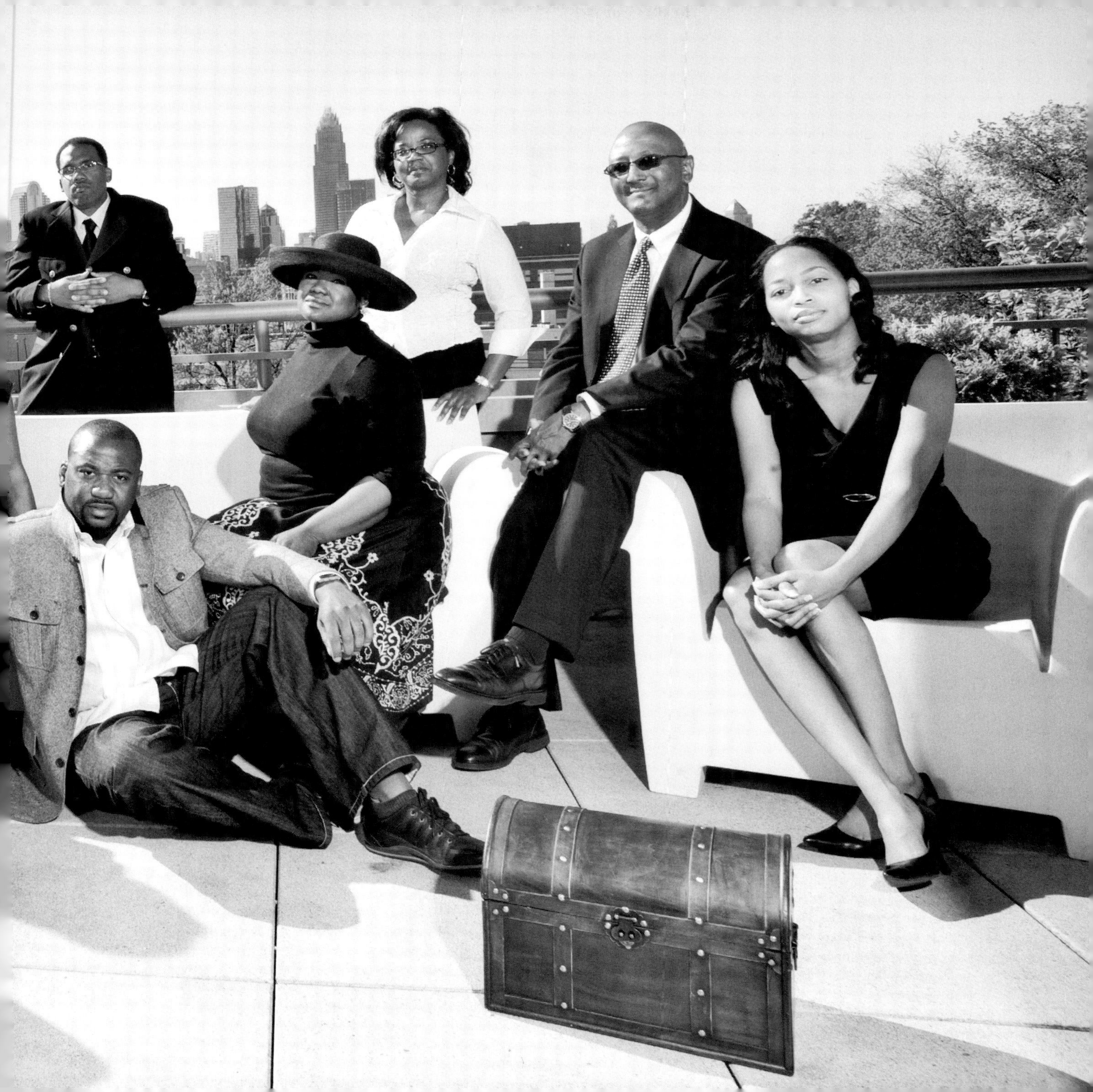

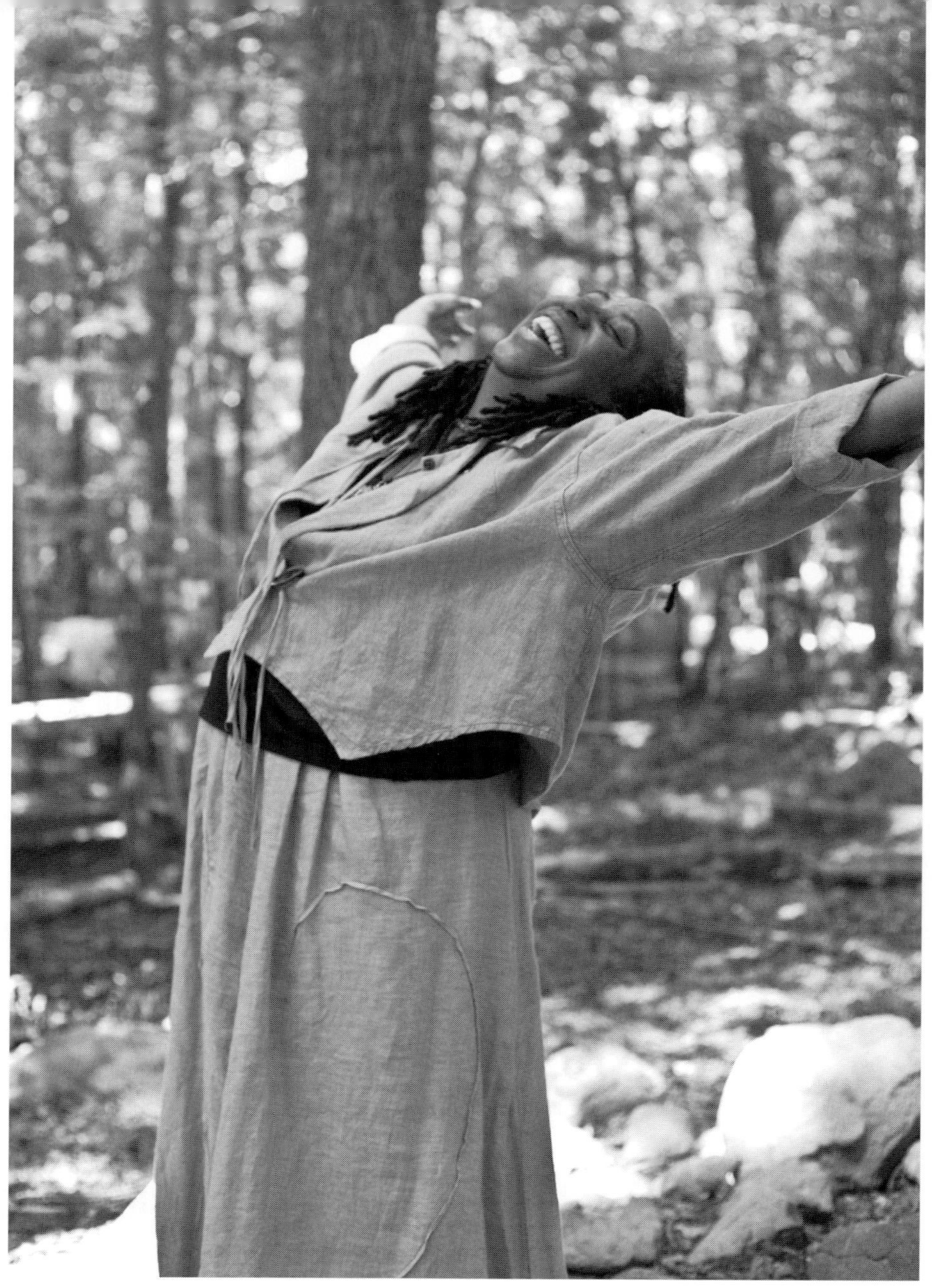

Feeling gratitude and not expressing it is like wrapping a present and not giving it.
— William Arthur Ward, American writer

Circle of Advisors

Project advisors and their philanthropic affiliations

Renee L. Bradford | *New Generation of African American Philanthropists*

Rashad Davis | *New Generation of African American Philanthropists*

Victor Fields | *African American Community Foundation*

DeAlva Glenn | *Harvey B. Gantt Center for African-American Arts + Culture*

Bridget-Anne Hampden | *Charlotte-Mecklenburg Community Foundation*

Gerald Johnson | *Charlotte Post Foundation*

Stoney Sellars | *John S. And James L. Knight Foundation*

Geraldine Sumter, J.D. | *Foundation For The Carolinas*

Project team

Valaida Fullwood, NGAAP-Charlotte (writing, art direction & project management)

Dimeji Onafuwa and India Simpson, Casajulie Visual Communications (web and book design)

Dawn Fisher, Diatra Fullwood and Jenene Seymour, NGAAP-Charlotte (fund development)

Charles W. Thomas Jr., Sankofa Photography (photography)

Sticks in a bundle are unbreakable.
— Kenyan proverb

Sponsoring Partners of the Giving Back Project

*Giving***Vision** Partners

Philanthropic organizations sponsoring the start-up of the Giving Back Project are:

FOUNDATION FOR THE CAROLINAS
www.fftc.org

JOHN S. AND JAMES L. KNIGHT FOUNDATION
www.knightfoundation.org

HARVEY B. GANTT CENTER FOR AFRICAN-AMERICAN ARTS + CULTURE
www.ganttcenter.org

CHARLOTTE POST FOUNDATION
www.thecharlottepost.com

NCGIVES
www.ncgives.org

COMMUNITY INVESTMENT NETWORK
www.thecommunityinvestment.org

BLUECROSS AND BLUESHIELD OF NORTH CAROLINA FOUNDATION
www.bcbsncfoundation.org

*Giving***Momentum** Partner

THE DUKE ENDOWMENT
www.tde.org

*Giving***Joy** Partner

PIEDMONT NATURAL GAS
www.piedmontng.com

Do real and permanent good in this world.

— Andrew Carnegie, Scots-born American industrialist

Wisdom lies neither in fixity nor in change, but in the dialectic between the two.
— Octavio Paz, Mexican writer, poet and diplomat

*Giving*Inspiration

Honorees featured in Tribute Vignettes

Cleon C. Arrington, Ph.D. †
Dora Atlas
Renee L. Bradford
Jeanne M. Brayboy
Annie Brewer
Robert J. Brown
Willette Chambers †
John Crawford
Elizabeth Ross Dargan †
Doris Ann Fullwood
Maldonia McGimpsey Fullwood †
Endia Brabham
Mary Harper, Ph.D.
Robert Harrington, J.D.
Jelani Haskins
Carlenia Ivory
Lois Jamison †
Adonis "Sporty" Jeralds
Carlotta and Johnnie Jones
Donna Murray Lacey
Darryl K. Lester
Nancy Moore
Shirley Oliver Nelson †
Emmanuel Ohonme
William Pretty Jr. †
Lucille Erwin Scott †
Eric Shelton
Byron A. Smith Sr.
Saundra Porter Thomas

† *deceased*

*Giving*Honor

Contributors & Sponsors of Tribute Vignettes

Michelle Arrington
Alexandré Bailand Bohannon
Renee L. Bradford
Joyce M. Brayboy
Ronald L. Carter, Ph.D.
Lisa Crawford
Rashad Davis
Dawn Fisher
Valaida Fullwood
Diatra Fullwood
Allen W. Fullwood
Harvey B. Gantt
Sharon Harrington, J.D.
Sandra Jamison
Melandee Jones
Coron Jordan
Rahsaan Lacey
Dionne Lester
Britt Brewer Loudd
Lisa Nannette Moore
Dimeji Onafuwa
Cathy Peterson
Reginald F. Pretty
Meka S. Sales
Eric Shelton
Reggie Singleton
David R. Taylor
Charles W. Thomas Jr.
Esther Witherspoon

Never doubt that a small group of thoughtful, committed citizens can change the world. Indeed, it is the only thing that ever has. — Margaret Mead

*Giving*Treasure

Donors to the Giving Back Project

as of June 1, 2011

Anonymous donor
Edwin Atlas
Brant Aycock
P. Jean Bligen
Brenda Erwin Brewer
Christa Carter, Ph.D.
Ruthye Cooley
Rashad Davis
Patrick L. Diamond
Ayanna Fisher, *in memoriam*
Dawn A. Fisher
Rosalyn V. Frazier
Valaida Fullwood
Karen Geiger, Ph.D.
Bridget-Anne Hampton
Bryan Hassel, Ph.D.
Arthur, Sandra and Sheila Jamison
Mary Klenz
Kathi M. Knier
Michelle S. Langdon
Candice Langston
Eric Law
Dee K. Lee
Dionne Lester
Myrna E. Lewis
Cori & Athan L. Lindsay
Bilenda Madison
Nettie McGimpsey McIntosh
Willie McIntosh Jr.
John F. McKinley
James Mitchell, *in memoriam*
Dorothy Murray
Lisa Nannette Moore
Edna M. Norwood
Pam Pompey
Reginald F. Pretty
Tracy Russ
Kathryn Sain
Tonya & Stoney Sellars
Octavia Seawell
Jenene Seymour
Shades of Brown Book Club
Jehan Shamsid-Deen
Geraldine Sumter, J.D.
Mildred Dwiggins Swift
Vonda K. Villines
Edward Wall, J.D.
Qiana L. White

*Giving*Love

CIN Giving Circles

Charlotte's New Generation of African American Philanthropists is encircled by support from members of the Community Investment Network (CIN), which comprises the following giving circles:

20/20 Sisters of Vision, *Durham, NC*
A Legacy of Tradition (A LOT), *Raleigh-Durham, NC*
Birmingham Change Fund, *Birmingham, AL*
Circle of Joy, *Atlanta, GA*
Heritage Quilters, *Warrenton, NC*
New Mountain Climbers, *Christiansburg, VA*
Next Generation of African American Philanthropists (NGAAP), *Raleigh-Durham, NC*
Sankofa, *Pittsburgh, PA*
Way Out, *Durham, NC*
Zawadi, New *Orleans, LA*

*Giving*Time+Talent

Friends of the Giving Back Project

Editing
Rebecca Gholson

Photo Shoot Assistance
Jasiatic Anderson
Nikea Flegler, JCSU intern
Phylicia Hartfield, JCSU intern
Patrick Tennin, JCSU intern
Micaila Thomas, Sankofa Photography

Book & Web Design
India Simpson, Casajulie Visual Communications

Make-up
Donah Tolson Ollila

Poetry
Quentin "Q" Talley, On Q Productions
Ava Wood

Kind spirits who provided support to our book project in multiple ways and at pivotal times
Arts and Science Council
Dianne C. Bailey, J.D. and Nichelle Nicholes Levy, J.D.
Bonita Buford
Trish Hobson and Linda Miller, Men's Shelter of Charlotte
Linetta J. Gilbert
Sandra Jamison
Sheila Jamison
Michelle Langdon, J.D.
Dee Lee
Darryl K. Lester
Michael Marsciano, Ph.D., David Snider and the Foundation For The Carolinas staff
Lisa Nannette Moore
Joy Paige and Benny L. Smith, Johnson C. Smith University
Susan Patterson, Knight Foundation
Mark Peres, Charlotte ViewPoint
Robinson Bradshaw & Hinson, P.A.
Amy Rogers
Adam Whalen, Loft 1523

They who give have all the things. They who withhold have nothing.
— Hindu proverb

Appendix I | List of Photographs

Photo shoot locations

We appreciate the people who assisted us in capturing photographs in locations mainly in the Charlotte region and also in Durham and High Point, North Carolina. The following is a list of locations for our photo shoots.

Afro-American Cultural Center
Bank of America Plaza
Center City Charlotte
Frazier Park
Friendship Missionary Baptist Church
Freedom Park
Graveyard at Torrence Grove AME Zion Church
Harvey B. Gantt Center for African-American Arts + Culture
Highland Mills
Home of Carlotta and Johnnie Jones
Home of Cathy Peterson
Home of Micaila and Charles W. Thomas Jr.
Home of Mary Harper, Ph.D.
Home of Thereasea Clark Elder
Home of Valaida Fullwood
Ivory Baker Recreation Center
Johnson C. Smith University
KIPP Charlotte
Levine Center for the Arts
Loft 1523
Men's Shelter of Charlotte
Marshall Park
Modern Salon & Spa at Phillips Place
Newell Rosenwald School
Offices of B&C Associates, Inc.
Reedy Creek Park
Residence Inn • Charlotte Uptown
Samaritan's Feet
Stewart Creek Greenway
Studio of Photographer Jeff Cravotta
The Green on South Tryon
The Males Place, Mecklenburg County Department of Health
Trinity Episcopal School
The Wadsworth Estate
Wallace Pruitt Recreation Center
Uptown Charlotte, North Carolina

Photographs

We are forever grateful to the scores of people who sat for portraits and participated in photo shoots over a two-year period. Below is a list of the people, places and objects, in the order they appear in chapters and pages of *Giving Back*.

The eye altering, alters all.
— William Blake, English poet and artist

List of photographs, *continued*

List of photographs, *continued*

List of photographs, *continued*

How beauteous mankind is! O brave new world. That has such people in't!

— William Shakespeare, English playwright and poet

Appendix II | List of Organizations

The following is a list of nonprofits organizations, educational institutions, foundations and community-based groups mentioned in stories throughout *Giving Back*.

20/20 Sisters of Vision, a CIN giving circle
A LOT: A Legacy of Tradition, a CIN giving circle
African American Women On The Hill Network
Afro-American Cultural Center (now Harvey B. Gantt Center for African American Arts + Culture)
Alabama A&M University
Alpha Kappa Alpha Sorority, Incorporated
Alpha Phi Alpha Fraternity Inc.
Atlanta University (now Clark Atlanta University)
Amateur Athletic Union • AAU Team Charlotte
American Red Cross
Anita Stroud Youth Development Center
Arts and Science Council
Auburn University
Bank of America Foundation
Bay Area Leadership Foundation
Be A Blessing Inc.
Bechtler Museum of Modern Art
Belmont Community Development Corporation
Bennett College
Bennett College • Western North Carolina Alumnae Chapter
Berklee College of Music
Bethune Women's Club
Birmingham Change Fund, a CIN giving circle
Black Benefactors
BlueCross and BlueShield of North Carolina Foundation
Boy Scouts of America • Troop 718
Brenner Children's Hospital
Burke County Historical Society
Carolinas Healthcare System
Central Piedmont Community College
Chantilly Pyramid Minority Student Achievement Committee
Charlotte Housing Authority Scholarship Fund
Charlotte Post Foundation
Charlotte ViewPoint
Circle of Joy, a CIN giving circle
Clark Atlanta University
Community Charter School
Community Investment Network (CIN)
Crown Jewels Chapter of The Links, Incorporated
Delta Sigma Theta Sorority Inc.
Dr. Cleon C. Arrington Scholarship for the Sciences
Duke University
Emmanuel Baptist Church, Brooklyn
Fayetteville State University
First Baptist Church, Winston-Salem
First Purse
Flynn Christian Fellowship Home
Ford Foundation
Foundation For The Carolinas
Friendship Missionary Baptist Church, Charlotte
Georgia State University Foundation
Girls on the Run
God City
Goodwill
Greenville Community Historical Society Inc.
Greenville Memorial AME Zion Church, Charlotte
Habitat for Humanity
Harvey B. Gantt Center for African American Arts + Culture
Heritage Quilters, a CIN giving circle
The History Museum of Burke County
Ivory Baker Recreation Center
J.T. Williams Middle School
Jacob's Ladder Job Center Inc.
John S. and James L. Knight Foundation

The best time to plant a tree was twenty years ago. The next best time is now.
— Chinese proverb

When one takes a broad survey of country, he will find the most useful and influential people in it are those who take the deepest interest in institutions that exist for the purpose of making the world better.

— Booker T. Washington, American educator, orator and political leader

List of organizations, *continued*

Johnson C. Smith University
Junior League
KIPP Charlotte
Koinoiah magazine
LATIBAH Collard Green Museum – Life and Times in Black American History
Lawyers' Committee for Civil Rights Under Law
Levine Children's Hospital
Levine Museum of the New South
The Light Factory Contemporary Museum of Photography and Film
Lindsay Legacy Fund
Louisiana Disaster Recovery Fund
The Males Place
McCrorey YMCA
Mecklenburg Bar Association
Men's Shelter of Charlotte
Morehouse College
Mount Carmel Baptist Church, Charlotte
NAACP Legal Defense and Educational Fund
National Association of Negro Business and Professional Women's Clubs
National PTA
National Urban League
NCGives
New Generation of African American Philanthropists • Charlotte, a CIN giving circle
New Mountain Climbers, a CIN giving circle
Next Generation of African American Philanthropists, a CIN giving circle
North Carolina A&T University
On Q Productions
Our Daily Bread Kitchen Inc.
Oxford Children's Home (now The Masonic Home for Children at Oxford)
Pecha Kucha Night • Charlotte
PEN Pals Book Club and Support Group for Children of Incarcerated Parents
Piedmont Natural Gas Foundation
Pilgrim Baptist Church, Durham
Project HealthShare • Charlotte Volunteers in Medicine
Project REAP: Real Estate Associate Program
Ronald McDonald House
Room in the Inn • Urban Ministry Center
Samaritan's Feet
Sankofa, a CIN giving circle
Sassafras All Children's Playground
Seversville Neighborhood Organization
Shaw University
Shiloh AME Church, Morganton
Silicon Valley Community Foundation
Special Olympics
Spelman College
St. Jude Children's Research Hospital
St. Luke Missionary United Methodist Church, Asheboro
Sweet Beginnings
Teach For America
TEDxCharlotte
Teen Health Connection
The Duke Endowment
The Links, Incorporated
United Negro College Fund (UNCF)
United Way
University of North Carolina at Chapel Hill
University of North Carolina at Charlotte
University of Southern Mississippi
Urban League Central Carolinas
Veterans of Foreign Wars
Wadsworth House Foundation
Wallace Pruitt Recreation Center
Way Out, a CIN giving circle
Weeping Willow AME Zion Church
Wesley Heights Community Association
WFAE 90.7 FM Public Radio
William Pretty Jr. Foundation
Women's Impact Fund
YMCA Black Achievers
Zawadi, a CIN giving circle

Index

Valaida Fullwood • Writing, Art Direction & Project Management

Described an "idea whisperer," Valaida brings a mix of unbridled imagination and a gift for harnessing wild ideas to her work as a writer, creative consultant and project strategist. Her client base ranges widely and her interests center on social innovation in philanthropy, education and the arts. A born-and-bred North Carolinian, Valaida has deep hometown roots in Morganton and is a graduate of the University of North Carolina at Chapel Hill, where she majored in International Studies with a focus in Economics. For nearly a decade, she managed international economic development projects for major corporations, living and working overseas prior to establishing a Charlotte-based consulting practice.

Valaida's primary passions are foreign cultures and international exploration. Perpetual wanderlust has inspired her to travel to more than twenty countries, four continents and counting. Closer to home, she throws delicious parties and thrives from social and philanthropic involvement with Charlotte ViewPoint, Community Investment Network, On Q Productions, Wesley Heights Community Association as well as the innovative forums Pecha Kucha and TEDxCharlotte. She is a founding member of New Generation of African American Philanthropists—a giving circle that gives back.

Charles W. Thomas Jr. • Photography

Artist, educator and entrepreneur, Charles is a native of Charlotte, North Carolina and director of education at TLF: The Light Factory Contemporary Museum of Photography and Film. At TLF, he challenges youth and adult students to create visual art that reflects the story of self, family and community.

Charles also is the owner of Sankofa Photography, which pursues an artistic mission based on an Akan philosophy: Go back and fetch the story of your past, to understand who you are today. Charles' images reflect his dedication to preserving the history and stories of individuals and communities. His current work focuses on Manhood. His work has been featured on the cover of *The Charlotte Post* and Charlotte's Cultural Calendar and in *The Charlotte Observer* and *La Noticia*. Exhibitions of his photography have appeared at the LATIBAH Museum, the Afro-American Cultural Center (now The Gantt Center), and Macy's department store.

A photographer and educator for over ten years, Charles graduated from Duke University with a degree in Economics and studied Photography at Central Piedmont Community College. His international travels include: India, South Africa, Mexico, Puerto Rico, several European countries, and most recently China.

Casajulie Visual Communications • Design

Dimeji Onafuwa is the founder and Creative Director of Casajulie Visual Communications. Since graduating Summa Cum Laude with a Bachelor of Arts, with majors in Advertising and Studio Art, Dimeji has worked in the design industry for over ten years. He holds a Masters in Business Administration with a concentration in Management from the University of North Carolina at Charlotte. He sits on the board of several Charlotte-based organizations, including the Belmont Community Development Corporation. Dimeji is also a figurative painter and is represented in Charlotte by Redsky Gallery and in Winston-Salem, North Carolina, by 5ive & 40rty Gallery. His paintings are in private and public collections. He is happily married to Bimpe, and they have a son.

India Simpson is Senior Designer at Casajulie and brings organization, energy and enthusiasm to the company. While at Johnson C. Smith University, where she studied Criminology, India won several awards, including "Stop the Gun Violence" art competition and "The Maya Angelou Women Ambassador Scholarship." She is fluent in sign language. India believes that process management is a significant part of implementing big ideas.

In recognizing the humanity of our fellow beings,
we pay ourselves the highest tribute.

THURGOOD MARSHALL
American civil rights activist and Supreme Court justice
(1908-93)